Backward Glances

ASIA-PACIFIC:

CULTURE, POLITICS,

AND SOCIETY

• • •

Editors: Rey Chow,

H. D. Harootunian, and

Masao Miyoshi

Backward Glances

· · ·   · · ·   · · ·

Contemporary Chinese Cultures

and the Female Homoerotic

Imaginary

FRAN MARTIN

Duke University Press

Durham and London

2010

© 2010 Duke University Press
All rights reserved
Printed in the United States
of America on acid-free
paper ∞ Designed by
Amy Ruth Buchanan
Typeset in Quadraat by Tseng
Information Systems, Inc.
Library of Congress Cataloging-
in-Publication Data appear
on the last printed page
of this book.

For Carol

· · ·

Contents

...

Acknowledgments

The research toward this book was made possible by an Australian Research Council Discovery Projects grant. Thanks to the many friends and colleagues who in different ways helped this book come into being: AD, Tomoko Aoyama, Chris Berry, Marion J. Campbell, Karen Chang Hsiu-min, Lisa Chen Xiuyu, Chen Xue, Yushin "Deadcat" Chen, Wen Cheng, Rey Chow, Chu T'ien-hsin, Naifei Ding, Hiromi Tsichuya Dollase, Brett Farmer, Garfield, Han Jia-yu, Chris Healy, Lai Zheng-zhe, Larissa Heinrich, Josephine Ho, Jubin Hu, Alison Huber, Lucifer Hung, Lucetta Kam, Olivia Khoo, Helen Hok-sze Leung, Pik-ki Leung, Tania Lewis, Li Yu, Jenpeng Liu, Joyce Liu, Yan Yan Mak, Mark McLelland, Meaghan Morris, Lisa Palmer, Amie Parry, Greg Pflugfelder, Shi Tou, Jessie Shih, Teri Silvio, Carmen Tong, John Treat, Yin Wang, James Welker, Angela Wong Yin Ni, Cuncun Wu, Taeko Yamada, and Zhuang Mingzhu.

. . .

Note on Translations and Transliterations

All Chinese–English translations are the author's except in cases where the work of other translators is cited.

This book uses the Hanyu Pinyin system of transliteration for Chinese words, names, and phrases, except in cases where a different conventional or preferred spelling or pronunciation exists, as is frequently the case in Taiwan and Hong Kong with personal names (for example, Tsao Jui-yuan; Wong Bi-kwan), character names in films or novels (for example, She Shih; Foon), place names (for example, Hualien), and other proper names (for example, Kuomintang).

Introduction

Love and Remembrance

On October 31, 1963, the streets of central Taipei were taken over by an impassioned crowd of hundreds of thousands of women, from middle-school students to young wives to grandmothers. In a rare upsurge of popular defiance to the Nationalist Party government's authoritarian regime, the mass of ordinary women brought traffic to a standstill and stretched the crowd control capacity of the military police to the limit. The crowd converged on a gaily decorated tour truck that for several tense moments it effectively held under siege, with police overpowered by the women's sheer numbers and unable to force a break in the throng to allow the truck to exit. On the truck, only just managing to maintain her professional composure, stood Ivy Ling Po, the freshly minted superstar of the Shaw Brothers' smash hit opera film *Liang Shanbo yu Zhu Yingtai* (The Love Eterne, dir. Li Han Hsiang, Hong Kong, 1962; figure 1). In the film, following southern Chinese all-female opera traditions, Ling cross-dressed to play the male romantic lead, Liang Shanbo, to Betty Loh Ti's Zhu Yingtai. Her performance was such a success that many women watched the film scores of times; others were reported to carry pictures of Ling in their purses like a sweetheart's portrait.[1] It was to be the first of a long series of such roles for Ling, and the film's spectacular box-office success marked the launch of her stellar career as screen heartthrob for a generation of Chinese women across East Asia, prefigured by this spontaneous and overwhelming expression of fandom in an otherwise strictly culturally regulated 1960s Taiwan.[2]

The tragic romance of Liang Shanbo and Zhu Yingtai is the best-known popular love story in the Chinese tradition. In the legend, Zhu rebels against

1. Ivy Ling Po's 1963 Taipei visit (image reproduced on
Shaw Brothers' bonus DVD accompanying *The Love Eterne*,
dir. Li Han-hsiang, 1962). The caption reads: "Brother
Liang's visit to Taiwan brings the whole city into the streets;
it has been likened to the passing of a giant typhoon."

her strictly Confucian father by cross-dressing as a boy to attend school. There
she falls in love with her classmate Liang, but the couple's romance is doomed
by class differences, and ultimately both lovers perish from broken hearts.[3]
That the definitive modern representation of this classic romance should be
emblematized by the screen image of the lovers played by two actors who are
both recognizably female is a rather remarkable fact (figure 2). Contrary to
the common assumption that romantic or erotic relations between women
must, by definition, be culturally marginal, the *Love Eterne* phenomenon suggests that representations of—and, in the fan response, experiences of—the
passionate love of one woman for another may occupy a position of unsus-
pected centrality in modern Chinese popular cultures.[4] It is this possibility
that this book sets out to investigate.

The continuing topicality of this issue today is reflected in the fact that
some four decades after the release of *The Love Eterne*, both the legend of Liang
and Zhu and the more recent cultural memory of the Shaw Brothers' film have
been reanimated in a new adaptation of the romance: independent Taiwanese
director Alice Wang's film *Fei yue qing hai* (Love Me If You Can, 2003; figure 3).
The film transposes the tale of Liang and Zhu onto a story of two contemporary Taiwanese young women who reincarnate the star-crossed lovers of the
legend. Ying (Ariel Lin), the reincarnation of Zhu, returns to the village where
she spent her childhood with her tomboyish cousin San (Alice Wang), the
reincarnation of Liang. Remembering her twofold love for San/Liang, Ying
tries to make San understand their true identities, periodically singing arias
from the original folk opera that punctuate the film's narrative as a kind of

2. Betty Loh Ti and Ivy Ling Po as the lovers Zhu Yingtai and Liang Shanbo (at this point, both costumed as male scholars) in *The Love Eterne* (dir. Li Han-hsiang, 1962).

intertextual commentary, their familiar melodies and tragic-romantic sentiment no doubt calling up, for regional audiences, memories of the 1962 film. But San's memory cannot be awakened, and seemingly unable to entertain the possibility of a female lover, she rejects Ying's romantic advances. Once again the story ends in tragedy with the death of both lovers. Yet the film's final scene indicates that death is no obstacle to Zhu's tenacious, transhistorical love: we see a new young woman arriving in what looks like the same coastal village, telling an unseen interlocutor that she is Zhu Yingtai and that she comes in search of a certain someone (figure 4).

Love Me is a film about love and remembrance; it is about a love that lives on, in, and as memory. On a diegetic level, memory and forgetting play a central part in the narrative development: while Ying remembers both her childhood love for San and her previous incarnation as Zhu to San's Liang, the film's viewer is constantly reminded that it is precisely the failure of San's memory on both of these counts that leads to the ultimate tragedy (figures 5 and 6). On an extradiegetic level, the film reanimates its audience's memory of the Shaw Brothers' version of *The Love Eterne* and the collective romantic adulation of Ivy Ling Po by a generation of women viewers—the mothers, aunts, and grandmothers of today's young viewers. But in addition to its evocation of love and memory in its plot and in its intertextual relationship with *The Love Eterne*, *Love Me* references the link between these ideas at a more basic conceptual level as well. This book's central contention is that in modern Chinese media and literary cultures, the topic of love between women has been constitutively linked with a memorial mode of representation: in the contemporary Chinese mass cultures of China, Hong Kong, and Taiwan, where erotic or romantic relations between women are depicted, one almost invariably finds a preoccupation with memory. In its depiction of the love of

3. Ariel Lin as Ying, Zhu's reincarnation, and Alice Wang as San, Liang's reincarnation, in *Love Me If You Can* (dir. Alice Wang, 2003).

4. Zhu Yingtai (Chu Yin Tai)'s second reincarnation at the conclusion of *Love Me If You Can* (dir. Alice Wang, 2003).

5-6. The centrality of memory in *Love Me If You Can* (dir. Alice Wang, 2003).

one woman for another in and through a memorial mode, *Love Me* thus exemplifies a central, structuring logic of modern Chinese female homoerotic representation, one that not only features in self-consciously lesbian texts but is also central to more mainstream depictions of women's intra-gender relations.

This book is about the epistemology of female homoeroticism—ways of understanding love between women—as it is played out in mainstream Chinese media and literary cultures today. It asks: What are the most common narrative, generic, and ideological patterns in representations of love between women in contemporary Chinese cultures? Have there been recurring themes and structures of feeling in these mass cultural figurations of women's same-sex relations? If so, what does the persistence of those themes and structures reveal about modern Chinese understandings not only of lesbianism, but, more broadly, of women's gendered experiences of love, sex, marriage, and intra-gender relations? Is the topic of women's same-sex love a merely marginal one, as is often assumed, or might it turn out to occupy a more central place than anticipated in Chinese mass cultures? What are the ideological functions of modern Chinese representations of women's love and desire for each other? Do they serve symbolically to stifle or to enable the public imaginability of love between women?

In response to the first of these questions, through analyses of a wide range of texts from pulp fiction to TV soap opera and from translated Japanese manga comics to teenpics, this book analyzes the centrality of a temporal logic in contemporary Chinese representations of women's same-sex love. It argues that a dominant modern Chinese discourse on female homoeroticism has asserted the impossibility of lesbian futures: sexual relations between women are culturally imaginable only in youth; therefore same-sex sexual relations may appear in adult femininity's past, very rarely in its present, and never in its future. As in *Love Me*, in a majority of mainstream Chinese literary, filmic, and other cultural production since the early twentieth century, loving relations between women have been represented as temporally anterior to the narrative present and available principally through memory's mediation. Following this logic, the book analyzes the dominance of an analeptic or backward looking mode of representation structuring the cultural appearance of female homoeroticism in this context.

As in *Love Me*, what is remarkable in most of the examples discussed in the chapters that follow—examples, let us be clear, that are overwhelmingly *not* marked out as self-consciously lesbian texts but are integrated into the mainstream of middlebrow women's mass culture—is the degree to which they openly acknowledge the pain and lingering regret associated with the forced termination of same-sex love between young women. The typical narrative trajectory of these stories sees socially mandated heterosexual conclusions, often enforced by a concerned mother, school counselor, or other external figure of social authority, superseding the same-sex love plots. Although such straightened-out endings may appear at first glance to be simply a means of de-realizing lesbian possibility, nonetheless the stories tend to cast their conclusions not as triumphant but at the very least as ambivalent and often as openly tragic, suggesting that the stories may have a more complex ideological function.[5] In light of this, one of this book's key propositions is that the common memorial narrative of young women's same-sex love, cherished then forcibly given up, has an important critical significance. Specifically, I argue that the markedly mournful cast of these stories' remembrance of same-sex love as a kind of paradise lost implies a critique of the social imposition of hetero-marital relations upon young women as a condition of feminine adulthood.[6] In Valerie Rohy's terms, the memorial female same-sex romance might be said to function as a marker of (proto-)lesbian "impossibility," where impossibility marks "a kind of vanishing point in both discourse and desire—not where these systems cease to exist but where they turn away from their own incoherence, where their success becomes their failure. As a name for an internal resistance, impossibility also describes the unacknowledged contradictions within hegemonic systems of sexuality, which patriarchal culture, in its will to meaning, displaces onto lesbian figures."[7]

My interpretation of these narratives perhaps has something in common, too, with Judith Roof's conceptualization of lesbian "configurations": "Operating as points of systemic failure, configurations of lesbian sexuality often reflect the complex incongruities that occur when the logic or philosophy of a system becomes self-contradictory, visibly fails to account for something, or cannot complete itself."[8] The incoherence and incongruity marked by the narratives I examine are those that dog the hetero-marital system itself: the narratives represent points of profound denaturalization of that system, points at which the system of adult hetero-marital sexuality recognizes the high subjective cost at which its aim is enforced.[9] But what distinguishes these Chinese examples from Rohy's and Roof's accounts of European and American lesbian representation is the degree to which mainstream, middlebrow mass culture *avows* the crisis of the dominant sex-gender system. For it is not the case here that the tensions and anxieties of hetero-marital feminine adulthood go unacknowledged in mainstream culture and are displaced onto the othered figure of the lesbian, nor that mass cultural representation is compelled vigorously to defend itself against the possibility of sexual love between women. Instead, the idealization of women's youthful same-sex love and desire, framed as a universal female experience, is remarkably common, and the pain caused by the renouncement of this love is frankly avowed, not simply papered over to enable an air of triumph in the stories' heterosexual conclusions. The protagonists in these stories do not so much "suffer from reminiscences," in Freud's famous formulation—precisely because their same-sex desires do not seem to be strongly suppressed in the first place; rather, they openly revel in the repeated, mournful narration of their treasured memories.[10] For these reasons, this book's argument is neither about the cultural repression of women's same-sex love nor about a marginal or subcultural resistance to a dominant structure. Instead, I propose that the criticism of the hetero-marital imperative that I read in these narratives is *central* to Chinese public cultures: the system of enforced adult hetero-maritality coexists alongside its own remarkably candid critique.

Alongside investigations in history and the social sciences, analyses of lesbian representation in the modern cultures of Western Europe and the United States form a central strand in lesbian studies as it has emerged since the 1980s. These studies have been concerned with how love between women has been represented in the modern West and how these representations have both reflected and shaped modern Western understandings of lesbianism. Key works have investigated the formations of lesbian representation and sexuality in literary narrative, popular and avant-garde cinema, and feminist and psychoanalytic theories, tackling both self-consciously lesbian texts and mainstream representations.[11] Too diverse in their approaches and conclusions to sum up simply, these works have addressed a wide range of issues, including questions of classification (what makes a text "lesbian"?), ideology (are particular representations of lesbian subjects conservative or radical?), form (how does narrative or cinematic structure impact on writers' and filmmakers' attempts to represent the lesbian?), philosophy (how is lesbian possibility figured or disallowed in the central theories of modern Western thought?), and historical specification (what is particular about the recurrent structures and tropes of modern Western lesbian representation?). Although a comparatively recent development in the academy and notwithstanding the polyvocal variety of its constituent works, the study of lesbian representation by now constitutes a recognizable subfield within English-language humanities scholarship.

In contrast, lesbian representation and epistemology in modern Chinese contexts have only very recently, and still incompletely, been addressed as objects of study. The major English publication to date in Chinese lesbian studies is Tze-lan D. Sang's pioneering work, *The Emerging Lesbian*.[12] Sang's book is a feminist historical study of the transition from premodern to modern understandings of same-sex sexuality in the People's Republic of China (PRC) and Taiwan, as revealed primarily through elite literary texts between the seventeenth century and the present. This work is groundbreaking not only in the richness of the range of literary representations of love between women that it uncovers, but also in the complexity of its historical argument regarding the gradualness and incompleteness of the transition from premodern Chinese sexual epistemologies to modern sexological taxonomies. Sang's analysis corrects the common view—espoused by writers including Chou Wah-shan and Bret Hinsch—that premodern Chinese societies were "tolerant" of same-sex behavior and that the introduction of European sexology in the 1920s and 1930s served mainly to instill a new homophobic impulse.[13] Instead, Sang shows that the transculturation of sexological science enabled homophilic as well as homophobic alignments by Republican Chinese intellectuals and that sexology's arrival led not to any epochal epistemic break with older conceptualizations of same-sex sexuality but instead to a gradual transformation with diffuse effects.[14] Broadly, Sang argues that although in premodern China homoeroticism between women was a source of some anxiety for the patriarchal power system and typically led to either recuperative or trivializing accounts of such attachments by male literati, it was not until the modern period, when for the first time women showed signs of gaining genuine social power, that female homosexuality became the focus of real and intense male panic.[15] Although she underscores the ideological complexity of the Republican Chinese engagement with European sexology, in the final instance Sang sees sexology in the hands of China's male intellectuals as principally a tool used to demonize erotic love between women.[16] Sang's analyses of contemporary lesbian texts and cultures in mainland China and Taiwan hinge on a similar opposition between an anxious male social power and lesbian relations conceived as a form of proto-feminist resistance to that power.

Although *The Emerging Lesbian* is dominated by literary textual analyses, the spirit of its approach has much in common with lesbian feminist historical studies, particularly the work of Lillian Faderman.[17] As the above account indicates, the questions that most occupy Sang in her approaches to the texts she analyzes are ideological ones about the politics of gender. And as in Faderman's *Surpassing the Love of Men*, Sang at times tends toward equating love between women in general with lesbian feminist politics in particular.[18] In response to her central questions about whether various literary representations of lesbianism imply positive or negative valuations, Sang assumes in advance that when penned by male authors, such representations are negative—belying cooptation, trivialization, anxiety, or voyeurism—whereas when written by female authors, lesbian representations are positive, almost by definition encoding a feminist politics.[19] Without wishing to detract from the genuine importance of *The Emerging Lesbian*, I think that this approach entails certain risks. First, the same criticism could be made of Sang as has been made of Faderman—that is, that the conceptual reduction of sexuality to gender and of lesbianism to lesbian feminism papers over the actually far messier and more complex sexual and cultural particularities of the various articulations of female same-sex love under discussion.[20] Second, the division of the material into the two neatly opposed camps of "dominant (male) power" and "subversive (lesbian) resistance" risks offering an essentializing vision of the complex relations between gender and sexual identity and between authorship and representations of homosexuality and foreclosing the possibility of textual tensions and ambiguities.[21] As I illustrate in the chapters that follow, mainstream and male-authored representations of love between women visualize its possibility just as much as subcultural and female-authored ones and as such may incite lesbian attachment even when they superficially appear to prohibit it. Likewise, lesbian-identifying women can and do draw upon mainstream discourses (and not always subversively or with a feminist spin) in their elaboration of alternative sexual selves and communities. It may be less useful, then, to imagine modern Chinese sexual culture as riven between sanctioned and repressed discourses than to see the whole tangle as the expression of a complexly interlinked system.[22]

This book does not presume in advance that gender will provide the magic key to the logic of modern Chinese female homoerotic representation—although gender does prove to be an important thematic in many of the examples discussed. The book is less interested in discovering the feminist politics underpinning certain "authentic" modes of lesbian representation than it is in understanding women's same-sex love more broadly as a topic within mainstream popular culture. Whereas Sang concentrates on textual analyses of lesbian themes in elite literature, *Backward Glances* shifts the focus to contemporary popular culture, asking how women's same-sex relations have appeared not just in highbrow literature but also in the more widely disseminated forms of women's mass culture: school stories, soap operas, the women's telemovie, pulp fiction, melodrama, women's autobiography, the teenpic.

Although a central aim of this book is to uncover some of the recurrent patterns and preoccupations in the contemporary representation of women's same-sex love in Chinese as distinct from Euro-American contexts, the book does not attempt a systematic comparison of Western with Chinese forms of lesbian representation. Rather, it seeks to offer an analysis of some of the central structures and logics of such representations in Chinese contexts on their own historical and cultural terms, approaching contemporary Chinese female homoerotic representation as a semi-autonomous, self-referential system distinct from—albeit everywhere in conversation with—modern Western forms.[23] The motivation behind this approach is both general—that is, to contribute to a scholarly appreciation of the multiplicity of sexual modernities coexisting in the world today—and specific—that is, to contribute to the development of the nascent yet fast-expanding field of critical, anti-homophobic Chinese sexuality studies by mapping some of the basic structures that shape the public cultural representation and conceptualization of love between women today. Thus, although selected concepts and theories from work on lesbian representation in Euro-American contexts have proven useful in the analyses that follow, this work is taken up and put down opportunistically, providing elements of a critical tool kit rather than being mined for a unified theory of "the" logic of Western lesbian representation (if this could ever be reduced to a singular logic) as a point of comparison for the Chinese examples.

Schoolgirl Romance and Secondary Gender

The memorial discourse on female homoeroticism that is this book's central subject can be traced in part back to the indigenization of European sexological theory in China during the 1920s and 1930s.[24] That period saw the introduction of Havelock Ellis's influential taxonomic division of female homosexuality into the mutually exclusive categories of situational/temporary (a universalizing model) and congenital/permanent (a minoritizing model). Zhang Jingsheng's *Sex Histories*, published in 1926 and greatly indebted to Ellis, develops the first of these views by presenting school-era homosexuality in girls as a nonstigmatic, temporary stage on the way to adult heterosexuality.[25] The volume includes a remarkably candid yet unpanicked account of temporary same-sex romance and sexual behavior among schoolgirls by its sole female contributor, Miss Ban, who writes in detail about the activities of pairs of "intimate friends" in the Jiangsu girls' school that she attended from the age of fourteen. In addition to falling in love with one another and being subject to romantic pining and fierce jealousy, according to Miss Ban, unbeknownst to the school authorities the lovers also routinely passed the night in one another's beds, causing "the beds in which the couples were lying [to] shake most severely" for reasons that were not at the time clear to the naïve young Miss Ban.[26]

Although the effects of the minoritizing view on female homosexuality are certainly present in some contemporary instances — notably in mass-cultural "tomboy melodrama" (the subject of chapter 4) — in post-1920s Chinese cultural production it is the universalizing view that Miss Ban's account exemplifies that is by far most commonly seen. Chinese mass-cultural representations of sexual love between women, both in the modernist fiction of the 1920s and 1930s and in the second wave of female homoerotic representations since the late twentieth century, have tended to dwell on the theme of the "temporary" same-sex love of a conventionally feminine young woman for one of her companions, a love that is forcibly severed by the incursion of socially mandated cross-sex relations, frequently in the form of the marriage of one of the partners.[27] The pervasive association of women's same-sex love with a specific time of life — the remembered past of adult femininity — is bolstered by the prominence of representations of intimate, sometimes erotic, friendships between girls and young women in modern Chinese cultures. Such emotionally intense and physically intimate female friendships, while relatively visible and at times valorized, nonetheless continue to bear an uneasy relation to the modern sexological category of female homosexuality (nü-tongxinglian).[28] This unresolved tension between an idealized view of intense and more or less erotic friendships between young women, on the one hand, and the stigmatization of "female homosexuality," on the other, is expressed in the continuing parallel presence of the two most influential models for conceptualizing female same-sex love in modern China: one based on same-sex romance, the other on secondary gender.[29]

Lesbian historiography in the West has turned up two central tropes of lesbian epistemology and social practice: the romantic female friendship that emerged initially in eighteenth-century Europe and systems of secondary gender, such as butch/femme, that crystallized in urban subcultural practice after the Second World War.[30] Two similar formations loom large in modern Chinese cultural interpretations and practices of women's same-sex love as well. Astutely, Sang points out the parallel between the social practice of intimate female friendship, as depicted by Republican-era Chinese women writers like Lu Yin, and romantic friendships between nineteenth-century intellectual women in Europe and the United States.[31] For both groups of "new women," as Sang observes, romantic friendships with other women enabled them to distance themselves from women's conventional roles in the family and advance their struggle for autonomy. Both groups of women were among the first generations to receive formal education; both were influenced by first-wave feminisms; both were drawn from the middle or upper classes; and both were born into societies in which intense and sensual female friendships constituted a culturally viable—albeit in some cases also anxiously policed—form of feminine sociality. A major project undertaken in this book is that of tracing the narrative logics and structures of feeling associated with the Republican-era model of romantic friendship through Chinese-language stories, films, and television productions that have appeared post-1970 through the genre that I term memorial schoolgirl romance.[32] Notwithstanding the influence of the sexological pathologization of female homosexuality, in Chinese cultural production the schoolgirl romance model has survived on into the present as a dominant strand within contemporary mass-cultural representations of erotic love between women, even bringing along with it a vestigial shadow of the Republican-era romantic idealization of "same-sex love" (tongxing'ai) as a sweet and ennobling experience for young women.[33]

In addition to this dominance of the memorial schoolgirl romance in contemporary Chinese mass-cultural figurations of women's same-sex relations, what emerges strongly from many (though not all) of the examples analyzed here is the conceptual and experiential centrality of secondary gender.[34] Gender in this sense differs from the sense in which Sang invokes gender in relation to lesbian representation. For Sang, gender refers primarily to the principle of social classification that divides men from women and unites women-loving women in their common opposition to patriarchal power. Secondary gender, by contrast, refers to a gendered distinction within the category of women who engage in sexual, erotic, or romantic relationships with other women. Although a majority of mass-cultural representations focus on normatively feminine protagonists, nonetheless in both popular representations and self-understandings on the part of self-identifying lesbians in China, Taiwan, and Hong Kong today, the gendered distinction between masculine and feminine women—in its broad outlines comparable perhaps to Western systems of butch/femme—is central. In mass-cultural representations since the Republican era, apparently conforming to an Ellis-style taxonomy, this gendered distinction commonly maps onto the distinction between "permanent" lesbianism (presumptively the preserve of the relatively rarely represented masculine woman, or tomboy) and "temporary" same-sex love (assumed to be the experience of the more frequently represented normatively feminine woman). This distinction in turn maps onto the further distinction between minoritizing accounts of lesbianism, commonly applied to the tomboy, and universalizing accounts, usually applied to the normatively feminine woman. I deem that the latter constitute a *dominant* form of representation because stories, films, and television programs presented from the point of view of "temporarily" same-sex loving, normatively feminine protagonists simply outnumber narratives that focus centrally on the experience of tomboys. Secondary tomboy characters do sometimes appear in the schoolgirl romance genre, frequently as the currently absent yet lovingly remembered school-era sweethearts of the feminine protagonists. However, because these characters do not serve as the focus of narrative attention and indeed tend to disappear altogether prior to the end of the stories, the central logic of that narrative remains one of same-sex love as a temporary stage preceding the feminine protagonist's reorientation toward adult cross-sex relations. The contemporary Chinese tomboy narrative—a term that I use to refer to texts that present the tomboy as protagonist rather than secondary character—is a distinctive form of representation with its own particular generic structures, notably those of the social problem melodrama (see chapter 4). It stands in contrast to the more common memorial narrative of same-sex love told from the perspective of a feminine protagonist, which tends instead to draw on the generic structures of tragic romance. In sum, while the memorial same-sex love story focusing on a normatively feminine protagonist is relatively mainstreamed and remarkably readily integrated into the broader cultural logic of romance, the tomboy narrative, by contrast, is relatively ghettoized; it is confined to a specific, "social problem" genre and thereby held at a greater distance than the schoolgirl romance from sexual and gender normativity.

Memory and Repetition

In *Love Me*, the final (re)appearance of "Zhu Yingtai" after Ying's death dramatizes the way in which memory—especially the memory of a tragically unfulfilled love—engenders repetition (figure 4). Since fate (or social convention) always intervenes to prevent Zhu and Liang's love from being realized, the film seems to say, their story will never be finished and hence must be repeated over and over again in perpetuity. This book proposes that a similar logic applies to the meta-narrative of women's same-sex romance in contemporary Chinese popular cultures. For the remarkable cultural pervasiveness of tragic-romantic stories of passionate love between young women cherished and then abandoned due to forces beyond their control does not equate in any concrete way to heightened "tolerance" for lesbian relations between adult women in the societies in question. On the contrary, there is a clear link between the proliferation of such narratives and the social prohibition on adult lesbianism. Just as in Wang's film, where the story of Zhu and Liang's romance is doomed to eternal repetition by virtue of its being prematurely truncated, I contend that the memorial narrative of same-sex love between young women proliferates endless repetitions of itself precisely because the social ban on adult lesbianism means that this particular love story cannot be granted closure.

This book argues that the ideological effects of the memorial mode of female homoerotic representation are twofold and contradictory. First and most straightforwardly, the persistent corralling of women's same-sex love and homoerotic desire into the past within Chinese popular texts can readily be understood as a recuperative de-realization of present or future lesbian possibility on the part of a dominant, patriarchal sex-gender system. Indeed, this is a critique that has often been made by local lesbian- and queer-identified commentators.[35] However, representing such relations as confined to the past does not actually confine female homosexual signification to pastness since memory and its narration take place, by definition, in the present.[36] Therefore, I argue that the attempt by the dominant culture of marital heterosexuality to de-realize lesbian possibility by memorializing it is, in a strict sense, doomed to failure. Against the commonsense assumption in popular post-Stonewall gay and lesbian discourse that happy endings to lesbian or gay stories are the sole means by which such stories can manifest critical potential, this book contends that the memorial discourse on women's same-sex love in these sad-ending love stories does indeed have a critical function, especially for its female consumers.[37] Rather than dismissing the memorial same-sex loving woman and her generic home, the sad-ending same-sex romance, as inherently "backward" formations, the chapters that follow strive to take seriously their ideological complexity both at the textual level and in their consumption by audiences. The apparent backwardness of these narratives turns out to make an important commentary on the present: attending closely to the repeated ideological construction of women's same-sex relations as an insistently memorable paradise lost, we discover a vigorous critical energy underlying this central theme in modern Chinese women's mass culture. The analyses reveal the rich polysemy of the memorial discourse on female homoeroticism; its capacity not only to close down the possibility of a lesbian erotics but also to open it up; its tendency simultaneously to naturalize adult heterosexuality and to foreground the tragedy of its imposition. They show how these complex cultural texts function not simply to seal the same-sex loving woman safely in the past but also to cause her to appear and reappear, ceaselessly, in the present.

Female Homoerotic Imaginary

In framing these arguments about the structural forms and ideological effects of the selected representations of same-sex love between women, this book also makes a broader claim about what I have termed the female homoerotic imaginary in contemporary Chinese public cultures. To clarify the precise valence of this invented term, it may be helpful to break it down into its two constituent parts. First, the phrase "female homoerotic" is intended to signify anything pertaining to sexual, erotic, or romantic love and desire between women. It has been chosen over what might initially appear a more likely candidate for the job — the word "lesbian" — for one major reason. The English word "lesbian," however carefully or strategically deployed, seems today to trail along with it an almost inevitable implication of self-conscious, minoritizing, Western-style lesbian identity: ways of imagining selves and interpersonal relations that have emerged out of the specific contexts of second-wave feminism and lesbian movements and politics in the United States and Western Europe since the early 1970s. But this book is for the most part less interested in self-conscious, minoritarian lesbian identities and subcultures than in the broader mainstream cultural representation of sexual, erotic, and romantic love between women, a realm indicated in my subtitle by the phrase "female homoerotic."[38] Expanding the purview of inquiry to include any representation of love and desire between women, and not only representations staked out in advance as representative of that quite particular, minoritizing category, lesbian (in Chinese, *nütongxinglian*, *nütongxinglianzhe*, or, more recently, *nütongzhi*), one finds a vast cultural reservoir of other representations of same-sex love between women.[39] Crucially, many of these representations feature universalizing rather than minoritizing representations of same-sex romance, figuring it as an ephemeral yet powerfully — often troublingly — memorable moment in a woman's life.[40] The nonidentitarian approach is intended to aid in exploring the distinctive cultural understandings of feminine same-sex love in this context without prematurely narrowing the terms of the inquiry with the a priori imposition of a homo/heterosexual dichotomy.[41]

Second, in using the term "imaginary" to designate the book's object of analysis, I mean to indicate not a theory of sexuality, not a theory of identity, not a theory of narrative, but rather a theorization of dominant ways of both representing and conceptualizing the female homoerotic within contemporary Chinese public cultures.[42] This book considers the activity of imagining in both personal and collective senses. With its intended implication of structured ways of thinking and feeling that are both embedded in everyday subjective experience and mediated through historically specific representations, my usage of the term "imaginary" perhaps has something in common with Raymond Williams's notion of the historically determined "structure of feeling" or with Teresa de Lauretis's concept of the "public fantasy."[43] The imaginary of the female homoerotic designates both the dominant ways in which women's same-sex relations are publicly represented and, as a consequence, the ways in which those forms of relationality become culturally intelligible for actual social subjects.

In light of the nonidentitarian approach outlined above, the selection of texts for analysis in the following chapters has not been guided by a judgment of the authenticity of these texts' lesbian credentials.[44] Rather, I have chosen a range of more or less widely circulated texts that have been recognized as thematizing women's same-sex romantic and erotic relationships by their readers and viewers, both lesbian- and heterosexual-identifying. Over the years during which the research for this work took place, numerous informal conversations, book reviews, scholarly papers, and Web discussions have thrown up this group of texts as likely candidates for inclusion in a popular canon of modern Chinese female homoerotic representation. The readers and viewers of these relatively widely circulated texts collectively interpret them as thematizing women's same-sex love; given that collective public judgment, they provide a logical place to begin mapping the hegemonic representational patterns that structure public fantasies on this subject. There is also an intentional focus, in most of the chapters, on texts that are relatively widely circulated and are neither necessarily written by known lesbian authors nor addressed primarily to lesbian audiences. This is because I feel that we need to gain a solid and adequately complex understanding of dominant patterns of female homoerotic representation before moving on to consider how these might be reconfigured by authors or directors with a conscious personal or political stake in producing enabling, subversive, or challenging representations of lesbian subjects.[45] This logic structures the progression of the chapters, with the final chapter mapping some recent cinematic responses to the dominant modes of representation sketched out in the previous chapters.

Sexual Histories and Geographies

The historical focus of this study is on female homoerotic representations in the contemporary period, between 1970 and the present. While chapter 1 shows that some key elements of these contemporary representations first emerged from the urban cultural and intellectual ferment of the 1920s and 1930s, this material is presented largely as contextualizing background for a study that is principally interested in the post-1970 period. Underlying this focus on twentieth- and twenty-first-century examples is my assumption that the modern period differs decisively from previous moments in the history of Chinese sexual epistemology due to the far-reaching transformative effects of intensified transculturation from Europe, the United States, and Japan from around the turn of the twentieth century. Therefore, this book has not attempted to construct an account of female homoeroticism through the ages of Chinese dynastic history.[46]

The book's bipartite chronology, with the initial focus on the Republican period followed by a jump to the post-1970 era, is not coincidental but reflects the contours of the public topicality of women's same-sex love in twentieth-century Chinese public cultures.[47] In mainland Chinese urban cultures in the 1920s and 1930s, the translation of sexological theory, the establishment of women's educational institutions, and the rise of the modern (heterosexual) romance narrative converged to provide the conditions for the literary emergence of same-sex schoolgirl romance in that period. However, with the political turmoil of the 1940s—the war of resistance against Japanese invasion and the civil war between the Nationalist and Communist armies—Chinese intellectual debates became overdetermined by pressing questions about national defense and political revolution, and the topic of women's same-sex love faded from view. Following the 1949 Communist revolution, strict political regulation of culture under Mao Zedong effectively kept the topic out of public discussion on the Chinese mainland between the 1950s and the 1970s, although as Harriet Evans observes, the official silence may have masked a widespread public condemnation of homosexuality (tongxinglian) as a violation of the "natural" biological laws of sex and gender.[48] Cultural censorship by the Nationalist government in Taiwan resulted in a comparable lack of public discussion during the 1950s and 1960s, aside from a scattering of scandal-mongering articles in the popular press that sensationalized male homosexuality as a monstrous inversion of "normal" gender.[49] Jens Damm's research shows that public discourse on male homosexuality in Taiwan between the late 1960s and the late 1980s, to the limited extent that the topic was discussed in popular journalism and medical publications, was split between pathologizing medical and psychoanalytic accounts and an emergent humanism that called for greater public understanding of homosexuals as an embattled sexual minority.[50] As on the mainland, however, very little public attention appears to have been paid to female homosexuality.[51] In Hong Kong, notwithstanding the modern tradition of playful gender ambiguity in popular cinema, male homosexual behavior remained illegal under British colonial law until 1991, and the extant studies indicate high levels of homophobia toward both male and female homosexuality.[52] The earliest of the late-twentieth-century examples discussed in this book are literary works that appeared in the mid-1970s in Taiwan: the young Chu T'ien-hsin's schoolgirl romance story, "Waves Scour the Sands" (1976), and Xuan Xiaofo's pulp novel of the same year, Yuan zhi wai (Outside the Circle), with its sympathetic depiction of a socially beleaguered tomboy protagonist.[53] Xuan's novel responds quite clearly to the then current humanist construction of homosexuality as "misunderstood" gender inversion, while Chu's story is a now classic contemporary adaptation of the schoolgirl romance narrative. The appearance of both these works, along with Beijing author Liu Suola's crypto-lesbian novella of 1985, "Lan tian lü hai" (Blue Sky Green Sea), foreshadows the late-century "second wave" of female homoerotic topicality that is this book's principal focus. This second wave coincides with the reemergence of the lesbian topic into public discussions in all three regions. Along with the slackening of previously harshly authoritarian regimes and the gradual reduction in the political regulation of culture in both the People's Republic of China and Taiwan, the late-twentieth-century reemergence of the lesbian topic can be linked to a spate of new popular and academic sexual studies during the 1980s, notably studies in sexual psychology in Taiwan and sexual sociology in the People's Republic.[54] But even more influential, since the early 1990s local movements and communities have emerged in all three areas responding to the global spread of lesbian identity politics. This factor more than any other underlies the regional "boom" in Chinese-language female homoerotic representations over the past fifteen-odd years.[55]

This book's rationale for considering the three distinct geocultural areas of mainland China, Taiwan, and Hong Kong together does not stem from any a priori presumption of their inherent similarity. The modern cultures of China, Taiwan, and Hong Kong are of course historically interlinked to a certain degree, both in a broad cultural and linguistic sense and through the more recent emergence of the various forms of Chinese modernity through the processes of conflict and reciprocal self-definition among the regimes of British colonialism, Chinese socialism, and Kuomintang party-state capitalism. Leading up to the 1949 Communist revolution, the late 1940s exoduses from China's cities to Taiwan (the Nationalist army and its followers) and Hong Kong (many artists and other professionals from Shanghai's then sizable film industry) effected a transplantation of some elements of the urban cultures and intellectual ferment of Republican China to these other locations.[56] Yet despite significant strands of historical connection, the contemporary cultures of the People's Republic, Taiwan, and Hong Kong are irreducibly plural. It is therefore worth emphasizing that although this book proposes the cultural dominance of a particular, temporal logic of female homoerotic representation and attempts to trace this logic across texts produced in all three areas, this logic does not exhaust the field of female homoerotic representation in any of them.[57] Rather than attempt the impossible task of formulating a theory capacious enough to account for every single instance of such representation in all three geocultural areas, this book identifies one highly pervasive cultural logic and traces it as it manifests at particular sites and in various ways in each area. One of the central questions addressed in the analyses that follow concerns how the temporal logic of female homoerotic representation is marked by the local historical and cultural particularities of each of the areas in which it manifests.[58] But in addition to localized inflections of this common discourse there also exist forms of representation in each area that are far more strongly marked by local particularity; examples include the all-female Taiwanese opera (koa-a-hi), with its attendant quasi-tradition of romantic and/or sexual relationships between actresses and between actresses and female fans; the comedic or carnivalesque representation of proto-lesbian characters in popular Cantonese cinema; and the normalization of intimate bonds between women workers under Maoism in mainland China.[59] The high degree of local specificity in such formations prevents them from being slotted neatly into the more general interpretive schema that this book proposes. The gaps that are apparent in the choice of examples analyzed here therefore point to the limits of the model proposed; like any analysis, this is a necessarily partial account, and such gaps indicate areas awaiting further research.

More than from any presumption of deep-rooted cultural similarity, the decision to consider female homoerotic representation across the People's

Republic, Taiwan, and Hong Kong arises from the observation of the intra-regional mobility of popular texts and discourses among these three areas in the present day. Since the mid-1980s, cultural flows between the People's Republic of China, Taiwan, and Hong Kong have steadily accelerated. Taiwanese fiction has become an area of major interest to both mainland Chinese and Hong Kong readerships and critics, and indeed some of the Taiwanese schoolgirl romance stories discussed here have been republished by mainland Chinese presses.[60] Likewise, queer-themed mainland Chinese and Hong Kong fiction has sparked the interest of Taiwanese readerships.[61] Short fiction from all three areas is also circulated to readers throughout the region more informally via the World Wide Web. Similarly lively trans-local cross-flows of media products like television programs and films from and to all three areas occur via the Internet and media piracy, as well as by more formal means like film festivals, campus screenings, and commercial theatrical release.[62] The map of contemporary Chinese cultures that emerges from this research thus resembles not so much the "living tree" of Tu Wei-ming's famous formulation, with its singular trunk of cultural tradition, as a cultural archipelago where media cross-flows—both within and beyond "transnational China"—interact with local histories to create distinctive yet interlinked contemporary cultural scenes.[63]

Black Skirts and White Blouses

This book's focus on the memorial narrative of schoolgirl romance reflects the remarkably pervasive conceptual linkage of female same-sex love with youth in contemporary Chinese cultural life, from pop psychology and media cultures to popular fiction by young lesbian authors and the experience of ordinary female students in their everyday school lives. By the early twenty-first century, the discourse of "temporary homosexuality" in same-sex schools is frequently enough invoked in Chinese public life that it may be considered a form of cultural common sense. Consider, for example, the following excerpt from an article published in 2001 entitled "Facing the Suspicion of Student Homosexuality," originally published in the *Ming Pao Daily* and reproduced on the Web site of the Family Planning Association of Hong Kong:

> In a girls' school, intimate behavior among female students tends to be relatively open; for example, holding hands to demonstrate the closeness of a friendship is commonly seen. Perhaps due to the narrowness of their social circle, adolescent boys and girls tend to develop emotional attach-

ments to friends of the same sex. It may be that intimate behaviors between [adolescents] of the same sex arise from fantasies about and desires for relations with the opposite sex. The temporary impossibility of directing these toward male-female romance may very well be sufficient to cause them to divert their feelings or sexual fantasies toward someone of the same sex. In reality, many adolescents pass through this deceptive phase of pseudo-homosexual same-sex attachment in the process of their development; it does not mean that when they have grown up they will be homosexuals.[64]

In this account, as in many similar ones to be found in sex education materials, parenting manuals, and colloquial interpretations of adolescent sexuality throughout China, Hong Kong, and Taiwan today, the recuperative insistence that teenage same-sex attachments are really heterosexual yearnings in disguise is accompanied by the enforcement of a heterosexual ending on the merely "pseudo-homosexual" story of adolescence, where same-sex love is constructed as a common but temporary phase in young women's development and thereby fated to become but the memory of adult femininity. A similar logic underlies the following account, published in 2002 by Shen Yuexing, a guidance counselor at Shanghai Number Three Girls' School, as a commentary on a confessional account of same-sex romance written by one of her students:

Something that is like friendship but is not quite friendship; something like love yet not quite love—these sentiments bring adolescent middle-school girls pleasure, but they bring also self-castigation resulting from a failure to adhere to the social standard that "it is not permitted for a girl to like another girl." . . . Allow me to discuss my opinion on this special kind of same-sex emotionality. . . . For the girl students who inhabit it, the environment of the girls' school lasts, after all, just three to seven years, and after this period they will all return to a mixed-sex environment. Even if same-sex love (tongxing de lianqing) does occur, it is but a transient phenomenon. . . . It disappears naturally with a change in environment, and afterwards it does not have any effect on the girls' normal relations with the opposite sex. Furthermore, in degree this is merely a psychological tendency toward infatuation with the same sex; there are neither obvious external behavioral symptoms nor situations involving sexual acts as between a cross-sex couple. Under most circumstances, this is a process that will end as readily as it began. . . . The schools and families of girls in all-girl schools should institute a wide spectrum of extracurricular activities to afford the students plentiful opportunities to communicate with and learn to understand the opposite sex and to experience cross-sex friendship. This will prevent innocent same-sex friendship from developing and deepening in the direction of homosexuality (*tongxinglian*).[65]

Here, as in the previous excerpt, the emphasis is on the ubiquity and temporariness of the (non-)homosexuality. Not only is it a passing phase destined to be superseded once adult (hetero)sexuality makes its inevitable claim, but also, supposedly lacking the component of genital sex, it is not a real but a "false" homosexuality, caused by mere circumstance rather than by an inherently different sexual orientation.[66] Yet although the intent of articles like these is to mark out a decisive boundary between youthful same-sex passions and "true" homosexuality, in trying to shut down the question of homosexuality once and for all, they stir up a hornet's nest of irresolvable questions. Where exactly does "false" homosexuality leave off and "true" homosexuality begin? If the situations that give rise to situational homosexuality produce young people who *continue* to prefer same-sex partners to opposite-sex ones and require careful coaxing toward the proper path with specially designed programs of extracurricular hetero-sociality, then how is the situational to be practically distinguished from the permanent? And so on. Despite their intention to establish a *cordon sanitaire* between true homosexuality and "same-sex emotionality" or the "deceptive phase of pseudo-homosexual same-sex attachment" between girls, the end result of such accounts is only to strengthen the conceptual link between feminine adolescence and a same-sex love that is fundamentally conditioned by its hot-and-bothered proximity to homosexuality proper.

The theme of romantic attachment between schoolgirls also appears, in slightly less anxious form, in texts consumed within contemporary youth cultures, notably in the Japanese manga and anime (comics and animation) and the Japanese and Korean girls' school horror movies that are consumed throughout Hong Kong, Taiwan, and mainland China. The distinct female homoerotic manga subgenre known as *shōjo ai* (girls' love) developed in Japan in the early 1970s, alongside the better-known male homoerotic *shōnen ai* subgenre.[67] Translated Japanese manga have a long history in both Taiwan and Hong Kong, where they have circulated for several decades in both pirated and (more recently) legal form; in mainland China, the manga craze gathered force in the mid-1990s with the widespread pirating of many popular Japanese series.[68] Some of these series have also been made into anime for broadcast on regional cable television.[69] Girls' love manga focus on romantic stories of love between wide-eyed teenage students; circulating throughout "transna-tional China" in Chinese translations, these popular manga, which empha-size the youth of the protagonists and fetishized school settings, contribute to the wider cultural association of same-sex love with female students. A similar preoccupation with Japanese-style black-and-white school uniforms, campus settings, and homoerotic possibility is found in the spate of Japanese and Korean girls' school horror movies that circulate in the Chinese-speaking societies under discussion as part of the late-century waves of Japanese and Korean popular culture throughout the East Asian region.[70] Like the campus-based girls' love manga, these films figure intense romantic or quasi-romantic relationships between schoolgirls; in distinction to the manga, their domi-nant note is anxiety and terror, as the girls' relationships seem inevitably to lead to a downward spiral of jealousy, possessiveness, violence, bloodshed, and even destruction of cosmic proportions.[71] This somewhat conservative tendency notwithstanding, the circulation of these popular genre films in China, Hong Kong, and Taiwan contributes to the widespread association of same-sex love with feminine youth.

The familiar popular cultural figure of the same-sex attracted girl or young woman has also recently found her way into materials produced by self-consciously lesbian-identified cultural producers directed at lesbian reader-ships. This is the case with the new wave of lesbian popular fiction that has arisen since the late 1990s. These novels and short stories are distinguished from earlier, more highbrow instances of "queer fiction" (*tongzhi wenxue* or *ku'er wenxue*) by their unapologetic populism and easy readability. They often appear initially as Internet fiction—a major arena of literary production in its own right in Chinese-speaking youth cultures—before being published in book form by dedicated gay-and-lesbian (*tongzhi*) publishing houses like Jihe in Taiwan and Huasheng in Hong Kong or other popular presses. A major genre of these lesbian-themed stories is the high school campus romance with its open and queer-affirmative celebration of same-sex love in "the era of black skirts and white blouses" (*hei qun bai yi shidai*).[72]

Recent ethnographic research in Taipei, Shanghai, and Hong Kong also reveals the important place of girls' same-sex romance within lived campus cultures.[73] Zhang Qiaoting's aptly titled *Xunfu yu dikang* (Campus Memory) presents the results of her research at Taipei First Girls' High School (Bei Yi Nü), Taiwan's most prestigious girls' school, established under the Japa-nese colonial administration on the model of European elite girls' schools. Zhang's study of ten lesbian-identifying Bei Yi Nü graduates reveals the exis-tence of an apparent quasi-tradition of same-sex romantic pairings in the face of school authorities' vigorous policing of students' sexuality. Sweethearts pair up in couples with one tomboy (T) and one feminine (po) partner; meet for clandestine dates and sex in secluded corners of the campus; write about their romances in thinly disguised form in stories submitted to the school magazine; and copy and circulate well-known schoolgirl romances by other writers, including Chu T'ien-hsin and Cao Lijuan.[74] Pik-ki Leung's research at the elite mainland Chinese state key school Shanghai Number 3 Girls' School (Shi San Nü Zhong) reveals a comparable culture of romantic same-sex friendships.[75] Leung's findings suggest that these students' views of intimate relations between girls are internally divided. On the one hand, when questioned directly about homosexuality, the students appeal to a disapproving, minoritizing discourse on lesbianism (nütongxinglian) as pathology, echoing the rhetoric of current Chinese popular psychology. On the other hand, in their own forms of cultural expression, including creative writing and the narrativization of their autobiographical experience in interviews, the students give voice to an alternative, idealizing and universalizing discourse on the beauty of romantic intimacy between young women. These students' ambivalent construction of same-sex love mirrors the double vision that this book proposes is characteristic of contemporary Chinese representations of women's same-sex love more broadly, split as these are between a universalizing view (schoolgirl romance) and a minoritizing view (tomboy melodrama). Lucetta Kam Yip-lo's and Carmen Tong Ka-man's studies of TB (tomboy) culture and same-sex romance in Hong Kong high schools reveal similar subcultural formations, as do the findings of the Hong Kong Women Who Have Same-Sex Desires Oral History Project.[76] Such studies demonstrate the degree of social embeddedness of contemporary schoolgirl romance narratives. Manifestly, these stories exceed the boundaries of the texts themselves to produce significant subjective effects for the girls and women who read, watch, write, exchange, reenact, and identify with their narratives.

All these examples demonstrate the high degree of cultural prominence enjoyed by the figure of the same-sex attracted schoolgirl or young woman in the contemporary Chinese cultures under discussion: she appears in both openly homophobic and proudly lesbian-affirmative instances, as well as in examples whose ideological valence is less immediately clear. It is in this context that the stories, television programs, and films analyzed in the chapters that follow have emerged and should be viewed; they are not idiosyncratic depictions of some obscure or marginal figure but reflections of a broader, fully mainstream cultural preoccupation.[77] Far from addressing a merely peripheral concern, the investigation of female homoerotic representation and epistemology illuminates central aspects of contemporary Chinese understandings of sex, love, gender, marriage, and the cultural ordering of human life.

Trajectory of the Text

The chapter that follows this introduction traces the early-twentieth-century origins of the Chinese schoolgirl romance narrative, or what I call the going-in story (marking an intentional ironic contrast with the Western, post-Stonewall coming-out story), due to its characteristic narrative structure in which adolescent same-sex love is superseded by cross-sex union at story's end. Focusing on modernist stories written in the 1920s and 1930s by Lu Yin, Ling Shuhua, and Yu Dafu, the chapter traces the literary roots of the universalizing mode of female homoerotic representation in Lu's and Ling's stories while also noting the concurrent literary emergence of a minoritizing discourse on the masculine lesbian in Yu's novella. I frame the emergence of the same-sex schoolgirl romance in the context of both the transculturation of European sexology into China in the early twentieth century and the generic conventions of popular cross-sex romance, which I argue Lu's and Ling's stories appropriate to present a markedly utopian vision of young women's same-sex love.

Chapter 2 charts the late-twentieth-century resurgence of the going-in story, analyzing two contemporary literary examples by Chu T'ien-Hsin and Wong Bikwan. Continuing the generic analysis begun in chapter 1, the chapter demonstrates how each story rehearses in a knowing manner the codes of modern Chinese-language tragic romance fiction. Chu's story, for instance, stages an ironic citation of the characteristically romantic-melancholic structure of feeling in tragic romance stories like those of Taiwanese "romance queen" Qiong Yao. Comparably, Wong's story reworks some central themes and aesthetics of the 1940s works of Shanghai/Hong Kong writer Eileen Chang. I propose that it is by means of such generic intertextuality that these stories critically interrupt, rather than merely reproduce, the naturalizing force of the heterocentric, sexological account of adolescent sexual development that also informs them.

The following chapter investigates the form in which the schoolgirl romance reappeared in the People's Republic of China in the immediate post-Mao era. The chapter frames female rock musician/author Liu Suola's 1985 novella "Blue Sky Green Sea" in the intellectual context of mid-1980s Beijing, the moment of "culture fever" when Chinese intellectuals were enthusiastically reengaging with modern Euro-American thought. The chapter shows how Liu's novella draws on a strongly Freudian vocabulary to dramatize the melancholia of adult femininity in this post-Mao social context in which the loss of female same-sex attachment could not be mourned. Although "Blue Sky" echoes the Hong Kong and Taiwanese works discussed in chapter 2 in its idealizing construction of young women's same-sex love as a universal yet fleeting experience, this chapter shows how the specific intellectual and historical context of the novella's production led Liu to express the utopian memorialism of the Chinese going-in story through the distinctive language of psychological humanism.

Chapter 4 picks up the thread on the minoritizing discourse on lesbian masculinity introduced in chapter 1. This chapter illustrates how in dominant representations, the tomboy's future has been strictly unimaginable; overwhelmingly, tomboy characters have tended either quietly to fade from narrative focus as the story progresses or to disappear by more dramatic means (most commonly untimely death). No less than the more common, memorial figure of the conventionally feminine same-sex-loving schoolgirl, then, the vanishing tomboy attests to the dominance of the temporal discourse on the impossibility of lesbian futurity. The chapter maps a genealogy of the tomboy narrative since the 1970s through pulp fiction (Xuan Xiaofo's Outside the Circle), soap opera (Ko Yi-zheng's Ninü [The Unfilial Daughter]), and teenpic (Yee Chih-yen's Lanse da men [Blue Gate Crossing]). It shows that the tomboy has tended to be represented in the melodramatic mode, marking a counterpoint to the going-in story's generic affiliation with tragic romance. A classically melodramatic image of the tomboy as emotionally wounded, socially besieged, and in need of feminine love emerges—an image that is interestingly answered by a recent wave of Taiwanese telemovies (discussed in the following chapter) centering on tomboy-loving feminine protagonists.

Chapter 5 analyzes viewer responses to two recent Taiwanese telemovie adaptations of memorial schoolgirl romance narratives. This chapter furnishes a concrete illustration of a cultural logic that is presumed throughout this book: the assumption that widely circulated forms of representation exceed the "merely" textual and have a material impact on how their consumers understand themselves and their place in social life. The chapter reveals that these two telemovies project a vision of mournful femininity with which their female viewers—heterosexual as much as lesbian—strongly identify. Focusing particularly on the enthusiastic identification of nonlesbian women viewers with these sorrowful same-sex lovers, I propose that these programs are engaged in the cultural labor of publicly mourning the closing down of future lesbian possibility in the lives of young adult women. Further, by unambiguously cuing female spectators to identify with their tomboy-loving protagonists, these programs frame the tomboy as the object of love of women in general. In this regard, they enable a profoundly reparative vision of the tomboy, rendering her lovable and lavishing collective feminine love upon her, in sharp contrast to the broader cultural abjection of lesbian masculinity dramatized in the tomboy melodramas analyzed in chapter 4.

It is only relatively recently that the lesbian subject has begun to be treated directly and seriously by young, independent film directors, and the book's final chapter focuses on the rise of Chinese lesbian-themed cinema since the late 1990s. This chapter marks a turning point in the book's focus and argument. We shift from analyzing the contradictory functions of the memorial discourse in more or less mainstream representations of female homoeroticism to exploring resistant responses to this pervasive discourse in some recent independent films that are consciously and clearly self-marked as "lesbian." This chapter thus shifts the previous focus on recovering the complexity and ambivalence of supposedly "backward" texts toward an attention to the actively "forward-looking" practice of queer filmmaking, with its commitment to forging new forms of representation. Following an overview of the ways in which the memorial mode has structured female homoerotic representation in previous, mainstream Chinese-language cinemas, this chapter reveals how recent films by young, independent women directors, including Chen Jofei, Mak Yan Yan, and Li Yu, are challenging the dominant construction of women's same-sex love as a memorial condition. In one sense, these directors' serious, anti-homophobic treatments of love between women reflect the impact of globalizing U.S.-style lesbian identity politics. But while their films undoubtedly respond to such global movements, the specificity of the ways in which they do so also illustrates a continuing preoccupation with temporality that, as the preceding chapters have illustrated, has been the hallmark of modern Chinese female homoerotic representation. These recent films approach this theme in new ways in order to reconfigure the Chinese female homoerotic imaginary away from the familiar memorial logic toward the present and future.

ONE

Tragic Romance

The Chinese Going-In Story

Over ten years ago, Bret Hinsch concluded his argument on the decline of premodern Chinese conceptualizations of same-sex sexual behavior with the gloomy assertion that "The fluid conceptions of sexuality of old, which assumed that an individual was capable of enjoying a range of sexual acts, have been replaced by the ironclad Western dichotomy of homosexual/heterosexual. Instead of . . . terms taken from [Chinese] history and literature, Chinese now speak of "homosexuality" (*tongxinglian* or *tongxingai*), a direct translation of the Western medical term that defines a small group of pathological individuals according to a concrete sexual essence."[1] Despite some scholarly disagreement with Hinsch's historical oversimplification, the view that modern Chinese cultures conceptualize sexuality primarily in terms of a rigid and indicatively Western dichotomy between the terms "homosexuality" and "heterosexuality" remains influential.[2] In the pages that follow, however, I want to propose a different framework for approaching Chinese sexual epistemologies in the context of twentieth-century modernization.

In relation to post-Foucaldian scholarship on the history of sexuality, Eve Sedgwick cautions that "the historical search for a Great Paradigm Shift may obscure the present conditions of sexual identity."[3] This warning is certainly apposite to the study of the history of sexuality in twentieth-century China: as Sang's work implies, an analysis like the one made by Hinsch is open to precisely this kind of critique in its simplistic construction of Westernization as effecting just such a radical, total, and irreversible break with "Chinese sexual tradition."[4] Further, pursuing the implications of Sedgwick's warning even more explicitly into the territory of cross-cultural sexuality studies, I would propose that the geocultural search for a great paradigm *divergence* between the West and its "others" — a search that implicitly propels many cross-cultural and sexuality studies — may obscure the conditions of sexual cultures in both places. Reducing the question to be asked of disparate sexual cultures to "How does the understanding of sexuality there differ from our understanding of sexuality in the modern West?" entails some specific risks.

First, such a formulation implies that sexuality in the modern West is a self-evident object of knowledge, whereas, as Sedgwick forcefully demonstrates, this is very far from the case; modern, Euro-American sexual epistemology is nothing if not multiple, discontinuous, and riven with internal contradictions.[5] The attribution of an ironclad dichotomy between heterosexual and homosexual to modern Western culture ignores the fundamental incoherence of the hetero/homo distinction in this context. To take an example from material close at hand: the chronic strain that Sedgwick observes between minoritizing and universalizing accounts of homosexuality is illustrated clearly in Havelock Ellis's anxious distinction between temporary and congenital female homosexualities, which, as this chapter will demonstrate, had a significant impact on Republican Chinese accounts of same-sex love. That strange category, "temporary homosexuality," has a peculiarly solvent effect on that supposedly unassailable fortress of modern Western sexual epistemology, the homo/hetero division. For surely the "temporarily homosexual" schoolgirl is, in effect, a kind of *homosexual heterosexual* or *heterosexual homosexual*. Through her, the supposedly hermetically sealed category of heterosexuality is infiltrated by the possibility of homosexual desires and behaviors; likewise, the outward appearance of homosexuality is belied by the potential of latent heterosexuality. The deconstructive critique of the homo/hetero divide that has been advanced by queer analysis reveals the extent to which modern Western sexual culture is genuinely anxious, genuinely unable to rule, once and for all, where the homosexual leaves off and the heterosexual begins.[6] What characterizes modern Western sexual culture, this work has shown, is not so much an ironclad distinction between homosexuality and heterosexuality as the repeated, panicked attempt to *impose* such a distinction on a body of knowledge and experience that is in reality defined by an uncontrollable indeterminacy. Given this, in approaching the transculturation of Western sexual knowledges into Chinese contexts in the early twentieth century, our first question should not be about how originally complex understandings of selves and bodies are reduced to something simple and ironclad. Rather, we should ask how the *already* complexly incoherent and anxious discourses of European sexology get transfigured into a related yet distinct set of incoherencies and anxieties in Chinese contexts.

The issue of cross-cultural conversations on sexuality relates to the second problem with the search for a great paradigm divergence between Euro-American sexual understandings and their "others": it implies that "other" sexualities will necessarily be meaningful primarily in terms of their self-evident *differences* from modern, Western ones. Yet given that in the modern period non-Western sexual knowledges are never entirely isolable from Western ones, it makes little sense to assume in advance that the most meaningful relation between modern Chinese and Western sexualities will be one of contrast; more often, the relation between them turns out to be one of *proximity*—neither identity nor otherness, but a complex relation of adjacency and interconnection.[7] Instead of asking how Chinese sexual paradigms decisively diverge from Western ones, then, it may prove more fruitful to ask which particular strands within modern Western discourses of sexuality are taken up and continued elsewhere. How are discourses that already begin life as multiple and internally contradictory translated and transcultured to produce the distinctive formations of Chinese sexual modernities? These are some of the questions addressed in this chapter.

Looking with a careful eye over the field of modern Chinese cultural production, in addition to a minoritizing understanding of female homosexuals as a distinct and finite group of sexually variant individuals, we also find alternative sexual epistemologies, ways of knowing feminine sexuality that resist articulation in the language of homosexual/heterosexual opposition.[8] The coming-out narrative, which retrospectively both describes and constructs the moment of the lesbian or gay individual's discovery of her or his "true" sexual identity, is a central one for modern Euro-American sexual cultures.[9] In fact, in its installation of a concrete and essential homosexual identity within its protagonist the coming-out story exemplifies the very sexual epistemology whose supposed supersession over older nonidentitarian Chinese understandings Hinsch bemoans. And with the late-twentieth-century emergence of lesbian and gay movements in mainland China, Hong Kong, and Taiwan, the coming-out story has indeed become a common narrative in these contexts. Yet alongside the coming-out story and its attendant minoritizing epistemology there also persists here another kind of sexual story. Over the three chapters that follow, I examine the influential modern Chinese narrative of temporary same-sex love between adolescent girls remembered after the fact; I call this the memorial schoolgirl romance or, in contrast to the coming-out story, the "going-in story" (as it narrates a going into rather than a coming out of heterosexual relations, or, alternatively, a going out of rather than a coming into homosexual ones). Although, like the rhetoric of minoritarian homosexual identity, the history of this narrative can be traced in part back to the Chinese translation of European sexology in the early twentieth century, this narrative produces female homosexuality on a universalizing model that notably distinguishes it from the homo/hetero opposition's instantiation of homosexuality as a minority identity.

I begin by sketching out the historical context of the going-in story's emergence in early-twentieth-century China before analyzing two literary examples of the narrative: Lu Yin's "Lishi de riji" (Lishi's Diary, 1923) and Ling Shuhua's "Shuo you zheme yihui shi" ("Once upon a Time," 1928). As these readings demonstrate, taking the going-in story seriously, as befits its remarkable cultural pervasiveness, throws into relief the multiplicity and complexity of modern Chinese sexual epistemologies. While such epistemic incoherence *structurally* parallels the condition of modern Euro-American sexual knowledges, nevertheless, as I will show, the distinctive emphases and generic preoccupations of modern Chinese sexual narratives make them irreducible to—if also intractably entangled with—their Euro-American counterparts. Through a discussion of Yu Dafu's novella "Ta shi yige ruo nüzi" (She Was a Weak Woman, 1932), the second part of the chapter traces some of the literary and cultural roots of what would in the late twentieth century become a minoritizing discourse on the tomboy as an embodiment of sexual and gender deviance. Yet as I will show, translated European sexological understandings were not straightforwardly or uncritically reproduced in Yu's novella any more than they were in Lu's and Ling's stories, for Yu's masculine, same-sex-desiring schoolgirl, Li Wenqing, cannot be interpreted as simply a Chinese version of the Euro-American mannish lesbian but represents a far more complex transcultural amalgam.

Transcultured Sexology: Sexual Modernity via Japan

Despite the common assumption that the Chinese invention of "homosexuality" as *tongxinglian* or *tongxing'ai* is a direct translation from European sources and hence best understood as a straightforward instance of cultural Westernization, in fact, as Sang has shown, the category *tongxing'ai* first entered modern Chinese in the 1920s not directly from European sexology, but rather refracted through the Japanese translation, *dōseiai*.[10] This double transculturation from English and German through Japanese to Chinese raises the possibility that early Chinese constructions of homosexuality may have been colored, in part, by Japanese selections and interpretations of the material.[11] In light of this Japanese connection, it is interesting to note that the coinage of the modern Japanese term *dōseiai* in the opening decades of the twentieth century was strongly linked with contemporaneous attempts specifically to describe romantic friendships between female students in modern educational institutions.[12] Sociologist Furukawa Makoto writes as follows: "Homosexuality among female students [in the first decades of the twentieth-century in Japan] encouraged the introduction of the term *dōseiai* (homosexuality) to express an erotic relationship between two partners of the same sex, since the existing terms, *nanshoku* and *keikan*, applied only to men. A number of terms developed, through the translation from foreign literature. . . . These terms gradually converged on *dōseiai*, with the nature of female homosexuality playing an important role in this process."[13]

The term *dōseiai* had become standard usage by Meiji sexologists by the 1920s.[14] It thus entered circulation just after the popularization of the modern term *shōjo* (girl), a novel category designating feminine adolescence as a distinct experiential period within a woman's life between childhood and adulthood. *Shōjo* was also inherently a sexualized category, as it implied the concept of virginity, not previously a defining characteristic of young female personhood.[15] As Tomoko Aoyama and others have pointed out, from the outset the concept of *shōjo* was associated with the consolidation of a distinct *shōjo bunka* (girls' culture), linked to the establishment of women's education, the translation of American girls' fiction and the publication of (frequently homoerotic) girls' stories by popular woman author Yoshiya Nobuko, the rise of a lively *shōjo* magazine culture, and the targeting of *shōjo* as consumers of a range of other commercial products.[16] The conceptual possibility of female homosexuality, in *dōseiai*, thus emerges in the same cultural moment as the idea and cultural practices of feminine adolescence in *shōjo*.[17] And as both Furukawa and Gregory Pflugfelder illustrate, early-twentieth-century Japanese discussions of *dōseiai* were indeed marked by a selective emphasis on discussions of romantic love between *shōjo*.[18] Over the course of the opening decades of the twentieth century, *dōseiai* became associated more and more with adolescent girls, ultimately producing an understanding in prewar Japan, Furukawa proposes, "of [*dōseiai*] as lesbianism."[19]

Pflugfelder emphasizes that early-twentieth-century Japanese sexologists, journalists, and feminists reached no consensus on the significance of intimate relations between girls, producing instead a "discursive fray" that, "through its very clamorousness, helped keep the schoolgirl at the forefront of early twentieth-century debate on gender and sexuality."[20] Pflugfelder's study reveals an intricate snarl of competing constructions of *dōseiai* between schoolgirls in early-twentieth-century Japanese public discourse, including not just those who, taking a cue from Richard von Krafft-Ebing, saw it in a pathologizing and minoritizing light as a congenital sexual defect, but also those who, taking up one strand of Ellis's thinking, normalized and universalized it as a situational behavior characteristic of feminine adolescence, in addition to commentators who reflected Freud's influence in constructing youthful *dōseiai* as a necessary stage in young women's psychosexual development toward heterosexual adulthood. Constructions of the schoolgirl same-sex lover produced her, at different times, on the model of both gender transitivity and gender separatism, and feminist commentators and sexologists alike were divided on the possible benefits and dangers of same-sex love among schoolgirls.[21] Yet despite this cacophony of competing constructions, which in part reflected the incoherencies intrinsic to the European sexological discourse itself, Pflugfelder observes a marked tendency among early Japanese commentators on schoolgirl *dōseiai* to presume as foundational the contemporaneous gender ideology, derived both from European sexology and popular Japanese gender typologies, that women were emotionally more sensitive yet sexually less desiring than men. Hence, *dōseiai* among schoolgirls tended to be constructed in a comparatively idealizing mode as more sentimental or spiritual (*seishinteki*) and less carnal or sexual (*nikutaiteki*) than *dōseiai* among schoolboys.[22]

The connection that was forged in the Japanese discourse between the two novel concepts of *shōjo* and *dōseiai* clearly appears to have been translated into the Republican Chinese context soon after its emergence in Japan, with Chinese discussions of *tongxing'ai* heavily indebted to the earlier Japanese debates, especially in their sharp focus on *tongxing'ai* among adolescent girls (*shaonü*) in modern-style educational institutions.[23] Direct Chinese translations of European sexological texts were made in the 1920s and 1930s, but this period also saw an intensive transculturation of the emergent modern Japanese sex discourse.[24] The Japanese influence took effect through actual Chinese translations of Japanese articles about *dōseiai* between schoolgirls; through Chinese authors' discussions of the Japanese "fashion" for such relationships; and, more broadly, through the high level of general familiarity that the Chinese authors showed with contemporary Japanese sexology.[25] Sang's research shows that like the Japanese discussions of schoolgirl *dōseiai*, the Chinese debates over *tongxing'ai* in girls' schools demonstrated a wide range of competing constructions of the phenomenon, including not just minoritizing accounts but also universalizing ones.[26] Directly evidencing the Japanese influence, in 1925 the intellectual women's magazine *Funü zazhi* published a Chinese translation of the well-known Japanese feminist educator Furuya Toyoko's influential 1922 article praising the pedagogical value of same-sex love in girls' schools, "The New Meaning of Same-Sex Love in Women's Education."[27] Pflugfelder observes that in the Japanese context, "Furuya's essay captures a historical moment when the concept of 'same-sex love' could still convey a remarkably positive meaning in the realm of public discourse," and he proposes that the essay implies an alternative—ultimately unrealized—vision of Japanese sexual modernity in which same-sex love among women would have an integral and valued role.[28] The translation of this article marks one concrete instance of the importation into China of the universalizing and idealizing Japanese discourse on love between schoolgirls. And given the remarkable longevity of the elegiac narrative of love between adolescent girls in modern Chinese literary and popular cultures, it is worth considering whether the alternative vision of sexual modernity that Pflugfelder discerns in Furuya's idealization of universalized same-sex love between schoolgirls may perhaps survive as one component of Chinese sexual epistemologies today. It is this possibility that the following chapters set out to explore.

In the context of the double transculturation of European sexology via Japan to China, Sang examines the emergence of a distinct modern-vernacular Chinese literary phenomenon in the 1920s and 1930s that she calls the "women's homoerotic school romance."[29] Through her analysis of works by elite, modernist women writers—including Lu Yin, Ling Shuhua, and Ding Ling—Sang traces the historical foundations of an influential modern Chinese literary discourse on homoerotic friendships between young women in modern schools and colleges. In the light of the marked Japanese influence in Republican Chinese discussions of tongxing'ai, it is worth underlining that the Chinese literary form of the women's homoerotic school romance is undergirded by the history of early-twentieth-century cultural flows between China and Japan. This is most especially the case in the Chinese reproduction of the conceptual linkage between the novel categories of adolescent girls (shōjo/shaonü) and homosexuality (dōseiai/tongxing'ai); both of these terms and the categories they designate—and, as we will see, the conceptual linkage between them—have persisted into early-twenty-first-century Chinese language and culture. The connection is also revealed in the Chinese reiteration of the idealizing tendency in Japanese female dōseiai discourse, a tendency that drew on the contemporaneous popular and sexological gender ideology constructing adolescent femininity as spiritually pure, passionately emotional, and sexually quiescent. This distinctively modern opposition between feminine/spiritual (seishinteki) and masculine/carnal (nikutaiteki) love remains a common one in contemporary Chinese schoolgirl romances, where the same Chinese characters are used for these terms (in Mandarin, pronounced *jing-shende* and *routide* respectively).[30] Indeed, the equation of adolescent female same-sex romance with "spiritual love" remains a prevalent feature of many contemporary Chinese schoolgirl romance narratives.[31]

Schoolgirl Romance and the Literary Romance Narrative

In addition to Sang's observation that the Republican-era Chinese school-girl romances cite the contemporaneous discourses of transcultured sex-ology, it is also interesting to consider the uses the stories make of romance itself, both as ideology and as narrative form. Approaching the Republican-era schoolgirl romance as a subset of the romance narrative more broadly not only reveals a further reflection of the ideological concerns of the May Fourth literary modernists—specifically their concern to transform feudal sex and gender relations through the modern idea of romantic love (*lian'ai*)—but also shows up formal links back to earlier forms of the Chinese liter-ary love story. Framing the schoolgirl romance through its generic affilia-tion with romance reveals how these stories appropriate stock elements of cross-sex love narratives, in their various, historically distinct generic mani-festations, to construct the modern Chinese literary discourse on same-sex love between young women. This generic linkage again underscores what a mistake it would be to assume that the pathologizing, minoritizing view of some European sexological accounts of homosexuality is the sole impetus for the cultural elaboration of the idea of female same-sex love in Repub-lican China. By implicitly paralleling same-sex romances between young women with the cross-sex love stories of popular romance, writers like Lu Yin and Ling Shuhua made female same-sex love part of a familiar narra-tive of "women in love," where "women" designates a broad and general category rather than the specific sexual minority that would be implied in the term "homosexuals" (*tongxinglianzhe*). Romance stories, in the broadest possible sense of narratives of obstructed love, have been part of Chinese popular and elite literary and entertainment cultures since medieval times. Prior to the twentieth century, such narratives appeared most notably in the classic tales of "scholar-beauty" (*caizi-jiaren* or *jiaren-caizi*) romance, which took the form of vernacular folk legends, popular dramas, narrative poems, and (since the mid-seventeenth century) novels.[32] Keith McMahon divides the genre in its eighteenth-century literary manifestations into two streams: the "chaste beauty-scholar romance," which idealizes the spiritual perfection of the woman, and the "erotic scholar-beauty romance," which glorifies the sexual potency of the man.[33] It is the former variant that is most pertinent to the literary genealogy I wish to trace here. Such narratives center on an idealized couple from gentry families: the young man is a handsome literary genius (caizi); the young woman (or women) (jiaren) is inwardly virtuous, as well as outwardly beautiful and possessed of unusual literary talent. Typically the central couple overcomes a series of external obstacles in order to achieve a happy marital union at the end of the story.[34] In light of the subsequent preoccupations of Chinese popular romance vis-à-vis the social regulation of gender (discussed below), it is interesting that the chaste beauty-scholar romances have sometimes been interpreted as socially progressive in their critique of traditional marriage practices: they have been read as promoting women's freer choice in marriage and as critical of other aspects of women's social restriction, such as their exclusion from education.[35]

Historically much closer to the appearance of the first same-sex schoolgirl romances in the 1920s, however, is a wave of romantic fiction produced in the 1910s by the authors of the popular "mandarin duck and butterfly school" (yuanyang hudie pai). Mandarin duck and butterfly fiction (hereafter simply butterfly fiction) was a form of commercial mass-entertainment literature published primarily in the newspapers, literary supplements, and new pop-literary magazines of China's treaty port cities, especially Shanghai. In his study of the "wave" of popular love stories that circulated in urban China during the 1910s, Perry Link observes that the plots of these stories converge into two standard narrative patterns: those with happy endings (yanqing xiaoshuo) and those with tragic endings (aiqing xiaoshuo); these subgeneric classifiers were commonly even printed alongside the stories' titles as a means of distinguishing the product for readers.[36] Link characterizes the tragic-love story of the 1910s—the variant most pertinent to the generic history I am tracing here—as passing through a series of clearly defined stages that comprise what he terms "the Romantic Route."[37] As in the earlier chaste beauty-scholar model, a strongly idealized young hero and heroine, both possessed of extraordinary inborn talents (cai) and emotional supersensitivity (duoqing)—the capacity to feel both great love (qing) and great sorrow (chou)—meet and fall in love with a spiritual passion that is characterized by its purity, in distinction from base bodily desire (rou yu).[38] But unlike in the beauty-scholar romances, in the popular tragic-love stories of the 1910s cruel fate intervenes to make the lovers' union impossible, leaving them prey to worry, sickness, and ultimately defeat—most commonly in death but sometimes in another kind of final parting such as flight to a monastery or nunnery or some far-distant place. The dominant affective note in this feminine subgenre is a melancholy one of romantic pathos; presumably for readers at the time, this is where much of its pleasure lay.[39] Summarizing the affective and aesthetic effects of this literature, C. T. Hsia proposes that it "lyricise[s] the kind of negative feelings the lovers may have when they are not together or when they entertain no hope of ever being united in wedlock, such as loneliness, despair, or grief, and celebrate[s] the true lovers in their courtship of martyrdom when confronted with a crisis."[40]

Most commentators trace a hybrid line of descent for the *aiqing* stories of the 1910s.[41] Hsia, for example, frames Xu Zhenya's wildly popular *aiqing* novel *Yu li hun*, (Jade Pear Spirit), 1912, within what he terms the "sentimental-erotic" tradition in Chinese literature, while also noting its reflection of European romantic fiction in some aspects of its literary form. In Hsia's account, the sentimental-erotic tradition stretches back to Tang poets (including Li Shangyin and Du Mu); includes classic works of drama and prose like *Mudan ting* (Peony Pavilion), *Taohua shan* (Peach Blossom Fan) and *Hong lou meng* (Dream of the Red Chamber); and later also annexes certain Western works through translation, most notably Lin Shu's 1899 classical Chinese translation of the younger Alexandre Dumas's *La dame aux camélias*.[42] Although they did not fully embrace the new vernacular literary language, authors of butterfly fiction explored many of the thematic preoccupations of Western literature, particularly the modern ideology of romantic love, and their stories drew from Western fiction a new preoccupation with psychological characterization.[43] In Hsia's analysis, the popular *aiqing* subgenre to which *Jade Pear Spirit* belongs thus amounts to a modern, semi-Westernized extension of a Chinese literary tradition.

Diverse analysts of butterfly romance concur that these popular narratives enact a series of ambivalent negotiations with conflicting models of gender and social conduct in Chinese cities in the culturally turbulent early years of the twentieth century. In Link's account, these stylistically hybrid romances enabled a public "thinking-through" of intensifying contradictions between residual-traditional and emergent-modern ideologies of femininity and social life. They typically invoked "social problems" arising from traditional gendered practices including widow chastity, child marriage, dowries, and arranged marriage and enabled their readers playfully to consider "new"— that is, modern and implicitly Western-inflected—solutions to such problems.[44] Thus, as Rey Chow (among others) has argued, despite its apparently conservative tendency to reiterate the value of traditional feminine virtue in the final instance, the popular romantic fiction of the early twentieth century begins, albeit indirectly, to explore the idea of modern femininity.[45] In Chow's analysis, butterfly stories achieve this by reconstructing the by then besieged tradition of feminine moral virtue in an implicitly critical mode.[46]

But it is the elite, modernist women's fiction written in the 1920s and 1930s as part of the May Fourth New Literature movement that provides the literary context from which the schoolgirl romance most obviously and directly emerges. Like the butterfly romances that many May Fourth authors so vehemently denounced, this wave of modernist women's fiction, in the new vernacular style and centering on subjectivist accounts of ordinary characters' inner lives, is also centrally concerned with love. But as Wendy Larson and others have observed, this writing differs significantly from butterfly fiction in ideological content, as well as literary style, in that it far more overtly critiques traditional gender relations — especially *de*, feminine "moral virtue" — and openly champions a self-consciously modern, Western-inspired ideology of romantic love (*lian'ai*).[47] For the May Fourth writers, recreating oneself as a modern subject necessitated firmly rejecting the traditional husband-wife relationship with its basis in familial hierarchy and hidebound ritual and instead "freeing" oneself for modern romantic love with its contrasting emphasis on interior, individualized sentiment and desire.[48] The New Woman (*xin nüxing*), once liberated from the debilitating fetters of traditional gender and family structure, could then exercise the strength necessary to make her contribution to building the modern Chinese nation.[49] But Larson also highlights the ambivalence of the new ideology of romantic love in the work of the modernist women writers, as the female characters in their fiction find themselves impossibly torn between lingering identification with the old moral virtue and the incompatible demands of the new romantic love.[50] While traditional gender relations are no longer tenable, the modern ideal of feminine gender and (hetero)sexuality remains, in Larson's reading of works by Lu Yin, Chen Hengzhe, Ling Shuhua, and Bing Xin, as yet powerless to emerge fully, as women characters struggle with unrewarding marriages, male double standards, and debilitating self doubt.[51]

It is in the context of such literary negotiations with the ideologies of modern femininity, romantic love, and marriage that the schoolgirl romance genre emerges in the 1920s and 1930s in works by modernist women authors including Lu Yin, Ling Shuhua, Ding Ling, and Xie Bingying. In stories that have been analyzed by both Sang and Larson, including "Lishi's Diary" and *Old Acquaintances by the Seaside* (1923) by Lu Yin and "Once upon a Time" by Ling Shuhua, same-sex love between female students is idealized as a pure, sentimental, and spiritual bond that contrasts favorably with adult marital relations, which are represented as socially compulsory yet emotionally stultifying compared with the joys of same-sex love between unmarried young women.[52] While managing the modernization of cross-sex love was often portrayed by the modernist women authors as an arduous and frustrating project, "same-sex love," that contemporaneous modern invention, was represented by some as offering a potential utopian alternative. As Larson observes, the new discourse on modern, romantic love thus facilitated the reformulation not only of understandings and practices of love between women and men, but also of love between women.[53]

Schoolgirl Romance as Tragic-Love Fiction in the 1920s: Ling Shuhua and Lu Yin

Interestingly, the new stories about young intellectual women's same-sex love borrow quite clearly from the conventions of heterosexual romance narratives, and while they readily invite interpretation as thematically modern and stylistically modernist stories, they also draw upon several of the thematic preoccupations and narrative patterns of earlier popular tragic-love stories. Larson demonstrates the former point briefly with an excerpt from Xie Bingying's *Autobiography of a Woman Soldier* (1936), which concerns a flirtation between the author and a classmate in a girls' boarding school. Xie's text, she shows, reproduces conventions of the modern cross-sex romance narrative in its inclusion of the generic elements of "intimations of sexual activity, secret devotion, professions of unrequited love, and the presence of a well-intentioned match-maker."[54]

Related observations could be made about Ling Shuhua's "Once upon a Time," which, typical of the emergent subgenre, tells of a romantic attachment between two late-adolescent schoolgirls (Yingman and Yunluo) that is encouraged by another classmate in the role of matchmaker but is in the end tragically curtailed by Yunluo's forced marriage.[55] In Chow's terms, Ling's story could be seen as dramatizing the enactment of a "virtuous transaction" between a woman character and the patriarchal social system, a transaction by means of which, at the cost of annihilating self-sacrifice, the woman attempts to ensure her own place within that system.[56] In these terms, Yunluo "agrees"—albeit more or less as the result of main force—to renounce her love for Yingman and marry the man her parents have selected for her. Indeed, in this respect Ling's story is typical of the schoolgirl romance genre more broadly, in both its early- and its late-twentieth-century manifestations. Collectively, the stories solicit interpretation as dramatizations of the wrenchingly painful process of precisely this "virtuous transaction": the renunciation of the same-sex sweetheart that a girl learns she must complete in order to gain access to the category "woman," with its definitional tie with cross-sex marital or proto-marital relations.

And yet, in contrast to the other stories that Chow discusses, in the schoolgirl romances such transactions tend to be marked by a notable lack of closure. This is the case not only because of the emotional agony that the enactment of the transaction so manifestly occasions in the partner who makes it most fully—that is, the partner who "goes in" to heterosexuality by agreeing to enter into marital or proto-marital relations, in this case Yunluo—but also because, almost without exception, the stories include the perspective of the other partner, who refuses the transaction altogether. In "Once upon a Time," Yingman simply refuses to forget her love for Yunluo, the news of Yunluo's marriage causing her to fall into a dead faint, as though in a willful self-absention from the impossible situation that confronts her. The only indication that Yingman may perhaps in future be induced to resign herself to the social system that has robbed her of her sweetheart is ambiguous in the extreme. The story's final line is spoken by a classmate, as Yingman regains consciousness: "It's all right, it's all right, she's coming to."[57] Perhaps, then, Yingman will "come around" from her impossible dream of lasting same-sex love—but then again, perhaps not. In its marked ambivalence about the possibility of the full interpellation of young women into their "proper," self-sacrificing role in this particular virtuous transaction, Ling's story is typical of the genre, which, as we will see, is marked by a lack of narrative and ideological closure on the questions of whether such "going in" is ever really final and whether women's adolescent same-sex love can be fully or successfully renounced in adulthood.

In its major elements, Ling's story's plot is similar to Lu Yin's "Lishi's Diary." Lu's short story is written in the form of a schoolgirl's diary discovered and made public by a friend after the diarist's death. As we will see in later chapters, the backward-looking cast of this narrative was to become characteristic in later examples of the Chinese going-in story.[58] In her diary, Lishi wrote in distinctly modern terminology of her growing "same-sex love" (tongxingde ailian) for a female classmate, Yuanqing, who was ultimately forced by her family into an arranged marriage that led the already sickly Lishi to will herself to die of grief.[59] In its modernist preoccupation with exposing the deleterious effects of the arranged marriage system on the nation's youth, the story is exemplary of Lu Yin's early fiction.[60] But although in this sense the story, like Ling's "Once upon a Time," is typical of the category of modernist "woman question" fiction into which it is often classified, it is interesting to note that as a student, Lu Yin herself had been deeply moved by the tragic-romantic butterfly novel *Jade Pear Spirit*.[61] Several plot elements in the ostensibly modernist, realist "Lishi's Diary" echo the form of the popular romances and in doing so recall the longer-standing generic conventions of the tragic-love story.[62] I propose that this generic echo is not merely coincidental but is in fact a constitutive feature of the schoolgirl romance genre as a whole as it has developed across both of its major "waves," first in the 1920s–1930s and again from the 1970s to the present. This proposition will be borne out more fully by the analyses of more recent examples in the next chapter. For the present, it will be useful to sketch out more precisely the ways in which "Lishi's Diary" performs its intertextual citation of popular cross-sex romance.

In the most general terms, "Lishi's Diary" conforms to the narrative form of the tragic-love story, in which the major aesthetic effect and readerly pleasure is derived from the pathos of the central lovers' final separation rather than from the triumph of their ultimate union. As noted above, this tragic narrative of ill-fated love in its cross-sex version was popularized closest to Lu Yin's time in the mass-entertainment *aiqing* stories of the butterfly school, of which Lu Yin herself was an enthusiastic consumer, but the broad thematic and narrative pattern of the modern tragic-love story also harks back to a much longer tragic-love tradition in Chinese literature. Further and more specifically, the plot device used in "Lishi's Diary" of lovers separated by the forced marriage (arranged by an elder relative) of one of them to somebody else is also common in earlier cross-sex tragic-love stories, as is the figure of the faithful, broken-hearted lover subject to languishment and melancholic illness — and often, as is the case here, death — as a result of romantic yearning.[63] Indeed, in her preface to the diary sections of the story, Lishi's anonymous friend even compares the late Lishi's pale cheeks to the white petals of the pear blossom, obliquely paralleling Lishi with Bai Liying (White Pear Image), the heroine of the butterfly romance *Jade Pear Spirit* who similarly willed herself to death as the result of an impossible love.[64] Further, in tragic-romantic butterfly fiction, as in "Lishi's Diary," the chastity of the lovers is key, their spiritual passion far outweighing the carnal — albeit in the former case, such chastity is framed as exemplary of the lovers' virtuous conformity to gender propriety while in the latter case the de-emphasis on the sexual element of the young women's relationships probably also reflects concurrent sexological accounts of women's relative sentimentality and inherent sexual passivity.[65] Lu Yin's story also echoes the conventions of the tragic-love story in the lovers' correspondence through passionate and eagerly awaited letters when they are separated and in the central role in the plot of flowers exchanged between the two.[66]

Moreover, in "Lishi's Diary" the appropriation of well-recognized tragic-love story conventions for the purpose of telling the new story of modern same-sex love is remarkably self-conscious: as well as drawing upon and re-functioning these familiar narrative elements, the story appears intentionally to draw attention to the process of their appropriation. For example, when Yuanqing sends branches of plum blossom to Lishi, the act that effectively inaugurates their romantic relationship, she includes a letter spelling out their intended meaning: "In dispatching someone to bring you these two branches of red plum blossom bought at the fresh flower market, I mean to draw upon [liaoxi] the significance understood by the ancients, who sent plum blossom to serve as a companion to a dearly missed friend."[67] More than anything else, the effect of Yuanqing's note is to underscore her own act of citation—an act that rescripts the gendered significance of the classical symbol since the plum blossom now serves as a romantic gift between female students rather than the male literati of the classical reference.[68] The transformative citation underlined so self-consciously in Yuanqing's letter is, I propose, a central tactic in the story as a whole, which reflexively highlights its own rescripting of the familiar patterns of the tragic-love story to tell a modern story of feminine same-sex love.

A similar effect is seen in Lishi's resolution to die of grief. She confides to her diary following Yuanqing's marriage: "Ai! The more I remember, the more heartbroken I become! Each time I write in this diary about Yuanqing's abandoning me, I'm filled with the urge to bid this world farewell upon the instant. But I haven't the courage for suicide—let me die of grief, then! Let me die of grief!"[69] Lishi's resolution to die of grief seems, once again, peculiarly self-conscious: the idea comes to her in the form of a clichéd set-phrase (yiyu er si) that would be familiar to readers of elite or popular Chinese fiction as the ultimate recourse of any number of pure and lovelorn romantic heroines, from Lin Daiyu in Dream of the Red Chamber to Bai Liying (Li Niang) in Jade Pear Spirit. There is something overtly stylized, almost obtrusively formulaic, in Lishi's enraptured repetition of this well-worn literary cliché. As with Yuanqing's emphatic citation of the sentimental significance attached to plum blossom by the ancients, Lishi's repetition of this set-phrase of tragic-love fiction mimics the tactic of the story as a whole, which is to appropriate familiar elements of cross-sex tragic love stories for the purpose of writing the new story of modern feminine same-sex love.

As the following chapter will show, both the appropriation of elements from cross-sex tragic-love stories and the reflexive reference to it are also characteristic of stories from the second wave of schoolgirl romances, from the 1970s to the present. In the later going-in stories, as in these early ones, the idealizing and implicitly universalizing literary construction of feminine same-sex love with reference to the generic structures of tragic romance fiction serves as a counterpoint to, and to some extent critically interrupts, the scientistic construction of homosexuality as a condition affecting a discrete group of individuals. Representing women's same-sex love through the familiar formulae of popular stories about sentimental women in love obviously has markedly different aesthetic and ideological effects from representing it as a case study in deviant sexuality. Even at the very moment that European sexology was having its most decisive impact on Chinese sexual epistemologies, then, the minoritizing model of female homosexuality was clearly not the only, nor perhaps even the dominant, construction in play.

The Tomboy's Prehistory

As will be demonstrated in the remaining chapters of this book, the universalizing construction of same-sex love evident in Lu Yin's and Ling Shuhua's stories that frames same-sex romance as a forcibly foresworn, retrospectively recalled pleasure of feminine adolescence was to become the dominant mass-cultural Chinese discourse on female homoeroticism for the remainder of the twentieth century. As influential as it has proven, however, this universalizing construction is not the only modern Chinese understanding of women's same-sex love; as in Western contexts, Chinese understandings of homosexuality—both male and female—are riven, albeit in distinctive ways, by an internal contradiction between universalizing and minoritizing accounts.[70]

In "Sexual Inversion in Women," a chapter in volume 2 of *Studies in the Psychology of Sex*, which was published in Pan Guangdan's Chinese translation in 1946 but had been in circulation among Chinese intellectuals in the English edition since the 1920s,[71] Havelock Ellis draws a distinction between two kinds of adolescent female homosexuality: the situational or "spurious" kind, to which temporary circumstances may lead conventionally feminine girls to fall prey (a universalizing view), and the "congenital" kind, which is a permanent condition in a minority of girls (a minoritizing view).[72] This taxonomy also underlies Ellis's appendix to the same volume, "The School-Friendships of Girls," which was published in Zhang Jingsheng's Chinese translation in 1927.[73] There, Ellis distinguishes between the temporary homosexuality of romantic friendships between schoolgirls and "real congenital perversion," which has an organic cause and persists lifelong.[74] As in this schema, in modern Chinese representations of female same-sex love the taxonomic distinction between situational lesbianism and its congenital counterpart tends to map onto a gendered distinction between conventional femininity and female masculinity.[75] And as with the universalizing construction of temporary, adolescent same-sex love, the minoritizing account of the "mannish," permanent lesbian, too, finds expression in literary form.

One notable example of a literary representation of love between young women that draws partly on the sexological theory of Krafft-Ebing and others to construct a locally inflected and markedly phobic literary prototype of the "mannish lesbian" is "She Was a Weak Woman," by the male modernist author Yu Dafu (1896–1945).[76] However, as the analysis below shows, what is particularly interesting about "She Was a Weak Woman" is that it does not simply mirror current European sexological theory but also draws on local folk beliefs about feminine sexual deficiency to create a hybrid account of a new and frightening kind of feminine sexuality that is part sexological theory and part indigenous folklore.

The first part of Yu's story takes place in a girls' school. The man-like girl Li Wenqing, daughter of a wealthy rural landowner, seduces the pretty but weak-willed petit bourgeois protagonist, Zheng Xiuyue, with expensive gifts and an impressive rubber dildo.[77] Li is described as "both tall and large," with a "loud and resonant, husky voice" and "snub nose," while "her face was covered in red-black freckles, and in size outdid that of a normal, huskily built middle-aged man"; she is also described as emanating "a very strange smell of rotting onions that simply suffocated you to death."[78] The first time Li coerces Zheng into an intimate exchange by forcibly pulling Zheng's hand over her own naked body, she reveals to the other girl's touch "skin like sandpaper; a pair of very broad, very saggy, downward-dangling tits; a few straggly hairs in her armpits; and congealed in those hairs, a mass of sticky sweat."[79] The influence of Krafft-Ebing's theory of female homosexuality as gender inversion is unmistakable in the horrifying literary personage of Li Wenqing. Yu's description attests to the capacity of the translated discourse of sexology to effect, in some instances, a regulatory and markedly phobic corporealization of lesbianism as a stigmatic, masculinized body. Equally, however, the characterization of the monstrous Li also appears to draw on the folk figure of the *enü*, or malignant woman, whom McMahon notes appears both in sex treatises dating back at least to the tenth century and in much later literature and folk wisdom. Enü, summarizes McMahon, "have ugly and inauspicious features that cause men harm—for example, coarse skin, masculine voice, large mouth, coarse and long pubic hairs, malodorous underarms, inability to have orgasm, excess sexual waters, and coldness of the vagina."[80] Possessing several of the inauspicious traits of the *enü*, Li Wenqing can be seen as an amalgam of the sexological inversion theory of the mannish lesbian and local premodern folk beliefs about the malignant woman who fails to conform to the cultural and corporeal codes of normative feminine gender.[81]

Interestingly, in this story Li Wenqing functions as a device by means of which the romantic love between Zheng Xiuyue and her elder female schoolmate, the revolutionary Feng Shifen, can be contrastingly guaranteed as "innocent" and "spiritual" and protected from the smirch of masculinized sexual desire as represented by Li.[82] Following Li's seduction of Zheng, Feng returns to their dormitory and asks Zheng to explain the strong stink of body odor hanging about their shared bed:

> Zheng Xiuyue didn't understand what she meant and asked her what body odor was. After Feng Shifen explained the symptoms of this disease, she burst out laughing and suddenly lifted her head and deeply, deeply kissed Feng Shifen's face for a long moment. She had been friends with Feng Shifen for almost a year, the two of them sleeping in the same bed separated by only a quilt, and this was the closest they had ever come to anything approaching lascivious behavior [*yinwude xingwei*]. Yet neither felt in her heart any other kind of excitement: they simply felt that this signified the deepest kind of affection [*qin'ai*], an affection that could not be expressed with words.[83]

The distinctly pathological body and moral decrepitude signified in Li—who only the previous night has, on the very same bed, unquestionably engaged with Zheng in "filthy behavior" and felt "other kinds of excitement"—enables a symbolic defense of the healthy, girlish love that exists between Zheng and Feng. As a caricatural monster, Li's effect is to hold Zheng and Feng's romantic friendship clear of the stain of her stigma. Indeed, the logic of the story seems almost to *require* a monstrous Li *in order* to construct the passionate schoolgirl love between Zheng and Feng, by contrast, as pure, innocent, and lovely.[84] In this way, Yu's story illustrates particularly clearly the bifurcating mechanism in modern Chinese representations of female homoeroticism that relies on an idealized same-sex love felt by gender-normative women in order to abject a demonized one felt by masculine ones.

Insofar as she is described plainly as a masculine woman who manifests a strong and active sexual desire for feminine women, Li Wenqing can be seen, perhaps, as a kind of prehistoric precursor of the contemporary tomboy sex-gender identity (the subject of chapter 4). However, it would be a mistake to think that Li simply equates in any straightforward way to the Republican-era sexological category "female homosexual."[85] First of all, same-sex relations are not the only kind in which Li engages: she also has sex with a series of (often effeminate) men throughout the course of Yu's narrative. Nor is same-sex sex the most outrageous of Li's sexual exploits: she also cheerfully engages in nonmarital (hetero) sex with one of her teachers, an underage boy, and her own father, among others. Li encapsulates her sexual belief system candidly in a letter to Zheng Xiuyue: "Love is sex and sex is love, and love shouldn't make distinctions regarding its object. Conventional criticisms of so-called incest and so-called cross-generational relations are just so much hot air. If one's going to love, then it doesn't matter whether the object is cat or dog, father or son—what's the matter with amusing oneself with any of them just as one pleases?"[86]

Perhaps even more strongly than the specific identity of female homosexual, then, Li's characterization implies the more generic category of perversion (biantai), which entered public discourse around the same time; homosexual behavior is only one of Li's several affronts to sexual normativity.[87] Moreover, as well as drawing on this sexological concept, as Chen Huiwen observes, Li's various affronts to sex/gender propriety also suggest the premodern, culturally abjected category of "lascivious woman," characterized by Naifei Ding as the view of women as "potent, powerful and dangerous sexual agents" that arises when feminine sexuality exceeds a merely reproductive function.[88] Chen argues that the distinction between Feng Shifen and Li Wenqing echoes the distinction in late imperial literature between the (good) talented woman (cainü) and (bad) lascivious one (yinnü)—the latter, indeed, is sometimes marked by her same-sex sexual behavior in classical fiction as well.[89] On this reading, the scene analyzed above, where Feng's pure love for Zheng is contrasted with Li's openly sexual attentions, calls up this premodern taxonomy of cainü versus yinnü just as readily as it also implies the sexological distinction between feminine/situational and masculine/congenital lesbianism.

In sum, then, Li Wenqing is an almost unmanageably polysemic figure with regard to her gender and sexual expression, calling up multiple and complex associations not only from within the translated discourse on sexual perversion (homosexuality, incest, pedophilia, gender inversion, promiscuity), but also from indigenous ideologies of proper and improper femininity (the figures of enü and yinnü/yinfu). Clearly, to describe Li Wenqing as a "lesbian" and leave it at that would be to do a great disservice to the complexity of the representation. Nonetheless, as chapter 4 will show, some forty-odd years later, certain aspects of Li's characterization—in particular her masculinity, her active sexual desire for feminine women, and her status as part of a sex/gender minority within the class of women as a whole—will reemerge, in different form, in popular late-twentieth-century representations of the tomboy.

The Republican-era stories discussed in this chapter illuminate something of the modern history of the two commonest constructions of female same-sex love in contemporary Chinese-language popular cultures and their definitional link with temporality: the universalizing model of the temporary schoolgirl lover and the minoritizing understanding of the lifelong tomboy. I have tried to demonstrate the multiple complexities of the historical emergence of these ways of understanding women's same-sex love. If one claims that these constructions are the product of sexological Westernization, then one must temper that claim by noting that the process of that Westernization is not direct but filtered through Japanese interpretations of the material, with the consequently intensified—and by no means wholly phobic—interest in the figure of the same-sex-loving schoolgirl. Even if one leaves aside the Japanese connection in order to concentrate purely on the direct influence of European sexological theories, those do not entail solely a minoritizing pathologization of homosexuality either; as we have seen, universalizing accounts of female homosexuality as a temporary condition also form an integral part of that body of knowledge. In considering the literary personage of the temporarily same-sex-loving schoolgirl, one must also concede that the Chinese elaboration of this figure draws not only on imported sexology but also on the locally embedded history of popular tragic-romance fiction. And even if, contracting one's claim yet further, one focuses more specifically still on the minoritizing construction of the masculine lesbian in Republican China, one finds that neither was her emergence simply a matter of the wholesale import of European models; equally it drew on local and markedly misogynist folk theories of auspicious versus malicious feminine gender. Further, the extent to which a figure like Yu Dafu's Li Wenqing can even accurately be described as "a female homosexual" is doubtful, given the carnivalesque polysemy of her character's sexuality; at most, one can say that *elements* of the sexual imaginary that produced Li Wenqing were later taken up and pressed into service for the creation of the cultural image of the lesbian as tomboy. The equally complex contemporary afterlives of these culturally and ideologically heterogeneous figures, the homoerotic schoolgirl and the tomboy, are the subject of the chapters that follow.

. . .

TWO

Voluble Ellipsis

Second-Wave Schoolgirl Romance
in Taiwan and Hong Kong

I'm not interested in narratives that end in
a full stop—I prefer an ellipsis . . .
—CHU T'IEN-HSIN

Like the institutions of women's education themselves, the modern Chinese narrative of schoolgirl romance has persisted well beyond the early-twentieth-century moment of its initial emergence. The narrative can be traced through contemporary works produced between the 1970s and the present in each of the three major areas of contemporary Chinese transnationalism: the People's Republic of China, Taiwan, and Hong Kong. Classic texts in the genre—like Chu T'ien-hsin's "Lang tao sha" (Waves Scour the Sands; Taiwan, 1976); Liu Suola's "Lan tian lü hai" (Blue Sky Green Sea; China, 1985); Cao Lijuan's "Tongnü zhi wu" (The Maidens' Dance; Taiwan, 1991); and Wong Bikwan's "Ta shi nüzi, wo ye shi nüzi" (She's a Young Woman and So Am I; Hong Kong, 1994)—to be discussed in this and following chapters, are persistent favorites among women readers, both lesbian and straight-identifying, from teenage schoolgirls to middle-aged married women.[1] These widely enjoyed works of "respectable" literature have also been joined, in recent years, by a profusion of Internet teen fiction that takes up the schoolgirl romance narrative in a more populist mode, as well as a spate of similarly themed television and film productions that will be discussed in later chapters.[2] What is there, then, in the ideological structure of the schoolgirl romance that remains compelling enough to keep the narrative flourishing decades after its emergence? What do contemporary Chinese publics *want* with the story of romance between young women? What kind of cultural labor is this narrative performing today? These are the central questions explored over the chapters that follow.

This chapter begins our exploration of contemporary manifestations of the schoolgirl romance narrative by asking how two post-1970 stories from Taiwan and Hong Kong continue the thematic, stylistic, and ideological work of the Republican-era examples discussed in chapter 1. How do these stories cite the romance genre and to what ideological effect? What is the characteristic narrative structure of these stories, and again, what is the ideological implication of such a structure? All in all, do these stories simply shore up hetero-normativity, as they may appear to do at first glance, or are they more ideologically complex?

Second-Wave Schoolgirl Romance

To begin with, it is worth identifying the key characteristics of the Chinese-language schoolgirl romance in its contemporary instances. Like the examples from the May Fourth period discussed in the previous chapter, the contemporary going-in stories have at their center intense sexual or romantic relationships between young women who meet in school or college. A defining feature of the narrative therefore remains the age of the primary characters at the time when they first know each other; the protagonists range in age from early teens to early twenties. Also like their early-century forerunners but unlike other examples of contemporary lesbian fiction and film in Chinese, these schoolgirl romances uniformly stop short of detailed representations of genital sex between women.[3] However, although they have been criticized by local lesbian commentators for their seeming desexualization and consequent despecification of lesbian relations, the contemporary stories in fact vary quite widely in their representation of the women's sexual desire for each other.[4] While some continue to impute to the young women purely spiritual as opposed to carnal love,[5] others linger in detail over the potent stirrings of sexual desire aroused by physical contact between young women.[6] As in the Republican-era examples, the stories' characterization of the young women's genders is also variable. Some tend toward a gender-separatist model in which the women's femininity is represented as a condition shared equally by both partners and not jeopardized by the erotic attachment between them.[7] Others foreground sexual attraction between the secondary genders of tomboy and po—comparable to, though not identical with, the English terms "butch" and "femme"—presenting the masculine-identified tomboy characters on a gender-transitive model.[8] Yet other examples include both gender-separatist

and gender-transitive models within a single narrative or represent their protagonists' gender ambiguously.[9]

Although contemporary instances of the schoolgirl romance narrative vary
with regard to their characterization of the young women's gender and sexual
desire, they are quite consistent in several other regards. Again similarly to the
going-in stories of the 1920s and 1930s, these narratives are characterized by
a marked utopianism.[10] Echoing the romantic construction of same-sex love
among schoolgirls in early-twentieth-century public discussions, the stories
represent love between adolescent women in a strongly idealized manner. It
is often nostalgically associated with spiritual purity, sexual innocence, and
moral integrity—a blissful, prelapsarian state from which the protagonists
have since reluctantly fallen into the corrupting experience of socially enforced marital or proto-marital relations.[11] Further, insofar as the schoolgirl
romance in the contemporary period remains a *failed* romance in which the
central couple is unable to come together in a happy union at the conclusion
to the story, it again recalls its forerunners in the 1920s and 1930s, as well
as echoing certain contemporary heterosexual popular romances, as will be
shown in detail below. The contemporary schoolgirl romances can be seen, I
propose, as a distinctive modern subgenre of the tragic-love story, in which
pathos and mournful yearning for an impossible love constitute the central
emotional pleasures and aesthetic effects.

Finally and most important for my concerns in the remainder of this chapter, the contemporary schoolgirl romances are related in what I call the *memorial mode*: developing a nascent tendency in the 1920s and 1930s examples, the
key events of the contemporary stories are related in the past tense, retrieved
from the past by a reminiscent third- or first-person narrator.[12] Further,
in distinction to the "tomboy texts" discussed in chapter 4, the reminisc-
ing narrator in the stories discussed in this chapter is characterized by her
feminine gender identification. Where the romance occurs between women
differentiated by secondary gender, the narrator is the feminine-identified
partner, not the cross-gender-identified tomboy; where both partners are
feminine-identified, the narrator is, of course, likewise feminine-identified.
These stories thus insistently underscore the mechanism of feminine rec-
ollection in representing desiring relationships between women. The relationships are without exception represented as having ended and as being
recollected with mournful nostalgia from the viewpoint of the present, in
which, after being abandoned by her beloved schoolmate, the protagonist
has generally entered—either apathetically or against her will—into some
form of heterosexual union.[13] The persistence of the memorial mode in con-

temporary feminine-narrated schoolgirl romances thereby produces feminine homoeroticism as something that is defined by its dredging, years after the fact, from a more or less distant but always intensely memorable past.[14] In this, the narrative produces a set of mutually reinforcing definitional bonds, precipitating a kind of ideological molecule binding femininity, memory, adolescence, and homosexuality. It is this insistent association of women's same-sex love with memory to which I now turn.

Memorial Lesbians

The European sexological theory of "temporary homosexuality" in girls' schools that was translated into Chinese in the early twentieth century establishes a firm connection between adolescent lesbianism and the workings of memory. In *Studies in the Psychology of Sex*, published in Pan Guangdan's Chinese translation in 1946, Ellis writes, "With girls, as with boys, it is in the school . . . that homosexuality usually first shows itself. . . . Two children, perhaps when close to each other in bed, more or less unintentionally generate in each other a certain amount of sexual irritation, which they foster by mutual touching and kissing. This is a spurious kind of homosexuality, the often precocious play of the normal instinct. In the girl who is congenitally predisposed to homosexuality it will continue and develop; in the majority it *will be forgotten as quickly as possible*, not without shame, in the presence of the normal object of sexual love."[15] Aside from its influential taxonomic division of schoolgirl homosexuality into the categories of situational and congenital—a bipartite conceptualization of schoolgirl homosexuality that, as we shall see, is reflected, to a degree, in the characterization of the central couples in the contemporary schoolgirl romances—what stands out most strongly in this passage is its construction of a defining relation between homosexuality and feminine memory. If the noncongenitally predisposed (that is, conventionally feminine) schoolgirl is to pass through her temporary adolescent phase of "spurious" homosexuality and emerge, triumphant, into a proper relationship to the "normal" object of (hetero)sexual love, she must not only forget her schoolgirl lover but must also do so, Ellis insists, *as quickly as possible*. Yet in sharp contrast to Ellis's uneasy prescription of amnesia and shame as the best cures for adolescent lesbianism, the contemporary Chinese schoolgirl romances under discussion here are narrated by adult women who, in effect, *do nothing but remember* their lost schoolgirl loves.[16]

In Freud's account of women's psychosexual development, too, female homosexuality is consigned to the past and to the realm of memory. Critics of

Freud's memorializing construction of female homosexuality have been quick to point out that this ascription of lesbian priority effectively secures the lesbian's secondary status in relation to a presumptively normative heterosexuality. Annamarie Jagose argues that in Freud, "the primacy of homosexuality perversely ensure[s] its secondariness" because pre-oedipal homosexuality in girls, figured as the "prehistory of heterosexuality," is thereby destined to be straightened out for a heterosexual outcome.[17] In a related manner, Diana Fuss underscores the internal incoherence of Freud's construction of female homosexuality as always and only a temporal "fall back" into the precultural, presexual time of pre-oedipality and primary identification.[18] Fuss proposes that "homosexuality is "inessential" in [a] double sense, positioned within psychoanalysis as an essential waste ingredient: the child's homosexual desire for the parent of the same sex, essential to the subject's formation as sexed, is nonetheless simultaneously figured as nonessential, a dispensable component of desire that ultimately must be repudiated and repressed."[19]

Angus Gordon makes a related argument on the strategic duality of twentieth-century Euro-American discourses on adolescence and homosexuality, which he proposes construct adolescence as a site of sexual plasticity while at the same time, contradictorily, foreshadowing heterosexuality as its presumptive conclusion.[20] Citing Freud's wry remark in the *Three Essays* that in puberty, the task for sexual object-choice to find its way to the opposite sex "is not accomplished without a certain amount of fumbling," Gordon proposes that Freud's model of adolescent sexuality constitutes a "strategy of *recuperation*, in which [homosexual] deviations are constructed . . . as mere 'fumbling,' as detours which can and probably will return in good time to the main road."[21] Thus, in psychoanalytic discourse on adolescence, "a climactic normality is achieved *by means of* a negotiation of various moments of non-normality."[22] While presenting its story as a neutral observance on sexuality, for its critics, Freudian psychoanalysis scripts its story's outcome to suit its own ends, tending to presume in advance the desirability of a heterosexual conclusion.[23]

Given that the work of Freud, Ellis, and other European sexologists was widely and influentially translated into Chinese in the first decades of the twentieth century, the currency of their theories of female homosexuality as a memorial condition undoubtedly had an influence on the memorialization of the lesbian topic in modern Chinese fiction and popular culture.[24] The contemporary schoolgirl romance echoes the preoccupations of sexology and psychoanalysis in several ways: both the prevalence of the memorial mode and the preponderance of marital outcomes to stories of adolescent lesbian romance parallel comparable tendencies in the European theories. My key question in the analyses that follow concerns *how*, precisely, the Chinese schoolgirl romances reflect and reinflect the discontinuous narratives of modern Euro-American sexual epistemology. Do they tend to reproduce an all-too-predictable recuperative narrative of adolescent lesbianism as merely a detour en route to a triumphantly heterosexual conclusion? Or can we also glimpse here the transfigured trace of an alternative sexual epistemology that implies not a reiteration but a critique of the familiar narrative that naturalizes heterosexual union as the proper conclusion for *all* stories? My exploration of the possibility that these narratives may complicate, rather than merely reproduce, a heterocentric and developmentalist account of young women's sexuality pays particular attention to two elements. These are, first, the stories' underscoring of the role of external social motivating factors (such as pressure from mothers, peers, and school authorities) in precipitating their protagonists' eventual heterosexual turn, and second, the stories' framing of thwarted same-sex love within the generic conventions of tragic romance.

"Waves Scour the Sands": Sex and the Sentimental Schoolgirl

Prominent Taiwanese author Chu T'ien-hsin's schoolgirl romance "Waves Scour the Sands" was first published in 1976, when Chu herself was still a schoolgirl—much to the shock of her classmates and teachers.[25] It is the earliest example of the late-twentieth-century second wave of highbrow literary renditions of the schoolgirl romance narrative, and it is often framed as something of a classic in the genre. Along with Chu's later literary representations of romantic love between young women—most famously in her autobiographical essay collection about her years at Taipei First Girls' School, *The Pushpin Song* (1984) (*Jirang ge*), and the short story "A Story of Spring Butterflies" (1992)—"Waves" has been read avidly by generations of Taiwanese women for whom Chu's writing resonates strongly with personal experience.[26] The story holds a significant place, too, within local lesbian subcultures. Illustrating this, in 1998 the first issue of the Hong Kong/Taiwan lesbian and gay glossy magazine *Together* carried a photo spread based on Chu's story, including quotations from key passages and featuring two wistful-looking young models in school uniforms arranged in a series of romantic poses in picturesque forest and urban settings (figures 7–8).

"Waves" centers on Little Qi (Xiao Qi), a first-year university student, and her successive romantic relationships with two tomboy schoolmates, Zhang

7–8. Excerpt from photo spread based on Chu T'ien-hsin's "Waves Scour the Sands" in *Together* magazine, 1998. Reproduced with the kind permission of Han Jia-yu.

Yan and Long Yun. The story is narrated by an omniscient third-person narrator, and the excitable sentimentalism of Qi's tone, marked orthographically in Chu's text by a proliferation of exclamation marks, recalls a similarly fervent expressive manner in Lu Yin's "Lishi's Diary."[27] In the story's present, Qi is romantically involved with Long Yun, whose shortcomings serve as a constant reminder to Qi of her enduring love for her former girlfriend, Zhang Yan, who has moved away to the south of Taiwan. Qi is portrayed as childlike, sentimental, and narcissistic, enjoying creating a persona for herself as a "cute little girl" as opposite number to her tomboy girlfriends, who are athletic, protective, and chivalrous and to whom Qi habitually refers with the masculine *ta* pronoun.[28] Much to Qi's consternation, however, as the story commences, her current tomboy sweetheart, Long Yun, has begun a flirtation with a local sailor. Finally, Long Yun takes Qi along to a party with the sailor and his gang, where Qi looks on in distress as Long Yun turns disappointingly girlish and kisses the boy. Qi, who has been forced to dance with the sailor's friend, flees the party in confusion, and the story concludes with her tearfully vowing never to marry but to remain eternally faithful to her girlhood love for her two tomboy classmates.

The memorial mode is instantiated most clearly in Qi's nostalgic remembrance of her love for the distant Zhang Yan. The narrative pattern of the story is such that the unfolding events involving Qi and Long Yun in the present are constantly interrupted by Qi's mournful backward gaze, which discovers traces of the lost paradise of her time with Zhang Yan all about her. Standing dazed in the street after fleeing the party where Long Yun kissed the sailor, as if seeking refuge from the dreadful present, Qi recalls a blissful summer afternoon spent with Zhang Yan: "Suddenly she felt like singing, like that summer when she'd sat under the banyan tree with Zhang Yan as the little banyan figs pattered to the ground all around them, pitter-pat. She'd sung 'A Tale,' with Zhang Yan accompanying in a low voice. They'd sung up to the line, 'How many times have the flowers of our dreams fallen to the ground?' and the two of them had looked up at the banyan figs falling on their heads and burst out laughing. Life had seemed truly boundless."[29] Such ecstatic remembrance of past summer intimacy from the vantage point of a desolate present has been characteristic of the schoolgirl romance genre since the publication in the 1920s of stories by women writers such as Lu Yin, discussed in chapter 1.[30] In Qi's memory, Zhang Yan, the long-ago summer, the nostalgic 1930s pop song, and the blissful sensation of "boundlessness" (*youchang*) combine in an image of a prelapsarian romantic utopia utterly lost to her in the present.

Yet ecstatic though Qi's memory is, the sense of loss and shattered hopes in the song's rhetorical question—"How many times have the flowers of our dreams fallen to the ground?"—carries an ominous significance as well. For Zhang Yan is lost to Qi not once but twice: even before she betrayed Qi's trust by moving to southern Taiwan to attend college, Zhang Yan had already "died" to Qi on the day of their high school graduation, when Qi discovered Zhang Yan at home, suffering from painful menstrual cramps:

> "I've brought you a rose. What's the matter? Your tummy hurts, h'm?" [Qi] drew each word out long and slow. The world seemed perfectly harmonious and utterly serene, making her sense with what tenderness, with what immeasurable tenderness, she must cherish it.
>
> "It's my damn time of the month, it's killing me! I've never had it this bad before. . . ." After that, she had no memory at all of what Zhang Yan had said nor how she'd replied. When she got home, all she could do was cry. She cried all night: so Zhang Yan was like that! So Zhang Yan was just a girl, like her, with a special time of the month! The world had played a great big trick on her! She cried till she had no tears left and could only sob dry sobs, gazing at the moon.[31]

Prior to this moment, Qi had loved Zhang Yan neither as a boy nor as a girl, but as a tomboy lover desirable precisely by virtue of his/her transgender allure, characterized by boyish features while at the same time clearly differentiated from ordinary boys ("Zhang Yan never spoke a word to boys—even if he did, he'd do it nonchalantly, with arms akimbo, by the side of the basketball court as though discussing business"). Once Zhang Yan's unsettlingly womanly, menstruating body is revealed to Qi, her tomboy lover is effectively lost to her. Thus, even before Zhang Yan moves south, Qi's relation with him/her is already a memorial one: even with Zhang Yan standing right in front of her, Qi's love for him/her is already nostalgic: "Before going south Zhang Yan had said to her, Qi, be good, h'm? The wind blew their hair about so it filled the whole sky. Looking at Zhang Yan, she felt she'd been peculiarly calm. She'd looked at Zhang Yan smiling at her and stroking her hair, and not felt excited in the least—and yet at the same time, deep in her heart, she'd been missing Zhang Yan, missing him so her heart ached. . . . Zhang Yan had died, she knew it."[32]

Qi's loving relation with Zhang Yan in the story's present, then, occurs at a double memorial remove: she must recall not only the Zhang Yan who preceded Long Yun but also the Zhang Yan who preceded Zhang Yan. The doubly removed relation is nicely expressed in the lines from Tang poet Li Shangyin's typically romantic-melancholic poetry, which Qi inscribes in Zhang Yan's yearbook on their graduation:

> Such feeling cannot be recalled again,
> It seemed long-lost e'en when it was felt then.[33]

In this story, *qing* (sentiment)—which might also be translated "love"—between women is always already long lost, receding ever further backward into memory's sorrowful abyss. Most powerfully present in the narrative through nostalgia's mediation, love between women is figured as the memorial subject *par excellence*.

Judith Roof has observed the tendency for representations of lesbian relations to remain confined to the middle section of narratives since, she argues, narrative itself strains toward sexual and formal closure in a triumphantly reproductive union that she proposes is structurally—as well as often actually, in content—aligned with a heterosexual outcome.[34] Yet Chu's "Waves," typical of the Chinese schoolgirl romance genre, differs from Roof's Euro-American examples of "hetero-narrative" insofar as although here, as there, a heterosexual conclusion supersedes the lesbian romance of the narrative middle; nevertheless in this case the encroachment of heterosexuality is anything but climactically triumphant. Rather than a natural or self-motivated progression from lesbianism, heterosexual dating is represented as largely an external social imperative forced on an unwilling protagonist by powers outside her control. Insofar as it constitutes a familially enforced obstacle to the love relationship between the central couple, the heterosexual imperative in Chu's story performs an analogous function to the arranged marriages that separate the young same-sex lovers in Lu Yin's and Ling Shuhua's 1920s schoolgirl romances discussed in chapter 1. By the late twentieth century, the traditional arranged marriage system is no longer operative as such; the hetero-marital system has become diffused, no longer concretized in the clearly delineated rituals of the past, yet our heroine finds it no less forceful for that.

Throughout the story, Qi's watchful mother is the primary enforcer of the heterosexual imperative, constantly berating her daughter for choosing to hang around with these strange, gender-ambiguous classmates, Zhang Yan and Long Yun ("who looks like I-don't-know-what") and praising her when, after Qi grows exasperated at the inconsistency of Long Yun's affections, she briefly withdraws from her. Qi's peer group—cruelly including Long Yun herself—acts as the other agent propelling the unwilling Qi toward cross-sex object choice. Yet despite the best efforts of her mother and her friends, the most enthusiastic praise Qi can muster for the sailor with whom the callous Long Yun pairs her up is that he is "nice" (hao)—a sharp contrast to Qi's sexually charged internal monologues on the irresistible tomboyish charms of Long Yun herself. And the story's conclusion finds Qi strenuously resisting the disciplinary directives of both her mother and her peer group as they struggle to redirect her toward a hetero-marital future:

> She decided that in future she'd wear a black dress, and in the summer a snow-white one. She wouldn't speak but would just sit, for evermore, quietly in a corner, ghostly pale and peaceful. And people would ask, Why has that beautiful girl not married? And people would answer, Ah, because in her life there are only two people, and she remains faithful to the friendship of her youth! . . .
>
> She decided that when she got home she'd write an entry in her new diary: In my life there are two people, and only two: Zhang Yan and Long Yun. Thinking of it, she couldn't help laughing. Let the tears overflow her cheeks—she wasn't going to wipe them away![35]

Qi's determination to remain chastely faithful to her love for her tomboy sweethearts in the face of increasing pressure to marry—readable, perhaps, as a kind of queer appropriation of the classical paragon of the virtuous widow who chooses celibacy over remarriage—is the story's final word.[36] Although the story could be read to imply that Qi will eventually, despite her misgivings, succumb to the mounting pressure to marry, such a conclusion does not strongly *naturalize* cross-sex object choice. Rather, it frames cross-sex union as a socially enforced ordinance brought to bear on a tragic heroine who, if free to pursue her own will, would most likely continue to be guided by her intense romantic attraction to her tomboy lovers.

Marking a distinction from the 1920s stories, however, it must be noted that "Waves" does suggest that its heroine internalizes the injunction against same-sex love to some degree. Following the traumatic shattering of Zhang Yan's illusion of tomboy masculinity the day of their high school graduation, Qi reflects: "It was funny: Zhang Yan looked just the same as before, mouth pulled down in a smile, and that tall form, in jeans, still made her heart leap; the sound of that call, 'Qi——!,' her name drawn out long and slow, still made her heart break. But now when Zhang Yan put an arm around her shoulders, she only found it creepy and disgusting."[37] Still drawn to the romantic memory of Zhang Yan as tomboy heartthrob—and, as her later relationship with Long Yun attests, still keen to pursue further romantic liaisons with tomboys—Qi nonetheless experiences a sense of "disgust" at the now conscious knowledge of her sweetheart's female body. The possibility of such a response is entirely absent from the early-century stories discussed in the previous chapter, and its appearance in this later story would seem to bespeak a new partial *interiorization* of a social imperative that previously manifested in a wholly exterior way, through social pressure to fulfill the familial obligation to marry.

As is clear from the overwrought sentimentalism of Qi's internal monologue at the story's conclusion (quoted above), "Waves" is marked throughout by an ironic distance between the narratorial voice and Qi's emotional experience. Indeed, the text often seems internally split between empathy for and affectionate mockery of its naïve and excitable young protagonist. This pervasive sense of ironic distance can, I think, be explained through closer consideration of the uses the story makes of the tragic-love story formula. It should be recalled that at the time when Chu wrote the story, the tragic-romantic structure of feeling was in wide popular cultural circulation in Taiwan, as can be seen in both the continuing cultural impact of the legend of Liang Shanbo and Zhu Yingtai as told in the enduringly popular 1962 Shaw Brothers' film *The Love Eterne*, and the massive popularity of the novels, films, and television serials of romance writer Qiong Yao (discussed below).[38] I propose that "Waves" is self-conscious in its citation of this popular narrative form; it represents not simply a further instance of the tragic-love story but a thoroughly reflexive appropriation of elements of that generic form. Hence the sense of ironic distance that pervades the story: the narrator leads the reader to observe Qi making use of the somewhat clichéd generic formulae of tragic romance as a template by means of which to narrativize internally her own experience of same-sex love. More explicit examples of the story's citation of these formulae will lend weight to this point.

In addition to the external obstacle to the lovers' union in the form of oblique parental encouragement to the heroine to make a (proto-)marital union with somebody other than her tomboy lovers and the heroine's final vow of lifelong celibacy in faithful memory of her true love(s) (discussed above), the exchange of letters and flowers between the lovers as tokens of their love also echoes stock elements in tragic-love narratives.[39] Qi also reflects on her love for Long Yun and Zhang Yan in language that strongly recalls the vocabulary of the popular tragic-love story: when at the beginning of the story she tearily "contemplat[es] this pure and faintly tragic love of hers," "tragic" translates *xunqing*, a stock term of tragic-love fiction meaning to die in self-sacrificing testimony to true love.[40] The overall tone of Qi's subjective construction of her relationships with Long Yun and Zhang Yan is saturated with the classic tragic-love mixture of *qing* (love) and *chou* (sorrow). When Qi recalls crying in front of Zhang Yan and "a wave of tender melancholy [*aichou*] [brings] to her mind all manner of tragic stories [*beizhuangde gushi*]," we might reasonably infer that Qi herself is a reader of popular tragic love stories. In 1970s Taiwan, the likeliest literary exemplars of the tragic-love discourse would be the stories of popular novelist Qiong Yao.

Qiong Yao remains the most widely read Chinese-language popular romance writer of recent decades. Her writing was widely adapted for film and television in the 1960s and 1970s and became a staple of Taiwan, Hong Kong, and diasporic Chinese entertainment cultures in those decades.[41] In her detailed study of Qiong Yao's social impact in Taiwan, Lin Fang-mei observes that Qiong Yao's fiction conforms in several respects to the narrative patterns of earlier Chinese love stories, in particular the "sentimental tradition" described by Hsia.[42] In keeping with this older narrative pattern, romantic heroines in Qiong Yao's novels are characterized by their emotional and aesthetic supersensitivity (*duoqing*) and are often fond of reciting classical poetry. Tragic plots are common, especially in Qiong Yao's works of the 1960s, with generational conflict frequently constituting the major external obstacle to the lovers' union. Here as in the popular tragic-love stories of the 1910s discussed in chapter 1, readerly pleasures center on the romantic pathos of the image of perfect yet thwarted love. Lin offers a detailed analysis of the widespread phenomenon of Qiong Yao fandom among adolescent girls in the 1970s, underscoring the intense anxieties that Qiong Yao's popularity aroused among defenders of masculinist literary high culture.[43] Such critics professed concern about the potentially harmful effects that pleasurable identification with the melancholic, lovelorn heroines of Qiong Yao's tragic love stories might have on the impressionable minds of young women.

Given the clear irony with which the narratorial voice in "Waves" treats its heroine's mournfully sentimental attachment to her tomboy sweethearts, I propose that the story can be read as a literary representation of the same high-cultural anxiety that Lin describes: it is as if Chu presents the character Xiao Qi as a fictional exemplar of the morbid effects of Qiong Yao–style romantic sentimentalism on young women readers.[44] Many of Qi's habitual ways of conceptualizing herself and her relationships with Zhang Yan and Long Yun mimic the conventions of Qiong Yao's romance novels (which themselves update the older tradition of popular tragic-love fiction) — for example, Qi's earnest enactment of the clichéd "love rituals" of poetry quoting, diary writing, and moon gazing.[45] Qi's conceptualization of her relationship with Zhang Yan, whereby Zhang Yan is constructed as masculine nurturer and Qi as his/her passive feminine counterpart, also recalls gender ideology in Qiong Yao.[46] Indeed, the parallel is made explicit in Qi's choice of metaphor; she muses: "She realized her eyes were moist. It occurred to her that she was but a weak, delicate vine; what she needed was a big, strong tree to climb upon. Pitifully, she stroked her own cheeks. Seeing the tears glistening in her eyes, she sighed, and walked slowly upstairs. She picked up the phone extension and dialed Long Yun's number."[47] The image of the feminine clinging vine that relies on a steady, masculinized tree for support is pointedly reminiscent of the structuring metaphor in Qiong Yao's 1964 novel *Tusihua* (The Dodder Flower).

Chu T'ien-hsin's early fiction has frequently been placed into the culturally deprecated category of *guixiu wenxue* (boudoir fiction)—fiction concerned with the trifling details of women's domestic and emotional lives—a category into which Qiong Yao's popular romances also, and much less ambiguously, fall.[48] But my point in drawing attention to the echoes between "Waves" and Qiong Yao's romances is not to argue that the two authors' works are substantially similar in either style or genre. Rather, I propose that in the figure of Xiao Qi, Chu's story enacts a self-conscious, reflexive *reference to* the mournfully romantic structure of feeling evoked in Qiong Yao's tragic-love fiction. "Waves" should be seen as a commentary on Qiong Yao–style popular romance rather than simply an example of it; the text does not *itself* fully subscribe to the sentimental romanticism it describes; instead, it frames for the reader Qi's pleasurable immersion in this familiar, bittersweet structure of feeling. What is most interesting about this story's intertextual relation with popular romance is the way it presses what might seem like an indicatively heterosexual structure of feeling and set of narrative conventions into service for the writing of a same-sex love story.[49] In this, like Lu Yin's and Ling Shuhua's stories discussed in chapter 1, "Waves" reveals how the modern, universalizing Chinese imaginary of young women's same-sex romance has drawn on the affective imaginary and narrative conventions of cross-sex romance narratives; in particular, the tragic-love story.[50]

In an interview with the author about this story, Chu T'ien-hsin observes that the theme of unconsummated adolescent female same-sex romance runs through much of her writing. Suggestively, Chu remarks in relation to this preoccupation, "I'm not interested in narratives that end in a full-stop—I prefer an ellipsis."[51] Chu links the repetition of female homoerotic ellipsis in her writing to her own life experience, specifically to a passionate adolescent friendship she enjoyed with a female classmate—a relationship that,

Chu explains, "never developed beyond friendship, as we both got married and things changed." For Chu, the elliptic (in)conclusion to her relationship with her classmate produces a thematic repetition compulsion in her writing: "Because our relationship ends in ellipsis, I keep repeating characters that represent my friend in my writing, from 'Waves Scour the Sands' to 'A Story of Spring Butterflies,' right through to 'Ancient Capital.' I have a feeling that she'll keep on turning up, too." In Chu's theorization of her own work, female homoerotic ellipsis, the memorial mode, and repetition are linked together in circular succession: female homoerotic memory must be narrativized in never-ending repetitions precisely because the schoolgirl romance is forever suspended, never reaching its conclusion.

Indeed, insofar as romantic liaisons between women constitute the principal subject matter in schoolgirl romances generally, and yet typically, as occurs in both "Waves" and Chu's own life story as she tells it, the romance is tragically cut short by the untimely incursion of the marital or proto-marital imperative, ellipsis—a sign of narrative suspension, abbreviation, and significatory failure—is typical of the narrative organization of the schoolgirl romances more broadly. Since the characters set up by the narrative as romantic partners fail to come together at the stories' end, the equivocal ellipsis, not the decisive full stop, is these stories' (in)conclusion—unconcluded, the stories must be endlessly repeated, as indeed they are in the ongoing repetition of the memorial same-sex romance narrative in contemporary Chinese cultural production.[52] This, however, is a peculiarly voluble ellipsis, less a refusal to name the homoerotic possibility than an underscoring of the forcible foreshortening of the homoerotic narrative such that marriage appears not as a satisfying conclusion but rather as a premature, violently enforced and tragic truncation of the "real" (same-sex romance) story.[53]

Another interview response from Chu suggests a similar interpretation. In answer to a question about why she wrote this kind of story, Chu responds: "Around that age, girls will often find themselves being courted by boys. And in that social context—where it seemed as if society was telling you that at a certain age, a girl *ought* to be with a boy—a lot of girls just went along with that."[54] Later, she elaborates: "I think a lot of girls have similar experiences in this regard: they just muddle along through adolescence, and before they've even had a chance to think about the question of their own sexual orientation they find themselves married with children."[55] These responses suggest that the problem indicated by the "why" in the interview question was interpreted by Chu as the problem of the story's heterosexual outcome, not its homosexual content; refreshingly, Chu interpreted the heterosexual conclusion as the narrative problem most self-evidently demanding an explanation. Her responses, like her story, suggest a theory of marital heterosexuality as a form of deviation in the lives of actual as well as fictional subjects, a peril liable to overtake the unwary young woman as the result of a combination of girlish absentmindedness and the social efficacy of the marital imperative. Thus, although the life stories of the girls to whom Chu refers, like her own autobiography and the schoolgirl romances that she authors, conclude with the imposition of the marital imperative on their protagonists, nevertheless by presenting that conclusion as a tragic deviation in the course of a love story that is really about the heroine's relationship with another woman, these stories implicitly underscore the disappointments of such an ending. Along with other contemporary Chinese-language schoolgirl romances, like Wong Bikwan's "She's a Young Woman and So Am I," discussed below, the memorial mode is mobilized here to suggest that far from representing a satisfying conclusion, externally imposed heterosexuality frustrates the proper narrative and sexual progression of the central, same-sex romance story.

"She's a Young Woman and So Am I": The Utopianism of Schoolgirl Romance

Wong Bikwan (Huang Biyun) is among Hong Kong's best-known and most prolific contemporary women writers. A key contributor to Hong Kong's 1990s literary "new wave," Wong has attracted sustained critical attention — and at times critical outrage — for her bleak literary visions of sex, death, and visceral violence, characterized by postmodernist experimentation with narrative structure and a resolute refusal to moralize.[56] The homoeroticism in Wong's writing has attracted relatively little attention, yet as Hou Li-zhen observes, "Amid the profusion of [stories] drenched in gore, semen, violence, and chaos, [representations of characters'] same-sex intimacy and mutual reliance shine, under Wong's pen, with exceptional earnestness."[57] Indeed, in the context of Wong's relentless dystopianism in the work for which she is best known, the idealizing representations of same-sex intimacy between women in both *Lienü tu* (The Picture of Female Virtue, 1999) and "Ta shi nüzi, wo ye shi nüzi" (She's a Young Woman and So Am I, 1994) are all the more notable for their strongly utopian cast.[58]

Wong's "She's a Young Woman and So Am I," the first short story in her collection of the same title, is narrated by a university student, Yip Saisai, who is romantically infatuated with her seductively feminine classmate Hui Jihang.[59] Saisai dreams longingly of living forever with Jihang in a simple yet fulfilling life of nonsexual companionship, but the two become estranged when Jihang loses out on a scholarship to Saisai. Jihang is determined to become a fashion model and begins sleeping with men in an attempt to get ahead in the business; Saisai retaliates by moving out of their shared dorm room and taking up with a male student to whom she is emotionally indifferent while remaining in love with Jihang. Saisai eventually returns to the dorm room she shared with Jihang, but when she discovers Jihang having sex with a man on her own bed, she tells the man that the relations between herself and Jihang are "special"; before fleeing, the man berates the pair as perverts. Soon after, the two young women are reprimanded by the dorm matron for their "abnormal" relationship. Jihang is forced to move out, the two lose contact, and Saisai is left mourning the unrealized possibility of their life together as she observes Jihang's progress in her modeling career and her public liaison with a male mentor in the industry.

The memorial mode asserts itself most forcefully in the story's final lines, as Saisai reflects on her loss of Jihang:

> I remember her *qipao* and her embroidered slippers. I remember her self-contained confidence when she was copying from my notes. I remember her smile when she softly pressed her bosom with her hand. I remember her lazy demeanor when she used to lie in bed reading Yi Shu.[60] I remember the time I was cold and she gave me her scarf to warm me up, and the time when I was proud and she had thrown coins at me. When I was cold and distant, she had held my hand tightly and said "The general has lost his wife and his army." I remember. I remember, I tied up her hair, cut her toenails, bought her a bouquet of gerberas. I remember I had once attempted to strangle myself; my eyes filled with tears. She had pulled away my hands and said, "Why do this?"
>
> Why do this. I thought I could spend the rest of my life with Jihang.[61]

The insistent repetition, here, of "I remember" (*wo jide*) serves once again to specify memory as the rhetorical frame for the subject of desiring attachment between women. In this final passage, the reiteration in such an emphatically memorial mode of events that have been narrated for the first time only a page or two earlier highlights the constitutive link between Saisai's romantic love for Jihang and the retrospective operations of memory. It also reminds us that the story's effort of remembrance is compelled by Saisai's mourning of the unrealized possibility of a life lived with her female lover—reinforcing this, the story's final sentence is a repetition of its first. In narrative terms, the story bites its own tail, forming a self-enclosed circuit rather than stretching forward in a linear trajectory. This unsatisfying conclusion bespeaks, once again, the workings of ellipsis; as in Chu's "Waves," the story's unsatisfying (in)conclusion results from the suspension of the central same-sex romance by the untimely incursion of a peremptory heterosexual ending.

Wong's story is exemplary of the utopianism that characterizes the school-girl romance. By contrasting Saisai's faithfulness to her love for Jihang with Jihang's self-serving pursuit of heterosexual relations, the story sets up a series of parallel oppositions whereby women's same-sex relations are to cross-sex relations as simplicity is to sophistication, spirituality is to worldliness, purity is to corruption, love is to sex, innocence is to experience, authenticity is to commodification, and cooperation is to competition. The story's utopian representation of same-sex romance is reinforced by the use of quasi-religious language in describing Jihang's and Saisai's respective characters. Jihang's entanglement in the world of heterosexual and commercial competition and exchange is described more than once with the related terms *shisu* and *sushi*, denoting that which is common, secular, or worldly (classically, in distinction from the Buddhist clergy).[62] In contrast to Jihang's association with the profane world of commerce and heterosexuality—and indeed the most direct confluence of the two in prostitution—Saisai is linked with qualities valued in folk Buddhism: purity or simplicity (*danchun*) and plainness (*jianpu*).[63] While the sophisticated Jihang continues to pursue heterosexual relations as a means of social and economic self-advancement, the simple Saisai, in contrast, narrowly avoids the perilous lure of marriage. Suggesting an idea similar to Chu's (above) about the dangers of young women being sidetracked into marriage through a kind of untimely lapse in concentration, Saisai recalls with alarm that she once almost agreed to marry the boyfriend for whom she felt nothing simply because he happened to offer her a handkerchief when she was drunk and teary.[64] Having escaped this trap—and appropriately, given the story's other allusions to folk Buddhism—Saisai memorializes her faithful love for Jihang through a nun-like sacrifice of the sensual pleasures of worldly existence.[65]

If one set of metaphors through which Wong's story articulates its utopianism is religious, another is economic. Jihang's fall from grace is not only a fall into heterosexuality, but also a fall into the deathly corruption of economic exchange. As Patricia Sieber observes, it is appropriate that Jihang and Saisai first bond in class over the Marxian notion of surplus value.[66] Jihang's education through the length of the narrative is really an education in self-exploitation, as she learns to work her feminine assets to turn a profit. Paralleling a similar theme in Eileen Chang's writing (see discussion below), through figures of self-interested exchanges of money and advantage the story directly equates heterosexual relations with prostitution.[67] Meanwhile, a brokenhearted Saisai watches Jihang's uniqueness being drained from her as the surplus value generated by her self-exploitation, so that ultimately Jihang appears as no more than a depthless spectacle of commodified femininity in a fashion magazine: "Later on, I saw her on the cover of a magazine. Her luscious lips. The smile. However, I did not open the magazine. She was merely one among many thousands of beautiful women, entirely different from the Jihang I had known."[68] In contrast to Jihang's self-insertion into the vampiric economy of exploitation, exchange, and profit, Saisai imagines a life for the two of them in which wealth accumulation is shunned for blissfully wasteful spending on oysters on the half shell, expensive cashmere sweaters, and hand-woven Persian carpets.[69] Through these chains of metaphoric association, while same-sex love is equated with spiritual purity and an ecstatic rupture of the laws of capitalist accumulation, cross-sex relations are linked with worldly corruption and entrapment within the deadening cycles of economic exchange and accumulation.

Here as in Chu's "Waves," the supplanting of same-sex romance by cross-sex relations at the story's conclusion—in this case, in the form of Jihang's liaison with a "big callow-faced fatso with a pair of flashy sunglasses," as observed by Saisai—is rather far from celebratory.[70] Anything but a jubilant return to some predetermined path of "natural" sexual and narrative development, the heterosexual ending is once again presented as a premature, tragic truncation of the central romance between the two women. In this story, the social and economic systems of patriarchy and capitalism themselves conspire to teach Saisai the "lesson" of the heterosexual imperative by robbing her of her beloved Jihang. But in addition to these impersonal structures, Wong's story also personifies social-sexual discipline in the figure of the dorm matron who reprimands Saisai for her "abnormal" relationship with her classmate. In her capacity as the coercive voice of the hetero-marital social convention that is the major obstacle to the two women's romance, the matron in this story performs an analogous function to Qi's censorious mother in "Waves." Saisai's interview with the matron is as follows:

> The television was on, with only muted pictures flickering past the screen. The dorm matron's face went bright and dark, blue and white. It was frightening. Amidst the play of light and shadows she held back for a little while, then spoke slowly, emphasizing each word, "I have received a letter reporting on the abnormal relationship between you and Jihang."

The oolong tea was scalding and burned the tip of my tongue. I lifted my head to look at her, and without knowing why, I had a smile on my face.

"University students not only have to have knowledge, they must also have high moral standards. . . ."

"I don't think this is anything degraded. Many men and women behave in a much more degraded way than we do." I looked straight into her eyes. She did not try to avoid my glance, but looked straight back at me.

"It is abnormal, what you two are doing; it obstructs the development of human civilization. The reason society as a whole can remain an orderly system is entirely dependent upon natural human relationships. . . ." I no longer heard her clearly, I just picked up bits and pieces. I was no longer looking at her; instead, I began to flip through the pages of [the women's magazine] Breakthrough.

Mingsum replies, "Ling, that you should destroy another's relationship is not right, but the Almighty God will forgive you. . . ." I was so frightened I hurriedly put the magazine away. After a long time, I said very softly, "Why impose your moral standards on us? We haven't harmed anyone." I don't know if she heard; at the same time, my voice was so soft it seemed as if someone else was whispering these words into my ears. I looked around in alarm, but there was no one else beside me.

"Dorm matron." I put down my teacup and said, "As long as Jihang won't leave me, I will certainly not leave her." Having said this, I abruptly got up and opened the door.[71]

This exchange between Saisai and the dorm matron provides an exemplary dramatization of the conception I have discussed throughout this chapter of heterosexuality as an externally imposed social edict. The eerie atmosphere at the beginning of the passage, with the blue and white flicker of the muted television lending the matron's face a preternatural luminosity, underscores both the symbolic weight of the scene and its uncanny psychic effect on our heroine. What is dramatized here is a scene of failed interpellation: the matron attempts to instill in Saisai the shame proper to an accusation of homosexuality, but Saisai fails to proffer the response demanded of her. Instead of the downturned face that marks shame's victory, Saisai gives the matron an unexpected smile and meets her gaze defiantly. Moreover, she not only tunes out to the matron's righteous sermonizing to flip idly through a magazine, but she also repeatedly counters the matron's shaming discourse on homosexuality's moral depravity with her own proud, idealizing one, which elevates women's same-sex love above the "degraded" behaviors of women with men. The matron's condemnation of homosexual behavior is itself interestingly hybrid. On the one hand, she appeals to "natural human relationships" (zirande renlei guanxi) in an implicitly biological-essentialist defense of the naturalness of cross-sex pairing. On the other hand, she appeals to the maintenance of an "orderly society" (wendingde shehui zhidu), implying an instrumentalist conception of the hetero-marital system's social utility. It is at this confusing moment that Saisai tunes out to read her magazine, but with the advice columnist's comparably moralizing take on love and sex, a confederacy of interlocking disciplinary institutions bent on regulating feminine sexuality begins, vertiginously, to bear down on her: the school; the Christian church; the commercial entertainment culture that is represented by the magazine and possibly also by the soundless television screen that projects its weird light onto the matron's face and seems somehow collusive with her reprimands. As if as a result of the psychic stress of resisting such a polyvocal, multidirectional hailing as a good feminine subject, Saisai now undergoes a disorienting subjective splitting so that her own protesting voice seems to belong to somebody else standing beside her. In sum, the postadolescent move toward cross-sex sexual practice and the concomitant turn away from same-sex desire could hardly be less interiorized than they are here. Even more clearly than in "Waves," in Wong's story, far from appearing as a spontaneous desire within the young feminine subject, heterosexuality is figured as the imperious demand of a set of exterior disciplinary institutions. This demand voices itself ever more insistently to Saisai as she enters adulthood, thereby forcibly suspending her own narrative of same-sex romance and effectively perverting the narrative flow of the story itself.

In contrast to the relatively direct citation of the tragic-love story form and aesthetic in Chu's "Waves," with its sentimental heroine and overt allusions to classical poetry, in Wong's story reference to this form is fragmentary and schematic. Elements of the generic narrative are certainly discernable: the pining Saisai enacts a kind of symbolic death for love (xunqing) when she stands over the sleeping Jihang and attempts to strangle herself with her own hands; she brings Jihang a gift of flowers; at the two women's final parting reference is made to a "final farewell like that of lovers parted by circumstance or death" (sheng li si bie); and after their parting, Saisai adopts distinctly nun-like behavior, immersing herself in her studies, giving up brightly colored clothing, quitting smoking, and adhering to a Buddhist-style vegetarian diet.[72] In a reflexive twist, Jihang herself is even a fan of Hong Kong novelist Yi Shu's popular romance fiction.[73] But although the broad generic outline of a classical-style tragic-love story remains discernible, Wong's story's clearest intertextual reference is far more specific: in both style and theme, the story recalls the fiction of one of the most widely read modern Chinese women writers, Eileen Chang.

Eileen Chang is an iconic figure in modern Chinese literature and public culture, famous for her appropriation of the form of popular romance fiction for "serious" yet immensely popular stories that tend to subvert rather than champion the ideology of romantic love.[74] Chang was born in Shanghai and began writing in the early 1940s. Her first stories appeared in *Ziluolan* (The Violet), a key magazine of the mandarin duck and butterfly school of popular fiction, and the young Chang soon rose to fame as one of the city's most prominent intellectuals.[75] The stories for which Chang is best known — including "The Golden Cangue" (*Jin suo ji*, 1943); "Love in a Fallen City" (*Qingcheng zhi lian*, 1943); and "Traces of Love" (*Liu qing*, 1945) — narrate in meticulous detail the everyday material and emotional lives of bourgeois women in the modernizing cities of Shanghai and Hong Kong. Suffused with pathos, Chang's stories deconstruct the decadent glamour of modern urban life to focus on the petty competitiveness and self-destructive behavior to which women are driven by oppressive social systems, especially the tenacious, entrapping structure of the gradually disintegrating traditional family system, aptly called by Lim Chin-chown the "iron boudoir."[76]

Chang's love stories end at best with their heroines' resignation to emotional compromise rather than the triumph of true love fulfilled, but instead of the high drama of tragedy, they evoke the quiet despair of desolation — *cangliang*, Chang's self-confessed favorite word.[77] On this distinction, Chang writes: "Tragedy is like the juxtaposition of bright red with bright green: a very intense contrast. But such a juxtaposition is more dramatic than suggestive. The reason why desolation produces a more lasting poignant effect is because it is like the juxtaposition of scallion green with peach red: a less predictable contrast."[78] The use of the visual metaphor here is characteristic. Stylistically, Chang's writing is marked by a quasi-fetishistic attention to the visual and sensual details of quotidian urban life; obsessively, her texts linger over the fabric and style of a woman's outfit; the color and texture of a wall; the appearance of a facial feature.[79] Rey Chow links this incessant detailing with Chang's central thematic concern with representing women's experience of modernity: the accumulation of seemingly trivial details undercuts the concerns of "serious" (and masculinist) modern Chinese fiction with the grand narratives of History, the Nation, and Revolution.[80] In presenting a feminine counter-perspective on the experience of modernity, Chang's focus on details can be seen as continuous with her implicitly critical exposure of women's entrapment within the binding disciplinary structures of gender and the patrilineal family system.[81]

Chang's influence on contemporary women writers in both Hong Kong and Taiwan, where her work has enjoyed lasting popularity from the 1960s to the present, can hardly be overstated, and it is not surprising to discover Chang's stylistic shadow in Wong's writing.[82] In an almost self-conscious reference to Chang's technique, "She's a Young Woman" pays insistent attention to the details of Jihang's clothing and body from Saisai's point of view.[83] Saisai's first encounter with Jihang is recalled through a description of the precise details of Jihang's appearance: she wears not just a dress and slippers but cut "a tightly fitting *qipao* dress" and "dainty embroidered," "bright red" slippers; her hair is not just bobbed but "trimmed evenly to just below the earlobes"; her nails are not just painted but are painted "peach red."[84] Saisai's experience of Jihang's presence is treated similarly throughout; later Jihang appears in a "loosely fitting, white and dark mauve cotton *qipao*"; there is "very fine" hair on her arms; she exudes a smell that is a mixture of "make-up, perfume, milk and ink"; and she always wears those same embroidered slippers, which are mentioned several times.[85] The text also lingers over the details of other quotidian objects — Saisai's pink size 32A Maidenform bra; a piece of stale bread that tastes like floury animal feed — but the descriptions of Jihang in particular perform a kind of compound reference to Chang's writing insofar as Jihang favors precisely the fashions of 1930s and 1940s Shanghai and Hong Kong that feature in Chang's stories. With her bobbed hair, *qipao*, and embroidered slippers, smoking Red Double Happiness cigarettes in the dorm room that the two call a "'smoke and flower alley,' punning on the name for the traditional haunts of courtesans," Jihang seems like a character from an Eileen Chang story transported across time to the Hong Kong of the 1990s.[86] Jihang's story, too, parallels those of Chang's heroines: in her desperate effort to better her social position by getting ahead in the entertainment and modeling business, Jihang falls into petty competitiveness with Saisai and self-destructive reliance on a string of male mentors to whom she offers sexual favors in the mostly vain hope that they will help her gain a foothold in the industry. In its focus on Jihang's gradual entrapment by a hostile social system as she struggles to improve her status and financial situation, the story suggests a historically transposed Chang-style critique. Now the entrapping structures are not concubinage, marriage, and the decaying clan system of the early twentieth century but a hyper-competitive, late-capitalist commodity culture where women are still forced into self-defeating sexual transactions in their attempt to secure a place within a system that is loaded against their interests.[87]

As observed above, some of Chang's stories contain elements of school-girl romance, but only as peripheral subplots and not as the central subject. In her posthumously published "Tongxue shaonian dou bu jian" (My Prosperous Classmates) (the story within the book of the same title), for example, while the adult narrator reveals that her own schoolgirl crush on a classmate was "washed away without a trace after [she] fell in love with a man," she realizes with a shock at the end of the story that her friend's unrequited same-sex love for another classmate has remained constant and that her friend's marriage has therefore essentially been a sham.[88] If for Chang, marriage and cross-sex relations serve more to frustrate and entrap than to satisfy women characters, then women's same-sex love appears, in its occasional fleeting descriptions in her writing, as a utopian but always unrealizable alternative. That construction of same-sex love—which also echoes, once again, the 1920s writings of Lu Yin and Ling Shuhua—is repeated in Wong's story. While marriage itself is no longer necessarily the focus of the ambitious woman's life plan, Jihang's pursuit of financial success and social status nevertheless draws her, like Chang's characters, decisively toward self-interested sexual/financial transactions with powerful men and away from her female sweetheart.

Going In: The Never-Ending Story

In some important ways, contemporary Chinese-language going-in stories repeat a standard modern sexological and psychoanalytic narrative organization. As in both Freud and Ellis, loving attachments between women are represented as bearing a defining relation to memory—indeed, the pervasiveness of the memorial mode tends to construct these attachments as available only through memory's mediation. Further, same-sex love, confined to the past, seems fated to be superseded by a marital or proto-marital heterosexuality that usurps its position at story's end. However, crucially, although these schoolgirl romances may appear simply to reiterate a psychoanalytic and sexological construction of female homosexuality as a prehistoric precursor to heterosexuality, nevertheless, in these stories this primacy stubbornly refuses to flip over into secondariness. The psychic anguish occasioned by compulsory "going in" is eloquently and ritually repeated, and going in is presented not as the effect of any natural predisposition but rather as the tragic result of an externally imposed social law forcibly directing young women's sexuality toward marital or proto-marital union. Presented in perpetual retrospect, the adolescent utopia of schoolgirl romance is always and by definition overlooked by the threat of its imminent prohibition. My argument is that insofar as they construct feminine adolescence as the decisive moment of socialization toward hetero-marital union and forcible renunciation of the pre-adult pleasures of same-sex eroticism, these stories mobilize the progressive function of memory: reminiscent narrators reconstruct the latterly prohibited pleasures of adolescent feminine same-sex love through a memorial narrative that reveals its radical potential as a critique of that prohibition.

As I have tried to show, the stories' critical function results not just from their presentation of adult heterosexual orientation as an externally imposed social edict, but also from their creative appropriation of generic elements of the tragic-love story. These elements critically interrupt another possible interpretation of the stories' conclusions—which I have argued against—as signifying the belatedly recognized but ineluctable "nature" or "truth" of the heroines' ultimate heterosexuality. In citing the formulae of the tragic-love story, the stories cue their readers to interpret them as to some degree stylized genre stories, rather than as realist coming-of-age stories. The oblique citation of generic formulae links these stories with a well-known literary tradition in which socially curtailed, unconsummated love is strongly idealized in a tragic-romantic mode rather than being seen, as in scientistic, developmentalist accounts of schoolgirl homosexuality, as merely a pointless sidetrack on the way to somewhere more consequential. In these ways, while the stories are clearly "aware" of *both* developmentalist constructions of adolescent lesbianism's giving way to adult heterosexuality *and* literary-generic constructions of tragic romance, the simultaneous appeal to such strictly incommensurable discourses results in a kind of critical interruption of the former by the latter, such that far from naturalizing the heterosexual conclusion to the adolescent same-sex love story, these stories implicitly question it.

In their utopian vision of love between young women and ready avowal of the tragic dimension of the hetero-marital imperative, these stories perhaps constitute a continuation of the alternative discourse first articulated in early-twentieth-century public conversations on the value of same-sex love (*tongxing'ai*) among girls. Sang proposes that the idealizing discourse on women's *tongxing'ai* in mainland China in the 1920s and 1930s—"an alternative modern discourse on homosexuality"—was ultimately driven underground by Maoism, to reemerge only in the late twentieth century through liberal feminism.[89] In this chapter, I have argued that this alternative discourse also reemerges in literary form in late-twentieth-century Hong Kong and Taiwan. Like the same-sex love story at the heart of the schoolgirl romance, the alternative, early-twentieth-century story exalting women's *tongxing'ai* seems to end in ellipsis, often appearing to have given way entirely to a modern, developmentalist sexual narrative that naturalizes heterosexuality as the sole satisfying conclusion. Yet as these stories teach us, ellipsis engenders repetition. Its continuing proliferation in contemporary Chinese literary and popular cultures shows that if the going-in story, like the early-twentieth-century idealizing discourse on schoolgirl same-sex love, is a story forcibly abbreviated, then by the same token it is also a story without end.

Postsocialist Melancholia

"Blue Sky Green Sea"

There are many things you have to know, even when you don't know them,
and many things you must not know, even when you do.
—LIU SUOLA, "BLUE SKY GREEN SEA"

Commentary to date on representations of women's same-sex love in post-Mao Chinese fiction has generally assumed that, mirroring the absence of lesbian (*nütongxinglian*) self-representation from the social sphere between the 1949 revolution and about 1995, the topic was also virtually absent from contemporary literature prior to the emergence of certain works by women writers, including Chen Ran, Lin Bai, and Zhang Mei in the late 1980s and 1990s.[1] In contrast, I argue in this chapter for the ambiguous yet discernable fictional pre-emergence of the theme of sexual love between women in a novella by Liu Suola, "Lan tian lü hai" (Blue Sky Green Sea), originally published in early 1985 in *Shanghai Literature*.[2] Liu's novella was published in an interstitial period with regard to the public representation of homosexuality in mainland China. While the Maoist state effectively excluded all mention of same-sex love (*tongxinglian*) from the media and other forms of public representation shortly after the 1949 revolution, by the Reforms Era of the mid-1980s the topic had begun gradually and unevenly to reappear in medical, psychiatric, popular health, and legal discourse.[3] By the early 1990s a new generation of young women writers had begun to publish overtly lesbian-themed stories, and by the end of that decade, recognizable lesbian (*nü-tongzhi*) subcultures were consolidating in China's larger cities. Published in 1985, "Blue Sky" thus appeared at a liminal moment with regard to the representation of women's same-sex love in post-Mao China, a moment at which the idea of female homoeroticism had only very recently and unevenly begun to reconsolidate after more than three decades of absence from public representation.

As its nonappearance in existing accounts of contemporary lesbian fiction from the People's Republic suggests, "Blue Sky" is not an obvious choice for the critic in search of literary depictions of lesbians.[4] Illustrating the liminal position that the novella occupies for such critics, mainland author Hong Ying, in the introduction to her 1999 Taiwan-published collection *Jing yu shui* (Mirror and water), paradoxically cites Liu's (allegedly non-) lesbian novella as proof of the fact that a lesbian story has hitherto been an impossibility:

> Before now, among Chinese women writers, over a period of thousands of years and including all the well-known and lesser-known women poets and all the female writers of rhymed fables set to music [*tanci*], not one has written on the topic [of sexual love between women]; neither have any twentieth-century women writers written on this topic. Among women writers who emerged slightly earlier than [those collected in this volume] and the mainland Chinese women writers of the mid-1980s, many championed women's rights, emphasized women's friendships, and implied that for women men were merely sexual tools, paling in comparison with other women. But the purpose of such a comparison was to propose that friendship and affection between women were more important than sex. The implication was that women would be better off casting "sex" aside, since the thing was impossible without men. The affection described between women in these works, which include Jiang Zidan's "Yesterday Is Already Ancient," Liu Suola's "Blue Sky Green Sea," and Liu Xihong's "You Can't Change Me," has no sexual overtones.[5]

Hong argues that in the realm of textual representation, sexual love between women "is something that, in Chinese culture, has not been ceded a position in which to exist" (*ta shi Zhongguo wenhua zhong bu neng geiyu cunzai diweide dongxi*).[6] Contra Hong, I will argue in this chapter that affection between women in "Blue Sky" in fact consists of *nothing but* sexual overtone—insofar as overtone, or connotation, is precisely the mode of signification that the novella takes up to represent sexual desire between women. Further, I hope to demonstrate that Liu Suola's novella is in a different sense actually collusive with Hong's argument insofar as it produces, by literary means, the same idea that Hong presents as a more direct theoretical critique: the idea that sexual desire between women is a fundamentally repressed and unspeakable element of "Chinese culture."

Compared with Chu T'ien-hsin's and Wong Bikwan's stories discussed in chapter 2, in Liu's novella the subject of women's same-sex love is rendered doubly elliptic: not only is it confined to the register of memory within the narrative, but it is also excluded from the denotative level of the text and appears only as highly encoded, "repressed" content. "Blue Sky"'s paradoxical strategy of female homoerotic representation is to effect a materialization of this subject without—more precisely *by means of not*—naming it as such. The novella is particularly interesting, I will propose, because as an instance of the schoolgirl romance in the memorial mode written in the "feverish" intellectual context of 1980s China, "Blue Sky" illustrates not only the geocultural pervasiveness of the mode but also the very specific inflection this mode takes on in this context.[7] Like other instances of the going-in story, "Blue Sky"'s representation of love between young women is characterized by its strongly utopian cast. But the particular form that female homoerotic memorialism takes in this novella—associated, on the one hand, with a subjective authenticity symbolized by the unconscious and, on the other, with an artistic authenticity embodied in the narrator's dead sweetheart—is unmistakably marked by the utopian yearnings characteristic of the intellectual and cultural renaissance that took place in the People's Republic during the mid-1980s. The aim of this chapter, then, is to investigate how and in what form the schoolgirl romance reemerged in late-twentieth-century China. Exploring the ways in which "Blue Sky Green Sea" reflects the particular cultural, historical, and intellectual context in which it was written, the chapter analyses the conditions of emergence of the distinctive interpretive framework that the novella proffers for its (non)representation of female homoerotic desire. The chapter also considers both divergences and continuities between the internal logic of female homoerotic representation in this novella and the late-century Taiwanese and Hong Kong examples discussed in the previous chapter.

Context: Cultural Enlightenment, "Borrow and Learn," New Humanism

Following the death of Mao Zedong and the fall of the Gang of Four in the late 1970s and the subsequent coming to power of Deng Xiaoping, the "New Era" (Xin Shiqi) of the 1980s in the People's Republic of China saw far-reaching transformations across the fields of economics, politics, cultural production, and intellectual life.[8] The mid-1980s cultural thaw that accompanied the Chinese Communist Party's (CCP) drive toward socialist modernization was characterized by a new wave of cross-cultural borrowing and syncretism as China's intellectuals made an enthusiastic engagement with modern and contemporary Western thought, which, as some cultural critics writing at the time observed, in many ways mirrored the earlier engagement made during the May Fourth cultural modernization movement of the 1920s and 1930s.[9] Intellectuals writing in this period make regular reference to selected nodal points of twentieth-century Euro-American philosophy and literature. Frequently cited are Nietzsche, Sartre, Camus, Gide, Kafka, Beckett, Salinger, Heller, and Bellow, as well as absurdism, black humor, the unconscious, stream of consciousness, the beat generation, Western modernism, and postmodernism. A common framing of the desire for intellectual interaction with Western philosophy and literature is in the language of *jiejian*, "borrow and learn."[10] The predominance of such a framing suggests that the Chinese intellectuals of the mid-1980s conceived of their project not as simply a straightforward adulation of the West but rather as a way of reinventing Chinese culture for the New Era by means of constructive and selectively appropriative interaction with Western thought.[11]

Concurrent with and related to the cross-cultural intellectual practice of "borrow and learn," a series of heated debates occurred in mainland China's intellectual circles in the mid-1980s on the question of individual subjectivity (*zhutixing*). At the center of these discussions were new critical interventions into Marxian theories of practice and the subject by the philosophers Li Zehou and Liu Zaifu.[12] The immensely influential work of these writers was aimed at elaborating an adequately complex theory of the human subject within a Marxian framework as a counter to, and indeed implicitly as a critique of, the effective erasure of the category of individual consciousness within the prevalent Maoist-Marxist-Leninist thought. The work of these philosophers was freighted with political significance in its turning away from the Maoist construction of the subject—as what Liu Zaifu, quoting a Maoist adage, disparagingly called "[a] mere screw in the machinery of the revolution"—and its optimistic return, once again, to the May Fourth discourse of cultural enlightenment and humanist values.[13] These theoretical discussions in academic circles were paralleled by popular versions of the new humanism that, as Lisa Rofel shows, constructed a universal human nature, marked by the supposed naturalness of dimorphous, heterosexual gender that had, so the discourse ran, hitherto been repressed by the dehumanizing and de-gendering effects of Maoist ideology and revolutionary practice.[14] A related return to the May Fourth enlightenment project and the resuscitation and passionate revalorization of a humanist model of the individual subject, constructed explicitly *contra* the presumptively repressive power of the state, were key elements, too, in the pro-democracy discourse of the 1989 student move-ment. The models of hitherto "repressed" human subjecthood constructed in these overlapping academic, popular, and political discussions were referred to variously as "self" (ziwo); "humanity" (renge); "the individual" (geren); and "subjectivity" (zhutixing), as well as in the universalizing language of a gen-eralized "humankind" (renlei). Although differing greatly in many respects, these new or freshly revalorized models of the human individual all, to a greater or lesser degree, implied a critique of the absence of any such cate-gory in official, national-collectivist constructions of "the masses" (dazhong) and "the people" (renmin) upheld by the Maoist and post-Mao state.

It was at this historical juncture that there emerged, as an aspect of the new wave of cross-cultural borrowing from Western thought, a critical re-engagement with Freudianism (Fuluoyide zhuyi), which had been absent from public and academic discourse since 1949, following its initial emergence in China's intellectual circles during the 1920s.[15] The mid-1980s saw a spate of new translations of Freud's major works, including An Introduction to Psycho-analysis, On Creativity and the Unconscious, The Interpretation of Dreams, An Autobio-graphical Study, Beyond the Pleasure Principle, The Ego and the Id, and Totem and Taboo, as well as increasing literary and literary-critical engagement with psycho-analytic theory.[16] This wave of "borrow and learn" from Freud worked in com-plex ways alongside the various intellectual, popular, and political projects of inventing a new, post-Mao individual human subject. Although in many ac-counts of the emergence of Euro-American modernism in the early twentieth century the Freudian theory of the unconscious is credited with inaugurating precisely the dissolution of the rational, self-determining subject of human-ist philosophy, in the postsocialist Chinese context, the "deep structures" of the human psyche that Freudianism proposed were able, to some extent, to work collusively with the reemergent discourse of humanist individualism in challenging the functionalist collectivism of official state ideology.[17] In other words, and as we will see below in the discussion of Liu Suola's fiction, a Freudian conception of the psyche could be and sometimes was appropri-ated for the utopian project of uncovering a new form of modern, individual subjectivity for the post-Mao era.[18]

Contemporary fiction and literary-critical commentary was a key staging ground for the mid-1980s debates on subjectivity and the new humanism.[19] In particular, the writing of the younger generation of Chinese modernists, among them Liu Suola, was often framed as being of significance especially in the unruly individuality and inward orientation of its characters. Thus, mainland Chinese critic Li Jie sees the primary goal of the narrator in "Blue

Sky Green Sea" as being "the search for the self" (xunzhao ziwo),[20] while Liu Xiaobo, a prominent cultural critic and later a leading democracy activist in the 1989 student movement, links Liu Suola's fiction explicitly with the proto-political project of "questing after independent humanity" (dui renge dulide zhuiqiu). In an essay on Liu Suola's "You Have No Other Choice" and works by Chen Cun and Xu Xing published in Literary Review (Wenxue pinglun, edited at the time by Liu Zaifu), Liu Xiaobo writes as follows:

> Conceding that the mockery in these three works holds a challenge with a definite objective, we cannot doubt that this challenge implies a spiritual pursuit. Reading these works closely reveals that neither their protagonists nor their authors are confused: they maintain a clear and active goal, the pursuit of independent human dignity, human creativity, and the true value of human life. . . . In the traditional Chinese value system, those who respect their father and mother are filial sons; those who revere the elders are good descendants; those who study to gain wisdom are true gentlemen; those who "overcome the self and attend to ritual" are righteous; those who are obedient in all matters are virtuous folk. But all of this depends fundamentally upon the abnegation of the individual; it is built on the foundation of deference to others. Do anything you like, only don't ask for independent humanity. . . . This value system has been shaken before, in the May Fourth New Culture Movement, but it was not destroyed, as its roots are deeply entrenched. It remains a force to be reckoned with until this day and has become an unconscious complex in the character of the Chinese people that exerts an invisible yet momentous constrictive power from moment to moment. In the New Era, with its reforms and opening up to the outside world, bursting free from the prison-house of traditional thinking has become a fundamental demand of the Chinese people, particularly the younger generation. And this demand is necessarily reflected in literature, particularly in the works of young writers. The three works that are the subject of this essay are clear evidence of this. Their common subject is the quest for independent humanity.[21]

Liu Xiaobo's appeal to May Fourth humanism as a cure for "traditional Chinese values" that subordinate the individual within a hierarchical social structure represents a veiled but unmistakable attack on the effects of Maoist collectivism. While the socialist state is not mentioned explicitly in Liu's critique, implicitly it cannot be anything other than the 1949 revolution that intervened, in this narrative, to curtail the May Fourth enlightenment project and return the nation's people to their subjection under the age-old "complex" of anti-individualist collectivism. What Liu criticizes directly in this article is the Party-approved target of "feudalism," but clearly the real target of his attack is the postfeudal socialist state. The subtext of this passage is that the political value of works like those by Liu, Chen, and Xu lies in their insurgent assertion of the value of the individual human subject against the "prison-house" of a hierarchical collectivism that is as patent in the structure of the modern socialist state as it was in China's presocialist past.

Maintaining this emphasis on the humanist impulse in Liu Suola and the other modernist writers, Liu Xiaobo argues later in the same article that unlike Western modernists, these writers were not concerned with representing the unconscious but were concerned instead with the conscious realms of the social and the moral.[22] Interestingly, however, despite his explicit assertion of the irrelevance of the Freudian conception of the unconscious to the humanist project of these new Chinese literary modernists, Liu Xiaobo's framing of the issue is itself colored by the language of Freudianism, particularly when he claims that hierarchical collectivism is "an unconscious complex in the character of the Chinese people that exerts an invisible yet momentous constrictive power" (*Zhonghua minzu xinggezhongde qianzai jiegou, . . . fahuizhe wuxing er you judade zhiyue zuoyong*). The infiltration of the interiorizing language of psychoanalysis into Liu Xiaobo's characterization of the modernist writers' radical humanism even while Liu himself seeks to deny the relevance of the unconscious to these writers' social and moral project illustrates not only the pervasiveness of proto-Freudian thinking at the time, but specifically the potential for a Freudian view of the psyche as a deep structure to support the utopian and emancipatory project of asserting the autonomous humanity of the individual subject.

It is in this mid-1980s intellectual context that Liu Suola wrote "Blue Sky Green Sea," a novella that has attracted relatively little critical commentary from mainland critics, who have tended to view it as less aesthetically and philosophically significant than Liu's better known works, especially "You Have No Other Choice" and "In Search of the King of Singers."[23] In what follows, I argue that this novella's representation of subjective interiority openly solicits a reading through a Freudian paradigm of repressed desire and unconscious processes, thereby implicating this proto-lesbian novella in the concurrent debates on Chinese modernity and human subjectivity in the immediate post-Mao era. Whereas the memorial schoolgirl romances from Taiwan and Hong Kong that were discussed in the previous chapter draw on the popular literary discourse of tragic romance to frame their stories of true love lost, "Blue Sky" makes use of psychological humanism to produce a vision of women's same-sex desire as both psychically and culturally repressed.

The examples discussed in chapter 2 and here draw on and develop different aspects of the discourses of cultural modernity that emerged initially during the May Fourth period. In the case of Chu's and Wong's tragic-romantic stories, these include the modern valorization of romantic love, the discourse on marriage modernization and the critique of traditional marriage practices, and the modern romance genre itself. Liu's proto-Freudian tale of female same-sex desire as unquiet inhabitant of the shadowy realm of the individual unconscious, meanwhile, draws on notions of individualism and modern subjectivity as well as the trend toward literary subjectivism that emerged initially during the 1920s and 1930s and resurfaced, in related but different form, in the People's Republic during the 1980s.[24] In addition to this common intellectual heritage from the cultural debates of the May Fourth period, the examples discussed in these two chapters also share a tendency to frame same-sex love through a characteristic utopian memorialism. What is particularly interesting to consider in examining these examples side by side is how the stories articulate this common structure of feeling through the distinct languages most readily available to the authors at the times and places of writing. As we have seen, for the Taiwan and Hong Kong examples, this language is that of popular tragic romance. This chapter will demonstrate that for Liu's novella, the available language for framing female homoerotic utopian memorialism in the People's Republic in the mid-1980s was that of psychological humanism.

"Blue Sky Green Sea"

Liu Suola, born in Beijing in 1955, published her first novella, "Ni bie wu xuanze" (You Have No Other Choice), in 1985. The story of a group of rebellious music students struggling to create authentic art under the rigid, unimaginative, and outdated instruction of their principal lecturer, "You Have No Other Choice" created an immediate name for Liu as the voice of the passionately idealistic yet deeply alienated—and, some charged, irresponsible and dissolute—post–Cultural Revolution generation of Chinese intellectuals.[25] Over the next two years Liu published two further novellas, "Blue Sky Green Sea" and "In Search of the King of Singers," as well as several short stories. These were collected in a volume entitled You Have No Other Choice, published in 1987, a year before Liu moved to London, where she continues to write. Liu's pre-1988 writing is generally classified as representative of the new 1980s modernist (*xiandai pai*) fiction, as distinct from realist fiction and from both the slightly later nativist "root-searching" school (*xungen pai*) and the avant-garde or experimental fiction movement (*xianfeng xiaoshuo* or *shiyan xiaoshuo*).[26] A popular singer and composer as well as an author, in the mid-1980s Liu became a kind of pop-cultural celebrity in the People's Republic, her fame spreading also to Taiwan, where *You Have No Other Choice* was published in 1988 as part of a series on mainland Chinese women writers.[27]

"Blue Sky Green Sea" is a seventeen-part first-person narrative chronicling a single day in the life of a young woman pop singer in which she waits endlessly in a recording studio to begin recording her first album. Stylistically the novella is marked as modernist by its use of nonrealist techniques, including stream-of-consciousness and nonlinear narrative structure. The singer's recording never begins since progress is impeded both by constant bickering among the members of the backing band and by the narrator's own obtrusive memories of her female best friend, Manzi, who died after trying to perform a home abortion. These memories leave the narrator incapacitated, lying most of the day prostrate on the floor, feeling all but incapable of speaking, let alone singing. Throughout the novella, Manzi is associated with the narrator's own reluctantly abandoned ideals of artistic integrity and auratic art; the second page reveals that while the narrator is unwillingly seduced by the lure of commercial success, Manzi never considered such things but only "sang with all her might—her voice could make you weep, like Christians seeing the face of God."[28] From the outset, then, the narrator aligns her dead friend with her forsaken ideals of authentic art and spiritual perfection, while seeing her own efforts as verging on mere vulgar commercial imitation.[29] In Manzi, Liu's novella parallels the perfect yet irretrievably lost value of artistic integrity and philosophical idealism with an equally perfect yet equally irrecoverable love between young women. This association of the lost female lover/friend with an authentic relation to art and the self exemplifies the characteristically utopian cast of the memorial schoolgirl romance.[30]

True to the memorial mode of female homoerotic representation, "Blue Sky"'s narrative circles back and forth between the present in the recording studio and the twenty-four-year-old narrator's remembered friendship with Manzi, dating back to the girls' primary-school days. Nostalgia for a shared trip to the seaside forms the symbolic cornerstone of the narrator's memory of her dead friend. It was there that she posed for a photograph in her yellow dress, identical to one that Manzi had. She recounts: "In the photo that'll be used for my album cover, I'm wearing a light yellow dress, too, and in the background are the blue sky and green sea. Manzi took that photo of me when we were taking a vacation together at the seaside. We were having a ball, in fits of laughter from morning to night—that's why in the photo I'm grinning from ear to ear."[31]

The narrator's fetishization of the seaside snapshot with its edenic vision of blue sky and green sea exemplifies Susan Stewart's observation on nostalgia and the photograph: "The nostalgic's utopia is prelapsarian, a genesis where lived and mediated experience are one, where authenticity and transcendence are both present and everywhere."[32] Stewart proposes that the nostalgia that attaches to personal souvenirs like photographs is driven by the absence of the souvenir's referent and nostalgia's object: the always already lost authenticity of experience.[33] Hence, "nostalgia is a sadness without an object."[34] Stewart's formulation is remarkably apposite to the melancholic structure of feeling evoked in Liu's novella, and in the pages that follow, I will propose that in addition to the general loss to which Stewart refers, the nostalgia of Liu's protagonist in "Blue Sky Green Sea" is bereft of an object in another, more particular way as well. This relates to the novella's construction of the narrator's relation with Manzi's memory as, quite precisely, a melancholic one, according to a Freudian paradigm. The novella prompts in its reader the idea that in losing Manzi, as well as losing a friend, the narrator has also lost something else that she does not know about, hence the "real" object of her persistent reminiscences remains opaque to her, confined to the unconscious level of the narrator's psyche and to the subtextual level of signification in the text.

Borrowing and Learning from Freud

Liu's writing, "Blue Sky" in particular, has sometimes been accused of being about nothing—of lacking a discernible plot or subject.[35] In what could be interpreted as a reflexive commentary on the elusiveness of its own motivation, "Blue Sky" ends with a seemingly unrelated anecdote about a writer of thrillers left in a state of terror because in the story he is writing, corpses are piling up apace with no sign of either a villain or the police. The novella's final words, spoken by the narrator after recounting this anecdote as she wanders aimlessly through darkening streets, are as follows: "I don't know how far I'll have to go before I find a crossroad, and there are no cops on this street."[36] While this statement could be interpreted as being about the narrator's feeling of helplessness at her friend Manzi's senseless death, it can equally be read as referring reflexively to the story itself. An entire novella has been written and yet somehow the real motivating force behind the story remains elusive, as much to its protagonist as to its reader.[37] Like the horrifying unfinished thriller, "Blue Sky" appears to be a story without a subject—or rather a story with a subject that remains concealed, leaving only encrypted traces of itself, like the thriller's ominously accumulating corpses, while refusing to show its face.

Given the conspicuous opacity of its subject and motivation, I propose that "Blue Sky" is not just concerned with "the search for the self" or "the pursuit of independent humanity," as others have suggested, but that it is concerned quite precisely with representing the unconscious according to a Freudian paradigm.[38] Beyond simply representing the unconscious in general as an aspect of the longed-for humanist self, however, Liu's novella figures sexual desire between women *in particular* as repressed content—as the novella's own missing subject, unconscious, or subtextual signified—thereby articulating the memorial utopianism of the schoolgirl romance narrative with the enlightenment humanism of the mid-1980s cultural renaissance movement. The story solicits interpretation through the Freudian theory of melancholia since the narrator's sexual desire remains unconscious in the narrator and subtextual in the story; hence neither narrator nor text has knowledge of what, exactly, has been lost with Manzi's death. In "Mourning and Melancholia," Freud writes:

> In [some] cases one feels justified in maintaining the belief that a loss of this kind has occurred, but one cannot see clearly what it is that has been lost, and it is all the more reasonable to suppose that the patient cannot consciously perceive what he [sic] has lost either. This, indeed, might be so even if the patient is aware of the loss which has given rise to his melancholia, but only in the sense that he knows *whom* he has lost but not *what* it is he has lost in him. This would suggest that melancholia is in some way related to an object-loss which is withdrawn from consciousness, in contradistinction to mourning, in which there is nothing about the loss that is unconscious.[39]

As we will see, this conception of melancholia as arising when somebody knows whom she has lost but not *what*—what precise sentiment, what possible relation—she has lost in losing the person resonates remarkably strongly with the representation of the narrator's experience in "Blue Sky." In its literary rendition of the psychoanalytic theories of melancholia and repression and in what amounts to its proposal of a repressive hypothesis on women's same-sex love, this story is self-consciously Freudian. And in structuring the schoolgirl romance narrative through this particular framework, the novella exemplifies the 1980s tendency to "borrow and learn" from Euro-American models. As I will show, true to the logic of the Freudian paradigm that so centrally informs it, the novella stages the return of its own repressed motivation through the displacement of female same-sex desire onto a number of peculiar narratorial and textual symptoms, the patent strangeness of which acts as an open invitation to readerly diagnosis.

In the first pages of "Blue Sky Green Sea" the narrator acts out a very clear metaphor for the mechanism of repression with reference to her memory of Manzi. She recalls that after publicly performing for the first time a song dedicated to Manzi, she felt the song so unworthy of her friend's memory that she was driven to cut a piece of adhesive tape and stick it over her mouth in order "to avoid my voice slipping crashingly out" and so that "I shouldn't continue speaking such self-flattering nonsense."[40] Following this initial metaphorical enactment of repression's mechanism, two neurotic symptoms triggered in the narrator by Manzi's memory also solicit interpretation in relation to the same theory. Significantly, the narrator's symptoms both relate to her voice, and hence to the novella's central problematic of speaking versus not speaking. First, the narrator suffers from a mounting hypochondriacal conviction that a cancerous tumor is growing on her vocal cords, a notion that arises initially the night of her first performance of the song she wrote in Manzi's memory. Second, following her own mention of Manzi's name after her death, the narrator suffers a fit of frighteningly violent, hysterical laughter that turns into uncontrollable sobbing.[41] With their troubling of the narrator's capacity for rational speech, both of these symptoms invite diagnosis through the Freudian paradigm of repression as somatic signifiers of an unconscious thought or wish in relation to Manzi on the part of the narrator.

That the narrator's repressed wish in relation to her friend may have a sexual character is suggested in a number of details that the narrator more or less casually lets slip about the history of the relationship between the young women. For example, the narrator recalls her jealousy when, in high school, Manzi mentioned a boyfriend: "One day, she suddenly told me she had a boyfriend. I was shocked. 'Are you scared?' She shook her head. 'Is it fun?' She burst out laughing. She came over to kiss me, but I turned away. I don't know why, but I felt disgusted. Thinking that her mouth and face had been kissed by a man I didn't know, I felt disgusted. But I still wrote her a love song. Often, when she closed her eyes and sang that song, I couldn't stand to look at her. Then she'd yell at me: 'Why can't you be happy? Why can't you be happy for me?'"[42]

In addition to the history of shared kisses, dedicated love songs, and jealous quarrels between Manzi and herself, the narrator casually recalls that she used to dress as a boy and walk with Manzi in the park at night with her arm about the other girl—in order, obviously, to circumvent unwanted attentions from local louts.[43] The two young women also planned trips away together, "just the two of us," without Manzi's boyfriend. "But really," the narrator muses, "she couldn't handle not seeing him for two days together. It occurs to me that only since the day she died has she finally returned to my 'jurisdiction.'"[44] The narrator herself also has a boyfriend, Lu Sheng, but she describes her relationship with him as "brotherly" (rutong shouzu) and reveals that "our memories of Manzi make it impossible for us to speak of marriage."[45] Throughout the novella, significant symbolic weight attaches to the narrator's and Manzi's wearing of identical yellow dresses at the seaside, where the photograph referenced in the novella's title was taken. Following Manzi's death, for example, the narrator reflects sadly that "Nobody would notice [now] that the two of us once wore the same clothes."[46] Paradoxically, the emotionally freighted homovestism of the two ecstatic young women in identical yellow dresses as readily connotes a homosexual relation as does their heterovestism when the narrator dressed as boy to Manzi's girl.

Close to the end of the novella, the narrator recalls an impulsive nocturnal bicycle trip the two women made together to the outlying suburbs, singing all the way, then returning at dawn to the city, where they napped on a park bench:

> When we woke up, we went to a natural pond to wash our faces. When we'd done that, I said, Manzi you're so pretty. Manzi said I was pretty, too. We were both so full of self-confidence; utterly self-absorbed, we jumped on our bikes and rode home, singing all the way. Back at home, Manzi and I lay on my bed, and she started chattering on and on about her boyfriend and about love. I only heard half a sentence before falling asleep, but I slept just the length of one sentence before I woke up again and answered "Mmm" to some question she'd asked. Until this day, she must believe I was listening all along that morning.[47]

In keeping with the Freudian logic of repression that structures the novella from start to finish, just as the narrator managed to answer in the affirmative to Manzi's crucial question while also believing that she *did not hear it*, so she also manages not to linger over what Manzi's question may have been, and as a result the reader, like the narrator herself, cannot know. (Although unlike the narrator, the reader is certainly free to speculate: in the drowsy morning after an ecstatic night together, after admiring each other's beauty, in bed together, and in the context of a conversation about love, what might it have been that Manzi asked her friend?) The weighty question of what it was that Manzi asked the narrator that morning becomes another aspect of the novella's mysteriously missing subject, a subject that, I have been suggesting, can hardly be other than the narrator's "repressed" desire for Manzi, albeit that this desire only appears in the story *as* repressed: it can be spoken only by not speaking, heard only by not hearing, and appear only by failing to appear as such.

The subterranean subject of homosexuality comes closest to surfacing when the narrator recalls visiting an artists' salon with Manzi and her music teacher, Mr. Ding; the incident leaves her with what she describes as "the most shameful memory of my life" (*yishengzhong zui xiukuide jiyi*).[48] Having just witnessed an execrable performance by a male singer who imitated the style of Japanese singer Sada Masashi, the narrator is covered in embarrassment: "All I could do was desperately try to hide my face behind my wine glass. Next up was a womanish man who played the guitar and sang as though intoxicated by his own passionate imitation of a Hong Kong woman pop star, which brought cheers from the men and women all around. Red in the face, Mr. Ding did his best to avoid my gaze. Through my wine glass, I saw Manzi looking at me. Expressionlessly, she wagged her long index finger, not so much as blinking an eye. I felt a little awkward and grinned at her. She lowered her eyes."[49]

The sudden appearance of this "womanish man" (*nüren moyangde nanren*) is met with a triple outpouring of shame: the narrator, already embarrassed, continues to cringe behind her wine glass; Mr. Ding turns red and avoids eye contact; Manzi, too, finally lowers her gaze. Although on one level it is the man's poor rendition of the Hong Kong pop song that causes everyone's embarrassment, on another level the trigger for this shame is surely his gendered performance as an imitation woman—a "womanish man"—an image that is strongly overdetermined by the culturally prevalent construction of homosexuality both as gender inversion and as mere imitation of a presumptively authentic and originary heterosexuality.[50] In the midst of this eruption of crypto-queer Cantopop, the narrator finds Manzi staring fixedly at her, making an enigmatic hand signal, all of which, for some reason, makes her feel "awkward" (*gan'ga*). Manzi's wagging index finger seems to carry a censorious significance, and especially given the text's lingering attention to the intense exchange of glances between the two women, the unspoken object of Manzi's censure could be interpreted as the singer's implied queerness as much as his poor singing.[51]

The proposal that the novella draws upon the Freudian theories of melancholia and repression is lent weight by its preoccupation with problems of the voice: speaking versus not speaking, singing versus not singing, hearing versus not having heard. The problem that most pressingly occupies the narrator's mind throughout her day at the recording studio is will she sing or won't she? The novella as a whole constitutes a series of variations on this theme; there is a pervasive sense of the proximity of a portentous something that remains just on the verge of being voiced. This is most clearly evident in the climax, when Manzi finally appears to the narrator—or rather, is heard by her—as a kind of auditory apparition, after the narrator fails, for the fourth time, to tell Mr. Ding that she will not be able to sing:

> Dispirited, I hang up the phone. I will never manage to say what I want to say.
>
> I walk to the corner of the studio where I left my folder, take out my sheet music, and leaf through it page by page. I want to make a sound.
>
> Manzi, what are you doing here?
>
> I hear everybody chattering away, all saying you're going to make it. I'm afraid you'll be too tired, once you're tired you don't feel like speaking, you'd better not refuse to speak, that's taking it too far. Don't take it too far, laughing everybody off, saying to everybody Manzi, Manzi, that's taking it too far. You'd better not refuse to speak, once you're tired, you don't feel like speaking, I'm afraid you'll be too tired. Everybody says you demand too much of friendship, you forgot to speak about the Manzi in the yellow dress, you just say "Manzi." . . . Must you refuse to speak, must you clack your mouth open and shut and Manzi, Manzi?
>
> What is it that you really want? Do you want to get something? Or get rid of something? Is it that you can't think what it is? Or can you think of it but don't dare say it? Or can you say it but not do it? . . . Why do you keep thinking endlessly on and on about Manzi, Manzi, endlessly on and on wondering if you're going to sing or not sing, sing or not sing? . . . What is it that you really want? Do you want to get something? Or get rid of something? Is it that you can't think what it is? Or can you think of it but don't dare say it? Or can you say it but not do it? Why don't you go put on that yellow dress, go back to the place we went together that year. Ah you, you.[52]

This excerpt, with its heavily psychologizing emphasis on the melancholic subject's nonconcatenated speech, pinpoints the narrator's problem throughout the novella: the impossibility of saying what she wants to say.[53] What she wants to say to Mr. Ding but cannot is that although she wants to sing, she cannot; the reason she cannot sing, in turn, is connected in some unspeakable, even unthinkable, way with her memory of Manzi. Although the narrator "wants to make a sound," she does not; instead, Manzi's raving voice returns from beyond the grave to speak in her place. But like the narrator's repeated, pointless telephone conversations with Mr. Ding, in which she fails, by failing to speak, to tell him that she cannot sing, Manzi's words seem like a circular nightmare of repetitious nonsense that never reaches its point. Yet in another sense, Manzi's repeated series of suggestive questions addresses directly (as directly as this subject can be addressed) the novella's central theme. This theme is not simply the *general* psychic paralysis of intellectual youth brought about by the spiritual dislocation of the post–Cultural Revolution era, as some commentators suggest; it is specifically a paralysis brought about by the refusal consciously to entertain some obscure but momentous knowledge connected with an intimate relationship between two women.[54] For finally, the disembodied, gibbering voice does reach its point, albeit indirectly: it emerges that this phantom Manzi has returned to relate that the key to the unthinkable, unspeakable, impossible something that has incapacitated the narrator and robbed her of her voice is to be found in the remembered utopia of the two women's seaside holiday. With its framing of the potent sentiment evoked by the memory of this holiday as obscure and unspeakable yet insistently interruptive, the passage implies that since neither the narrator nor the text itself can become conscious of the nature of the attachment between the two women that was lost at Manzi's death, this repressed content is doomed endlessly to return in displaced form—in the form, for instance, of a babbling ghost. In the Taiwanese and Hong Kong stories discussed in chapter 2, the interruptive potential of female homoerotic memory was treated rather literally as the effect of a "true love" reluctantly renounced due to social pressure, following and adapting a tragic romance formula. Here this interruptive potential is presented more abstractly—yet equally emphatically—through the language of psychological humanism. Through this language, Liu's novella articulates the rediscovered Freudian theory of unconscious desire with the literary form of the schoolgirl romance to produce a theory of sexual love between women as fundamentally repressed. The textual organization of the novella itself works as a synecdoche of repression's mechanism, so that just as the desire of the narrator for her friend is not available directly to her conscious mind but only indirectly as a series of neurotic symptoms, so the subject of women's same-sex desire is not present at the denotative level of the text but instead forms the text's own wordless, subtextual "unconscious."

"Blue Sky"'s representation of female homoerotic desire as repressed and unconscious repeats the familiar tendency, in modern Chinese cultural production, to "utopianize" women's same-sex love in at least two ways. First, no less than in other instances of the repressive hypothesis, the effect of such a theory in this instance is to produce that which is "abusively reduced to silence"—in this case, love between women—as an inner core of subjective truth that persists in spite of the heavy hand that enforces its repression.[55] In representing sexual desire between women as the repressed desire and thereby as the elusive content of the individual unconscious, "Blue Sky" produces this desire in particular, and not just sexual desire in general, as subjective truth—as that secret content of the individual psyche that it is, in Foucault's words, "at the same time difficult and necessary, dangerous and precious to divulge."[56] Second, as outlined above, the unconscious, as a key site of both the psychic and the sexual life of the individual that elite and popular cultures in postsocialist China were intent on liberating, is in this historical and cultural context already heavily loaded in itself with connotations of authenticity.[57] In mid-1980s China, the Freudian depth-model conception of the individual psyche constituted a significant challenge to the official collectivist-functionalist ideology of the very recent past. By producing female same-sex desire as the foremost inhabitant of the individual unconscious, "Blue Sky" thus consigns that desire to a doubly utopian location. On the one hand, female same-sex desire is produced as the ultimate subjective truth in a general sense by the repressive hypothesis's own internal logic. On the other hand, that desire is produced as truth in a historically particular sense by the novella's overdetermination by the contemporaneous discourse positing individual consciousness as the authentic counter to political repression by the Chinese state.[58]

Female Homoerotic Memorialism and Post-Mao Utopianism

Framing Liu Suola, and "Blue Sky Green Sea" in particular, as representative of the existential mood of the post–Cultural Revolution generation of modernist Chinese intellectuals in the mid-1980s, Jing Wang characterizes both author and novella as caught between nihilism and fervent belief, between ennui and a euphoric faith in the spirit of the new humanism: "Liu Suola's characters, however cynically they reject redemption, have souls that await epiphany. . . . No matter how hard they tried, Liu Suola and the Chinese *xian-dai pai* [modernists] could never trivialize their blasphemy as effortlessly as the experimentalists. She and her fellow travelers uttered curses as part of the religious ritual dedicated to the true believers."[59] In this chapter, I have tried to suggest that if there are utopian elements in "Blue Sky Green Sea"—the elements of epiphany and belief to which Wang alludes—they cluster most densely around the figure of Manzi and the implied relationship that the narrator remembers with her. That is, the novella's utopianism crystallizes precisely around the (repressed) memory of women's same-sex love.

At first glance, this novella's appeals to the proto-Freudian discourses of repression, melancholia, and the unconscious would seem to present a marked contrast to what I proposed in the previous chapter was a key structuring discourse in Chu T'ien-hsin's "Waves Scour the Sands" and Wong Bi-kwan's "She's A Young Woman and So Am I"—namely, the popular literary discourse of tragic romance, which I argued served precisely to interrupt a psychoanalytic interpretation of psychosexual development. Yet counter-intuitive though it may seem, in the context of Liu's novella I would argue for a continuity between these apparently incommensurable discourses in their structure and "spirit," if not their content. If, as we have seen, the tragic-romance formula constructs youthful love between women as "true love lost" that returns to haunt the adult "heterosexual" woman in the form of dogged memory, then the Freudian formula appealed to in Liu's novella constructs such love analogously, as "authentic desire repressed," latterly returning in disturbing, symbolic forms, as the repressed is wont to do. As I have pointed out, both discourses are markedly utopian—even romantic—with their drive to retrieve a lost or obscured affective and erotic authenticity in the province of memory.[60] That the utopian memorialism that is such a defining characteristic of modern Chinese female homoerotic representation should take these two different forms in these distinct locales reflects the different cultural languages available to the authors in their particular times and places. In these ways, at the same time as it unmistakably reflects the very particular cultural and intellectual context out of which it was produced, "Blue Sky" attests, too, to the long-lasting and far-reaching currency—moreover, the remarkable transcultural flexibility—of the modern Chinese discourse on female homoerotic memorialism.

. . .

FOUR

No Future

Tomboy Melodrama

In lived lesbian cultures in mainland China, Taiwan, and Hong Kong today, the secondary gender of "tomboy"—designating a same-sex attracted girl or woman who embodies a form of female masculinity—is among the central features of subcultural social organization and individual sex-gender identification. In Taiwan and mainland China, tomboy is abbreviated colloquially to T and in Hong Kong to TB, while the tomboy's feminine lover is known in Taiwan and mainland China as *po* (meaning woman or wife); now often abbreviated to P and in Hong Kong as tomboy girl (TBG). These folk categories coexist alongside the newer designations *bu fen* (meaning "not distinguishing," used in Taiwan and mainland China) and the English "pure" (in Hong Kong), which are sometimes taken up to signify feminist resistance to the gender dimorphism and presumed "heterosexual ideology" of T/*po* roles.[1]

In Taiwan, T and *po* constitute a system of secondary gender that, up until about the mid-1990s, structured most of the island's female homoerotic subcultures. In the subcultural practice of the "T bar" (lesbian bar) since the mid-1980s, Ts have marked their identity by adopting selected masculine-coded signifiers, including masculine dress; short haircuts; aftershave; and masculine bodily gestures, language use, and drinking style, as well as by modifying feminine attributes—for example, by breast-binding. Po style, meanwhile, appropriates sartorial and behavioral signifiers of normative femininity to produce the feminine counterpart to the dapper masculinity of the T. Detailed histories and theorizations of T/*po* cultures in the bar scene, girls' high schools, and informal friendship networks have been written by Antonia Yengning Chao, Gian Jia-shin, and Zheng Meili respectively.[2] They show that the terms T and *po* were first coined in the mid-1960s by the owner of a gay bar in Taipei who knew the English term *tomboy* through his acquaintance with the American GIs who were at that time a constant presence in Taipei on rest and recreation leave from the war in Vietnam.[3] The ethnographic research of both Chao and Zheng suggests that between approximately the 1960s and the mid-1980s, T identification tended to equate quite strongly with transgender masculine identification, with Ts considering themselves men, sometimes undergoing gender reassignment surgery, favoring men's rather than women's public toilets, and frequently passing as men in everyday life.[4] Taiwan's first T bar opened in Taipei in 1985, and others soon followed. As Chao's research demonstrates, the fuller development of T/*po* subcultures around the bar scene seems to have led to a shift in many Ts' gender identification, from being cathected through male-bodied masculinity to being self-reflexively directed toward the achievement of what Chao calls "T-ness": a recognizable subcultural style that equates neither to normative femininity nor exactly to normative masculinity—though it certainly draws on masculine sartorial and behavioral conventions—but is perhaps a gendered whole qualitatively different from the sum of its masculine and feminine parts.[5] Around the mid-'90s, as both Zheng and Gian show, following the impact of contemporary feminist theory, there occurred a renewed appropriation and proliferation of T/*po*-modeled subcultural styles by a generation of younger, intellectual, and middle-class women whose adherence to T/*po* roles was arguably less strict than that of the women in the bar subculture a decade earlier. This spawned a plethora of semi-humorous micro-categories like "sensitive new age T" (*xin hao* T), "nellie T" (*niangniang* T), and "super-*po*" (*nüqiangpo*).[6]

Ethnographic research conducted in Hong Kong by both Carmen Tong and Lucetta Kam reveals that comparable organizations of secondary gender are signified there in the categories TB and TBG. Tong's research, carried out in the late 1990s, included detailed interviews with, and participant observation of, a group of six TB-identifying high schoolers in the working-class district of Sand Bay.[7] Tong found that the girls constructed their TB identity through a range of social behaviors that marked them out as rebels against the model of conventional femininity in which the education system attempted to school them: they favored boys' clothing and short, boyish haircuts; they interacted socially in a rowdy, boyish manner and enjoyed swearing and using slang; they smoked cigarettes, played basketball, referred to each other as "brothers," and pursued romances with their conventionally feminine classmates (TBGs). Kam's research focuses on masculine women in Hong Kong more broadly. Her distinction between the Cantonese term *naam dzai tau* (boy-head) and TB is useful: the former refers to a more or less socially sanctioned form of female masculinity in adolescence (hence is closer to the English usage of the term "tomboy"), in contrast to the strong association of the more marginal category TB with same-sex desire and its broader definitional scope, including adult women as well as adolescents.[8]

It is only in the past decade that relatively large-scale, interconnected sexual subcultures based on lesbian identification have emerged in mainland China. Detailed research into the histories of this emergence is still being carried out, but it is clear that the concurrent rise of Internet communication in everyday urban life during the late 1990s has been of central importance in the contemporary formation of imagined or virtual lesbian communities in the People's Republic.[9] And interestingly, the Internet has facilitated the spread of the Taiwanese sex-gender categories T, P, and *bu fen* into mainland Chinese lesbian subcultures.[10] In a survey on Chinese-language lesbian Internet use that I conducted in 2003–4, one respondent, a Taiwanese professional then working in Shanghai, made the following observation:

> I've discovered that the lesbian communities in Taiwan, Hong Kong, and mainland China have been able to engage in a considerable degree of communication and exchange as a result of the Internet. Even many aspects of language usage are becoming similar, like the identity roles of T, P, and *bu fen*, and the term *lazi* [lez], etc. I was really shocked to discover this after arriving in Shanghai; it turned out that lots of mainland Chinese lesbians had begun the initial process of self-identification after visiting Taiwanese *lazi* Web sites. And on Shanghai-based *lazi* Web sites, I've also been able to get to know friends in Hong Kong and discovered that we have no problems at all in communicating — it's great ☺.[11]

While for some respondents, the shared sex-gender categories of T and P mark out a connection among lesbian communities in Hong Kong, Taiwan, and mainland China, tellingly, for others, the prevalence of these categories marks a distinction between Chinese and American organizations of lesbian life. For example, one respondent in my survey, who was born in Taiwan and emigrated to Hong Kong at the age of ten and then later to California, writes the following:

> Basically in the Taiwanese lesbian circle there is certain culture of the T/P (Taiwanese version of butch/femme gender roles). . . . Since this is the first source of information that I had access to, and only source when I first came out (only online, not really in real life in my heterosexual circle)

therefore I bought into it. It shaped my understanding of what lesbians are, how they socialize, etc. This kind of culture influenced how I identified myself. I have identified as P and learned how to as a P [sic] since my partner was butch and she had certain expectation of me as P. I now identify as in-between who looks feminine. Getting in contact with the Asian lesbian community here in Los Angeles and their different perspective has definitely shaped my sexual identity and my understanding of the butch/femme dynamics. I now have a more liberal view of the T/P dynamics and don't really buy it anymore.[12]

These responses reveal that the secondary gender of tomboy, and the particular forms of erotic and social organization that it entails, are, for these respondents, a central—even a defining—feature of contemporary lesbian life in the Chinese-speaking world.

Yet despite tomboy identity's key role in lesbian subcultures, as I have emphasized throughout the preceding chapters, the most commonly seen figure in Chinese mass-cultural representations of love between women has been not the tomboy, understood as a distinct sex-gender minority, but rather the same-sex attracted, conventionally feminine young woman, understood as a kind of anywoman.[13] As I have shown, the temporality of the schoolgirl romance narratives discussed in the previous three chapters is retrospective since the normatively feminine same-sex attracted young woman's future is defined, in advance, as marital or proto-marital; from the perspective of this kind of adult femininity, her youthful same-sex love appears always as memorial. But the question of the "permanently lesbian" tomboy's future has proven much more troublesome for the popular imagination since it cannot be effectively resolved by heterosexual marriage in the same way as that of the normatively feminine woman. This chapter argues that in dominant representations, the tomboy's future has been strictly unrepresentable, a kind of blank space in the popular imagination. Overwhelmingly, tomboy characters have tended either quietly to fade from narrative focus as the story progresses or to disappear by more dramatic means (most commonly early death). No less than the memorial feminine same-sex attracted schoolgirl, then, the vanishing tomboy attests to the cultural dominance of the temporal discourse on the impossibility of lesbian futurity. In light of this, this chapter asks: What representational strategies has popular culture employed to deal with the tomboy and her troubled relation to time and futurity? Which kinds of affective, narrative, and generic structures has the tomboy's representation tended to draw upon? How do these forms of representation differ from those that structure the cultural appearance of the conventionally feminine same-sex attracted schoolgirl, and what do such differences reveal about the ideological structuring of both gender and sexuality in these contexts?

My main proposal in response to the first of these questions is that in popular representations since the 1970s, the tomboy has tended to be represented in a melodramatic mode. In their essay on literary T/po representation in two 1970s Taiwanese pulp novels—Xuan Xiaofo's *Yuan zhi wai* (Outside the circle, 1976) and Guo Lianghui's *Disan xing* (Outside of Two Kinds; a.k.a. The Third Sex)—and contemporary writer Lucifer Hung's queer vampire narratives, Liu Jenpeng, Ding Naifei, and Amie Parry have proposed realist melodrama as a framework through which to interpret these texts' representational strategies.[14] My consideration of melodrama is partly inspired by this work, but it takes a slightly different direction. I am interested in the way in which the "tomboy texts" I will discuss draw upon the affective, narrative, and generic structures of melodrama defined as a mode that is centrally concerned with moral legibility (in Linda Williams's phrase) and with the representation of suffering virtue.[15] The chapter charts the emergence and development of contemporary tomboy melodrama, beginning with Xuan Xiaofo's pulp novel, then moving on to Du Xiulan's popular novel *Ninü* (The unfilial daughter, 1996) and its adaptation as a high rating commercial television drama series (dir. Ko Yi-zheng, 2001), and then to the more recent filmic adaptation of the tomboy narrative in the teenpic genre in Yee Chih-yen's *Lanse da men* (Blue Gate Crossing, 2002). Through this analysis, this chapter seeks to map the internal logic of a series of representations that both construct and reflect the ways in which the sex-gender category "tomboy" is understood and experienced in contemporary Chinese cultures.

Subjective Injury and Tomboy Identification

Before we move on to consider more recent examples, it is worth looking back for a moment to the fictional personage of Li Wenqing in Yu Dafu's 1932 story "She Was a Weak Woman"; Li was put forward in chapter 1 as possibly a distant literary ancestor to contemporary tomboy representations. Despite the passing of time and the seemingly outdated ideological framework, Yu's violently phobic descriptions of the masculine, same-sex attracted schoolgirl are shocking. Extrapolating from my own response to Yu's characterization of Li (who, let us recall, is described as having "skin like sandpaper; a pair of very broad, very saggy, downward-dangling tits; a few straggly hairs in her armpits; and congealed in those hairs, a mass of sticky sweat," and so forth), I suggest that these descriptions will trigger in some readers a very uncomfortable, almost panicked sense of being under attack, either in one's own person or on behalf of others whom one loves.[16] For certain readers, Yu's descriptions will bring with them all the force of an insult—ridiculously overstated, laughable in its very exaggeration, and yet an insult that somehow one cannot quite laugh off. The insult finds its mark; for these readers, the consonance between the fictional personage of Li Wenqing and contemporary attitudes toward masculine same-sex attracted women will seem to channel immense energies of actual social hostility and aggression toward oneself personally or toward people whom one loves. Conceding that the cultural energies arrayed against the masculine same-sex loving woman remain considerable today—if not always as conveniently overstated as we find them in Yu's text—we can pose the question: What will it.mean to come to understand and experience oneself as the subject of such a powerful insult?

At the end of Situating Sexualities, I proposed a theory of homosexual subject formation as a process based on identification with a prohibited or abjected category (tongxinglian: the category "homosexuality" itself); hence, I suggested, the shame produced by identification with this culturally stigmatized category becomes a keystone of the gay or lesbian self. In other words, in a context in which the shaming charge of the term tongxinglian remains immense, homosexual identity is necessarily based on a foundational injury: the subjective injury of recognizing oneself in the shameful accusation, "Tongxinglian!" That theory of homosexual subject formation in and through psychic injury has something in common with Didier Eribon's more elaborated theorization in his recently translated book Insult and the Making of the Gay Self. Eribon writes: "Insult is more than a word that describes. It is not satisfied with simply telling me what I am. If someone calls me a 'dirty faggot' . . . that person is not trying to tell me something about myself. That person is letting me know that he or she has something on me, has power over me. First and foremost the power to hurt me, to mark my consciousness with that hurt, inscribing shame in the deepest levels of my mind. This wounded, shamed consciousness becomes a formative part of my personality."[17]

The immediate question, then, concerns what responses are available to those who bear the force of interpellation through insult. Analyzing the work of the late Taiwanese lesbian author Qiu Miaojin, among others, I suggested in Situating Sexualities that one response to the predicament of finding one's identity based on shameful identification with such an abjected category is lavishly to display one's wounded subjectivity in an attempt to solicit the sympathetic gaze of the social collectivity that inflicted the initial injury. The tactic of gay and lesbian pride promulgates "positive images" against "negative stereotypes" and uses a discourse of pride in a principled denial of the power of queer shame. In contrast, I argued, the tactic we find in works like Qiu's *dwells upon* queer shame in an attempt to repair the initial injury to the queer subject by means of the sympathetic, loving response that the spectacle of queer injury solicits from the reader. In that sense, I read Qiu's literary representations of anguished tomboy subjecthood as an indirect response to the painfully subjectivating power of the insulting discourse on the "mannish lesbian," elements of which we glimpse in embryonic form in Yu Dafu's characterization of Li Wenqing.[18]

Here I want to elaborate further on this theorization. First, in the case of modern Chinese representations of female homosexuality in particular (as distinct from homosexual representation in general), one notable kind of representation of sex/gender subjecthood as based on a foundational injury is found in texts that center on tomboy protagonists. The image of the same-sex loving woman as someone definitionally associated with injury and framed for the sympathetic gaze of a collective spectator is very central in two of the tomboy texts I discuss below, *Outside the Circle* and *The Unfilial Daughter*. It appears that the combination of sexual *and* gender rebellion that is embodied in the figure of the tomboy, plus the pervasive notion that the tomboy is doomed to have no future, associate this figure with a state of injury especially strongly and in characteristic ways.[19] The second elaboration I will work through is to connect my earlier ideas about the drive to spectacularize queer suffering with current theories of melodrama, especially the theorization offered by Linda Williams in *Playing the Race Card*.[20] We thus arrive at the formulation in this chapter's title: tomboy melodrama.

Melodrama and the Spectacularization of Suffering Virtue

In *Playing the Race Card*, Linda Williams focuses on "black and white" racial melodrama in the history of American cinema to argue that melodrama, conceived not as a discrete genre but rather as a dominant cultural mode, has constituted the most important means through which the question of race has been thought through in American mass culture.[21] Although her central subject is American racial melodrama, Williams's book also enables a rethinking of the melodramatic mode more broadly and can shed light on the functioning of this mode in other contexts. Williams extends the work of Peter Brooks in *The Melodramatic Imagination* to formulate her characterization of melodrama as a mode that is centrally concerned with "moral legibility"—that is, with rendering visible the virtue of a central character whose virtue had been occluded, whether to other characters or to the reader or spectator. As Brooks writes, "Melodrama typically . . . not only employs virtue persecuted as a source of its dramaturgy, but also tends to become the dramaturgy of virtue misprized and eventually recognized. It is about virtue made visible and acknowledged, the drama of a *recognition.*"[22] Closely linked with the melodramatic mode's effort to effect moral legibility, then, is its tendency to render as spectacle the image of suffering virtue. Further, in the melodramatic mode, the act of suffering functions as a *proof* of virtue.[23] Williams writes: "If emotional and moral registers are sounded, if the narrative trajectory is ultimately concerned with a retrieval and staging of virtue through adversity and suffering, then the operative mode is melodrama. . . . Sympathy for another grounded in the manifestation of that person's suffering is arguably a key feature of all melodrama."[24]

The melodramatic mode, in various forms, has been a central feature of Chinese filmmaking since the shift from opera films and traditional spoken-word dramas to more Westernized genres in the early 1920s.[25] And Williams's definition of the melodramatic mode, with its characteristic enactment of the drama of the recognition of virtue besieged, makes very compelling sense of instances of tomboy representation in the post-1970 era.[26] As I have argued before, the lingering attention to the spectacle of queer suffering that we find in such works seems to beg for the loving recognition of the reader/spectator (the denial of love and recognition at a broad social level being the root cause of the protagonist's suffering), and in that plea for the collective recognition of concealed and tormented virtue we can now recognize a paradigmatically *melodramatic* gesture.[27] Even more specifically, I suggest that tomboy narratives like those found in *Outside the Circle* and *The Unfilial Daughter* can usefully be seen as "social problem" melodramas. Christine Gledhill underscores the capacity of the melodramatic mode to translate the real dramas and contradictions of social life into fantasy form: "Melodramatic modality, personifying social forces as psychic energies and producing moral identities in the clash of opposites, is committed to binaries which bring the 'others' of official ideologies into visibility. The body images of liberation and struggle created by the women's movement, black power, and gay liberation . . . provide material to melodrama for enactments of heroic resistance against tyranny and of world-transforming hope to counter the terrible fascinations of power at work."[28] But, unlike the optimistic examples to which Gledhill refers here, the tomboy melodramas in which I am interested tend to be of the "sad ending" variety, in which, as Williams writes, "victim-heroes . . . achieve recognition of their virtue through the more passive 'deeds' of suffering and/or self-sacrifice."[29]

Outside the Circle: Tomboy Pulp

Outside the Circle is a tomboy-centered *Bildungsroman* by Taiwanese woman author Xuan Xiaofo, who is best known as a writer of romance novels for the low-cultural rental book market.[30] Notable for her somewhat unconventional heroines, Xuan published no fewer than eighteen novels in the 1970s, five of which were adapted into films and two of which provided the basis for television serials. With such an impressive output, the social impact of her works may have been quite extensive, but her marking as a commercial romance novelist places Xuan at a considerable distance from the realm of elite and official culture, by which her writing has generally been ignored.[31] The paperback copy of *Outside the Circle* that I read at the Taiwan National Library is printed on coarse, pulpish paper, seemingly creased and stained by the hands of innumerable previous readers, perhaps attesting to its former life as a rental book. The print quality is poor, with frequent typographic errors, missing characters, and characters misprinted in a sideways orientation. The front pages of the book carry an advertisement for six of Xuan's romances published by the same popular press, Nanqi.[32]

The novel's sympathetically presented first-person narrator, Yu Ying, is an attractive, talented, precocious young woman from a wealthy family who, from an early age, has identified with masculinity while feeling nothing but scorn for actual boys. As Yu Ying enters adolescence and after the tragically premature death of her mother, she becomes emotionally and sexually attracted to her sweet-natured classmate, Tang Meijia, with whom she begins a relationship that lasts through the two girls' remaining school years and into college. With the refreshing candor of the pulp novel, the text indicates unambiguously that there is a strong connection between the death of Yu Ying's mother and Yu Ying's love for Meijia. As Yu Ying mourns her mother and is comforted by Meijia, Meijia's demeanor is described no less than four times in five lines as "maternal"; if this weren't clear enough, on the following page, Yu Ying flatly states the following:

> Had my mother not passed away at that time, my heart's longing for Tang Meijia would never have been so strong, so fierce. If my mother had been there, at most I would just have run out into the rainstorm and had a good cry and unburdened myself to [my friend] Cao Yueling. Then I would have

gone home to my mother's warm love and sesame-paste dumplings. The reliant love that I felt for my mother would at the very least have reduced the strength of my feelings for Tang Meijia.

But my mother *did* go: she was gone forever, and the seat of my flourishing love was vacant, leaving me fiercely empty, fiercely in need of someone to occupy that space. And so, and so . . . my possessive feelings for Tang Meijia became like the rising waves at high tide. Before I had time to realize what was happening I was already drowned.[33]

After Meijia's parents discover the sexual nature of the two young women's relationship and Meijia is excommunicated from her family by her father, who places a public notice in the newspaper formalizing the split, Yu Ying and Meijia move out to a rented apartment. Later, Meijia dumps Yu Ying twice: first for a male student who had been attempting to court Yu Ying, then for their mutual friend, tomboy singer Kong Xiaojiang, whom Yu Ying had befriended in a bar. Yu Ying then gets together with a second female partner, nightclub singer Cheng Xiujun, nicknamed Jun-jun. Finally, Yu Ying becomes a filmmaker and resolves to make a brilliant movie that will demonstrate her talent to the world before committing suicide at her life's most glorious moment in order, as she puts it in her suicide message relayed to the press via Jun-jun, "to show you all how laughable you really are. For if she didn't leave, it'd be she who was laughable."[34]

The novel commences with a brief rhetorical framing device, as follows: "There is a kind of love: solitary, difficult, lonely. For a very long time, it has been cast outside the circumference of the circle. That is—the third kind of love, a love doomed to eternal tragedy (*yige yong zhui yu beiju de ai*)."[35] The circle of the novel's title, then, as Liu, Ding, and Parry observe, refers to the parameters of normative (hetero) gender and sexuality, outside of which the tomboy falls and from the perspective of which, they propose, the reader is invited to observe her exotic being as if looking out through the "window-frame" of sex-gender normativity.[36] Early on in the novel, Yu Ying herself offers a version of the popular conceptual distinction between temporary/feminine and permanent/tomboy same-sex love that is similarly structured by this inside/outside dichotomy. Yu Ying speaks as follows about Meijia to her other school friend, Cao Yueling, whose elder brother Yu Ying has agreed to try dating, at his relentless insistence:

[Cao Yueling asked]: "But what if [after you date my brother], your opinion about boys changes [and you begin to like them]—then what will you do about Tang Meijia?"

[Yu Ying replied:] "If that really happened, then I'd apologize to her, and she'd very quickly regain her interest in boys, because her rejection of boys isn't as deep-rooted as mine. It's me who's made her reject boys. In the unlikely event that I changed my opinion [and started liking boys], she'd recover—with me out of the picture, she'd soon start liking boys again."[37]

The truly exotic being in this novel, the one most completely outside the circle, is Yu Ying; according to Yu Ying's own pop-sexological logic, Meijia is merely a "circumstantial" rather than an essential outsider.[38] In fact, this inside/outside split is suggested by the novel's opening lines about the tomboy's fated tragedy (quoted above) in more ways than one. For it is not clear who voices these sentiments; it could, of course, be Yu Ying herself, the first-person narrator of the rest of the novel. But then again, their generality and their indirect relation to the novel's story suggest that equally these words might be spoken by the author or by some further meta-narrator speaking from inside the circle from whose circumference Yu Ying and her kind have been expelled. The impression that the words are spoken by someone other than Yu Ying is strengthened by the temporal register of the pronouncement: its speaker knows *in advance* that the young Yu Ying's ultimate fate will be a tragic one. This proleptic device, framing Yu Ying from the outset as doomed to tragedy and casting her story over the 330 pages that follow as a flashback seen from the point of view of her eventual, inevitable demise, will be interesting to bear in mind later when we consider in detail the temporal structure of tomboy melodrama.[39]

Outside the Circle projects a reader, too, who is presumptively an "insider." For although the narrative is presented as a first-person account from the tomboy's perspective, in contrast to the memorial schoolgirl romances with conventionally feminine protagonists discussed in the previous chapters, in *Outside the Circle* the reader is not strongly encouraged to identify with the story's protagonist. Yu Ying, excelling to a virtually superhuman degree in almost every respect—a track and field star, an effortlessly outstanding student, popular, irresistible to both women and men, possessed of an intelligence uncannily beyond her tender years—is a figure who invites admiration more than identification. She is presented as an all-round prodigy, the oddness of her transgender identification a logical echo of the oddness of her preternatural talent and charm. But quite early on, the novel does offer the reader a model of the kind of relation in which she might imagine herself vis-à-vis Yu Ying: the role of sympathetic friend.[40] Consider the following scene, which takes place after Yu Ying has been initially rejected by Meijia and has fled in distress to the hill that overlooks their school, where she is met by her other friend, Cao Yueling:

Cao Yueling's face was covered in raindrops—that face, so full of understanding, was covered in raindrops. All my usual strength and independence slipped away. I was no longer boyishly proud; what I needed was something to lean upon. I needed to lean upon the understanding of another person. I no longer held back my tears but abandoned myself to weeping. In that moment—that moment that so betrayed my original nature—I let flow all the tears that had been without opportunity for release for so many years, so very many years.

"I don't know why I hate boys so. . . . I don't understand it, I really don't understand it."

Listening ever so quietly, ever so closely, Cao Yueling mulled over every phrase, every word. She thought back carefully over all of the Yu Yings of the past: the way Yu Ying spoke, the way Yu Ying thought, the way Yu Ying moved; everything about Yu Ying.

"I really don't understand myself, I don't understand myself, Cao Yueling—I don't understand myself at all. I—perhaps I've done something wrong. Have I done something wrong?"

"No, Yu Ying, you have done nothing wrong. Truly. It's just that your talents are too outstanding—you're so talented that there's no boy who can match you."[41]

In this passage, Yu Ying emphasizes the atypical character of her response to Cao Yueling: normally she is masculine and strong, whereas now she becomes feminine and tearful. Yet it is precisely in the unusualness of Yu Ying's response that its interest lies, for here, the text unambiguously prompts, we are given access to Yu Ying's "real" self—vulnerable, suffering, and in need of feminine understanding—a self that is usually hidden behind her practiced front of tomboyish independence. In this besieged, wounded, "real Yu Ying," whose virtue is misrecognized by society but is clear to us and is perhaps now proven by our privileged knowledge of her suffering soul, we can hardly fail to recognize melodrama's classic victim-hero. Further, the text openly invites us to occupy a particular position in relation to this victim-hero: the role of the sympathetic friend whose understanding is precisely what our hero most deeply craves and who is able to reassure the hero that she recognizes the virtue that others fail to see: "No, you have done nothing wrong. Truly." Following this reading and since Cao Yueling is a conventionally feminine "ordinary schoolgirl," in her own words, the position that the reader of *Outside the Circle* is invited to take up is as a sympathetic onlooker situated *within* the circle of normative gender from which Yu Ying is excluded. The reader is invited to feel empathy for the plight of the novel's beleaguered tomboy protagonist and to supply her vicariously with the understanding that is denied by the wider social context that she inhabits.

The novel's stream-of-consciousness-style ending, which records Yu Ying's final, fevered thoughts as she drives her car off a cliff in a dramatic suicide, again highlights the novel's structuring melodramatic framework, identifying the agent of Yu Ying's torment as a persecuting social order emblematized in the mass media. The novel's final paragraphs read as follows:

> The crashing grows louder and louder, there are lots of newspapers flying around, every one of them in flames. . . . A big pack of reporters surrounds Jun-jun, and Jun-jun doesn't open her mouth. There are lots and lots of microphones all pointing at Jun-jun, and Jun-jun's eyes stare stupidly off into the distance. Stupidly, she voices a single statement: Her leaving is just to show you all how laughable you really are. For if she didn't leave, it'd be she who was laughable. The racket rises all around, the microphones are everywhere, . . . it's going to explode, it's about to explode; there are lots of waving hands, lots of microphones crowding in everywhere, the racket is immense, ear-piercing and head-splitting. . . . Bang! It explodes. . . . Through this most exulted of deaths, a piece of eternity—perhaps not understood by others—is attained. Through this most exulted of deaths, a statement is left behind: Her leaving is just to show you all how laughable you really are. For if she didn't leave, it'd be she who was laughable.[42]

The imagined pack of reporters, crowding microphones, and flaming pages of newsprint that persecute Yu Ying in her final moments are intended clearly enough to represent the broader social collectivity that misrecognizes Yu Ying's worth, finding her merely freakish or laughable. Thus, as Liu, Ding, and Parry observe, this conclusion—rewritten to great effect as the conclusion to Qiu Miaojin's novel *Eyu shouji* (The Crocodile's Journal) almost twenty years later—unambiguously prompts interpretation as social critique.[43] Thinking back to Yu Dafu's violently phobic descriptions of the same-sex attracted masculine woman in "She Was a Weak Woman," we might say that where Yu's text *enacts* the insult heaped upon this personage, by means of its lavish descriptions of Li Wenqing's physical monstrosity, Xuan's text *dramatizes* the scene of this insult, casting the social violence directed against the tomboy as the villain in its melodramatic narrative of virtue misrecognized.

The Unfilial Daughter: *Tomboy Soap*

Two and a half decades after the publication of *Outside the Circle*, tomboy melodrama returned to Taiwan's mass-cultural scene with *The Unfilial Daughter*, a five-part television drama series directed by Taiwan New Cinema director Ko Yi-zheng for Taiwan's free-to-air TTV station. The series is based on the novel of the same name by Du Xiulan, which won the Crown Prize for Popular Fiction in 1996.[44] *The Unfilial Daughter* was a surprise ratings hit. The initial weekday evening screening of the first hour-long episode in 2001, rated at 2.17, had about 477,000 viewers; this was such a successful result that after multiple repeats on TTV and pay-per-view webcast, the series was bought by the Dong Sen (ETTV) cable network.[45] The series has also made an impact beyond the shores of Taiwan: Internet discussion boards reveal the sale of pirated DVD copies in mainland China and an enthusiastic audience in self-identifying mainland Chinese lesbians for both the series and the novel.[46] In the 2003–2004 survey on Chinese-language lesbian Internet use referred to above, six out of fifty-three mainland Chinese respondents mentioned *The Unfilial Daughter* as an example of a lesbian-themed film or book that they remembered watching or reading, making it the most commonly recalled such text for this group of women.[47] As Wang Chun-chi argues in a recent study of the audience response to the series, despite what might appear to be a wholly "negative" representation of tomboy abjection, *The Unfilial Daughter* has nonetheless played a significant role in facilitating individual identification, topical debate, and online community formation among lesbian-identifying viewers both within Taiwan and beyond.[48]

The Unfilial Daughter, like *Outside the Circle*, is narrated by a sympathetic first-person tomboy narrator, her verbal framing of events included in the TV series by means of voice-over. The plot is also similar to that of *Outside the Circle* in several respects. Like Yu Ying, Ding Tianshi (Angel Ding, played by Liu Yue) grows up in a difficult family situation, this time owing not to her mother's absence but to what are presented as the mother's character defects: Angel's mother (Qiu Naihua) is shrill, domineering, and vulgarly working class, and she dotes on Angel's elder brother, Tianhou (Wang Wei), while alternately ignoring and physically and verbally attacking Angel and her little brother, Tianming (Li Fengjia). In the boarding school where Angel finally manages to enroll in an attempt to get away from her miserable family life, she begins a romance with a middle-class female classmate, Zhan Qing-qing (Pan Huiru), a relationship that ends in disaster when the two girls are discovered in bed together by the school's disciplinary officer. When Zhan

Qing-qing's family forbids her to see Angel, Zhan commits suicide, leaving Angel heartbroken. Later, Angel discovers the world of the T bar through a tomboy friend she meets by chance, Sister Xu (Fan Ruijun), and in the bar Angel meets her second lover, Maggie (Xiang Liwen). Angel, Maggie, Sister Xu, and Sister Xu's girlfriend move out together into a rented apartment, but Angel remains tormented by her family life: her mother is working up to full-blown, flamboyant insanity, and her father is descending into abject alcoholism. Ultimately, Angel is diagnosed with cancer and rapidly sickens and dies in her mid-twenties, supported throughout the process by Maggie's unfaltering love (figure 9).

The first few minutes of *The Unfilial Daughter*'s first episode reveal that the key elements of the tomboy melodrama as seen in *Outside the Circle*, both in narrative structure and in structure of feeling, remain in place here. Accompanied by the wistful strains of the melancholy theme tune, the first scene is a flash-forward that shows us in advance what will also be the series' final scene: supported by Maggie, our feeble, terminally ill tomboy protagonist, Angel, rereads the suicide note left by her girlhood sweetheart Zhan Qing-qing—"We have not harmed anyone, why do other people want to harm us? I'm leaving"—before ritually releasing the note onto the wind out the window of the car where Angel and Maggie sit (figure 10). With a cut to a scene of a gaggle of ragged children playing in a rubbish dump beside a paddy field, Angel's voice-over introduces us to the unhappy world of her childhood, with her henpecked ex-soldier father, her spoiled and arrogant elder brother Tianhou, her sweet and neglected younger brother Tianming, and, overshadowing them all, her cruel and abusive mother: "As for my mother, well, all those positive words that people usually associate with mothers— 'kindness,' 'warmth,' 'loving care,' 'sanctuary'—she's got nothing at all to do with words like that." In the following scene, Angel and little Tianming, covered in mud from the rubbish dump, return to the village, where they are met by their furious mother, who beats them with a stick and subjects both them and their sympathetic father to a brutal Minnan-language tongue-lashing (figure 11).[49] As the onslaught of verbal and physical abuse from her mother tails off, little Angel begins obediently to pump water from the well to wash her younger brother; the sentimental theme tune swells once again as the camera moves in for a mid-shot focusing on Angel's tearstained young face in profile. As this opening demonstrates, partly as a result of the formal properties of audiovisual representation, *The Unfilial Daughter* is, if anything, yet more emphatic than *Outside the Circle* in its melodramatic framing of the tomboy as virtuous victim for whom the audience's empathy is solicited. With

9. The melodramatic tomboy: Angel lies terminally ill with cancer, tended by Maggie, in TTV drama series *The Unfilial Daughter* (dir. Ko Yi-zheng, 2001).

10. *The Unfilial Daughter's* first and last scene: Angel ritually releases the suicide note left by her childhood sweetheart Zhan Qing-qing, supported by her current girlfriend, Maggie: "We haven't harmed anyone, why do other people want to harm us? I'm leaving" (dir. Ko Yi-zheng, 2001).

11. The privatization of social violence: the young Angel is beaten and cursed by her mother in *The Unfilial Daughter* (dir. Ko Yi-zheng, 2001).

her abusive mother, unhappy family, poverty, terminal illness, and deviant gender/sexuality, Angel is framed as the victim-hero *par excellence*, and pathos is certainly the central affective note struck by the series as a whole.

Love Gone Wrong: The Tomboy and the Bad Mother

To a far greater degree than *Outside the Circle*, *The Unfilial Daughter* exemplifies melodrama's propensity to transform broad social issues into private familial or personal ones.[50] A peculiar logical inversion thus occurs. Whereas I have argued that *Outside the Circle* underscores the social system's victimization of its tomboy protagonist for her sex/gender nonconformity, in *The Unfilial Daughter*, the tomboy protagonist's sex/gender nonconformity is explained as the result of her having been victimized—not by the social system, but by her mother. The overdetermination of the tomboy narrative by the narrative of a nuclear family "perverted" by a villainous mother thus effects both a melodramatic privatization of the social and an inversion of cause and effect.[51] Although, as we have seen, *Outside the Circle* accounts for Yu Ying's homosexuality in part through reference to a problematic relation with her mother, this pop-psychological discourse is far stronger in *The Unfilial Daughter* in the absence of the other discourse of quasi-supernatural, supra-feminine genius that runs alongside the maternal explanation for the tomboy's sexuality in *Outside the Circle*. *The Unfilial Daughter*'s title reads as strongly ironic: it is not the daughter who has wronged the mother, but the mother who has fatally wronged the daughter and who is blamed not just for Angel's tragically misoriented sexuality but also, symbolically, for her early death and all of the other various torments that beleaguer Angel throughout her short and painful life.[52]

Both *Outside the Circle* and *The Unfilial Daughter*, and especially the latter, contribute to a pervasive tendency in Chinese mass cultures more broadly to attribute the existence of same-sex loving adult women, particularly tomboys, to deficient mothering. Indeed, this discourse—part pop psychology, part folk misogyny—turns out to be all but ubiquitous in modern representations.[53] In addition to these instances, one is reminded, for example, of Lishi's motherless condition in Lu Yin's "Lishi's Diary" (China, 1923; discussed in chapter 1);[54] the tomboy Zhang Yan's lower-class, gambling mother in Chu T'ien-hsin's "Waves Scour the Sands" (Taiwan, 1976; discussed in chapter 2); the protagonist Tong Suxin's frail and bedridden mother and her tomboy girlfriend Zhong Yuan's neglectful, promiscuous one in Tsao Jui-yuan's telemovie adaptation of Cao Lijuan's "The Maidens' Dance"; and the tomboy Shen Yijun's embittered mother with her disastrous marriage to a bigamous husband in Lisa Chen's telemovie *Voice of Waves* (the last two Taiwan, 2002; discussed in chapter 5); or again, Taiwanese writer Chen Xue's 1995 story, "Searching for the Lost Wings of the Angel," with its complex conflation of lesbian and mother-daughter love. Each of these examples links the same-sex attracted woman with the bad, absent, or otherwise deficient mother in a slightly different way. While in Lu Yin's story the link is faint and implicit at best and in *Outside the Circle*, "Waves," "The Maidens' Dance," and *Voice of Waves* it is explicit yet not strongly emphasized or presented as wholly determining, in "Searching for the Lost Wings of the Angel" the link is very explicit but its meaning is far from clear, implying as readily a queering of familial love as a reduction of lesbian desire to mother love gone wrong.[55] In *The Unfilial Daughter*, however, the link between deficient mothering and the production of the tomboy daughter is both explicit and flatly accusatory. Here popular melodrama's Manichean logic of suffering virtue and oppressive persecutor effect an all but total displacement of an actually social violence against tomboys onto the scapegoat of an individual evil mother. We will return to this symbolic displacement of public hostility toward tomboys by the attribution of private mistreatment of daughters by mothers later in this chapter. First, it is necessary to consider how the bad endings that seem the inevitable fate of these badly mothered mass-cultural tomboys relate to this book's broader argument on the temporalities of female homoerotic representation.

No Future: The Temporality of Tomboy Melodrama

I have argued throughout this book that the dominant metaphor in modern Chinese female homoerotic representation is temporal. A key question then arises: How does tomboy melodrama figure temporality? Linda Williams draws on the work of Franco Moretti and Steve Neale to propose that melodrama is centrally concerned with the question of time and the experience of time's passing; its characteristic pathos arises from the experience of time lost—the temporality of the "too late"—while the satisfaction of the happy-ending melodrama is rooted in the fantasy that time can be defeated and desire fulfilled.[56] And indeed, the pathos of the too late is everywhere apparent in both of the examples I have discussed so far. Consider, for example, the scene at the end of *Outside the Circle*, where a tearful and near hysterical Jun-jun begs Yu Ying not to end her life, all to no avail, for Yu Ying's mind is made up, the decision already made. Or recall the identical first and last scene of *The Unfilial Daughter*, where we reread Zhan Qing-qing's suicide note along with Angel in the knowledge that just as the note shows all too clearly the too lateness of any desire to save Qing-qing's young life, so too it is already too late for Angel herself, who even now teeters at the brink of death.

But the temporal logic of tomboy melodrama is not exhausted by the classic melodramatic temporality of too late; there is also another dimension that is worth exploring. As illustrated above, the narrative structure of *The Unfilial Daughter*'s beginning echoes that of *Outside the Circle*, with the same flash-forward device informing the audience in advance how the protagonist's story will end (in both cases in early death). In contrast to the TV adaptation, Du Xiulan's original novel does not conform to this structure, but a foreword written by the popular romance novelist Zhang Manjuan performs a similar function. The final lines of Zhang's foreword are as follows:

Angel Ding is no unfilial daughter.
She merely confronts an irreversible fate.
Nonetheless, she struggles to reverse it.
Her struggle is a hopeless one, yet it's also beautiful.[57]

Like the rhetorical framing device at the start of *Outside the Circle* that warns the reader in advance that Yu Ying is "doomed to eternal tragedy," Zhang's framing of *The Unfilial Daughter* as a story of Angel's irreversibly tragic fate sets up a particular temporal pattern for the tomboy's story in which the unfolding of events in the narrative present is always overshadowed by the reader's foreknowledge of the tomboy's bad ending. The temporal structure associated with these proleptic beginnings constitutes a variant of melodrama's characteristic too-late temporality that might be called the temporality of *no future*. Illustrating a popular intuition of this temporal logic, responding to Du's novel on an Internet book review site, one reader writes as follows: "Amid the endless sea of people, [Angel] couldn't find a complete person to fill the void within her soul; she tried to define herself by seeking out lesbians *and yet she couldn't envisage homosexuality's future*, the bitterness of her family life and the cruel pressure of society meant that death was the only possible ending for Angel: this is the book's unavoidable conclusion."[58] In laying out this folk theory of the novel's meaning, this response is particularly revealing in its assumption—not directly supported by any actual statement by Angel in the novel—that Angel "couldn't envisage homosexuality's future" (*kan bu dao tongxinglian de weilai*).[59]

I have argued in previous chapters that in the case of memorial school-girl romances with conventionally feminine protagonists, the temporality is retrospective because the protagonists' future is defined in advance as marital or proto-marital. But in dominant representations of the tomboy, we now find, her future has been strictly unimaginable—a kind of blank space in the popular imaginary, commonly dealt with by the most expeditious means of having tomboy protagonists die young.[60] My suggestion is that these vanishing tomboys furnish a literalization of the general cultural unimaginability of the tomboy's postadolescent future: where her feminine lover's future is marriage, the tomboy's own future is, simply, unthinkable. At the conclusion of *Outside the Circle*, Yu Ying's desire to commit suicide specifically by driving off a cliff into thin air can be read as symbolic of this failure in the popular imagination: "My ideal route would take me to a cliff accessible by car. There, any other person, any other car, would be forced to stop—but I, calmly, peacefully, would keep on driving. I'd just drive on and on."[61] There's a certain logic to Yu Ying's final drive out into the thin air beyond the edge of the cliff: metaphorically she drives out into the void of tomboy (non)futurity. Thus, to the temporality of too late that characterizes tomboy melodrama, mass-cultural tomboys' ineluctable tendency toward bad endings and early deaths that seem always to be foreseen before the fact adds a further dimension: the temporality of no future.

This overshadowing by the terrifyingly blank space of the tomboy's (non)future undoubtedly contributes to the miasma of melodramatic pathos that hangs about this figure's mass-cultural representation. As much the victims of cruel fate as of bad mothers, these tomboy heroines solicit the reader's or spectator's empathy in a number of different registers, all of which, I propose, can be seen as displacements of the social forces that con-spire to make real tomboys' lives genuinely difficult. If these tomboy narra-tives are saturated in violence, then, this is not simply for the generic reason that melodrama requires violence in order to produce a victim-hero worthy of our empathy, but also for the cultural reason that such texts are engaged in the symbolic labor of processing the real social hostility directed toward tomboys.[62] Perhaps, indeed, popular tomboy texts tend to take the form of melodrama *because* they are at root representations (however thoroughly dis-guised) of actual social violence.[63] It is worth underscoring, however, that this observation does not equate to a criticism of these popular texts for fail-ing to be more overtly political. For despite their at times heavy camouflaging of broader social relations as private, familial ones, these texts nonetheless represent tomboy lives in ways that clearly strike a chord for many tomboy-identifying viewers and readers, affirming the worth of the tomboy self even as, taken literally, they may appear to naturalize her suffering and attribute it, dishonestly, to bad mothering.[64] In the final section of this chapter, however, I turn to a more recent tomboy text that transforms the melodramatic mode and its associated temporality of no future to produce a different representa-tional and ideological structure.

Blue Gate Crossing: *Tomboy Teenpic*

The Taiwanese/French co-production *Blue Gate Crossing*, (Lanse da men, 2002) directed by young U.S.-trained male director Yee Chih-yen, opens to a black screen with a voice-over conversation between two high school girls, Lin Yue-zhen (Liang Youmei) and her best friend, Meng Kerou (Guey Lun Mei).[65] Yue-zhen is trying to teach Kerou to visualize her future, but while Yuezhen easily conjures up a fantasy scenario of herself in ten years' time, complete with a dream husband and cute daughter, Kerou repeatedly complains that she just can't see anything at all (figure 12). This imaginative failure begins to make sense when we learn that Kerou is in fact secretly in love with Yuezhen. While a vision of marital heterosexuality appears effortlessly as the future promise of Yuezhen's girlhood, same-sex attracted, tomboyish Kerou understandably has a harder time visualizing her own future. Indeed, the empty screen and voice-over from Kerou—"I can't see anything, I can't see anything at all!"—serve as an economical crystallization of the tomboy temporality of no future that I have been elaborating throughout this chapter.

Blue Gate Crossing, whose style is a kind of mix of TV teen drama and art film, is a coming-of-age/love triangle narrative that centers on the intertwined

我還是什麼都看不到

12. Meng Kerou complains, "I still can't see anything at all [of my future]," in *Blue Gate Crossing* (dir. Yee Chih-yen, 2002).

stories of three high schoolers, school hunk Zhang Shihao (Chen Bolin), beautiful popular girl Yuezhen, and tomboyish Kerou, from whose point of view the story is presented.[66] At the beginning of the film, Yuezhen has a crush on Shihao, and Kerou is secretly in love with Yuezhen; soon enough, Shihao becomes attracted to Kerou. Tensions build as Yuezhen begins to suspect that Kerou is seeing Shihao, whom Kerou has indeed agreed to date in the desperate hope that a kiss from a boy will cure her of her homosexual desire for Yuezhen.[67] Finally, Kerou confesses her love for Yuezhen to Shihao; at first he refuses to believe her, but he seems to grow used to the idea as the film progresses, and his relationship with Kerou subtly shifts from a quasi-romantic liaison to a more buddy-like friendship. Kerou dutifully sets Yuezhen up on a date with Shihao; he rejects her, and she bids farewell to her long-standing crush. Finally Kerou works up the courage to steal a kiss from Yuezhen, who from then on refuses to have anything to do with her. The film ends with Kerou and Shihao reflecting on the future and the passing of the summer. Although her own future is still unclear to her, Kerou has gained a friend in Shihao and has taken the difficult first step of facing up to her same-sex desires; the logic of the rite-of-passage narrative tells us that this is the central significance of Kerou's own "blue gate crossing."

A significant context for the appearance of a film like *Blue Gate Crossing*, with its focus on the sexual awakening of a sympathetic, nontragic young tomboy, is the rise of Taiwan's lesbian and gay, or *tongzhi*, movement since the early 1990s, which prompted a wave of lesbian- and gay-themed cultural production across the fields of fiction, film, graphic art, theater, and political and activist cultures. Like other examples of contemporary popular schoolgirl romance such as Internet fiction and cheap, pop-fiction novels, this film effectively articulates the modern Chinese schoolgirl romance narrative with postmodern Taiwanese lesbian (nütongzhi) culture—a culture that itself represents a localization of a globally extensive, late-twentieth-century lesbian and gay style and politics that initially emerged in Europe and the United States.[68] Another important context that sets this film apart from the other texts discussed in this chapter is its marketing toward international audiences likely to be more familiar with a globalized, post-Stonewall discourse of gay and lesbian identity politics than with the histories and conventions of Chinese-language tomboy melodrama or schoolgirl romance. Given all this, I have argued elsewhere that the film, together with the tie-in popular novel that was published to coincide with its domestic release, effects a hybridization between the Chinese schoolgirl romance narrative and the Euro-American coming out story. Kerou's character may be interpreted according to either framework (or both), depending on the cultural positioning of the film's various audiences, domestic as well as international.[69]

Reflecting the historical context of its production, Blue Gate Crossing's framing of the tomboy differs quite markedly from that found in any of the earlier texts discussed so far. The melodramatic mode is not strongly in evidence here: Kerou is not singled out as especially tormented or psychically wounded, and the emotional stress she suffers as a result of her same-sex crush on Yuezhen is paralleled, not contrasted, with Yuezhen's torments over her own secret heterosexual crush on Shihao. Nor is Kerou tortured by a cruel, mad, or absent mother. The film's narrative and temporal structure, too, marks a contrast with the other tomboy texts discussed above. Missing is the proleptic device at the beginning foretelling the tomboy's ultimate doom; instead, the film commences with a more distanced, ambiguous invocation of the dominant cultural logic that dictates that the tomboy has no future, in the scene described above where Kerou fails to visualize her future. However, having made reference to this all too familiar logic, the film then goes about refuting it by focusing on Kerou's successful negotiation of this difficult period and her eventual launching, at the film's conclusion, into a still unknown but nonetheless hopeful-looking future.

In one sense, the film's tone is reminiscent of the memorialism characteristic of schoolgirl romance. The sentimentality of its lyrical piano soundtrack; the "cuteness" of its simple, TV-style visual language; the frequent interposing shots of Shihao riding his bike bathed in a golden-sepia glow; and repeated verbal references to the bittersweet experience of being seventeen and in love for the first time all combine to suggest that although the action of the film takes place in the narrative present rather than in flashback, nevertheless the film's events might already be the memories of an adult looking back wistfully on her vanished adolescence. Despite this, however, the film is groundbreaking in its attribution of a possible (if unspecified) lesbian future to its tomboy protagonist. For if the film's nostalgic tone makes its story feel always already memorial, the film nevertheless refuses to specify what kind of an adult does the remembering: a heterosexual Kerou or a lesbian one. For although Kerou is ultimately rejected by her friend Yuezhen, the film's ending, in which Kerou and Shihao speculate lazily on what lies ahead for them, is a very open one that certainly allows for the possibility that Kerou will remain attracted to women in adulthood.[70] Moreover, the entire orientation of the final scene is toward the future. Kerou muses in beatific voice-over addressed to her friend Shihao: "I wonder, after three years, or five years, or even longer, what kind of grownups will we turn out to be? Will we be like the gym teacher? Or like my mom? Even though when I shut my eyes I still can't see myself, I can see you."

If the characteristic form of the schoolgirl romance narrated by a conventionally feminine woman is a memorial narrative that looks back on youthful same-sex romance from the point of view of marital adulthood, then Blue Gate Crossing effects a reversal of this in several senses, with its final scene showing a same-sex attracted tomboy schoolgirl looking forward to potentially lesbian adulthood. Even if one interprets the film, as I have suggested above, as an implicitly memorial narrative—a teenage story recalled by an adult Kerou whom we are not shown—nonetheless it remains significant that in this case, it is a tomboy who does the remembering, with no suggestion either that, as with the reminiscent feminine protagonists of so many other schoolgirl romances, she has married or that, as with the other tomboy protagonists we have encountered so far, she has died. Blue Gate Crossing thus stands as a surprisingly hopeful, forward-looking culmination to a century of mass-cultural representations of the tomboy as defined precisely by her lack of future prospects.

As will be demonstrated in chapter 6, this tactic of invoking then reworking the dominant temporal logics of modern Chinese female homoerotic representation to produce more reflexive representations in the present is not limited to Blue Gate Crossing. It can also be seen in other examples of recent Chinese-language lesbian-themed films, some of which speak back even more directly and critically than Blue Gate Crossing to earlier forms of representation. Through such critical citation and resignification of older forms of representation—the melodrama of the tragic, no-future tomboy and the memorial story of schoolgirl romance, along with their characteristic narrative structures of prolepsis and analepsis; the premonition of impending doom and the wistful remembrance of a vanished past—the central temporal logic of modern Chinese female homoerotic representation remains in play, albeit in distinctive new forms.

. . .

FIVE

Television as Public Mourning

Taiwan's Sad Young Women

Taiwan's television screens have lately become host to a spate of surprisingly popular local productions featuring same-sex romances between young women characters. Since 2000, three programs have brought the schoolgirl romance narrative to the island's network television. These include the thirteen-part soap opera Ninü (The Unfilial Daughter), produced by Taiwan Television Enterprise (TTV) and first aired in 2001 (see chapter 4), and two eighty-five-minute telemovies made by the Taiwan Public Television Service (PTS): Tongnü zhi wu (The Maidens' Dance, dir. Tsao Jui-yuan) and Nanian xiatiande langsheng (Voice of Waves, dir. Lisa Chen Xiuyu), both of which screened for the first time in 2002. The schoolgirl romance narrative has also made it to the big screen in the Taiwanese-French co-production discussed in chapter 4, Blue Gate Crossing (figure 13), among others, and these screen productions join an ever-increasing abundance of contemporary popular and elite fiction about romantic love between adolescent girls.[1] Although all of the above-mentioned programs were produced in Taiwan, their influence extends beyond the shores of the island to reach regional Chinese-speaking audiences. VCD and DVD recordings of these televisual and filmic adaptations of the schoolgirl romance narrative are readily available to viewers outside Taiwan via online purchase, as well as through informal FTP download and as black market discs sold by entrepreneurial media pirates in mainland China. According to discussions in Chinese lesbian Internet forums, the productions have been enthusiastically consumed by self-identifying lesbians not only within Taiwan but in Hong Kong and on the Chinese mainland as well.

Undeniably a significant context for the emergence of these post-1990s Taiwanese screen productions is the rise of the tongzhi (lesbian and gay)

13. Schoolgirl romance in *Blue Gate Crossing* (dir. Yee Chih-yen, 2002).

movement since the early 1990s.[2] The literary works on which several of the productions are based—notably Du Xiulan's 1996 popular novel *The Unfilial Daughter* and Cao Lijuan's prize-winning 1991 story "The Maidens' Dance"— are frequently cited as exemplary of the new *tongzhi* fiction that has flourished as an integral aspect of the new public *tongzhi* movement.[3] Within the diegesis of both *The Unfilial Daughter* and *The Maidens' Dance* we find some characters represented as participating in recognizable lesbian (*nütongzhi*) subcultures—for example, by frequenting lesbian bars and explicitly defining their sexual relationships according to T/*po* secondary genders.[4] Thus although, as I will discuss below, conceptually the going-in story of temporary adolescent same-sex love appears to undermine the minoritizing identity politics of *tongzhi* discourse, nevertheless in practice, the new wave of schoolgirl romance adaptations has worked closely in concert with the emergent *tongzhi* public culture.

My focus in this chapter is on the two schoolgirl romance telemovies released by PTS, *Voice of Waves* and *The Maidens' Dance*. PTS is Taiwan's first independent nonprofit television broadcaster, and it joined the four existing free-to-air commercial networks in 1998.[5] In the tradition of public broadcasting, the station's mission statement emphasizes indigenous content in the face of media globalization, "quality" programming, and social service in the form of public education.[6] In recent years, PTS has become a key producer of local queer-themed programming—another highly successful drama from PTS is the male homosexual-themed *Niezi* series (Crystal boys, based on Pai Hsien-yung's classic 1983 novel of the same name), also directed by Tsao Jui-yuan, and first screened at prime time in 2003. Jessie Shih, PTS's chief of program planning, explains PTS's remarkable decision to produce no less than three queer-themed dramas within two years as resulting partly from the station's desire to promote young local directors and partly from its responsibility to cater to social minorities, although the station does not have any formal policy of supporting lesbian and gay content.[7] Given that PTS's ratings are consistently well below those of the commercial networks, as is standard for a public broadcaster, both of the schoolgirl romance telemovies did reasonably well in that regard. *The Maidens' Dance* scored its highest ratings to date at 0.15, or about 33,000 viewers; *Waves* reached 0.18, or about 39,600 viewers, and PTS reported no conservative backlash from viewers critical of the programs' representation of young women's same-sex love.[8] The available data on audience demographics suggest that the majority of the telemovies' viewers will have been women.[9]

Schoolgirl Romance as "Women's Television"

The Maidens' Dance and *Voice of Waves* have much in common in style, narrative organization, and genre, as well as in their common theme of schoolgirl romance. Stylistically, as is typical of PTS drama productions, both telemovies are more self-consciously cinematic than standard commercial television dramas. In contrast to TTV's much higher-rated lesbian-themed series *The Unfilial Daughter*, which in both narrative and style conforms closely to a familiar soap opera/melodrama formula, the pace of *The Maidens' Dance* and *Waves* is much slower and the mise-en-scène more stylized, and the aesthetic of the productions draws on the art cinema tradition as much as, or even more than, that of popular TV drama. Thematically each production instantiates the memorial mode by means of a flashback structure and first-person voice-over narration, telling the story of a passionate attachment between adolescent girls as recalled by an adult woman protagonist who has, in the narrative present, entered ambivalently into proto-marital relations.[10] Generically both films can be seen as instances of the "woman's film" (or, relatedly, "women's television"). Most obviously, this generic affiliation is signaled by the programs' feminine point-of-view, their focus on an "ordinary woman's" emotional experience, and their central theme of a tragically impossible love culminating in climactic scenes of pathos and loss.[11]

As the discussion of women viewers later in this chapter will illustrate, the schoolgirl romance telemovie as women's television brings into being a new kind of feminized community of consumption. It is interesting to compare this community of viewers and the ways it uses the telemovies as mediators of personal same-sex romance memory with the ways that the stories by Chu T'ien-hsin and Wong Bikwan (discussed in chapter 2) project specifically lit-

erary modes of homoerotic schoolgirl sociality. At a textual level, the latter do this through their thematic preoccupations with characters' practices of diary writing and popular romance reading—practices that are replicated in the activities of actual young women who copy and circulate literary school-girl romances by these well-known writers, as well as pen and publish their own versions.[12] This chapter shifts the focus from such literary practices of schoolgirl romance to the related yet distinct practices of spectatorship and e-discussion enabled by the audiovisual and electronic media of television and the Internet. Such a comparison makes clear the extent to which the formal specificity of the media in which the schoolgirl romance appears impacts on the ways in which the narrative is available to be taken up and worked on by its audiences.

Cao Lijuan's short story on which Tsao Jui-yuan's *The Maidens' Dance* is based is a contemporary literary example of the schoolgirl romance narrative and, like Chu T'ien-hsin's school stories, something of a classic among Tai-wan's lesbian readerships. Both story and film take the form of an extended flashback, as the young woman Tong Suxin (Su Huilun) recalls the roman-tic friendship of her schooldays with her tomboy best friend Zhong Yuan (Chen Bozhen) in their home village in central Taiwan.[13] In the telemovie, the narrative is bookended by a fantasy shot, at the beginning and the end, of Tong Suxin dressed as a bride, hanging in the supersaturated blue air over the village.[14] The memorial cast of the film is established in this first frame, where we find our narrator fantastically suspended above the village while her schoolgirl self walks down the shade-dappled summer street beneath (figure 14). The film underscores its own status as memorial by presenting us with the proleptic device of two Tong Suxins, so that we understand from the out-set that the film's narrative results from the grown-up Tong recalling her own memories as a schoolgirl. But the fact that our floating narrator is dressed *as a bride* also secures the narrative's status as memorial in another way: insofar as the narrative's central subject is a same-sex romance, this prefiguration of the narrator's ultimate matrimonial fate serves conceptually to produce such loving attachment between young women as the memory of adult marital femininity—a standard move in the schoolgirl romance narrative.

In the film's flashback sections, we learn that Tong Suxin and Zhong Yuan met one morning on the school bus and became passionate friends; Tong Suxin's voice-over tells us that she has been romantically infatuated with Zhong Yuan ever since she was sixteen. But when Zhong Yuan kissed her sud-denly one day, Tong Suxin became confused and broke off their relationship; soon after, Zhong transferred to a different school. The years that follow are

14. Opening shot from *The Maidens' Dance*: The bridal Tong Suxin floats above her schoolgirl self in the street beneath (dir. Tsao Jui-yuan, 2002).

compressed into a series of scenes in which Zhong sporadically reappears in Tong's life: first, pregnant and seeking an abortion; later, with a series of female lovers whom she deserts, one after the other, without explanation. In college, Tong herself acquires a boyfriend, but again her voice-overs make it clear that her true love all along has been Zhong Yuan, and she spends months desperately searching for her vanished sweetheart. At a school re-union, Zhong reappears, and Tong learns that she will soon emigrate to the United States with her family. Just prior to Tong's wedding and Zhong's de-parture overseas, Zhong visits Tong at her family's home. In her girlhood bedroom, a tearful Tong poses to Zhong the question that has preoccupied her throughout their relationship: "Can two women make love?" Breaking down in tears herself, Zhong sobs her reply—"No—they cannot!"—before the two collapse into each other's arms and Tong kisses Zhong. At the end of the film, we see Zhong Yuan wistfully watch as Tong Suxin is driven off to be married; decked out in her wedding dress and veil, Tong gazes longingly back at Zhong from inside the car. The film's final shot reprises the opening shot of our reminiscent bridal narrator floating in the sky—but Tong is ulti-mately joined not, as we might expect, by her fiancé, but instead by her girl-hood sweetheart, Zhong Yuan, dapper in a formal black suit (figure 15). This fantasy ending presents both a graphic literalization and a wishful reversal of the romantic ellipsis that structures the film's narrative. We see Tong and her tomboy lover literally "left hanging" at the film's conclusion, mirroring the fate of their truncated romance. At the same time, however, the fantasized wedding between the two women undermines the force of the heterosexual conclusion to Tong Suxin's story: the blunt full stop of marriage—that all-too-expected narrative terminus—is forestalled by the ellipsis of Tong and Zhong's less conventional union.[15]

15. Closing shot from *The Maidens' Dance*: Tong Suxin as bride and Zhong Yuan as groom (dir. Tsao-Jui-yuan, 2002).

Like *The Maidens' Dance*, Lisa Chen Xiuyu's *Voice of Waves* is organized through a flashback structure and first-person voice-over narration. Here again, an adult, conventionally feminine protagonist, Lu Manli (nicknamed Xiao Li, played by Zhou Youting), recalls her past intimacy with a tomboy classmate, Shen Yijun (Huang Xiaoruo). The film's title sequence presents a montage of oceanic imagery: a uniformed schoolgirl stands on a beach calling to a figure swimming out through the surf, her voice drowned out by the crashing of waves (figure 16); a tightly curled female figure floats among streams of ascending bubbles in turbulent blue water; a schoolgirl splashes in slow motion through the shallows on a nighttime beach. The following shot reveals that these images have been dreamed by the adult Xiao Li, whom we now see tossing and turning in her single bed in a bluish nocturnal light. In the film's present, Xiao Li resigns from her office job of seven years, without plans for future employment, for a reason that she can't quite explain: "I just felt like changing my life somehow. Actually, I wasn't really feeling anything. Sometimes, I didn't even feel like being Lu Manli." As in *The Maidens' Dance*, Xiao Li's memories of her village girlhood are dramatized in flashback. While in the film's present Xiao Li remains confined to her apartment, ignoring phone messages from an increasingly irritated fiancé, in flashback we watch a teenage Xiao Li becoming fascinated by Yijun, a reclusive tomboy classmate. Intrigued, Xiao Li observes Yijun's romantic relationship with another girl, Lin Long (Chen Liqin); gradually Xiao Li and Yijun draw closer, and Xiao Li replaces Lin Long as the object of Yijun's affection. The two girls enjoy a period of intimacy; Yijun likes to swim in the ocean, and there is a repeated scene in which Xiao Li sits on the beach watching Yijun swimming, Xiao Li's face suffused with beatific contentment. But Xiao Li's solicitous mother and gossipy classmates dislike Yijun, and after Xiao Li is injured when Yijun crashes the bike the two girls are riding, these other women succeed in preventing Xiao Li and Yijun from meeting. The following year, the two are placed in separate classes and drift apart. After graduation, Xiao Li moves north for college. The next she hears of Yijun is when she receives a letter from Lin Long telling her of Yijun's (unexplained) death. The flashback narrative now catches up with the present as Xiao Li travels south to her home village to attend Yijun's funeral. There, Lin Long, who has been living at Yijun's family home since graduation, makes Xiao Li a present of Yijun's wallet; inside, Xiao Li finds a drawing of her young self accompanied by a love heart. Following this posthumous revelation of Yijun's love for Xiao Li, the film concludes with a sequence of oceanic images similar to that with which it began. The final shot, before the credits roll over an image of nocturnal waves, is of the young Xiao Li's loving gaze at Yijun as she swims (figure 17). Like *The Maidens' Dance*, then, with its flashback structure, *Waves* exemplifies the memorial mode of the schoolgirl romance. Both telemovies illustrate the typically elliptic form of the going-in story, in which the central same-sex romance is prematurely abbreviated by the forceful intervention of social convention—a traumatic injunction that nevertheless ensures the lost same-sex love's potent memorability in the narrative present.

Visualizing T/po Romance: Textual Dynamics

As I have suggested throughout my discussion of the memorial schoolgirl romance, much of the narrative's interest lies in its enduring popularity and relatively wide dissemination in modern Chinese cultural production. This, I have suggested, raises the possibility that the narrative is symptomatic of a particular form of modern sexual epistemology that is distinct, in some respects, from the organization of knowledge on sexuality in Euro-American modernity. However, several writers have drawn attention to a subgenre within Euro-American film that appears in some senses analogous to the Taiwanese productions under discussion here. I am thinking of what Chris Holmlund has called the "mainstream femme film": "a hybrid subgenre of the woman's film and the lesbian drama" that emerged in the early 1980s in American and European cinema, including films like *Personal Best* (Robert Towne, 1982), *Lianna* (John Sayles, 1983), *Entre nous* (Diane Kurys, 1983), *Desert Hearts* (Donna Deitch, 1986), and *Fried Green Tomatoes* (Jon Avnet, 1992).[16] There are several structural similarities between the Taiwanese schoolgirl romance films and the Euro-American femme films. Both can be seen as subgenres of the "woman's film"; both imply a universalizing understanding of women's

16. A young Xiao Li calls out to Yijun as she swims; in title sequence of *Voice of Waves* (dir. Lisa Chen Xiuyu, 2002).

17. Xiao Li gazes beatifically at Yijun as she swims; near the conclusion of *Voice of Waves* (dir. Lisa Chen Xiuyu, 2002).

same-sex desire in which female friendships shade into sexual relationships; both draw the identification of lesbian- and straight-identifying female audiences alike; both favor conventionally feminine protagonists; in both, for the most part, mid-narrative same-sex relations are ultimately supplanted by heterosexual conclusions.[17] But rather than see the Taiwanese telemovies as merely far-flung exemplars of this Euro-American subgenre, I want to explore further the generic specificity of *The Maidens' Dance* and *Waves*, elaborating what makes them distinct from, as well as similar to, the late-twentieth-century Euro-American femme films. Such an elaboration will allow us to see the extent to which these telemovies bespeak a distinct sexual epistemology, with its own characteristic forms and tendencies corresponding to its geo-culturally particular history and present. Below I elaborate some characteristics of the Taiwanese schoolgirl romance telemovies, aside from their already distinctive emphasis on actual school settings, which set them apart from the Euro-American examples analyzed by critics of the femme film.

First, unlike the films discussed by both Holmlund and Hollinger, with their uniformly feminine lesbian characters, the central couples in the Taiwanese telemovies are organized by dimorphous secondary gender; while the protagonists Tong Suxin and Lu Manli are feminine—or *po*-like—women, their partners, Zhong Yuan and Shen Yijun, are distinguished by their complementary tomboy style. Second, as I will show, exploiting the distinct formal properties of the visual medium, the Taiwanese films foreground the desiring gaze of the feminine protagonist at her tomboy partner in such a way that the spectator's gaze is aligned with that of the films' protagonists; hence— very interestingly—the spectator is interpellated as *herself* desiring the tomboy who is the object of the protagonist's gaze. Finally, as with the literary examples of the schoolgirl romance narrative discussed in chapters 1–3, the ideological subtext of these telemovies is markedly differentiated from the commonplace cultural wisdom that "lesbianism [is] an unsatisfactory stage on the road to more fulfilling heterosexuality."[18] Instead, the films figure proto-marital heterosexuality as a traumatic social injunction that prematurely truncates the "real" same-sex love story.

The reading I propose for *Voice of Waves* and *The Maidens' Dance* has something in common with Patricia White's interpretation of Kimberley Peirce's American teen romance *Boys Don't Cry* (1999), although the films themselves differ very significantly from *Boys* in a number of respects. Observing that *Boys'* centering subjectivity, with which the spectator is consistently invited to identify, is that of the transgendered Brandon Teena's conventionally feminine lover, Lana, White proposes that *Boys* forges "an insistent link between the . . . transgendered figure and the romance genre."[19] A similar set of proposals can be made about the Taiwanese telemovies. Sitting, like *Boys*, firmly within the romance genre, these films at all times frame their tomboy characters, Zhong Yuan and Shen Yijun, from a perspective that could be—and most of the time straightforwardly is—that of their feminine girlfriends.[20] In both films, the look of the protagonist at her tomboy girlfriend is foregrounded and aligned with that of the spectator (figures 18 and 19). In figure 20 from *The Maidens' Dance*, for example, the spectator is positioned close alongside Tong Suxin in a tight over-the-shoulder shot that makes us almost the object of Zhong Yuan's intensely desiring look at her girlfriend. This sequence is shot entirely from Tong's perspective—there is no answering close-up over-the-shoulder reverse-shot from Zhong's side of the exchange, which underscores the film's invitation to the spectator to identify with Tong. Interestingly, the visual alignment of the spectator with Tong Suxin occurs perhaps most clearly at the moment when Tong kisses Zhong on the night before her own wedding (figure 21). The kiss is caught in the mirror on Tong's bedroom wall, and the mirror's inverted optics produce some interesting effects for spectatorial identification. Although both women's eyes are closed, the camera angle projects the spectator very clearly into the position of Tong Suxin, to the right of the mirror, being kissed by Zhong Yuan, who now only *seems* to have her back to us by virtue of the mirror's optical inversion. Zhong Yuan occupies the center of both the mirror's frame and the camera's, held as firmly in our field of vision as she is in Tong's embrace, and framed as the object of desire for both Tong Suxin and ourselves.[21]

In other scenes, the protagonist's gaze dominates the frame, as it does in *Waves*, with Zhong Yuan positioned as the object of Tong's look. One such instance occurs at a key turning point in the narrative: the moment when Tong Suxin first becomes aware of her sexual desire for Zhong Yuan. Interestingly, in the literary work on which the telemovie is based this moment is represented in strongly scopophilic terms. Cao Lijuan writes as follows:

> In the dim twilight I searched for Zhong Yuan in the swimming pool. Suddenly the lamps by the side of the pool lit up, one after the other, and I caught sight of two slick, shiny arms slicing through the foaming water, swimming toward me. When she reached the edge of the pool Zhong Yuan leapt from the water, all soft and shiny, like a fish. The water dripped from the hair of this upright fish, flowing down her face, her neck . . . all the way down to form a puddle at her feet. I looked up at Zhong Yuan—she was a lot taller than me—and her wet black hair was plastered flat to her head,

走啦... 快去吃冰啦

lending her face a slick luster. The veins on that neck, the water droplet hanging from the point of the chin, those lips, the nose, the eyes, the eyelashes . . . I was transfixed. The Zhong Yuan before me was a translucent statue, emitting from within it a soft, steady light that at sixteen, I had never seen before. Suddenly, as if bewitched, I was compelled to reach out and touch the source of that light.[22]

In the following paragraph the language turns tactile, as Tong Suxin's fingertips touch Zhong Yuan's "lustrous, elastic, breathing skin" and "a hot flush mingling wonder, horror, excitement and shame passed swiftly through [her] body," but the logic of the passage quoted above is visual rather than haptic. As dim twilight turns to electric brilliance, the illuminating power of the poolside lamps is transposed to Zhong Yuan's body, experienced by Tong Suxin as a montage of wet, translucent skin surfaces that seem lit from within. Tong's gaze processes Zhong's body as a piecemeal series of visual impressions—slick, shiny, slicing arms; dripping hair; face; neck; feet; veins in the neck; point of the chin; lips; nose; eyes; eyelashes—punctuated by suggestive ellipses. This eroticizing fragmentation of Zhong Yuan's body mimics a cinematic logic: Tong Suxin's gaze works like the camera of classical narrative cinema, eagerly fetishizing the body parts displayed before it. Yet, of course, this is a scopophilic gaze with a difference. Not only is it wielded by a woman over the body of another woman, but it is the feminine partner who directs the gaze at the tomboy body of her sweetheart; Tong's look elides any markers of corporeal femininity to concentrate instead on the tomboy-masculine signifiers of Zhong's relative height and athleticism. The passage presents a compelling literary figuration of the active sexual desire of the *po* for her tomboy lover.

Given its highly cinematic sensibility, this literary passage appears ripe for a filmic adaptation to direct spectatorial attention toward the eroticized

---

18. Yijun (right) with Lin Long in *Voices of Waves* (dir. Lisa Chen Xiuyu, 2002). The following reaction shot aligns the spectator's gaze retrospectively with the point of view of Xiao Li.

19. Xiao Li watches the sweethearts, entranced, as her classmate A Fen drags her reluctantly off on a date to eat shaved ice with some boys. *Voices of Waves* (dir. Lisa Chen Xiuyu, 2002).

20. A young Zhong Yuan gazes intensely at a shy Tong Suxin in *The Maidens' Dance* (dir. Tsao Jui-yuan, 2002).

21. Tong and Zhong's final kiss on the eve of Tong's wedding, framed in a mirror in *The Maidens' Dance* (dir. Tsao Jui-yuan, 2002).

tomboy body. Yet while this moment in the narrative is indeed foregrounded in *The Maidens' Dance* telemovie adaptation, the filmic treatment of the scene is quite different from what Cao's short story would lead us to expect. While the scene does include a few seconds of blue underwater shots of Zhong Yuan swimming, the overwhelming visual emphasis is on Tong Suxin's activity of *watching* Zhong Yuan (figure 22). After Zhong leaves the water, her body is quickly obscured by her towel, while Tong's face remains in frame at all times. Never are we offered a point-of-view shot attributed to Tong; instead, we watch the spectacle of Tong watching and touching Zhong (figure 23). Mary Anne Doane's classic analysis of the distinctive structuring of the gaze in the woman's film is apposite here:

> Because the "woman's film" obsessively centers and re-centers a female protagonist, placing her in a position of agency, it offers some resistance to an analysis which stresses the "to-be-looked-at-ness" of the woman, her objectification as spectacle according to the masculine structure of the gaze. . . . The textual assumption of a specifically female spectator also entails that she does not adopt a masculine position with respect to the cinematic image of the female body. In other words, because the female gaze is not associated with the psychical mechanisms of voyeurism and fetishism, it is no longer necessary to invest the look with desire *in quite the same way*. A certain de-spectacularization takes place in these films, a deflection of scopophiliac energy in other directions, away from the female body.[23]

In the case of *The Maidens' Dance*, the generic conventions of the woman's film see scopophiliac energy deflected away from the tomboy body—its proper object—and reinvested in the spectacle of her feminine sweetheart's desiring look. What is foregrounded in this scene, in other words, is the protagonist's visual agency and subjectivity; Zhong Yuan's body is eroticized only insofar as the spectator is prompted to identify with Tong Suxin's activity of watching and desiring it. Thus, although in one sense this scene is undeniably concerned with the erotic desirability of the tomboy body, unlike in Cao's literary text, here the spectator/reader is not invited to desire that body directly on its own merits but is prompted rather to desire it at a second remove, by identifying with the feminine protagonist in *her* desire. Here, as throughout both of the telemovies, the emphasis is squarely on the affective experience of the protagonist.

This marked tendency in both *Voices of Waves* and *The Maidens' Dance* to invite spectatorial identification with the feminine protagonist in her desire for the

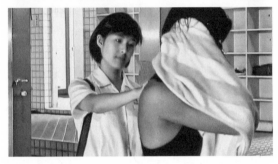

22. Tong Suxin watches Zhong Yuan swimming in *The Maidens' Dance* (dir. Tsao Jui-yuan, 2002).

23. Tong Suxin touches Zhong Yuan by the pool in *The Maidens' Dance* (dir. Tsao Jui-yuan, 2002).

tomboy has at least two important implications. First and most obviously, as White argues in relation to a comparable tendency in *Boys Don't Cry*, this strategy makes the feminine, transgender- or tomboy-attracted protagonist's "desire and way of seeing *count*."[24] It marks the telemovies as "*po* texts," which authorize, foreground, and revel in the particular pleasures of the tomboy-attracted feminine woman. Placing this form of subjectivity and desire at the center of the frame is particularly significant given the general cultural tendency to discount this type of desire not once but twice: first, insofar as feminine subjects in general tend to be constructed as the objects rather than the subjects of sexual desire; second, insofar as the feminine woman's love for the masculine one is all too easily discounted as merely a displacement of or precursor to her proper desire for "real" masculinity. Further, if, as I propose, these telemovies can be said to school their viewer in the pleasures of loving female masculinity by inviting her to identify with their protagonists' love for the tomboy, then they also enact a powerfully reparative tactic in relation to the tomboy herself. As we have seen in previous chapters, in the monstrously gender-inverted proto-lesbian of Yu Dafu and her psychologically anguished mass-cultural descendants of more recent years, there exists a powerful and historically entrenched modern Chinese discourse on the masculine lesbian that constructs her precisely as unlovable. In the face of that mode of representation, these films could be said symbolically to "repair" the masculine woman by positioning her as the object of the *po*'s—and the spectator's—love and desire. The popularity and cultural ubiquity of these and similar *po* narratives suggests that however influential the minoritizing construction of the masculine lesbian as an unlovable monster, that construction is nonetheless answered by an at least equally pervasive discourse that frames the masculine woman as the proper and cherished object of a universalized feminine love.

The Tomboy Vanishes—Again

But what do our feminine protagonists see when they look at their tomboy sweethearts? Closer attention to the formal organization of the telemovies reveals that there are in fact two distinct types of *po* looks. One, on which I have focused so far, is an appreciative, desiring, or contented gaze that expresses positive affect (figures 17, 22, and 23). This look dominates in the first part of each film. The second kind of look, by contrast, is characterized by negative affect; it is a sad, despairing, or anguished look that predominates in the latter part of each film as the tomboy begins, sometimes literally, to disappear from her girlfriend's field of vision. In their thematic focus on the tomboy's disappearance, these telemovies seem again to answer to the mass-cultural tomboy texts discussed in the previous chapter. Whereas, as we have seen, examples like *Outside the Circle* and *The Unfilial Daughter* chronicle the painful process of the tomboy's premature demise from the tomboy's own point of view, these programs view the tomboy's disappearance from the perspective of her feminine sweetheart.

The "vanishing tomboy" narrative is effected in *Voice of Waves* through the persistent implication that Shen Yijun is on the point of disappearing—or has already disappeared—into the ocean. This is suggested not only in the strong implication that Yijun ultimately committed suicide by drowning herself at sea, but also through the film's formal organization in the flashback scenes where the young Xiao Li watches Yijun swimming. Figures 24–27 describe a sequence near the end of the film in which the protagonist's anguished look at her disappearing tomboy lover is central.

The implication of this sequence that Yijun has swum out to sea, never to return, cannot be literally true since we know that Yijun died only recently, when Xiao Li was already an adult. Nevertheless, the mournful mood created by the scene of Yijun disappearing out to sea, leaving Xiao Li gazing hopelessly after her, dominates the film. Through insistent repetition, the scenario of the disappearing tomboy is presented as a kind of primal scene that haunts the adult Xiao Li's dreams, compelling her to resign from her job and dump her fiancé to revisit the site where Yijun disappeared from her life. The film's narrative logic implies, in turn, that this recurring image of Yijun disappearing, watched by a helpless Xiao Li, represents the affective impact on Xiao Li of the injunction ultimately issued by her mother and classmates that she stop seeing Yijun (figure 28). In Xiao Li's imagination, Yijun disappears out to sea; in Xiao Li's life, it is instead the possibility of loving Yijun that disappears, as a result of social prohibition. In its critical staging of the painful renunciation of same-sex love that a young woman learns she must complete as a rite of passage into the social category of "woman," this contemporary telemovie recalls the early-twentieth-century literary examples of schoolgirl romance discussed in chapter 1.[25]

The vanishing tomboy also features in *The Maidens' Dance*. Indeed, the narrative of this film is centrally structured by Zhong Yuan's repeated disappearance and sporadic reappearance in Tong Suxin's life. From the moment when the young Zhong kisses Tong and Tong becomes confused and suggests that

宜君，快上來

宜君，快上來

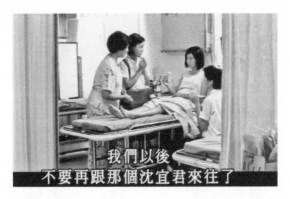

28. Xiao Li in hospital after the bike accident with Yijun. Xiao Li's mother, backed up by her classmates, advises: "Let's not hang around with that Shen Yijun anymore." *Voices of Waves* (dir. Lisa Chen Xiuyu, 2002).

they break up, the relationship between the two is presented as a sequence of scenes in which Tong searches in vain for the elusive Zhong only to have her reappear—and again disappear—when least expected. Zhong's trademark disappearing act is presented in the film with graphic literalness: following the two girls' breakup, as Tong's voice-over recounts receiving a curt note from Zhong—"I'm switching schools. Goodbye."—we watch from the tearful Tong's perspective as Zhong literally vanishes from the screen (figures 29–31).

The film's preoccupation with Zhong Yuan's tendency to vanish is reprised in the penultimate scene, in which Tong Suxin looks out the back window of the car that is taking her away to be married toward a Zhong Yuan whom we know is watching her departure but who is already lost to sight (figures 32 and 33). This shot figures visually what I propose is the underlying logic of these films' shared preoccupation with the vanishing tomboy. While in

---

24. An adult Xiao Li gazes out to sea after Yijun's death, with a voiceover from her young self: "Yijun, come back!" *Voices of Waves* (dir. Lisa Chen Xiuyu, 2002).

25. Flashback to the young Xiao Li calling Yijun in *Voices of Waves* (dir. Lisa Chen Xiuyu, 2002).

26. Yijun hears Xiao Li calling but does not turn back to shore in *Voices of Waves* (dir. Lisa Chen Xiuyu, 2002).

27. The young Xiao Li turns despairing as Yijun seems to disappear out to sea in *Voices of Waves* (dir. Lisa Chen Xiuyu, 2002).

29–31. A tearful Tong Suxin watches Zhong Yuan disappear in *The Maidens' Dance* (dir. Tsao Jui-yuan, 2002).

32. Zhong Yuan watches as Tong Suxin is driven off to be married in *The Maidens' Dance* (dir. Tsao Jui-yuan, 2002).

33. The bridal Tong Suxin looks back toward Zhong Yuan, already lost to sight, in *The Maidens' Dance* (dir. Tsao Jui-yuan, 2002).

many of the other shots in which the protagonists are gazing mournfully after their disappearing tomboy sweethearts, they look straight ahead, in this shot, Tong Suxin looks *behind* her for her final glimpse of her vanishing lover. Tong's backward glance captures graphically the temporal logic of the memorial mode that, as I have argued throughout this book, characteristically structures the schoolgirl romance narrative. As the tomboy lover disappears visually behind Tong Suxin's bridal car, she also disappears temporally into the adult, ambivalently "heterosexual" Tong Suxin's past. Insofar as both *Voice of Waves* and *The Maidens' Dance* are structured by the memorial mode and both, like the literary narratives analyzed in chapters 1 and 2, represent heterosexual marriage as the result of an enforced social imperative rather than as the spontaneous outcome of the protagonists' sexual development, the disappearing tomboy in both films functions as a personification of the disappearance of the possibility of same-sex love from the lives of the feminine protagonists. That, as exemplars of the generic logic of tragic romance, these programs unambiguously cue their viewers to experience the disappearance of this possibility *as tragic* suggests once again that contemporary schoolgirl romance narratives imply a critical stance toward the heterosexual social system, whose inevitability they simultaneously seem to presume.

Remembering Schoolgirl Romance: Viewer Responses

If through their formal and narrative organization *The Maidens' Dance* and *Voice of Waves* solicit spectatorial identification with their reminiscent, feminine, tomboy-attracted protagonists, then how is this textual suggestion taken up in the responses of actual audiences? Judging by the viewers who posted their responses to the programs on PTS's BBS forum, the programs' invitation to identification is remarkably successful. The memorial cast of the telemovies produces a markedly mimetic effect among viewers: there is a strong tendency in the viewer responses to these telemovies to write personal memory narratives. Consider the following responses to *The Maidens' Dance*:

> I myself am a girl
> And I have loved a girl
> I will always remember that gym class in junior high
> When a cool girl basketball player whom I didn't know led me in a waltz
> After a dizzy turn about the floor
> I really missed that flowing feeling
> I guess that must be the feeling of first love.[26]

It's not important to me what other people think about the movie. I experienced its intended effect very strongly; it was just like my own complex emotions in high school. . . . It was like watching my own story.[27]

This film truly does represent the emotional attachment between two women; many people, in the process of coming to identify as lesbian [tongzhi], go through this kind of phase; I myself went through it, and I was touched and moved to see someone telling this kind of story with the camera.[28]

I'm not a lesbian [nütongzhi], but . . . seeing The Maidens' Dance and The Unfilial Daughter has reawakened a memory that has been slumbering in some corner of my memory: in primary school, I fell in love with a girl classmate. . . . Today this is only a memory, but I think that's a beautiful experience for a girl [shaonü] to have.[29]

And consider the following in relation to Voice of Waves:

In this film, my own student days and the environment I grew up in find an echo . . . [that] once again stirs the secret memories in my heart.[30]

It portrays those subtle, simple feelings between one girl and another; although the feelings are without desire . . . yet they so stir the heart . . . It's as though one is emotionally transported back to those pure, midsummer years, back to the limpid days of that time . . . that fluttering heart . . . on account of that girl . . . those surging yet repressed emotions.[31]

Although I'm a heterosexual, I have a memory of high school that's just like Xiao Li's. The whole class cared only about gossiping, and "she" was just like Yijun in the movie: solitary yet intelligent and better than the other girls at math. I used to always ask her questions and seek out any chance to get a bit closer to her, to get to know her. . . . That's three or four years ago now, and I've since had several heterosexual love affairs, but . . . deep in my heart, the middle-school "she" still resides. . . . Perhaps regret is the most beautiful emotion.[32]

As these quotations demonstrate, such personal memorial narratives are written in response to the telemovies both by heterosexual-identifying women, who often preface them with "Even though I'm not a lesbian . . ." or "Even I, a heterosexual woman, still recall . . . ," and by lesbian-identifying women, who tend to frame these memories as indicative prehistories of their lesbian presents. In other words, these programs offer points of purchase for a range of sexual and gendered identifications that may be based either on a minoritizing understanding of essential lesbian identity or on a universalizing understanding of an adult "heterosexual" femininity that incorporates same-sex attraction and cross-sex sexual practice without producing a lesbian or bisexual (or indeed a straightforwardly heterosexual) identity per se.[33] From the perspective of queer popular culture studies, the enthusiastically identificatory response to the programs by straight-identifying female viewers is possibly the more interesting one by virtue of being less expected, and it is this response on which I concentrate here. However, given that self-identifying lesbian viewers also produce memorial narratives in response to these programs—narratives that certainly do shore up adult lesbian identity—it would be a mistake to presume that the universalizing sex-gender epistemology of tomboy-attracted femininity is the only one available to the programs' viewers. Rather, the duality of responses to the programs by both lesbian- and straight-identifying viewers bespeaks a nonsingular epistemological field, where conceptualizations of sexuality based in a metaphysics of sexual identity (homo versus hetero) coexist alongside other, nonidentitarian models of sexual subjecthood.[34]

One of the most interesting things about these televisual going-in stories, then, is that they lend support both to minoritizing lesbian identity politics and to a universalizing sex-gender epistemology that would seem logically to trouble lesbian appeals to a metaphysics of sexual identity.[35] To a significant degree, in the programs themselves the distinction between minoritizing and universalizing constructions of sexual love between women is mapped onto the distinction between the secondary genders of the main characters. Tomboys are constructed on a minoritizing model; as is also the case in the tomboy texts discussed in chapter 4, they form a distinct and recognizable sex-gender minority. But the tomboys' feminine sweethearts are represented according to a universalizing paradigm; effectively, any woman might love a tomboy.[36] In the remainder of this chapter, I will be most interested in the memorial narratives of the "temporarily homosexual" protagonists. These stories' proposal of pleasurable homoerotic adolescent memory as a foundational psychic experience for adult "heterosexual" women seems to me to offer promising potential for unraveling the meanings of straight femininity itself in this cultural context, thus productively complicating our understanding of what superficially may appear too obvious to warrant critical scrutiny.[37]

In his extended study of personal sexual narratives, *Telling Sexual Stories*, Plummer draws out some important further questions:

[In contemporary sociological interpretations] no longer do people simply "tell" their sexual stories to reveal the "truth" of their sexual lives; instead, they turn themselves into *socially organized biographical subjects.* They construct—even invent . . .—tales of the intimate self, which may or may not bear a relationship to a truth. Are their stories really to be seen as the simple unfolding of some inner truth? *Or are their very stories something they are brought to say in a particular way through a particular time and place?* And if so, where do they get their "stories" from?[38]

In Plummer's terms, the interpretive community that gathers at the PTS Drama BBS board to narrate its personal memories of adolescent same-sex love "gets its stories" from a wider historical and social context where such narratives both fit into and contribute to an existing coherence system and hence make cultural sense.[39] This coherence system, I suggest, is constituted by the particular sexual epistemology whose contours I have been tracing throughout this book. While the tomboy is seen as a sex-gender minority, this epistemology understands the feminine woman's love for the tomboy in universalizing terms, such that this form of love is generalizable to any woman; and for any woman, the potent memorability of that latterly proscribed form of love is judged likely to remain a notable component of adult psychic life.

Thus, although these narratives aptly illustrate the general structure of Plummer's sociology of stories, the details of the narratives themselves differ in important respects from his characterization of the prototypal modernist sexual story, of which the coming-out story is one example.[40] Conspicuously absent from going-in stories told from the point of view of "heterosexuals"-to-be is the scanning of the past for clues to the narrator's essential sexual being; the "sense of an identity . . . hidden from the surface awaiting clearer recognition, labeling, categorizing"; and the atmosphere of solitude, secrecy, and silence that in Plummer's account characterizes personal narratives produced by those in search of a (homo)sexual identity.[41] In short, for the fictional recollectors Tong Suxin and Lu Manli and the nonlesbian-identifying women viewers who identify with them, the memorial narrative of adolescent same-sex romance is not centrally concerned with coming to inhabit a minority sexual identity. Unlike the modernist sexual stories discussed by Plummer, for their feminine protagonists and nonlesbian viewers, these memorial narratives do not produce sexual identity in the present (either homosexual or heterosexual) as a primary effect—in fact, chief among their effects is precisely a problematization of the seeming transparency and opposition of those terms. Also in distinction to the coming-out story as characterized by

Plummer, this narrative is not *necessarily* productive of a strongly demarcated subcultural interpretive community, precisely because its implicit theory of tomboy-attracted femininity is a universalizing rather than a minoritizing one; under certain conditions, the story of love between adolescent girls can thus be encompassed by, rather than challenging to, the dominant culture of femininity. What kind of an "any woman," though, is produced by this universalizing discourse on remembered adolescent tomboy love? What are the effects of the memorial schoolgirl romance for the nonlesbian-identified adult feminine subject whose identification these narratives so successfully solicit?

Mournful Femininity

The relative prominence of memorial schoolgirl romance narratives in the literary and popular cultures of mainland China, Hong Kong, and Taiwan today raises interesting questions about the public mourning of the loss of adolescent women's same-sex erotic attachment in social contexts where adult heterosexuality remains, as the narratives themselves clearly indicate, effectively a compulsory requirement. Judith Butler's work on melancholia, gender identification, and the culturally prescribed renunciation of homosexual attachment in Euro-American contexts resonates suggestively here.[42] Taking up Freud's theorization of melancholia as involving the subject's identificatory incorporation of a lost object, Butler proposes that melancholic identification with the same-sex parent—barred from the young child as an object of libidinal attachment, hence effectively "lost"—may be seen as central to the ego's assuming of a gendered character. Hence, "the girl becomes a girl through being subject to a prohibition which bars the mother as an object of desire and installs the barred object as a part of the ego, indeed, as a melancholic identification."[43]

In the context of the present attempt to theorize the cultural labor performed by Chinese schoolgirl romances in the memorial mode, I am not interested in empirical claims about the psychosexual development of individuals that might be made or refuted on the basis of Butler's proposals. I am more interested in the *cultural* ramifications of rethinking the complexly overdetermined relationship between same-sex love and memory.[44] Several times in her 1997 essay "Melancholy Gender/Refused Identification," Butler emphasizes that the theory of melancholic identification illuminates "the predicament of living in a culture which can mourn the loss of homosexual attachment only with great difficulty."[45] Linking her argument explicitly with a particular and limited cultural and historical context, that of North American late modernity, she elucidates a key point: "To the extent that homosexual attachments remain unacknowledged within normative heterosexuality, they are not merely constituted as desires which emerge and subsequently become prohibited; rather, these desires are proscribed from the start. . . . As such, they will not be attachments that can be openly grieved. This is, then, less a *refusal* to grieve . . . than a preemption of grief performed by *the absence of cultural conventions for avowing the loss of homosexual love*. And this absence produces a culture of heterosexual melancholy."[46]

The question that arises from this theory in relation to the adolescent girls' romance narrative in contemporary Chinese literary and screen cultures is whether this narrative, with all its relative public visibility, may in fact constitute just such a set of cultural conventions for collectively avowing the loss of homosexual love between women—the very conventions Butler fails to find in contemporary North American contexts. Unlike the situation Butler describes, in which the possibility of homosexual attachment is not so much prohibited as foreclosed, "proscribed from the start," rendering lost homosexual attachment ungrievable and hence generative of melancholia, these stories seem quite precisely to bespeak an open cultural *recognition* of same-gender libidinal attachments between adolescent women.[47] Could we not read this pervasive narrative of love between adolescent girls tragically lost and latterly recollected as a critical dramatization of the psychic trauma caused by the prohibition on sexual relations between adult women—in effect, as a kind of public, ritualized *mourning* over the forceful imposition of the hetero-marital imperative?

Moreover, if the relative prominence of adolescent girls' romance narratives in contemporary Chinese popular cultures reveals a situation in which the possibility of same-sex love is figured not as preemptively foreclosed but instead as belatedly prohibited after its initial, intensely memorable emergence, then what are the implications of this for dominant forms of "straight" feminine subjecthood? We seem to be left with an adult "heterosexual" feminine subject whose identity, unlike that of her American counterpart in Butler's account, is decidedly *not* based on her unwillingness to avow her prior homosexual attachment and hence her inability to grieve it.[48] Instead, the "heterosexual" feminine subject that emerges from these narratives, both as the characters within them and as the many straight-identifying readers and viewers who continue enthusiastically to engage with the stories in fictional, televisual, and filmic forms, is based on the reluctant forced abandonment of homosexual attachment and the ongoing ritualized mourning of this lost attachment. This mourning is then publicly enacted in the compulsion to write, read, watch, exchange, discuss, and otherwise consume and produce the narrative of schoolgirl romance in the memorial mode. In other words, the sexual and gendered formation that these narratives imply is one of "heterosexual" femininity in a mournful rather than a melancholic mode.[49] This formation is thus distinguished both from melancholic heterosexual femininity as discussed by Butler and from the melancholic sexual and gendered subjectivity of the narrator of mainland Chinese author Liu Suola's novella "Blue Sky Green Sea" (discussed in chapter 3). Unlike melancholic femininity, mournful femininity knows what it has lost—and never stops grieving it. Its pictorial analogue is found in figures 27, 29, and 33 above, where the sad young women Tong Suxin and Lu Manli gaze with intense, mournful yearning back toward the vanishing tomboy sweethearts of their adolescence.[50] To link the textual representations with the social function that they perform for their audiences, one might say that the consumption of these texts functions as a practice of women's social memory.[51] In this sense the texts archive a particular structure of feeling; in their circulation, consumption, and constant rewriting, an individual affective experience of same-sex love lost and mourned becomes collectivized and publicly acknowledged within the field of women's popular culture.

Schoolgirl Romance as Embedded Critique

But where does this leave us? Is a mournful femininity any the less robust in its heterosexual effects than a melancholic one, any the less conventional in its feminine ones? Does the prevalence of semi-public, ritualized mourning for the loss of women's same-sex attachment translate into any weakening of the "heterosexual matrix" or any heightened cultural "tolerance" for same-sex attachments in Chinese societies more broadly, along the lines that some commentators have proposed?[52] Does this mode of female homoerotic representation have a critical function in positing adolescence as a moment when the possibility of alternative, utopian sexual futures is decisively raised only to be defensively—and always incompletely—quashed by the heteromarital imperative? Or, on the other hand, is the confinement of the same-sex loving woman to memory and adolescence in these narratives an inherently reactionary ploy, barring her appearance in the present and in adulthood, as has been claimed by some local lesbian critics? Given the continuing active discouragement of homosexuality in actual young women by families and school authorities in the Chinese societies under discussion, might these stories in fact perform the function of "inoculations" against the cultural threat of sexual relationships between women? Could one speculate, in that case, that far from becoming destabilized, heterosexual power may in fact be rendered more supple and comprehensive by this repeated public avowal of the painful—though implicitly inevitable—renunciation of homosexual attachment by young women?

The virtual autoproliferation of such questions indicates the ease with which arguments could be advanced in support of either proposition; doubtless such consideration would lead ultimately to that ubiquitous third alternative: the conclusion that the phenomenon in question is partly disciplinary, partly resistant.[53] But perhaps the most interesting questions here do not concern the extent of conservatism versus transgression of the sexual and gendered subjecthood that the schoolgirl romance posits. Nor am I interested in posing again that all-too-common default question of an emergent comparative queer studies: "How repressed is homosexuality there, as compared to here?"[54] Instead, I want to ask how particular representations produce sexual and gender knowledges in the first place. The key question then becomes: What kind of a "heterosexual" femininity is both inhabited and defined by the openly avowed memory of an idealized, adolescent same-sex love whose intensity, it readily concedes, can never be approximated in heterosexual relations in the present? The point in posing that question is not to imply that such a sexuality is somehow inherently subversive. But both in their own structure and in the social uses to which contemporary audiences put them, these narratives do project a model of adult femininity whose internal organization vis-à-vis both gender and sexuality is historically and culturally distinctive. As I have proposed, the contemporary Chinese schoolgirl romances rest on an implied theory of sexuality in which straight femininity is more the result of an externally enforced social imperative prohibiting the further pursuit of adolescent same-sex relations than it is the spontaneous outcome of the individual's psychosexual development. Moreover, as this chapter has shown, the form of adult femininity advanced by this implicit theory is defined by a persistent, mournful yearning for the latterly prohibited but openly memorable same-sex attachments of youth.

The most useful framework for considering the remarkably pervasive narrative of schoolgirl romance may be in terms of the distinctively inflected form of modern sexual culture that it implies: a sexual culture that incorporates an enduring critique of its own regulation of feminine sexuality.[55] To underscore the critical potential of these stories' powerfully denaturalizing representations of the hetero-marital imperative and their radical uses of nostalgia is not the same as claiming for them either a culturally unique or an inherently "resistant" function. I have tried to show that the critique implied by these schoolgirl romances does not function in simple opposition to, but is itself a notable strand embedded within, the intricate warp and weft of modern Chinese sexual epistemology. Hegemonic organizations of sexuality and gender in modern Chinese contexts, in other words, are irreducibly multiple in their very substance; they do not merely mandate marital heterosexuality but also deplore it; they do not only forbid same-sex attachments but also invite them.[56] In response to the question raised above in this book—What do contemporary Chinese publics *want* with the story of romance between young women?—one might speculate, then, that the schoolgirl romance is wanted by contemporary Chinese publics not only for its function as a catalyst for women's practices of social memory, but also more specifically for its readily accessible critique of the modern disciplining of women's gender and sexuality. In longingly invoking the only-ever-imagined future of adolescent women's same-sex love, the narrative's characteristic ellipsis gestures toward those compelling alternative possibilities that are at once prohibited and produced by modern regimes of sexual regulation.

. . .

SIX

Critical Presentism

New Chinese Lesbian Cinema

If, as the foregoing chapters have argued, the dominant metaphor shaping female homoerotic representation in transnational Chinese popular and entertainment cultures today is a temporal one, then one would expect to see this temporal preoccupation reflected in the medium of film. This chapter examines a selection of Chinese-language films made in recent years in the People's Republic of China, Hong Kong, and Taiwan to gauge the extent to which the memorial mode informs their depictions of love between women. A special focus in the latter part of the chapter will be on a recent wave of films made by a new generation of young, independent women filmmakers in which lesbian relations, openly and unequivocally represented on screen, form the cornerstone of the story.[1] Whereas chapter 5 read "against the grain" of the relatively mainstream, mass-cultural form of the made-for-television schoolgirl romance drama to uncover the latent critical function of this popular narrative, this chapter turns to the arguably more marginal form of women's independent cinema, including Chen Jofei's *Hai jiao tian ya* (Incidental Journey; Taiwan, 2001); Mak Yan Yan's *Hudie* (Butterfly; Hong Kong, 2004); and Li Yu's *Jinnian xiatian* (Fish and Elephant; China, 2001). Here we find a more reflexive and overtly critical reconfiguration of the memorial mode itself. Following a brief survey of the ways in which female homoerotic memorialism has informed Chinese-language cinema more broadly, the chapter considers how this new crop of independent, lesbian-themed films both references and complicates this familiar mode of representation. How do these films' representations of time—by means of style and technique, as well as narrative—underscore and play off the inherent ideological instabilities in the memorial mode of female homoerotic representation? How do the films' representations of lesbian relations resist the memorial mode's dogged (if never fully successful) attempts to impose a linear temporal structure that forces bygones to be bygones, quarantined from the narrative present by time's ineluctable forward march? In sum, how do these films reproduce the temporally fixated representational and ideological structures that culturally frame women's same-sex love in these societies while at the same time critically transforming those familiar structures?

Female Homoerotic Memorialism in Chinese Cinemas

Echoing a similar preoccupation in Western lesbian theory more broadly, a highly influential approach to analyzing lesbian representation in American and European cinemas takes as central the visual logic particular to the medium, asking questions about lesbian visibility versus invisibility, on the one hand, and voyeuristic versus counter-voyeuristic images of lesbians, on the other.[2] Teresa de Lauretis's path-breaking analyses of Sheila McLaughlin's film She Must Be Seeing Things (1987) exemplify this post-Mulveyan approach of interrogating the gendering and sexuality of vision itself as a means of unlocking the inner logic of lesbian representation in Western cinema. Framing McLaughlin's film as representative of lesbian resistance to the masculinism and heterosexism of dominant forms of visual representation, de Lauretis argues that such works strive to "devis[e] strategies of representation which will . . . alter the standard of vision, the frame of reference of visibility, of what can be seen."[3] In highlighting the problem of visual representation itself, McLaughlin's film both reflects and critically responds to Euro-American visual culture's subjection of women's sexuality, and therefore lesbian sexuality, to dominant, phallocentric gender ideology. Patricia White's UnInvited makes a different use of the post-Mulveyan emphasis on the politics of visuality in analyzing lesbian representations in cinema. Focusing on films made during the years of the Production Code, which prohibited any direct or implied reference to "sex perversion" on screen, White argues that these films both provided opportunities for lesbian spectatorial pleasure in decoding their queer subtexts and contributed to the construction of modern lesbian identity itself.[4] As White observes, the Production Code era (from the mid-1930s until the 1960s) coincides closely with the cultural elaboration of the lesbian as a social personage; Hollywood cinema, both as filmic texts and as a set of social practices, was central to defining what the lesbian was to mean for twentieth-century Western culture. Given this, it is not the case for White that by not representing the lesbian directly, classical Hollywood cinema *failed* to represent her or "repressed" lesbian meanings; rather, this cinema constructed the lesbian as precisely a problem of visualization.[5] A significant strand of work on lesbian representation in post-1960s Western film has analyzed how lesbian and anti-homophobic filmmakers respond to the visual problematics outlined in different ways by de Lauretis and White. For example, Andrea Weiss's chapter on independent lesbian filmmaking in her book *Vampires and Violets* is centrally concerned with how lesbian filmmakers have sought to counter lesbian invisibility by rendering the lesbian visible in their films.[6] On the other hand, Weiss also underscores these filmmakers' attempts to deflect the voyeuristic gaze on lesbian sex that has characterized the masculinist European art cinema tradition—an exploitative spectacularization that amounts to the inverse problem to the lesbian's de-visualization in classical Hollywood cinema.[7] Thus, as a result of the particular histories of Western dominant, alternative, and resistant filmmaking practices, questions about visuality have seemed particularly urgent to ask of lesbian representation in Western cinema. Have lesbians been rendered visible, invisible, exploitatively hyper-visible, or paradoxically visible in their very erasure? And how can lesbian filmmakers, audiences, and critics respond to these conditions of lesbian visualization?

In the Chinese-language cinemas of the People's Republic of China and Taiwan, strict government censorship directed mainly at political but also at "moral" content rendered the onscreen representation of sexual love between women an impossibility from the midcentury until relatively recently; in Hong Kong film, too, lesbian characters and plots appeared very infrequently prior to the 1990s.[8] Superficially these histories might suggest parallels with the situation of American cinema: a long period of lesbian "erasure" followed by a period in which it becomes possible for the first time to visualize the lesbian on screen.[9] Yet despite this superficially comparable history, I argue in this chapter that the visual logic that has shaped many of the major discussions of lesbian representation in Western cinemas may not be the most productive framework to apply to the recent crop of lesbian-themed Chinese-language films, for close attention to the films themselves reveals that collectively, a question that concerns them at least as much as the question of visibility is that of temporality. These films seem to ask not so much "How has the image of the lesbian been structured by her erasure from dominant representations, and how should lesbian films today respond to that?" as "How has the image of the same-sex loving woman been structured by her relegation to pastness and memory in dominant representations, and how should lesbian films today respond to that?" Indeed, once one becomes alive to the conventions of the modern Chinese memorial mode of female homoerotic representation, one sees with what startling regularity it crops up in the films; collectively these films are highly "aware" of this mode, and it is a structuring presence in almost all of them. Following the lead of the films themselves, then, this chapter proposes the importance of asking questions about temporal logic in contemporary Chinese-language lesbian film. As White argues in relation to lesbian (in)visibility in classical Hollywood cinema, the pervasive theme of temporality in these recent films implies a broader significance for cultural understandings of women's same-sex love. Just as the preoccupation with lesbian (in)visibility in Western film reflects, contributes to, and sometimes challenges the familiar figure of the "invisible lesbian," so these films' preoccupation with temporality simultaneously echoes, reinforces, and complicates the dominant modern Chinese construction of female same-sex love as a memorial condition.

That the memorial mode of female homoerotic representation has pervaded the medium of film has already been seen in this book's introduction through the discussion of Alice Wang's *Love Me If You Can*.[10] The mode is equally—if differently—apparent in Hong Kong "art film" director Jacob Cheung Chi Leung's 1997 film *Ji sor/Zi shu* (Intimates). This film explores the cultural history of the practice of "self-combing"—marriage resistance and sworn sisterhood among women—that was prevalent in southern China in dynastic through Republican times. The film is structured around a series of flashbacks, as Wan (Ah Lei Gua/Carina Lau) recalls her younger days as the eighth wife of a silk factory owner and the loving bond that she formed with the "self-combed" girl who became her maid and later her intimate friend and lover, Foon (Yeung Choi Nei). Scenes with the elder Wan set in present-day Hong Kong and Canton alternate with scenes depicting Wan and Foon's young lives in the 1930s and 1940s, until finally in the film's closing scene the two women, now both in late middle age, are reunited after their decades-long separation. Reflecting the paradigmatic mode of modern Chinese female homoerotic representation, the film's flashback structure effectively renders the story of Wan and Foon's love as a series of backward glances into the distant past. Reinforcing this, when the two women are ultimately reunited in the present, their contemporary clothing magically reverts to the old Republican-era styles and their now elderly faces and bodies transform into their youthful forms as they embrace before walking, hand in hand, away from the camera as though back into their past. Thus even when Wan and Foon's relationship is at last permitted entry to the film's narrative present, it nonetheless remains symbolically condemned to a condition of essential pastness (figures 34 and 35).[11]

A similarly memorial logic is notable in Taiwanese director Lin Cheng-sheng's 1997 film *Meili zai chang ge* (Murmur of Youth). The film follows the growing friendship, which ultimately becomes a sexual relationship, between two young women in contemporary Taipei, both of whom are named Meili. Lin Meili (Jing Tseng) lives with her impoverished extended family in a traditional brick house in the mountain suburb of Xizhi, while the middle-class Chen Meili (Rene Liu) lives in her family's apartment in the city. The two Meilis are depicted as living parallel lives. The film commences with a cross-cut sequence that shows both women getting their period on the same night, and soon the two meet when they both take jobs selling tickets at a city cinema. Like *Intimates*, this film is centrally concerned with a historical exploration of social (as well as individual) memory; in this case, the subject matter is local Taiwanese cultural history.[12] Chen Meili uncovers the story of her now silent, listless father's youth as a sapphire miner in the remote southeastern Taitung region of the island, while Lin Meili hears from her father the tale of her grandmother's bitter past as a sing-song girl who married an itinerant laborer. Lin Meili's grandmother is now an elderly woman and is regularly visited by the spirit of her dead husband, who she says is calling her to her grave.

In contrast with the memorial narratives of these elder relatives, the relationship between the two Meilis initially seems to operate according to a presentist logic of coincidence and simultaneity; however, the old memorial logic reasserts itself very powerfully at the film's conclusion. After the two Meilis have sex one night in Chen Meili's bedroom, Chen awakes in the morning to find Lin gone and a note left beside the bed. She reads the note, whose contents we are not yet shown, and begins energetically sweeping her bedroom floor. While she cleans, she listens to a radio broadcast on which a female announcer informs us of the bright new day that is dawning and goes on to relate intimately to her audience, "You know, one day I woke up in the morning and realized: I'm a grown-up now. . . . It's true, growing up can be a little painful." Crying, Chen Meili sits down and rereads the note from Lin, whose contents we are now shown. The note reads: "I woke up at 4 a.m., and as I sat gazing at your beautiful naked body, I realized that even when I'm old I will always remember this young, beautiful you. I thank you for all the happiness you've given me. But it's enough; I'm afraid that if you gave me any more, I'd be unable to bear it, and so I've gone. I'm going home and I won't be coming back to work at the cinema. Goodbye." The combination of

34. An elderly Wan and Foon in *Intimates* (dir. Jacob Cheung Chi Leung, 1997).

35. Foon and Wan transformed into their youthful selves at the conclusion of *Intimates* (dir. Jacob Cheung Chi Leung, 1997).

the radio monologue on the painful process of growing up and Lin's note's construction of the two women's hours-old sexual relationship as already a distant past event, remembered from the perspective of old age, expresses the familiarly memorial logic that frames same-sex love as a temporary phase in feminine youth.

But the film goes even further in the scenes that follow. From Chen Meili's apartment, we now cut to Lin Meili's house, where Lin is bathing her grandmother, helping her choose which clothes to wear, dressing her, combing her hair, and clipping her fingernails; her grandmother explains calmly that she is preparing for death. We now cut to a shot of Chen traveling on the same train that we have often watched Lin take home to Xizhi; she must be coming in search of Lin at home. As Lin and her grandmother sit on the rooftop balcony, Lin's grandmother turns her face toward the camera and gazes, smiling, at something that she seems to see approaching her. Previous scenes lead us to understand that what she is seeing is the ghost of her dead husband coming to take her to her grave (figure 36). Fascinatingly, the film now cuts to a shot of Chen Meili walking toward the camera. Despite the narrative non sequitur, the cut unmistakably prompts us to read this as a point-of-view shot from the grandmother's perspective. Moreover, Chen is dressed all in black, and the shot of her walking is accompanied by a rather horror-filmish sound track of ominous cello and piercing violin—all of which adds to the strong sense that Chen is being paralleled with the ghost of the dead husband whom Lin's grandmother awaits (figure 37). This curious sequence suggests a parallel between the relationship between Lin's grandmother and her dead husband and the relationship between Lin and Chen: Chen is fated to haunt Lin as her grandfather haunts her grandmother, like the ghost of the past. As in *Intimates* and many other Chinese-language films thematizing women's same-sex love, in *Murmur of Youth* the representation of love between women ultimately remains overdetermined by associations with pastness and memory.[13]

Incidental Journey: *The Presence of Landscape*

A recent crop of films by young, independent directors across the PRC, Taiwan, and Hong Kong has begun to complicate this familiar representation of female homoerotic temporality as epitomized by the backward glance of memory. Lesbian director Chen Jofei's *Incidental Journey* (16mm, 60 mins) provides an interesting example of a more recent film that exemplifies yet also complicates the memorial mode. Made on a tiny budget of NT $880,000 after

36. Lin Meili's grandmother watches the arrival of her dead husband's ghost in *Murmur of Youth* (dir, Lin Cheng-sheng, 1997).

37. In place of the ghost, Lin Meili's lover, Chen Meili, approaches in *Murmur of Youth* (dir. Lin Cheng-sheng, 1997).

tax (less than U.S. $24,000) provided by a grant from the Government Information Office, *Incidental Journey*, Chen's second film, is framed by its director as a self-consciously lesbian endeavor.[14] While she also hopes that the themes in the film could speak to a broader audience, Chen relates that she particularly wanted to make a film about the older generation of lesbians who came of age under often difficult circumstances in pre-queer-movement Taiwan. Chen explains that she hoped to make this generation of women feel loved by seeing their own image on the screen portrayed in a loving manner.[15] Based on the positive responses of local film festival audiences, Chen judges that her objective has been realized.

Incidental Journey presents a lyrical exploration of the relations among three women over several days in the Taiwanese countryside. Ching, fleeing from a painful breakup with her girlfriend in Taipei, heads to the island's east coast, where she picks up Hsiang, a forty-something tomboy hitchhiking to her own ex-partner's house near Hualien. Hsiang's ex-partner, Ji, is now married and living an idyllic rural life in the mountains with her husband, Fu. The two women stay with the married couple for several days, during which time they begin to fall in love; however, Ching has not yet recovered from her recent breakup, and after spending the night together, she and Hsiang finally part ways, both enriched by their brief relationship. The film's style is "soft" and emotional. Chen explains that she sought to reach as broad an audience as possible and to avoid making an inaccessible "art film" by simply mimicking the Taiwan New Wave style. Instead of the challenging aesthetics of long takes, static framing, and the withholding of extradiegetic music that characterize that cinema, *Incidental Journey* uses a gently mobile camera, more frequent cutting, lots of facial close-ups and point-of-view shots, and a sweet, slightly sentimental piano and cello sound track to convey the subjective experience of the three central women characters.

As in the two films discussed above, the memorial mode is a structuring presence in Chen's film. In addition to the inherently memorializing framework outlined by the director—the desire to honor the experience of an older generation of Taiwanese lesbians—the film memorializes the topic of women's same-sex love in a very familiar way in its presentation of Ji and Hsiang's memories of their relationship. As Ji and Ching wander in Ji's orchard, to the accompaniment of soft, extradiegetic music, Ji tells Ching, "You know, Hsiang was in love with a girl, long ago. . . . But the girl got married." It is clear to both Ching and the spectator that Ji is talking about her own prior relationship with Hsiang, and the way in which this relationship is represented here—as the poignant memory of a youthful same-sex love that was ultimately terminated by one woman's marriage—provides an economical distillation of the dominant mode of modern Chinese female homoerotic representation as discussed throughout this book. But what distinguishes *Incidental Journey* from the other examples discussed thus far is that the memorial narrative of Hsiang and Ji's previous love is joined now by another story: that of the new love between Hsiang and Ching in the present.

The sense of time in the scenes in which Hsiang and Ching are alone with each other is closely connected with the representation of landscape. Chen reveals that for her, the function of landscape in the film—which, as she notes, is so central that it might be considered an additional character—has something in common with the treatment of landscape in traditional Chinese *shanshui* (mountain-and-water) watercolor painting. And indeed the composition of the frequent exterior shots of mountains, rivers, and lakes—the backdrop to Hsiang and Ching's growing intimacy—clearly evokes that aesthetic. Ching removes her top and sits, back to the camera, gazing out at a misty lake while, unseen by her, Hsiang watches her from behind; the scene is accompanied by birdsong and punctuated by interposing shots of the densely wooded mountainside across the lake. In a shot that is repeated at the end of the film, the two women wander lazily away from the camera over lush green grass toward a distant, misty view of sky and mountains; the tableau is framed by the sculptural form of a small tree on the right hand side of the frame, and when the women shout out over the gorge to hear the echo of their voices, the camera cuts away to pan across the contours of the mountains, where fragments of cloud drift unhurriedly over the peaks. Another scene begins with a long pan across the green, rippled surface of a lake; we then see Ching sketching and watch Hsiang begin to sketch Ching's form into the landscape sketch that she herself is making. In this final example, the analogy between the filmic technique and the tradition of landscape art is quite unambiguous: just as Hsiang frames the sketching Ching in her own sketch, so the camera frames both women in its own *shanshui*-style graphic composition.

On first blush, this filmic evocation of the aesthetics of traditional Chinese painting would seem to echo a familiar nostalgic logic; in that reading, the "ancient cultural tradition" of *shanshui* aesthetics would function as an analogue for the individual memory of female same-sex love. Yet such a reading is not quite adequate to the film itself, for the camera's repeated cutting away to rippling water, drifting cloud, and distant mountain slopes evokes not only the backward glance of nostalgia but also a reflective gaze at the leisurely unfolding of a kind of eternal present in the flows and rhythms of an aestheticized nature. Thus, although it becomes clear at the end of the film that Hsiang and Ching's nascent love is indeed fated soon to become only a memory, in a strong sense, these *shanshui*-style shots foreground the sensual, emotional, and even philosophical experience of *presentness*. To explore further the tantalizing sense of presentness that is interwoven with the familiarly memorial tone in *Journey*, I turn now to two other examples of recent lesbian-themed films in which this presentism is even more marked.

Butterfly: Memory's Radical Potential

Mak Yan Yan's feature *Butterfly* in a sense takes up and extends the project of both *Blue Gate Crossing* (discussed in chapter 4) and *Incidental Journey*. Like those films, *Butterfly* both references and complicates the memorialism of modern female homoerotic representation, but, as we will see, the relationship it figures between past and present is even more suggestively complex.

Butterfly, Mak's second feature film, was financed jointly by the Hong Kong Arts Development Company and the Filmko company, though Mak notes that the film's lesbian subject matter scared off many potential investors and consequently the film was two years in the making (though only six weeks in the shooting), as it was delayed by the search for finance. The final budget was HK $2,000,000 (about U.S. $250,000). As well as exemplifying the practices of independent women's filmmaking, *Butterfly* also exemplifies the transnational turn in Chinese-language film production. Based closely on a 1996 novella by Taiwanese lesbian author Chen Xue, "Hudie de jihao" (The Mark of the Butterfly), the film is set in Hong Kong and directed by a young, Hong Kong-based woman director, while one of its stars hails from mainland China (musician Tian Yuan, who plays Yip, is originally from Wuhan and currently based in Beijing).[16]

The film's story centers on thirty-something wife and mother Flavia (whose Chinese name, Die, means "butterfly"; played by Josie Ho), a high school teacher who finds herself falling unexpectedly but passionately in love with a free-spirited musician, Yip, a woman around ten years her junior. Flavia's relationship with Yip brings back memories of her childhood sweetheart, Jin (Joman Chiang), with whom she was forced to break up when the two girls were discovered in bed together by Flavia's mother; Jin later moved to Macau and became a Buddhist nun.[17] True to the genre of the memorial schoolgirl romance, Flavia has been continuously haunted in her adult married life by memories of her youthful love for Jin. Ultimately Flavia resolves to divorce her husband to be with Yip, resigning herself to a custody battle for her young daughter, and the film concludes with a beatific scene of Flavia and Yip together on the balcony of their shared apartment, looking toward a bright if unknown future, implied in the final fade-to-white.

Stylistically Butterfly is a fascinating hybrid of experimental technique and slick fashionability. It is an overwhelmingly lush production, both visually and aurally. The hyperactive camera; multiple, contrasting film stocks; color filters; opulent sets and costumes; interposing nondiegetic extreme close-ups (of an ornament depicting a pair of girls with blue butterfly wings; of Flavia's hands under running tap water); shifting focus; and distorted reflections lend the film a certain MTV-ish air. The sound track, which features among others the music of Tian Yuan's band, Hopscotch, is equally luscious: rich electronic instrumentation and other-worldly female vocals produce a sugary-sweet yet eerie soundscape that complements the sensuous, dream-like quality of the film's visual style.

As in Intimates, the memorial mode is established in Butterfly by means of a flashback structure. The film proceeds contrapuntally, with scenes of a thirty-something Flavia in the present with Yip alternating with flashback scenes of a youthful Flavia (Isabel Chan) with Jin around 1989, the year of the Tian'anmen Square massacre, against which Jin was involved in protesting in Hong Kong.[18] This structure is concisely illustrated in the film's title sequence. The opening shot with Yip singing as she looks out her apartment window over Hong Kong is followed by a silent shot of the young Flavia with Jin, giggling uproariously as they climb the old Portuguese fort in Macau. This second shot uses a contrasting film stock: the image, produced by digital manipulation of Super-8 film, is grainy, high-contrast, and dominated by red and yellow tones.[19] The film now cuts to a black screen with the first of the titles; next, it cuts to an adult Flavia teaching a roomful of uniformed high school girls; she is teaching mainland writer Yu Qiuyu's poem "The Weight of Thirty Years," in which Yu recalls his own schooldays under Maoism. The remainder of the title sequence is composed of a series of ten crosscuts, back and forth between Flavia's present-day classroom (in the high-definition film stock representing the present) and the flashbacks to Flavia and Jin's school-days (in the grainy, high-contrast Super-8 film representing the past). The soundscape across the whole sequence is a mix of Flavia's students' voices reciting Yu Qiuyu's poem and Tian Yuan/Yip's voice singing.

Evidently, this sequence is organized around two of the key features of modern Chinese female homoerotic representation: the school setting (Flavia and Jin in the past; Flavia's classroom in the present; Yu Qiuyu's school memories) and the memorial mode (the flashback structure; the memorial theme of Yu's poem). One of the most potent signifiers of the film's pervasive memorialism is the second shot, with Flavia and Jin in Macau (figure 38). This image of youthful ecstasy, recalled through memory's stylizing filter, functions similarly to an early scene in Wong Kar-wai's Happy Together, as analyzed by Rey Chow. Chow proposes that in Wong's film, the black-and-white shots of the two male leads having sex function as a constant reference point: they index the film's structuring nostalgia in their representation of an Edenic "remembered but enigmatic other time" to which the characters long, impossibly, to return.[20] Similarly in Butterfly, Flavia and Jin's visit to the fort at Macau is a recurring image—a kind of primal scene, in Chow's terms, of a remembered moment of bliss that Flavia yearns to revisit.[21] The image has a number of analogues throughout the film, including the repeated interposing shots of the ornament of the two "butterfly girls" and of Flavia and Jin lying on the grass in their school uniforms (figure 39).

Significantly, however, the memorial mood that is signaled in the title sequence's Macau shots by means of the Super-8 film subsequently spreads to incorporate ostensibly nonmemorial elements of the film's narrative—notably scenes depicting Flavia's new relationship with Yip in the present. This happens, for example, in the scene where Flavia first encounters Yip and takes her out for coffee; as Flavia tells Yip about her memories of Jin, suddenly Flavia's own image, and then Yip's, appear in the grainy, high-contrast film that signifies memory (figure 40). Mak remarks of this spread of the Super-8 film into the present sections of the narrative as follows:

People have asked me about the Super-8 sections, because it's actually quite weird: not all of those sections were shot by Jin; some of them happen in the present. The reason I did it like that was because for Flavia, the sound and the image-feel of the Super-8 film are linked with the time she was with Jin. Although Jin didn't shoot all of [the film's Super-8 sections] herself, for Flavia, that kind of sound and image are connected with the most important time of her life, when she was young, so now, when she meets Tian Yuan (Yip), the same feeling, the same colors, the same sound come up again.[22]

This incursion of the memorializing filter of the Super-8 film into the narrative present initially suggests a logic similar to that seen in Intimates and Murmur of Youth. Women's same-sex relations in the narrative present are represented as if they were a memory, as though the force of the dominant mode of

38. Flavia and Jin's lost utopia in *Butterfly* (dir. Mak Yan Yan, 2004; in Super-8 film).

39. Analogous shot of Flavia and Jin's lost utopia in *Butterfly* (dir. Mak Yan Yan, 2004; in higher-definition 35-mm film).

40. Yip appears to Flavia as a memorial image in *Butterfly* (dir. Mak Yan Yan, 2004; in Super-8 film).

female homoerotic representation were strong enough to overpower both realist temporality and narrative logic in its drive to figure the lesbian as inherently memorial.

Yet closer attention to the formal organization of the film as a whole reveals a more complex structure. For in fact it is not only the case that selected moments of the narrative present are represented as if they were in the past through the use of the Super-8 film, but also many of the flashback scenes are shot using both the Super-8 film and the clear, high-definition 35-mm film that elsewhere signifies the present. In other words, both the narrative present and the flashback past alternate between Super-8 and 35-mm film stock, confusing any neat demarcation between past and present. The film cuts constantly back and forth between the two types of image, frequently juxtaposing the same shot in both modes (as with the two contrasting images of Flavia and the two close-ups of Yip and Flavia, in figures 41–44). If the device of the Super-8 film stock offers another way of representing memory in addition to flashbacks, then as a *modality* of the image, rather than image content, it arguably enables a more complex representation of the relation between past and present than the simple narrative alternation enabled by the flashback structure. Specifically it enables not only a memorializing of the present—a predictable enough move in a contemporary Chinese lesbian-themed text, as we have seen—but also, and more radically, a "*present-ing*" of the past.

In this way, *Butterfly* underscores the inherent instabilities and contradictions in memorialism as a regulatory discourse. In one way, as we have seen, the insistent relegation of the female homoerotic topic to the past can be understood as a symbolic de-realization of present or future lesbian possibility enforced by a hegemonic, hetero-marital sex-gender system. However, such representation cannot *actually* confine the topic to pastness since memory and its narration must take place in the present.[23] In this sense, the attempt by the dominant culture of marital heterosexuality to de-realize women's same-sex love by memorializing it is doomed to failure; to confine female homoeroticism to the memorial register is at the same time to ensure its persistent interruption of the present. As was demonstrated in the preceding chapters on classic late-twentieth-century texts of female homoerotic memorialism, like Cao Lijuan's "The Maidens' Dance" (and its telemovie adaptation by Tsao Jui-yuan) and Chu T'ien-hsin's "Waves Scour the Sands," these stories already carry within them the radical potential of female homoerotic memory insofar as they illustrate its disturbingly interruptive effects within the narrative present of "heterosexual" femininity. In

Butterfly, however, the persistent presentness of female homoerotic memory is far more vigorously foregrounded; what is implicit in the earlier texts here becomes explicit as Flavia's marital present becomes saturated and finally overwhelmed by the potently revenant memory of her past schoolgirl romance. The film's restless flashback/flash-forward oscillations, coupled with the constant cutting between the memorial Super-8 image and the presentism of the 35-mm film stock in both flashback and present scenes finally frustrate any desire for a clear demarcation between past and present. The film thus represents through both narrative and technical means memory's impingement upon present experience and the way in which memory actually links and melds, rather than separates, past and present.

The point is underscored in the film's narrative as well. For *Butterfly*'s narrative diverges significantly, both from that of *Happy Together* (in Chow's analysis) and from those of lesbian-themed films discussed so far, in its insistence on the possibility of actually realizing memory's yearned-for utopia in the present. In a way like *Incidental Journey* and *Blue Gate Crossing* and yet even more emphatically, *Butterfly* rehearses the old drama of women's same-sex love as an essentially memorial condition only to upstage that familiar scene with a new narrative that brings lesbian possibility unambiguously into the here and now. Underscoring this rescripting of the valence of lesbian memory, the butterfly theme in both Chen Xue's novella and Mak's film adaptation solicits interpretation as an intertextual reference to Chu T'ien-hsin's famous memorial lesbian love story "A Story of Spring Butterflies" (1992)—indeed, Chen conceptualizes "The Mark of the Butterfly" explicitly as a response to Chu's earlier story.[24] Chu's story, like Chen's, concerns a married woman who is haunted by memories of her adolescent love for her female best friend. However, Chu's story is written not from the woman's own perspective but from that of her husband, who has discovered, much to his disquiet, a love letter written by his wife to her old friend. It is the husband who refers to the young same-sex lovers as "spring butterflies," an image that is meant to convey the girls' youthful innocence and purity. In repeating both the butterfly image and the situation of the central character, Chen's story takes up Chu's theme and plot but rescripts both the perspective and the ending significantly

41. Flavia in Super-8 film in *Butterfly* (dir. Mak Yan Yan, 2004).

42. Flavia in 35-mm film in *Butterfly* (dir. Mak Yan Yan, 2004).

43. Yip and Flavia in 35-mm film in *Butterfly* (dir. Mak Yan Yan, 2004).

44. Flavia's face in Super-8 film in *Butterfly* (dir. Mak Yan Yan, 2004).

so that here, unlike in Chu's story, the married woman who is haunted by memories of her teenage tomboy sweetheart ultimately chooses a new female lover over her husband.

In the story of Flavia's and Jin's young love, cut short by Flavia's mother's decree and Flavia's consequent dutiful acquisition of a male fiancé, Butterfly presents a version of the familiar, memorial narrative in which love between young women is forcibly terminated by exterior social forces only to recur incessantly as the memory of adult femininity. To this well-worn story, though, there is now added another: that of Flavia's relationship with Yip in the narrative present. And the film's conclusion suggests unambiguously that Flavia's new relationship with Yip has a future: as the two women horse around gleefully on their balcony in the film's last scene before the final fade-to-white, the film's theme song swells on the sound track—a Cantonese/English song by Hong Kong girl band AT17 entitled "The Best is Yet to Come." The film's narrative thus echoes and reinforces the implications of its technique, discussed above. Referencing the familiar narrative of love between women as an inherently memorial condition, it dramatizes the radical potential of that narrative by literalizing memory's enactment within, and capacity materially to transform, present experience.[25]

Fish and Elephant: Critical Presentism

This Summer clearly represents the simple, present moment—neither the distant past nor some longed-for tomorrow or future. . . . The story that took place this summer could only have taken place this summer.—CUI ZI'EN

Fish and Elephant (Jinnian xiatian [This Summer], 2001, 16mm) is the first lesbian-themed feature film to emerge from the People's Republic of China. The film contrasts markedly with all of the films discussed thus far insofar as it eschews the memorial mode completely in favor of a strong focus on representing the present moment, which it achieves, as I will show, through both narrative and stylistic means.

The filmmaking debut of young, heterosexual woman director Li Yu, Fish and Elephant, with a budget of about U.S. $60,000 raised from one private investor and Li Yu's private savings was made "underground."[26] This means that the film, like so many of the recent Chinese films to attract international critical attention, was made without a permit from the Film Bureau; hence it could neither be funded by the government nor approved for domestic theatrical release. However, in one sense the moniker "underground" is misleading. The fact that a director makes a film without the sanction of the Film Bureau does not preclude its being seen by domestic audiences. Rampant DVD pirating means that street markets and other audiovisual retail outlets are regularly and openly awash with copies of the latest "underground" films. This was certainly the case with *Fish and Elephant* in late 2003; my own bootleg copy of the DVD—its cover breathlessly proclaiming the film to be "the first ever female-female same-sex love story in the history of Chinese cinema"—was purchased in a major state-run bookstore in Beijing. Li Yu even ironically expresses her gratitude to the DVD pirates for ensuring that her film found a domestic audience outside of the handful of students who saw it at a few special college screenings.[27] According to Li Yu, to the extent that audience responses are known, the film was highly controversial within China. Audience response at the campus screenings was quite polarized: older Party apparatchik types echoed the Film Bureau in decrying the film's exposure of the "dark side" of Chinese society in its depiction of lesbian relations, while college students were more likely to defend the lesbian topic as legitimate subject matter.

Li Yu's professional background is as a documentary filmmaker at China Central Television. However, after making *Fish and Elephant*, she was pressured either to give up making underground films or to resign from her job in state media; she chose the latter option, with a view to dedicating herself full time to filmmaking.[28] On being questioned on her motivation for making a lesbian-themed film, Li frames the film first and foremost in terms of gender, as a "women's story": "The documentaries I've made before now have all been about women's lives and family relations. I think the question of women's status in Chinese society is a very interesting one. . . . So I'm very interested in exploring relations between women, as well as the relations between women and society. I thought that the most direct way of exploring these questions was to focus on lesbians since their world is effectively composed entirely of women."[29]

As Li's response suggests, what is most interesting about *Fish and Elephant* is the way in which it uses the lesbian topic to probe broader questions surrounding marriage, the family, feminine subjectivity, and women's relationship with the masculinist state apparatus. One of the film's lead actresses, Beijing-based lesbian artist and activist Shi Tou, reveals that some queer audiences in the United States complained that the film wasn't "lesbian" enough and included too much social context, which, they felt, obscured the "main story" of the romance between the two lead characters.[30] Against this view, however, I would argue that the film's sustained linkage of lesbianism with women's social experience more broadly results not in a blunted but a heightened attention to the specificities of female same-sex love and the available cultural language for representing it in the particular social and historical context of early twenty-first-century Beijing.

Stylistically *Fish and Elephant* is very recognizably a product of its time and place of production. Like many of the so-called "sixth-generation" Chinese films of the late 1990s (and in sharp contrast to the unapologetic emotionalism of both *Incidental Journey* and *Butterfly*), it uses "art house style"—long takes, static framing, documentary-style hyper-realism, an unvarnished sound track, and nonprofessional actors—to present the stories of socially marginal characters in urban post-Mao China. The film focuses on the experiences of three young women one summer in Beijing. Xiao Qun (Pan Yi), who works as an elephant keeper at the zoo, is busy fighting off her mother's concern at her unmarried yet aged state (she is almost thirty). Her mother (Zhang Jilian), living in distant Sichuan Province, presses the extended family into service to organize a series of dates for Xiao Qun with prospective spouses. This is particularly irksome to Xiao Qun since, as she puts it to an appalled male cousin in an early scene, she "has no feelings for men," preferring women. Xiao Ling (Shi Tou) is a clothing designer who sells her wares in a local market and lives with her boyfriend in a joyless relationship. After meeting at Xiao Ling's stall, Xiao Ling and Xiao Qun strike up a flirtatious friendship that soon progresses to intimacy and sex, and Xiao Ling leaves her boyfriend to move into Xiao Qun's small apartment. Then one morning, Xiao Qun's ex-girlfriend, Wu Junjun (Zhang Qianqian), turns up at the zoo asking Xiao Qun for sanctuary. It emerges that she has fatally shot her father, who had been sexually abusing her since she was a child, and is on the run from the police. Around the same time, Xiao Qun's mother arrives in town to begin in earnest the process of matchmaking for her daughter. On one of the "dates" that Xiao Qun's mother organizes, she herself hits it off with the prospective groom—a widower around her own age—and the two begin seeing one another in secret. Soon enough, Xiao Ling catches sight of Xiao Qun with Junjun, believes Xiao Qun is cheating on her, and moves back to her boyfriend's place. Meanwhile, Xiao Qun and her mother are having an emotionally freighted lunch, during which Xiao Qun's mother reveals her plan to remarry, at which Xiao Qun expresses her congratulations, and Xiao Qun reveals her sexual orientation, at which her mother expresses her confusion. Xiao Ling soon returns to the apartment and apologizes to Xiao Qun; the lovers are reunited, and soon after, Xiao Qun's mother reconciles with her daughter by telling her that she supports her choice to be with Xiao Ling.

Finally, Junjun is discovered living in Xiao Qun's quarters at the zoo. She is surrounded by police in a siege that ends in the death of one officer, shot by Junjun, and ultimately Junjun's arrest. Crosscuts reveal Xiao Qun and Xiao Ling having sex at the same time the siege is taking place. The final scene is at Xiao Qun's mother's wedding, where the bride waits anxiously for Xiao Qun to arrive, which—ominously—she never does.

Horizontal versus Vertical Time

I observed above that Fish and Elephant stands out from the other films discussed in this chapter for its failure to take up the memorial theme that so centrally structures the other films; instead, I propose, along with Cui Zi'en, that the film is concerned with elaborating an image of lesbian presentness. As with Mak's Butterfly, Fish and Elephant's exploration of alternative modes of female homoerotic temporality happens at the level of film style as well as narrative. To further this consideration of the role of style in these films' representations of women's same-sex love, the film theory of American avantgarde filmmaker Maya Deren proves useful. In her influential analysis of "poetic film," which, as several commentators have noted, anticipates Gilles Deleuze's theory of movement-image and time-image, Deren distinguished between two dimensions of the filmic text, which she called the horizontal and vertical dimensions.[31] In Deren's schema, the horizontal dimension of a film refers to its narrative trajectory; it encompasses the action of the film, the unraveling of the story, and drama (similarly to Deleuze's movement-image). The vertical dimension, by contrast, is the film's lyrical component; in the vertical dimension, stasis replaces action, the "depths" of the isolated moment are emphasized over narrative progression, and poetry dominates drama (similarly to Deleuze's time-image).[32] Deren explains as follows:

> The poetic construct arises from the fact, if you will, that it is a "vertical" investigation of a situation, in that it probes the ramifications of the moment, and is concerned with its qualities and its depth, so that you have poetry concerned . . . not with what is occurring but with what it feels like or what it means. . . . In other words, it isn't that one action leads to another action (this is what I would call a "horizontal" development), but that they are brought to a center, gathered up, and collected by the fact that they all refer to a common emotion. . . . Whereas, in what is called a "horizontal" development, the logic is a logic of actions.[33]

Deren's examples of moments when the vertical dominates the horizontal axis include the opening passages of some films, where location and mood are established through montage, and dream sequences, in which, again, narrative is secondary to mood.[34] In Deleuze's later development of a similar analytic framework, he observes the dominance of the time-image over the movement-image in the postwar European and American New Wave cinemas; indeed, the privileging of vertical rather than horizontal dimensions, in Deren's terms, is a notable feature of the "art film" style, in distinction to Hollywood cinema's emphasis on continuity and narrative development.[35]

Although she does not dwell on this aspect, Deren's horizontal/vertical schema implies a particular structuring of cinematic time; this is a point that is drawn out more fully in Deleuze's later, related theory of the "chronosigns" of postwar art cinema, in which, he proposes, time dominates movement.[36] In Deren's horizontal development, story time moves ineluctably forward; the narrative trajectory is structured by a cause-and-effect chain of events unfolding in linear time (time as progression, in Deleuze's terms).[37] In Deren's vertical development, the emphasis is not on narrative but on "the ramifications of the *moment*"; isolated from the forward surge of the narrative, the single moment is plumbed for its poetic or subjective significance, held apart from the onward flow of the story (time directly presented, in Deleuze's terms).[38] Since in the context of the present study the most interesting aspect of *Fish and Elephant* is its representation of temporality, it will be useful to examine the film with reference to Deren's schema, especially this distinction between horizontal and vertical time.

The above précis of the film's story shows that the action—the film's horizontal component—is propelled in large part by two parallel narrative trajectories. First, there is the narrative of Xiao Qun's mother and her quest for marriage, initially for Xiao Qun and later for herself. Second, there is the narrative of Junjun's flight from the police. This, too, is at root a story about marriage—that of Junjun's parents, in which, as Junjun relates, her father regularly raped her while her mother colluded by turning a blind eye, ultimately leading Junjun to murder her father. In a sense, the film is structured by a dialectical tension between these two narratives concerning marriage and family life: the light or optimistic story of Xiao Qun's mother and her happy midlife remarriage and the dark or pessimistic narrative of the horrific consequences of Junjun's parents' abuse of their daughter. But surely there is also a third narrative here: the love story between Xiao Qun and Xiao Ling; moreover, as the film's American audiences insisted, surely that is really the film's *central* narrative? While not denying the central importance in the film of the relationship between Xiao Qun and Xiao Ling, in what follows I will nonetheless argue that this relationship is represented not so much through narrative, but rather precisely through *narrative suspension*: the interruption of the forward-hurtling horizontal time of the two marriage stories with their ineluctable end points (Xiao Qun's mother's marriage, Junjun's arrest) by the ecstatic stasis, or vertical time, of the women's same-sex romance.

Lesbian Space, Vertical Time

How does *Fish and Elephant* represent female homoerotic time? As the epigraph from Beijing-based gay filmmaker, author, and cultural critic Cui Zi'en suggests, the film is particularly notable for its efforts to situate women's same-sex love not in some distant past moment but instead firmly within the here and now of the present. As much is implied in the film's Chinese title, *Jinnian xiatian* (This Summer), which provides a fortuitous but nonetheless significant contrast with the Chinese title of the Taiwanese telemovie discussed in chapter 5, *Nanian xiatiande langsheng*: "The Voice of the Waves That Summer." In addition to the film's title, Cui's comment refers to the overt localism and presentism of the film's *mise-en-scène* and sound track, which consistently foreground the unmistakable textures, sounds, and sensory density of everyday life in early-twenty-first-century Beijing. The film is full of interposed street scenes, with pedestrians, trucks, buses, bicycles, cars, and delivery carts flowing across the frame, accompanied by a gritty sound track recording the auditory rush and hum of a Beijing summer: voices, footsteps, a distant television, cicadas, engines, bicycle bells, construction racket, birdsong, snatches of music. The first sex scene between Xiao Qun and Xiao Ling, in particular, underscores the co-presence of the lovers within the local space and present time of the city. A long take in which the two women draw together on Xiao Qun's bed and shyly kiss is followed by an exterior long shot in which a man, walking on the hot road, finds his shoe sticking to the bitumen, prizes it free, and continues walking toward the camera. The sound track here is dominated by loud cicada song, and the light is harsh summer sunlight. The following shot shows Xiao Qun and Xiao Ling lying together after sex, the softer cicada song in the background and the sunlight falling on the two women's skin indicating continuity with the previous street scene. While ordinary people go about their everyday business, this sequence seems to say, hidden from view, lesbian lives are being lived, right here, right now, in this city (figures 45–47).

Later in the same article from which the epigraph is taken, Cui offers a more complex formulation of the film's presentism: "Li Yu has intentionally distanced [the Pan Yi and Shi Tou characters] from the orthodox narrative chain. To put it another way, she allows them, to a certain degree, to break

45. Xiao Qun and Xiao Ling's first kiss in *Fish and Elephant* (dir. Li Yu, 2005).

46. Interposing street scene in *Fish and Elephant* (dir. Li Yu, 2005).

47. Xiao Qun and Xiao Ling lie together after sex in *Fish and Elephant* (dir. Li Yu, 2005).

the narrative chain's completeness, so that the independent, internal space [that they occupy] may remain uninterrupted by the narrative progression."[39] Although Cui's metaphor here is spatial rather than temporal, his remarks resonate interestingly with Deren's formulation of film's horizontal versus vertical dimensions. In suggesting that the independent, internal space that the lovers occupy ruptures the narrative chain, Cui implies that the representation of the lovers is of an order distinct from—and interruptive of—the horizontal progression of the story. And indeed, in a sense, the sequence discussed above could be understood to imply a distinction and separation between the two spheres of street and bedroom as much as a temporal and spatial connection between them. The exterior scene with the man and his stuck shoe takes place "out there," amid the incessant movement and urgent busy-ness of the summer streets: the rickshaw driver strains at his pedals; the bystander with the parasol waits for the arrival of something or someone; bicycles pass in a steady stream; the pedestrian is caught up in his own private narrative trajectory involving himself, his shoe, and the sticky bitumen. The interior scene with Xiao Qun and Xiao Ling, meanwhile, takes place "in here," in the distinct space of the bedroom. The relative quiet and stillness that distinguish these interior shots imply that the bedroom and the two women's relationship occupy a space and a time contiguous with, yet *at a certain remove from*, the space and time of the world "out there." Indeed, the first shot to visualize Xiao Qun's and Xiao Ling's intimacy—cutely enough, a shot from the perspective of Xiao Qun's elephant in her barred enclosure—implies precisely this kind of spatial distancing by means of architectural framing: the women appear in a small square of light, separated from the spectator by the bars of the elephant's enclosure (figure 48). And throughout the film, Xiao Qun and Xiao Ling's intimate moments take place in spaces that are similarly demarcated from the exterior spaces of the world "out there." Like those discussed above, these scenes are characterized by a certain stillness, quiet, and lack of narrative momentum; frequently they take place in the softly lit greenish space of Xiao Qun's bedroom. The two women's occupation of this space is several times paralleled metaphorically with the lazy circling of the fish in their rectangular tank, which is often either partially visible in shot or else fills the frame in a visual lead-in to these scenes.

In addition to this spatial demarcation there is also a temporal dimension to the scenes of Xiao Qun and Xiao Ling's intimacy that contributes to the sense that Cui describes of the two women's world tending progressively to drift free of the forward momentum of the two "orthodox" (marital) narratives. In Deren's terms, in these scenes—as happens similarly in the *shanshui-*

48. Xiao Qun and Xiao Ling's intimacy occupies "another space" in this shot of Xiao Ling giving Xiao Qun her phone number, from Xiao Qun's elephant's point of view, in *Fish and Elephant* (dir. Li Yu, 2005).

style landscape shots in Chen's *Incidental Journey* and the lushly subjectivist visuals in Mak's *Butterfly*—vertical development dominates horizontal.[40] Rather than the teleological chain of cause-and-effect events associated with the film's horizontal movement, the scenes dwell on the subjective and poetic qualities of the isolated moment, with little action or narrative progression. Time in these scenes is not linear and horizontal but static and vertical. In *Fish and Elephant*, this sense is created by the use of leisurely takes—generally the shots are of about sixty seconds' duration, and there is one very long shot of almost five minutes—static framing, and a general lack of either movement within the frame or narrative progression through dialogue (figures 49–52).[41]

Of course, this film style with its long takes and static framing—what Deleuze would call the dominance of the time-image—is common in the noncommercial cinemas of both the PRC and Taiwan and indeed in noncommercial cinemas throughout the world.[42] It might be argued that the use of this style, with its tendency to emphasize the poetic or vertical over the narrative or horizontal, results simply from Li's adherence to the "art film" formula that has so often characterized the work of women filmmakers concerned with representing lesbian themes.[43] Questioned about *Fish and Elephant*'s style, Li observes:

> This is the kind of film style that I personally favor: an objective, cool, detached gaze. But the film's story is extremely melodramatic. There's one girl who refuses to get married, so her mother comes to pressure her into getting married—but in the end it's the mother who gets married, not the

49–52. Static, vertical time in *Fish and Elephant* (dir. Li Yu, 2005).

girl. Then there's Junjun, who was raped by her father as a child, and so she rejects men and has become a lesbian and ends up under siege by the police; her story is a tragic one. It's all highly melodramatic. But I used a documentary style to cut back the melodrama, so the film took on a more objective, more distant feel. This was intentional; it was the style I felt the film needed. So although it's made in a documentary style, it's actually a highly stylized film.[44]

Li's response echoes Cui's observation about the film's dual character. For Li, the film is marked as stylized by the split between its melodramatic story—consisting of the two familial/marital narratives outlined above—and its documentary style, with the detachment implied by an immobile camera, long takes, and so on. And it is precisely this split between story and style that marks the particularity of Fish and Elephant's female homoerotic representation. For it is in the contrast with the forward movement of the familial/marital narratives (melodrama) that the stasis of the scenes of same-sex intimacy, achieved through camera style (documentary) becomes meaningful. In other words, if Fish and Elephant appropriates an art film style that is especially pronounced in the scenes of same-sex intimacy, the appropriation is a hybrid one, mixed as it is with the more conventional narrative structure of the familial/marital stories that unfold in other scenes.[45] Moreover, seen in the broader context of the conventions of modern Chinese female homoerotic representation, the film's stylistic foregrounding of the present moment in the "vertical" time of Xiao Qun and Xiao Ling's intimacy takes on a special significance that is not simply reducible to Li's adherence to art film style. That is, the emphatic presentism of these scenes can be interpreted as a resistant response to the persistent memorialism of modern Chinese female homoerotic representation.

Cui's insight about the distancing of Xiao Qun and Xiao Ling's world from the film's narrative progression makes good sense of the film's enigmatic conclusion, in which Xiao Qun and Xiao Ling fail to appear at Xiao Qun's mother's wedding. In the film's penultimate shot, we see the two women lying in each other's arms, shot through Xiao Qun's bedroom window (figure 53). Thus, when the film cuts to the final shot outside the restaurant where the wedding celebrations take place (figure 54) and we hear Xiao Qun's mother wondering aloud where her daughter could possibly be, in a sense we have just been shown the answer: instead of attending the wedding she is lying in cozy intimacy with Xiao Ling. As in the earlier scene shot from the elephant's point of view (figure 48), the penultimate shot frames the two women from a

53. Xiao Qun and Xiao Ling's intimacy is again projected into "another space" in penultimate shot of *Fish and Elephant* (dir. Li Yu, 2005).

54. Xiao Qun's mother and her groom anxiously await Xiao Qun's arrival at their wedding in final shot of *Fish and Elephant* (dir. Li Yu, 2005).

perspective outside the space that they occupy; their relationship is thus figured once again as taking place "somewhere else." And in Xiao Qun's failure to appear in the wedding scene, it is as though the alternative space and time of Xiao Qun and Xiao Ling's same-sex relationship had finally floated entirely free of the space and time of the marriage narrative. Xiao Qun's nonappearance in the final scene—as though she now remains suspended, eternally, in the two women's "other" space and static time—literalizes the film's final separation of the vertical from the horizontal dimension.

Critique of State Masculinism

Yet while the formal logic of the film prompts this symbolic reading of the conclusion, Xiao Qun's failure to show up at the wedding can also be explained in more literal, narrative terms. Junjun—now a double murderer—has been arrested at Xiao Qun's quarters at the zoo; the next step the police will take will surely be to search out Xiao Qun herself and charge her with harboring a fugitive. Furthermore, if the police now go to Xiao Qun's flat, they will find her in bed with Xiao Ling—which can hardly help her case, especially since Junjun's arresting officer was himself one of Xiao Qun's former arranged "dates." Thus, there is a more ominous significance to Xiao Qun's failure to appear at the wedding; while at our last sight of her, she was suspended in the alternative space and time of her intimacy with Xiao Ling, nonetheless, according to the film's narrative (rather than formal) logic, we must now presume her to be locked up in police custody facing an extremely uncertain future. Interpreted this way, Xiao Qun's nonappearance at her mother's wedding bespeaks not the separation of lesbian from marital time, but rather the final, fatal crossing of the two narratives outlined above: the light narrative of Xiao Qun's mother's wedding project and the dark narrative of Junjun's family history and its consequences. Given this, it is worth considering the significance of Junjun's role in more detail.

Junjun is presented primarily as a (justified) rebel against the system of the patriarchal family, patricide being the most extreme expression of a refusal to cleave to this structure's demand for properly reverent and obedient daughterly behavior. What is particularly interesting in the film's representation of Junjun's violent rebellion against her father is the way in which the patriarchal family, in which the father abuses his position of authority, is paralleled with the PRC state. Thus Junjun is framed as a rebel against not just the patriarchal familial system but also an amalgam of both familial and state power that we might call state masculinism. In the siege scene, Junjun's rage shifts concretely from its earlier target, her abusive father, toward the state system that seems to side with him against her. Upon surrounding her in her bunker in Xiao Qun's quarters, the police set up a relentlessly repetitive call through a loudspeaker: "Wu Junjun, you are surrounded. Give yourself up within three minutes and the authorities will look generously on your case; if you refuse, your path can lead only to death. Wu Junjun, you are surrounded. . . ." Et cetera. After several repetitions of this harsh, male-voiced officialese, Junjun picks off the offending officer with her revolver. The film then cuts to a shot of the blood-spattered loudspeaker lying in the grass, on which the camera lingers for a full seventeen seconds while the loudspeaker's final feedback wail dies feebly out and a buzzing fly alights to feed on the spattered blood (figure 55). This emphatic image of the motionless, bloodied loudspeaker—one is tempted to refer to it as the loudspeaker's "corpse"— stands as a potent symbol of the enraged woman's violent revenge against masculinist state/familial authority. Similarly, when Junjun holds a second officer at gunpoint, it is his condescending and highly gendered statement, "You're a woman; this conduct is unbecoming," that prompts her to pull the trigger—though by now she's out of ammunition (figure 56).

The projected interruption of Xiao Qun and Xiao Ling's beatific space-time at the end of the film by the consequences of Junjun's life-and-death struggle with her abusive father and his symbolic representative, the state, implies the ultimate impossibility of women remaining secure within the film's imagined alternative, lesbian realm. In Fish and Elephant, then, female same-sex love is framed as ultimately insupportable by the officially sanctioned sex-gender system, which is shown to be far stronger and more ruthless than the fragile alternative worlds created between women.[46]

In contrast with the alternative reading of the film's ending, above, which was based on the film's formal rather than its narrative logic, this might seem a rather negative conclusion. Yet interpreting the ending in this way under-scores the film's potential as a strongly critical commentary on the very impossibility that it dramatizes. In this regard, like Butterfly, Fish and Elephant takes up and develops an existing tendency in earlier instances of Chinese female homoerotic representation. Where Butterfly literalizes the radical potential of lesbian memory as interruptive of hetero-marital femininity, Fish and Elephant offers a critique of the existing sex-gender system's limitation of women's sexual and affective choices that echoes and amplifies a comparable critique in earlier narratives of female same-sex love. As we have seen in previous chapters, in the Republican-era schoolgirl romances by Lu Yin and Ling Shu-hua, the target of the implied critique was the arranged marriage system that tore the young same-sex lovers apart. The critique in Chu T'ien-hsin's and

55. The masculinist state's silenced mouthpiece in *Fish and Elephant* (dir. Li Yu, 2005).

56. Police officer lectures Junjun, "You're a woman; this conduct is unbecoming," prompting her to pull the trigger in *Fish and Elephant* (dir. Li Yu, 2005).

Wong Bikwan's later works targets the family and the school as agents of young women's sexual discipline toward "properly" marital adulthood. *Fish and Elephant* continues this tradition of female homoerotic representation as critique of the social regulation of feminine sexuality, but it does so in an even stronger voice. Reflecting the context of its production, the target of its critique is the collusion between the patriarchal family and the post-socialist state in punishing women who fail to conform to their expected social/familial roles as obedient daughters and dutiful wives.

I have argued in this chapter that films like *Incidental Journey*, *Butterfly*, and *Fish and Elephant* (and the list could certainly be extended) can be seen as critical responses to earlier forms of modern Chinese female homoerotic representation. It makes historical sense that films like these, with their relatively overt challenges to habitual ways of figuring women's same-sex relations, should emerge at a time when organized lesbian movements had been active in Hong Kong and Taiwan for around a decade and had begun to emerge in mainland China. Although not all of these films were made by self-identifying lesbians, nevertheless their serious, anti-homophobic treatment of love between women certainly reflects the impact of globalizing, post-Stonewall lesbian identity politics. Yet I have also tried to show that while these films respond to a global sex-cultural environment, the modality of their responses also bespeaks their linkage to the longer, more localized histories of modern Chinese female homoerotic representation. Just as Euro-American instances of critical lesbian self-representation, with their preoccupation with rendering visible the invisible, remain bound to the visual rubric that is also the problem they want to fix, so these Chinese examples remain centrally preoccupied with questions of pastness, presence, and futurity even though—indeed precisely because—it is the temporal obsession of dominant forms of female homoerotic representation that they aim to critique. The films thus attest to the persistent hold of a way of understanding women's sexuality that, while everywhere in dialogue with modern Western sexual epistemologies, is not merely some far-flung echo of these but is instead the expression of a culturally distinct metaphoric fixation.

Epilogue

In the spring of 2005, the memorial same-sex loving woman made her presence felt once again with the concurrent release of Tsao Jui-Yuan's television and film adaptations of Pai Hsien-yung's 1970 short story "Gu lian hua" (Love's Lone Flower). Tsao's lavish, sixteen-episode costume-drama adaptation of Pai's memorial narrative of one woman's love for two successive female sweethearts, spanning time and space to link late-Republican-era Shanghai with 1950s Taipei, was screened on Taiwan's CTS network between 9:30 and 10:30 Sunday evenings, and the film redaction was released in commercial cinemas around the island in May 2005. Throughout April and May, Pai Hsien-yung, Tsao Jui-Yuan, and a group of the production crew from the costume designer to the composer of the original score undertook a multicity promotional tour, screening a "making of" DVD and selling the sound track CD and a folio-format commemorative book featuring a selection of glossy stills, commentary from actors and crew, and a reprint of Pai's original story.[1] In addition to illustrating again the remarkable popularity of locally produced gay- and lesbian-themed television drama in Taiwan, the Love's Lone Flower phenomenon furnishes an apposite closing example of the continuing hold that female homoerotic memorialism maintains on the Chinese mass-cultural imagination (figure 57).

Love's Lone Flower is a historical drama focusing on love between sing-song girls. The protagonist Yun Fang's (Anita Yuen) first love is Wu Bao (Angelica Lee), a singer/escort with whom she worked in 1940s Shanghai and for whose affections she competed with the male Taiwanese musician Lin San-lang (Tou Chung-hua).[2] Wu Bao died young, however, in the chaos of the exodus from Shanghai to Taiwan following the Communist victory in the civil war, and she

57. Anita Yuen (left) and Angelica Lee in Tsao Jui-Yuan's memorial lesbian costume drama *Love's Lone Flower* (dir. Tsao Jui-yuan, 2005).

appears in Pai's story only in memorial flashback. After fleeing to Taiwan, Yun Fang eventually embarks on a second same-sex relationship, this time with Juan-juan (Suzanne Hsiao), a sing-song girl who reminds Yun Fang of her former love and who works in the Taipei wine house that Yun Fang manages during the 1950s. With her hard-earned savings, Yun Fang buys an apartment and brings Juan-juan to live with her there. But physically abused and forced into morphine addiction by a possessive gangster client, Ke Lao-xiong (Kao Chieh), Juan-juan is finally driven mad, violently murders Ke, and ends up in an insane asylum. The story ends with Yun Fang requesting Lin San-lang to sing for her the song "Love's Lone Flower," which both Wu Bao and Juan-juan used to sing. The narrative thus concludes on a note of mournful nostalgia, demonstrating once more this book's central contention that the topic of love between women in modern Chinese mass cultures has been, and continues to be, overdetermined by a temporal logic that is most commonly expressed through a memorial mode of representation.

Love's Lone Flower also illustrates this book's second and related claim: the widespread influence of a universalizing understanding of female same-sex love. As conventionally feminine women who love another woman but are also depicted as capable of cross-sex sexual relations and perhaps love, both Wu Bao and Juan-juan exemplify the universalizing model of the same-sex loving woman—the image of the woman-loving woman not as a distinct sexual minority but as a kind of "anywoman"—whose cultural prominence I have been tracing throughout this book. Their recent screen debut echoes a century of comparable characters in the literary, televisual, and filmic examples I have discussed in the foregoing chapters: recall Lu Yin's Lishi and Yuanqing; Ling Shuhua's Yunluo and Yingman; Yu Dafu's Zheng Xiuyue and

Feng Shifen; Chu T'ien-hsin's Xiao Qi; Wong Bikwan's Yip Saisai and Hui Jihang; Liu Suola's nameless narrator and her beloved friend Manzi; Xuan Xiaofo's Tang Meijia and Cheng Xiujun; Du Xiulan and Ko Yi-zheng's Zhan Qing-qing and Maggie; Cao Lijuan and Tsao Jui-yuan's Tong Suxin; Lisa Chen Xiuyu's Lu Manli and Lin Long; Chen Xue and Mak Yan Yan's Flavia; and Li Yu's Xiao Ling.

As the conspicuous absence from the above list of such tomboyish characters as Yu Dafu's Li Wenqing, Chu T'ien-hsin's Zhang Yan and Long Yun, and Mak Yan Yan's Jin (to name a few) reminds us, it is not the case that the universalizing understanding of women's same-sex love as the experience of a conventionally feminine anywoman is the only understanding in play in modern Chinese representations. Indeed, the foregoing chapters have shown that a very common pairing in contemporary narratives of love between women sees the conventionally feminine anywoman fall in love with a tomboy sweetheart, whose sexuality and gender, contradictorily, are framed as the property of a distinct minority. However, as I have argued throughout this book, although modern Chinese representations of love between women, like their Euro-American counterparts, are structured by an internal tension between universalizing versus minoritizing and gender-separatist versus gender-transitive models (to borrow Sedgwick's terms), what is distinctive is the relative emphasis.[3] Basing our evaluation on the number and popularity of texts that center on normatively feminine protagonists—thereby taking into account not just the fact that a character appears in a text but also the extent to which the text encourages its audience to linger over the subjective experience of that character—we find that in these contexts, unlike in Euro-American ones, the cultural image of the same-sex attracted anywoman is far more extensively developed and finely detailed than that of the masculine lesbian.

Excited by the prospect of a new instance of queer(ish) cinema, I went to see Love's Lone Flower with a group of six Taiwanese lesbian friends the first weekend of its theatrical release, at Warner Village Cinemas in east Taipei. After the film, the Saturday night crowd in the plaza outside the multiplex looked perhaps a little queerer than usual, with a sprinkling of dapper tomboys—ranging in sartorial style from '50s rockabilly to contemporary hip-hop—among the usual tide of trendy teenagers. Our group's post-film discussion focused on attempts to interpret the film's story and characters according to our own everyday understandings of lesbian identity. Some expressed the view that despite her stylish feminine costumes, Yun Fang should properly be interpreted as a tomboy (T), given her protective and chivalrous behavior toward her sweethearts, her competence in the masculine world of business, the general poise and dignity of her bearing, and her clear romantic preference for women over men. But a more difficult question presented itself: could Wu Bao and Juan-juan be classed as "lesbians"? On the one hand, it seemed, not really, because after all Wu Bao did seem to fall in love with the musician and probably only stayed with Yun Fang out of a sense of duty, and by the end Juan-juan was too destroyed by the morphine to even know what she wanted. But then again, maybe they sort of *were* lesbians since they both undoubtedly loved Yun Fang and in the end were more faithful to her than to their male lovers.

I think our inconclusive discussion that night demonstrates how the same-sex loving anywoman retains her capacity to trouble a sexual epistemology based on the opposition and mutual exclusivity of heterosexual and homosexual behavior and desire. In a sense, the minoritizing system of lesbian identity politics to which we were appealing, which informs everyday understandings of sexuality by younger, self-identifying lesbians in Chinese-speaking societies as well as Western ones, doesn't know—*can't* know—how to place this by now familiar figure.[4] Is she, or isn't she? Is she one of us or one of them? Is she a "real" lesbian or a false one? One of my central arguments throughout this book has been that the dogged cultural persistence and remarkable pervasiveness of this figure bespeaks precisely the incomplete hold of the homo/hetero binary and sexual identity politics (with which this model nevertheless continues, uneasily, to coexist) and the continuing presence of a different way of understanding women's sexuality.

In addition to the remarkable persistence over time of this distinctive mode of female homoerotic representation, the mode is achieving an increasingly wide geographic reach as well. This is the case, first of all, across the immediate Chinese-speaking worlds of China, Taiwan, and Hong Kong. Particularly with the aid of electronic dissemination via the Internet, a majority of the texts discussed in the foregoing chapters circulate reasonably readily among these three locales so that the memorial narrative and its associated structure of feeling reconsolidates in the present through transcultural media flows, its mobility helping to keep it alive. This transnational cast is evident both in intertextual elements within the texts and in their transnational patterns of consumption. We might, for example, consider how *Voice of Waves*, a 2002 Taiwan telemovie (discussed in chapter 5), in its story of a rebellious same-sex attracted woman's ultimate suicide by ocean drowning echoes a very similar plot element in the earlier Hong Kong movie *Twin Bracelets* (Huang Yushan, 1991)—itself based on a story by a mainland Chinese author.[5] Or again, consider how central thematics in the 2007 Taiwan film *Spider Lilies* (Zero Chou) — tattooing, memories of schoolgirl romance reanimated for lesbian plots in the narrative present—recall similar elements in the 2005 Hong Kong film *Butterfly* (discussed in chapter 6).[6] Both films also embody Chinese transnationalism at the level of production, with their mix of Taiwanese, Hong Kong, and mainland stars, and both draw together audiences from across all three areas in online discussions at fan forums.[7] The memorial mode even retains some degree of presence in films made by diasporic directors outside of China, Hong Kong, and Taiwan. For example, in Alice Wu's 2004 film about Chinese women in New York, *Saving Face*, the central lesbian couple, Wil and Viv (Michelle Krusiec and Lynn Chen), knew each other as children, and Viv confesses to harboring a romantic memory of Wil defending her honor in an argument and then kissing her. Here it is as if the Chinese schoolgirl romance and memorial mode have atrophied to the point of becoming a minor detail in what is overall a more global-style lesbian narrative. In the schoolgirl romance substory within Singaporean director Eric Khoo's 2005 film *Be with Me*, however, the imprint of these forms is clearer. The film shifts to the memorial mode at the conclusion of the substory, when in a by now familiar vision of vividly reanimated memory, brokenhearted Jackie (Ezann Lee) seems to see herself and her sweetheart Sam (Samantha Tan) sharing a cherished kiss in the prelapsarian moment before Sam abandoned her for a boyfriend. Through its geographic mobility, the Chinese memorial mode of female homoerotic representation is thus continually made and remade in the present, linking together Hong Kong, Taiwan, China, and the worldwide Chinese diaspora even as the locally distinct modes of female homoerotic culture that persist in each place also distinguish them.[8]

At the beginning of chapter 1, I speculated that 1920s and 1930s public dialogues on, and literary representations of, the value of young women's same-sex love may have implied a nascent alternative sexual epistemology in Republican China in which women's same-sex love would be not stigmatized but embraced. The analyses performed in the foregoing chapters have shown that this perhaps unexpectedly calm and positive view of women's same-sex love is not an "alternative" view in the sense of being one that was never realized or remained merely minor and marginal. Rather, the ongoing salience in Chinese texts of relatively unpanicked depictions of the young same-sex loving woman as an anywoman—including (perhaps especially) in texts that have sometimes been dismissed by their critics as ideologically "backward"—shows that such a view is a continuing strand within mainstream Chinese sexual epistemologies today. For reexamining the field of modern Chinese representations of love between women, we find, perhaps in spite of initial expectations, that romantic and erotic love between women is very frequently taken seriously and presented as a complex, deeply felt, troublingly memorable affective experience. Often, as we have seen, it is framed as continuous with, rather than antithetical to, normative femininity; it acts as a catalyst for women's social memory practices; it functions as a critique of the social regulation of women's sexuality; and it is aesthetically idealized. As I hope the foregoing chapters have made clear, by highlighting all this, I do not mean to imply either that the commonness of such representations necessarily indicates that these societies are more "tolerant" of actual self-identifying lesbians or that homophobia is not *also* a central component of contemporary Chinese sexual epistemologies and cultures. But I do propose that the homo/hetero binary, the minoritizing view of lesbian identity, and the homophobia that often accompanies these cannot be assumed to exhaust the field of modern Chinese understandings of women's same-sex love. For if we do as the discourse of female homoerotic memorialism prompts us and look back—indeed, even if we simply look around us today—we discover everywhere a quite different vision of women's same-sex love, most often framed through memory and yet at the same time insistently present.

Appendix

Interview with Shi Tou, Beijing

December 24, 2003

What follows is the edited transcript of an interview conducted by the author with Shi Tou, lesbian artist, lead actress in Li Yu's film *Fish and Elephant* (discussed in chapter 6), and one of the best-known lesbian activists and public figures in the People's Republic of China. The discussion is wide-ranging, touching on topics including the public response to *Fish and Elephant*, Shi Tou's role as a "public lesbian" in China, and the rise of lesbian activism in Beijing. It offers a glimpse of the recent emergence of a minoritized lesbian identity and community in mainland China: social formations that at once draw upon, reconfigure, and coexist alongside the universalizing formations of women's same-sex love discussed in the preceding chapters.

. . .

Fran Martin: I know that several years ago you came out publicly to the media; could you tell me about that?

Shi Tou: It was a program screened in 1990 on Hunan Satellite TV. The topic was "Approaching Homosexuality" (*Zoujin tongxinglian*); the program was called *Speak Your Mind* (*You hua hao shuo*). They invited me, [the gay author and filmmaker] Cui Zi'en, and [the sexual sociologist] Li Yinhe as special guests; Cui and I were there in the capacity of homosexuals; Li was there as a scholar on this topic. The purpose wasn't for us to come out; it was just to have a discussion on the topic of homosexuality. But, through that, of course in fact we did go public.

Was the program seen only in Hunan Province or right across China?

Right across China, since it was a satellite channel; it might even have been received overseas. I heard there were 300 million viewers! Many people have told me that they saw this program.

Weren't there call-in questions from the audience, as well?

It was filmed before a live studio audience, and they directed questions at us.

What did they ask?

As I recall, there were three major groups. First, university students. They had a very accepting attitude toward homosexuality; they saw it as quite natural and opposed the idea that it's a kind of illness. The second group was middle-aged cadres; they all said that homosexuality went against nature, that it violated natural laws; everything they said was connected with reproduction, biology, and so on. Then there was one woman who said to me, right now you're still young, but won't you want to have children when you're older? I think she really was concerned for me; she wanted to understand how I felt about this and what my future would be like, whether I'd regret things when I got older. Those were the three main types of responses.

What reactions from people around you did you receive after appearing so publicly on this program?

It didn't really have a very big impact. I guess some people I knew found out about my sexuality through the program. My close friends worried a bit about what impact it might all have on me, but actually, since I am living in Beijing, it wasn't so bad—things are relatively open here. Back in my hometown, Guizhou, I used to worry what my friends would think—whether they might reject me because of my sexuality. But it's not so bad here in Beijing.

What do you think the general public in China today thinks about the idea of lesbianism? I realize this is kind of an unanswerable question, but I'm interested in hearing your thoughts.

Well, there's almost no information about it in the televisual media. Occasionally, columns appear on the topic in the newspapers, and we sometimes write things for the papers too, and some journalists also write fairly open-minded columns on the topic. In magazines, the topic arises occasionally. A year or two ago, *Contemporary Civilization Magazine* (Xiandai wenming zazhi) did a special issue on homosexuality. And then Cui Zi'en published his own book, about himself. I think it's a gradual process of people coming to understand what homosexuality is.

So would you say that it's generally more accepted in the big cities whereas the countryside is more traditional?

Yes, you could say that the countryside is more traditional. People in the country might not even understand the concept of "homosexuality." For example, I took my girlfriend back to my hometown in the country and told my female relatives that she was my partner. Well, I didn't say that we were lesbians; I just told them that we were planning to spend the rest of our lives together. My relatives thought that was great. So that kind of thing can happen. But I think we still don't know enough about how homosexuals actually live in small towns in the countryside if they don't leave for the city. A few years ago, when I was involved in the Beijing Sisters group, we were extremely active. We did all kinds of things, including setting up a newsletter and a telephone hotline. We often received calls from women in outlying areas; it was great; we felt that through the hotline, we could really reach out to a wider group of lesbians. But later on the group kind of stalled, and the hotline's not running any more. These days, the Internet is the most important medium in this regard. People in outlying areas can get to know one another and exchange information via the Net. But we really know nothing about what life must be like for rural lesbians who don't have access to the Internet.

As I understand it, there's yet to appear a fully developed, public lesbian movement on the Chinese mainland. Is that correct?

Yes, it's strange. In 1998 we organized the First National Gay and Lesbian Conference (Di Yi Jie Nan Nü Tongzhi Dahui) in Beijing; people came from all over the country; I was one of the organizers and also a chair for some of the panels. Then that same October, we also organized a national lesbian conference. We were all full of enthusiasm and planned to create a national alliance and organize lots of future activities. But afterwards, we didn't really continue with it. Beijing Sisters organized a kind of lesbian cultural exhibition, but it got closed down by the Public Security Bureau (PSB). They'd invited a lot of media and a lot of celebrities — that's one way of doing things, I guess, but I'm not sure that it was the most appropriate way under the circumstances. Anyway, after the exhibition got closed down by the PSB, the movement kind of stalled. The leader of Beijing Sisters went to the United States right around that time, and I guess other people's confidence was really dented by being busted by the PSB.

So under what law did the PSB close down the exhibition?

I don't know for sure. It may have had to do with the fact that legally you need to apply for a permit to organize a public demonstration or a public meeting. Actually, the PSB doesn't even need a concrete legal reason—if they don't like what you're doing, they can just prohibit you from doing it. Even if you've been granted a permit and everything's in proper order, they can still close you down if they don't like the content of your activity. This happens with art exhibitions as well.

So although there's no specific law against homosexuality in China, the PSB can pick a law at random to prevent certain activities from going ahead?

That's right. One thing that's changed in law enforcement in China lately is that the authorities are less prone to interfere in people's personal lives. But they're still sensitive about public activities involving big groups of people.

In your opinion, what's the biggest problem facing lesbians in China at the moment?

I think it varies depending on whether you live in the city or in the country-side. I think the thing that has the greatest impact on individual lesbians' lives is their relations with their family, as well as with the society more broadly. Right now, there's absolutely no system in place to make life livable for homosexuals—no form of state protection at all. I think in China, sometimes individual lesbians have the impression there's nothing at all wrong with their situation—they feel that their lives are perfectly happy and don't realize what obstacles they face until they actually come face to face with them. The social problems faced by lesbians also include the problems faced by women in general. So "the biggest problem faced by lesbians today" actually includes multiple different problems around general social disadvantage.

Just now, you mentioned how you told your relatives in the countryside that you wanted to live with your female partner all your life, and they thought that was great. I find it very interesting that they should think that if you don't marry but nonetheless have someone to look after you for your whole life, then that's enough. It seems as if in that view, marriage is primarily a very practical arrangement that protects one from being left alone in one's old age. Is their response based on that kind of thinking, would you say?

Yes, that's right. Country people are very preoccupied with who will take care of one in one's old age. Actually, it's quite understandable. Because in the countryside, people have even less legal protection from the state than we do in the city—basically, they have none at all. Oftentimes, when we hear that you can get government support for this and that, we're shocked! When [country people] have a daughter rather than a son, it's a great worry. One has to bring her up and then marry her off, and she's not as strong a worker as a boy would be. And what will her parents do when they're old, with her married into someone else's family and unable to take care of them? The government needs to put more resources into changing this pattern. It's not something that can be changed just by telling people they should change; concrete action has to be taken.

> In the West, and also in Taiwan, the rise of public lesbian movements has been intimately connected to the emergence of nongovernment feminist organizations. Is a similar link apparent or possible in China?

Actually, the group I was in before had a close relationship with nongovernment feminism. Around 1995 and 1996, lesbian groups in Beijing began to emerge at the same time as feminist groups were also emerging. There was an English woman here at the time, Susie, and she kind of got everyone together socially.[1] Then we started a reading group to bring together Chinese and Western thinking on feminism. In the group we also discussed lesbian topics, and there were several lesbians in the group as well. We were all friends. We used to organize activities every week—we were so busy! I forgot all about my art for a while. We'd hold discussions, go to films, have parties. . . . Everyone was equal; there was no leader, and the group was quite unofficial. Not everyone necessarily knew everyone else; people came along by introduction—you'd bring along friends who were interested. There were more Chinese than foreigners, also some Chinese people who'd studied overseas and spoke to the group about what they'd learned overseas. Everyone had the chance to discuss their own research, and people like me could discuss our art, and so on. It wasn't connected to any particular university, although professors from various universities used to attend. So there truly was a link between feminism and the emergence of that lesbian social group.

> Do you think it's possible that in the future, there will emerge a public lesbian movement in China? Do you think that would be desirable?

I've thought a lot about this question: what a lesbian movement in China would look like and what methods we could use to work toward establishing one. Maybe we can learn from other countries where the lesbian movement is already established so that we don't have to reinvent the wheel. We need to choose which strategies are most appropriate to our situation. I think it's inevitable that lesbian culture in China will develop further—there's no way it can simply stay at the level it's at today.

So you think it will emerge naturally as society transforms?

Well, not necessarily "naturally"—we'll have to actively create it! I don't know how we should approach this task. At the moment, what I'm able to do is limited to my capacity as an individual; before, I had the strength of numbers, by belonging to a collective organization. I don't know whether or not we'll be able to return to the collective model. We'll have to wait and see.

Do you keep in contact with lesbian groups in Taiwan and Hong Kong? Do you see that as important?

I used to be in contact with a Chinese lesbian group in the United States. And I've had occasional contact with people in Taiwan and Hong Kong. People from Hong Kong and Taiwan attended our National Gay and Lesbian Conference, and we stayed in touch and occasionally exchanged information and news. But now, maybe because there's no longer an organized lesbian group here in Beijing, our contact has fallen away. People's contact is more at a personal level. In the last few days, the lesbian film director Yau Ching visited from Hong Kong—we've both seen each other's films.[2] Last year, some women also came up from Taiwan.

Ah, so you've seen Yau Ching's film. Have you seen other lesbian films in Chinese from Hong Kong or Taiwan?

I don't get to see them much unless friends bring them over to me. Recently, I've seen a Taiwanese lesbian documentary. . . .

So you do have an interest in seeing these films?

Yes—I definitely watch them whenever I get the chance.

You said that you had contact with lesbian groups in the United States. Is that more or less important, do you think, than keeping contact with lesbian groups in Hong Kong and Taiwan?

Actually, I think you're making a good point with that question. I think it's particularly important for us to keep in contact with groups in Hong Kong and Taiwan, since we have many things in common. But lately, I've had more contact with groups in the United States because last year, a Chinese lesbian group in California organized for me to go on tour over there, with the film, to New York, Chicago, and San Francisco. Actually, it was in the United States that I met lots of Taiwanese lesbians!

So how did you come to act in Fish and Elephant?

I think it was through Cui Zi'en's introduction. The director got in touch with Cui, and he got in touch with me. I said I'd organize a party and invite some lesbians and let them take a look for who they thought might be most suitable to act in the film. But before we even had the party, I introduced two other girls to them. They chose me and the girl who acts Xiao Qun as the most suitable.

How about Jun-jun?

They found her themselves—they got another group of girls together and picked her out.

So it's not necessarily true that the three major actresses are all lesbians?

That's right—not necessarily.

In my view, Fish and Elephant *is an extremely significant work since it's the first feature-length film on a lesbian topic ever to have been made in the People's Republic of China; it has a certain political significance. Would you agree?*

Yes, I think that making a lesbian film was extremely significant, a great thing to do. That's why I was willing to act in it. Previously, another director had approached me and asked me to act in another film on this topic, but I found I didn't really like the way he was treating the topic. Since Fish's director is a woman, I thought it might be easier to communicate with her, so I agreed to look at the script, and I thought it wasn't bad. I see it primarily as an artwork, an artwork with a lesbian theme. I think they probably asked me since I'm a lesbian myself, so presumably I'd be better able to understand the story. If they'd asked a straight woman to act the part, it would've been a lot harder—especially since the director is straight, as well; who would tell whom how to act the part? Of course, I listened to the director's advice, but I was also able to bring my own experience and way of thinking to the role. With me acting in it, the film really is certifiably lesbian—right? [Laughs.] So yes, I do think it's a most significant film.

You know, when we screened the film in the United States, a lot of people felt that the two major lesbian characters were loaded up with too many other problems—almost as if the film was trying to "explain" why they became lesbians. At first, I didn't agree with those viewers—I thought that the problems the women experienced were just part of the characters' general social background. But after thinking about it some more, I think maybe those viewers were right! Because the three main characters have all had terrible pasts, right? Xiao Qun's father kept a mistress; my character got along badly with her boyfriend; and Jun-jun was sexually abused by her father as a child. Some people thought the story was problematic in this regard.

> Actually, when I saw it, I felt that the story was pointing toward the kind of problems that ordinary women might face in society—whether lesbian or straight, these problems are quite commonly encountered, to some degree, by many women. So I didn't think that was a problem—I even felt it gave the film a kind of feminist slant.

I guess everyone sees it in their own way. When we screened it at Beijing University and had a discussion with the audience afterwards, Li Yu said quite strongly that she felt the film had nothing to do with feminism or whatever, that it was purely an artwork. Everyone has their own view.

> And it's certainly not always the case that the director holds the key to the meaning of a film!

Yes, indeed.

> I feel that another very interesting thing about the film is the way it links the topic of family relations with that of lesbian relations—for example, with the appearance of Xiao Qun's mother in Beijing and that subplot involving Xiao Qun's relationship with her mother. Some commentators have noted that this is actually a feature of East Asian gay and lesbian films: they tend to focus on family relations. In contrast, Western gay and lesbian films often leave these out altogether and construct a kind of total "queer world" as if the family didn't exist at all. I think one really does notice that tendency in Chinese queer-themed films. I don't mean to make some essentialist argument about the meaning of "Chinese culture," but this difference is actually undeniable.

I guess that family relations are extremely intimate in China, and that's a bit different from the West. For example, some children never leave their parents' home, even when they've grown up.

> Am I right in thinking the film was made in secret, without official sanction, and that it never got theatrical release within China?

Yes, it's an underground film. The filmmakers put up the money themselves — that's what you call truly independent filmmaking! We filmed it in public places, but we didn't tell anyone that we were making a lesbian film. The director and her boyfriend just told people they were filming something for China Central Television (CCTV) because they really did work for CCTV.

So in that case, it definitely never had official theatrical release domestically; only private screenings.

That's right. We screened it in some bars, at a couple of festivals, at Beijing University, and so on. But right now, you can see it everywhere on VCD and DVD — both official copies and pirated ones.

Yes, I'm puzzled about that. If it was an underground film, made without official permission, how come the DVD got such a public release? It's bizarre!

Yes, it is pretty strange. But there's one advantage: it does mean that an independent film gets to reach a far wider audience.

Yes, I agree — it's definitely a good thing. I'm just puzzled about how it came about, how it was allowed.

Maybe the authorities just can't control it. I guess they could prohibit the public release if they wanted, but they'd never find all the pirated copies or who made them.

I see. I bought my DVD of the film at the Beijing Book Center, and in the title credits it says it was released by something called the Shandong Cultural Audiovisual Publishing Company. When I read that, I thought, my god, it really is an official release!

I guess maybe the government is becoming more permissive.

Yes, it certainly seems so. So all this means that the film must have reached a much wider audience by now. What responses have you had from people who've seen the film, whether lesbian or straight?

Well, lots of people have told me that they've seen the film, but I guess I feel too embarrassed to ask them what they thought of it! We got lots of feedback from Chinese American audiences when we were on tour, as I said, but I really haven't heard much detailed feedback from audiences within China. I guess I should ask them. You know, the first time I saw myself up there on the screen, I was really embarrassed. And people used to tease me and say, "Aiya! Look, there are even nude scenes!" [Laughs.] Lots and lots of people have told me they've seen it, but that's kind of all they say.

So you haven't had any feedback from local lesbian audiences either?

Hmmm ... I'm trying to think of other responses. I already told you about the criticisms from the audiences in the United States. . . . There was also another reaction: some viewers felt the film wasn't "lesbian" enough. They wanted a film about lesbians and nothing else. This film has more social context in it. Actually, I like the inclusion of the social context.

Yes, so do I.

I think the film foregrounds certain kinds of social prejudice against lesbians. But some girls just want to watch lesbian love stories. Of course, those films are good too. Like, what's the name of that Canadian lesbian film, *When Night Is Falling?* In films like that, the world is all rosy; everything is perfect — you know what I mean.

Yes, that's exactly what I meant when I spoke just now about some Western queer films that totally leave out any social context or family relations — as if the world were simply a queer world. Of course, films like that are good; the world they create is very nice. But I guess I prefer films that include some kind of social context.

Some viewers say that our lives as lesbians are hard enough — can't we have some less depressing films? I understand their point, but I say to them, fine — then go make those films yourselves!

Was Fish and Elephant *reviewed by any mainstream film critics in the newspapers or wherever?*

There were some overseas but very few in China. Just a few simple introductions to the film, not anything very critical — the most in-depth analysis was the article Cui Zi'en wrote. Maybe the mainstream critics felt they didn't know enough about the homosexual topic to really comment on it.

You mean they were kind of afraid to touch it?

I think it's more that they didn't really understand it. They probably need more time to learn about the topic.

So what are your plans for your own filmmaking?

Actually, I'm making videos all the time. I've had a couple of screenings this year. I made one when I was in the United States, of a pride march — I filmed it, then edited the film, and stuck on Chinese translations of some of the really out-there placards that people were carrying. The viewer response here was excellent, from all viewers, male and female, straight and queer—but especially from women viewers. Because, you know, when they have those marches, the women marching are really free to express themselves very openly. They say things like "We love lesbians"; "We are sisters"; and then there were some placards with things like "Asian lesbians: Serving our community"—and lots of individual people's personal statements. The response at my screening was great—women viewers here just went wild over it.

> Yesterday I bought several of Professor Li Yinhe's books, including her collection of translated queer theory. It's really great that this material is now available in the People's Republic. I'm sure it will have a great impact—at least within academic circles.

Yes; she's written a lot of valuable material on this topic. You know, lots of lesbians read her works before they've come out, and through reading them, they come to understand their own feelings much better. They realize they're not alone—that there are many others like themselves.

List of Chinese Characters

Note: Character names are listed only where the names are explicitly discussed in the text. Entries are listed by first Chinese character, rather than by pinyin letter-by-letter alphabetization.

aichou	melancholy	哀愁
aiqing	tragic love	哀情
aiqing xiaoshuo	tragic-love fiction	哀情小說
aiqing	romantic love	愛情
anfen	obedient	安分
beizhuangde gushi	tragic stories	悲壯的故事
biantai	perversion, pervert	變態
bu fen	not distinguishing (colloq.; i.e., between T and *po* gender roles)	不分
cai	(literary) talent	才
cainü	talented woman	才女
caizi-jiaren	scholar-beauty romance	才子佳人
cangliang	desolate	蒼涼
chou	sorrow	愁
chuan zong jie dai	continue the family line	傳宗接代
dazhong	the masses	大眾
danchun	simple, pure	單純

de	traditional feminine virtue	德
dui renge dulide zhuiqu	quest for independent humanity	對人格獨立的追求
duoqing	sensitive, sentimental	多情
enü	malignant woman	惡女
Fuluoyide zhuyi	Freudianism	弗洛伊德主義
gan'ga	awkward	尷尬
geren	the individual	個人
guixiu wenxue	boudoir fiction	閨秀文學
hao	nice, good	好
hei qun bai yi shidai	the era of black skirts and white blouses	黑裙白衣時代
Huaren tongzhi jiaoliu dahui	Chinese Tongzhi Conference	華人同志交流大會
jiaren-caizi	beauty-scholar romance	佳人才子
jianpu	simple, plain	簡譜
jiejian	borrow and learn	借鑒
jiemei fuqi	sister spouses	姐妹夫妻
jingshen lian'ai	spiritual love	精神戀愛
jingshende	spiritual	精神的
kan bu dao tongxing-lian de weilai	could not see homosexuality's future	看不到同性戀的未來
koa-a-hi	Taiwanese all-women opera	歌仔戲
ku'er wenxue	queer fiction	酷兒文學
lazi	lesbian (colloq.)	拉子
lian'ai	romantic love	戀愛
liaoxi	to cite, to draw upon	聊襲
mijiao	secret religion	密教
mofang nüren changge de nü nanren	woman-man who imitated a woman singing	模仿女人唱歌的女男人
moyan kuanrong	silent tolerance	默言寬容
naam-dzai-tau	tomboy, boyish young girl (Hong Kong usage)	男仔頭
niangniang T	nellie T	娘娘T

nüqiangpo	super-po	女強婆
nüren moyangde nanren	womanish man	女人模樣的男人
nütongxinglian	female homosexuality; lesbianism	女同性戀
nütongxinglianzhe	female homosexual; lesbian	女同性戀者
nütongzhi	female comrade; i.e., lesbian	女同志
nüxing qingyi pianzi	female friendship film	女性情誼片子
nü xiang	"women facing"	女相
po	woman, wife; femme (colloq.)	婆
qipao	qipao, cheongsam	旗袍
qin'ai:	affection	親愛
qing	feeling, love	情
re	fever	熱
renge	humantity	人格
renlei	humankind	人類
renmin	the people	人民
routide	carnal	肉體的
routi lianai	carnal love	肉體戀愛
rou yu	carnal desire	肉慾
rutong shouzu	like brothers	如同手足
san di tong xin	three places, one heart	三地同心
shanshui	Chinese watercolor landscape painting	山水
shaonü	adolescent girl	少女
shennü	goddess	神女
sheng li si bie	final farewell	生離死別
shisu	worldly ways; ordinary	世俗
shiyan xiaoshuo	experimental fiction	試驗小說
sushi	the vulgar world	俗世
ta	he	他
Ta shi Zhongguo wenhua zhong bu neng geiyu cunzai diweide dongxi	It is something that may not be ceded a place to exist in Chinese culture	它是中國文化中不能給予存在地位的東西
tanci	rhymed fables set to music	彈詞

Tianshi	Angel (character name)	天使
Tong Suxin	Pureheart Child (character name)	童素心
tongxing'ai	homosexuality	同性愛
tongxingde ailian	love of the same sex	同性的愛戀
tongxingde lianqing	loving feelings toward the same sex	同性的戀情
tongxinglian	homosexuality	同性戀
tongxingliande fengqi . . . sheng	the fashion for homosexuality was strong	同性戀的風氣 . . . 盛
tongxinglian shide duixiang	homosexual-style partner	同性戀式的對象
tongzhi	comrade; i.e., lesbian or gay	同志
tongzhi wenxue	lesbian and gay fiction	同志文學
wei xiandai pai	the pseudomodernist school	偽現代派
wendingde shehui zhidu	stable social system	穩定的社會制度
wo jide	I remember	我記得
xiandai pai	the modernist school	現代派
xianfeng xiaoshuo	avant-garde fiction	先鋒小說
xin hao T	sensitive new age T	新好T
xin nüxing	the New Woman	新女性
xin shiqi	the New Era	新時期
xinli	psychology	心理
xungen pai	the root-searching school	尋根派
xunzhao ziwo	to search for the self	尋找自我
xunqing	tragic death for love	殉情
yanqing xiaoshuo	romance fiction	言情小說
yige yong zhui yu beiju de ai	a love doomed to eternal tragedy	一個永墜於悲劇的愛
yishengzhong zui xiukuide jiyi	the most shameful memory of a lifetime	一生中最羞愧的記憶
yixinglian	heterosexuality	異性戀
yiyu er si	to die of grief	抑郁而死
yinfu	lascivious woman	淫婦

yinnü	lascivious woman	淫女
yinwude xingwei	filthy behavior	淫污的行為
youchang	boundless	悠長
Yuanqing (character name)		沅青
yuanyang hudie pai	the mandarin duck and butterfly school	鴛鴦蝴蝶派
Zhonghua minzu xing-gezhongde qianzai jiegou, . . . fahuizhe wuxing er you judade zhiyue zuoyong	an unconscious complex in the character of the Chinese people that exerts an invisible yet momentous constrictive power	中華民族性格中的潛在結構，. . . 發揮著無形而又巨大的制約作用
Zhong Yuan (character name)		鐘沅
zhutixing	subjectivity	主體性
zirande renlei guanxi	natural human relations	自然的人類關係
ziwo	the self	自我

. . .

Notes

1 Interview by Cheng Pei-pei of Ivy Ling Po on the Shaw Brothers' bonus DVD accompanying *The Love Eterne*.

2 This account is based on "Sanqian li renchao bo guang lian yan," a report that appeared the following day in *Lianhe bao* (United Daily News).

3 For a detailed account of the legend's multiple theatrical and operatic instances, see S. Li, *Cross-Dressing in Chinese Opera*, 109–34.

4 For a discussion of the queer potential of *Love Eterne*, see Tan and Aw, "*Love Eterne*"; Zhang Aizhu, "Xing fanchuan, yizhi kongjian," esp. 146–48; and C. L. Chan, "'Interesting' Gender-Crossing."

5 This tendency distinguishes these examples from some Euro-American narratives in which lesbianism is cast as merely an immature "stage" on the journey to a triumphantly heterosexual conclusion; see, for example, Judith Roof's discussion of the "foreplay" trope in soft-core pornography in *A Lure of Knowledge*, 15–89.

6 Cf. Mandy Merck's broadly comparable argument that the BBC production *Portrait of a Marriage* uses homosexuality as a "lens" through which heterosexual marriage can review its own shortcomings and hence shouldn't be discounted as simply a drowning-out of lesbian by heterosexual themes. *Perversions*, 101–17.

7 Rohy, *Impossible Women*, 4.

8 Roof, *A Lure of Knowledge*, 5. Roof's theorization of the configuration assumes a tripartite structure: it encompasses the representation of lesbian possibility, a symbolic defense against that representation, and the exposure of the anxiety and fragility of the heterosexual ideology that is so vigorously defended against the threat of lesbian knowledge (1–14). My citation of the term does not indicate that my theorization of the memorial same-sex romance narrative follows Roof's theory in all of these details (I find the defensive element less marked, as is dis-

cussed below). It is the idea of the lesbian configuration as marking a point of crisis in dominant sex-gender systems on which I chiefly wish to draw.

9 The persistent previousness of women's same-sex love in the Chinese examples perhaps also shares something in common with both Rohy's and Roof's observations that European and American lesbian representation tends to function as resistance to closure and is often associated with penultimateness, with both its radical and conservative implications (Roof, *A Lure of Knowledge*, 5; Rohy, *Impossible Women*, 144).

10 Cf. Tania Modleski's argument on Max Ophuls's film *Letter from an Unknown Woman*, where she highlights Lisa's "open memory" and voluntary, even joyful, evocation of reminiscences, in distinction from Freud's hysteric and her repressed desires ("Time and Desire in the Woman's Film").

11 See Farwell, *Heterosexual Plots*; Meese, *(Sem)Erotics*; Zimmerman, *Safe Sea*; Roof, *Come As You Are* and *A Lure of Knowledge*; Hoogland, *Lesbian Configurations*; Rohy, *Impossible Women*; Castle, *The Apparitional Lesbian*; Jagose, *Lesbian Utopics* and *Inconsequence*; Mayne, *Framed*; Merck, *Perversions*; de Lauretis, *The Practice of Love*; and White; *Uninvited*. See chapter 6 for more detailed discussion of Western lesbian film theory and criticism.

12 The small amount of extant writing in Chinese about lesbianism in mainland China and Hong Kong is largely ethnographic; it includes Li Yinhe's ethnography of a handful of mainland Chinese lesbian and bisexual women's responses to her survey on women's sexual experience (*Xing wenhua yanjiu baogao*, 117–31); Chou Wah-shan's introductory essay on the lack of public space for lesbianism in mid-1990s Beijing (*Beijing tongzhide gushi*, 101–21); a handful of mainland Chinese women's life histories collected in Wu Chensheng and Chou Wah-shan, *Women huozhe!*, and An Keqiang, *Hong taiyangxiade hei linghun*; and some Hong Kong women's personal narratives included in Mak, Chou, and Jiang, *Xianggang tongzhi zhan chu-lai*, and Kam, *Yueliang de saodong*. Following the boom there in queer scholarship in the humanities over the past decade, there exists a wider array of critical lesbian studies from and about Taiwan, with which I engage in detail in the chapters that follow.

13 Chou, *Tongzhi*, and Hinsch, *Passions*.

14 Sang, *The Emerging Lesbian*, 99–126.

15 Ibid., 24 and 63–65.

16 Ibid., 15–16. The question of sexology's role in demonizing lesbianism in the West has been vigorously debated among feminist historians. For a complication of the common view, expressed by Sheila Jeffreys, Margaret Jackson, Lillian Faderman, and others, that sexology was primarily repressive and inherently anti-feminist, see Doan, "'Acts of Female Indecency.'"

17 Indeed, Sang's historical argument on the modern Chinese abjection of lesbianism reflecting male anxieties about women's social power quite closely echoes Faderman's argument on the ideological effects of sexology in the West. Sang, *The Emerging Lesbian*, 24; cf. Faderman, *Surpassing*, 239–53 and 411–15.

18 Sang's analyses of Taiwanese lesbian cultures and the late author Qiu Miaojin illustrate particularly clearly her investment in reading lesbian feminist-style politics in the material (*The Emerging Lesbian*, 225–74); cf. Faderman, *Surpassing*, 411–15.

19 This is especially the case in chapter 5 (127–60). Confessing to this predisposition, Sang writes:

> My strategies for reading [May Fourth era representations of love between women] . . . differ, depending on whether the author is male or female. Of men's graphic depictions of female-female sex, I insist on asking, What strategies does the author employ, not only to conjure up the spectacle of female-female sex voyeuristically, but also to suppress its threat so that a vertiginous masculine pleasure does not turn into a truly subversive feminine power? Of women's depictions of female-female sex . . . I ask, How can female-female sex be culturally significant—recognized as physically gratifying and ecstatic without, at the same time, being demonized or deemed degenerate? (*The Emerging Lesbian*, 132–33)

20 See Moore's critique of Faderman in this regard, "'Something More Tender Still,'" 23–24. Sang convincingly defends herself against the possible charge of desexualizing lesbianism (*The Emerging Lesbian*, 8), but my point here is not simply about desexualization; it is about the conceptual vulgarization inherent in assuming that sexuality is explicable simply as a function of gender or that, a priori, "gender analysis is the most effective and appropriate means for understanding the importance of female homoerotic writing in the Chinese-speaking world" (Sang, *The Emerging Lesbian*, 7–8). Cf. Sedgwick's critique of this tendency in some feminist scholarship on homosexuality, *Epistemology of the Closet*, 27–35. For an account of a truly messy relationship between lesbian writing and feminism, see Martin, "Stigmatic Bodies."

21 Cf. Zimmerman's more complex combinatory, multifactorial approach to defining what constitutes an authentically lesbian text, *Safe Sea*, 14–16.

22 Foucault, *The History of Sexuality*, 100.

23 Indeed, given the extremely complex, messy confluence of cultural and intellectual influences at work in the forging of modern Chinese sexual categories and knowledges in the nineteenth and early twentieth centuries (Chinese, Japanese, European, American), any attempt at a comparative approach would need to eschew a simple X-versus-Y binary logic in favor of an appreciation of the complex inter-relationality between "Western" and "Chinese" modern sexual knowledges. See the beginning of chapter 1 for a more extended discussion of the problems inherent in straightforward comparativism between "Chinese" and "Western" sexualities.

24 The Chinese transculturation of sexology in this period has been traced in detail by Sang, *The Emerging Lesbian*, 99–126.

25 Leary, "Sexual Modernism" 228–31, 332–44, and 370.

26 Chang Ching-sheng, *Sex Histories*, 51–56.

27 The Chinese obsession with homoerotic relations involving feminine young women in schools perhaps has something in common with a comparable preoccupation in modern French literary and filmic lesbian representation, as observed by Mayne (*Framed*, 46).

28 The stigmatizing and minoritizing connotations of *tongxinglian* today stand in contrast to the broader, more positive usage of the earlier but synonymous sexological term *tongxing'ai*, which, as Sang observes, intellectual women in the Republican era willingly and openly used to describe their romantic friendships with one another, apparently with minimal anxiety about the term's possible stigma (*The Emerging Lesbian*, 136–37).

29 As chapter 1 demonstrates in detail, these parallel models draw both on the schemas of Ellis-style sexology—with its situational, temporary, and feminine lesbians, on the one hand, and its congenital, permanent, and masculine ones on the other—and on local understandings of proper versus malevolent feminine gender. The very tangledness of this web illustrates once again the inadequacy of the view of Chinese sexual modernization as a simple case of "Western pathologizing sexology" replacing "tolerant Chinese tradition." For in the Republican Chinese context, Ellis-style sexology facilitated the cultural elaboration of a relatively valorized form of female same-sex love—the kind felt by a young feminine woman for an intimate friend—as well as a pathologized form; and as well as "tolerance" for female intimacy, "Chinese tradition" also reveals extremely negative valuations of physically "unfeminine" and sexually desiring women.

30 Vicinus, "They Wonder," 236. In Western lesbian historiography, these two formations have often been set up in opposition to one another, as Vicinus details. Additionally, each formation taken separately has been the center of debates; for example, see Moore's refutation of Faderman's and Smith-Rosenberg's arguments on the relative cultural "tolerance" for romantic friendships in the eighteenth and nineteenth centuries in "Something More Tender Still." On the romantic friendship model in England and the United States, see also Faderman, *Surpassing*; Smith-Rosenberg, *Disorderly Conduct*, 53–76; Vicinus, "Distance and Desire," 212–29; and Newton, *Margaret Mead*, 176–88. The term "second gender" is used by Newton (*Margaret Mead*, 197) to refer to lesbian butchness; Newton follows Robertson's use of "secondary gender" in relation to the male-role actresses in the all-female Takarazuka Revue in Japan (*Margaret Mead*, 286n1).

31 Sang, *The Emerging Lesbian*, 135.

32 Cf. ibid., 270.

33 Ibid., 136–37.

34 Leung, "Thoughts on Lesbian Genders."

35 See, for example, Hong Ling, "Leise yu bianzi de jiaohuan," esp. 95–97.

36 Jagose, *Inconsequence*, chapter 1.

37 This book's argument on the surprising centrality of idealized representations of women's same-sex love to modern Chinese media and literary cultures perhaps

has something in common with an important trend in Euro-American queer studies toward recuperating the productive potential of seemingly hegemonic cultural forms through deconstructive interpretations of their subtext, thereby uncovering the inherent queerness of MTV, classical Hollywood cinema, 1970s television sitcoms, and so on. See, for example, Burston and Richardson, *A Queer Romance*; Creekmur and Doty, *Out in Culture*; and Doty, *Making Things Perfectly Queer*.

38 This marks a distinction from my earlier work on Taiwan's queer cultures in *Situating Sexualities*. In cases where I want to designate self-conscious or minoritarian lesbian identities, politics, or texts—as in chapter 6 and the first part of chapter 4—I use the term "lesbian" in distinction to "female homoerotic."

39 Cf. Day Wong's critique of the minoritizing model of lesbian identity and her espousal of a universalizing concept of "women who love women" as a framework for the Hong Kong Women Who Have Same-Sex Desires Oral History Project. Wong writes:

> By presenting the stories of same-sex desires among women who are single, married or divorced, who claim to be heterosexual, homosexual or bisexual, who are housewives, workers or middle-class professionals, this project reinvents women who have same-sex desires as [ubiquitous]. . . . The project incites not only the identification of sexual minorities, but also the vast majority's reflection upon their own same-sex desires, the experience of which can be unacknowledged, unsettling, or memorable and pleasurable. The oral history in effect helps to shift the affiliations of ordinary people away from the heterosexist order. ("Beyond Identity Politics," 15)

This book's inquiry into same-sex love between women as a central rather than a marginal cultural experience shares much in common with the spirit of Wong's remarks here.

40 Also cf. Rohy: "Resisting the impulse to define lesbian specificity may help lesbian theory avoid the boundary policing that defines disciplinary mechanisms of heterosexual culture—or at least, to consider with open eyes the risks of adopting, in the name of lesbian identity, an exclusionary logic that also structures the homophobic repudiation of lesbian sexuality" (*Impossible Women*, 146).

41 For examples of similar reasoning in relation to historical studies on love between women, see Vicinus, "Introduction," 2–3; Smith-Rosenberg, *Disorderly Conduct*, 58–59; and Carter, "On Mother-Love."

42 Cf. the use of "imaginary" vis-à-vis geographic imaginings—for example, in Connery, "The Oceanic Feeling and the Regional Imaginary."

43 R. Williams, *The Long Revolution*, 48ff.; de Lauretis, *The Practice of Love*, xix.

44 Cf. Zimmerman, *Safe Sea*; Farwell, *Heterosexual Plots*; and Meese, *(Sem)erotics*.

45 In its intentional focus on broadly mainstream representations, the project has something in common with the approaches taken by Rohy (*Impossible Women*) and Roof (*A Lure of Knowledge*). There is a historical logic here as well. A type of cultural

production broadly comparable to that which Zimmerman treats in *Safe Sea*— that is, fiction by authors who self-identify as lesbians, write openly about lesbian subjects, and address a lesbian readership, which has burgeoned in English since the late 1960s—only began to appear in quantity in Chinese in the mid-to-late 1990s, with the consolidation of lesbian movement politics in Taiwan and Hong Kong. So the mainly earlier texts that chapters 1–5 of this book discuss (including their later televisual adaptations) speak from prior to the moment of emergence of a significant body of self-defined lesbian (or queer) writing, when readers in search of lesbian-like meanings had to find them elsewhere.

46 Cf. Hinsch, *Passions*, and see Sang's analysis of "lesbian" meaning in premodern China, *The Emerging Lesbian*, 37–95. This modern focus need not simply reduce modern Chinese sexual epistemologies to the effects of Westernization. In the modern period we see instead a muddy confluence of local and trans-local elements in sexual cultures, narratives, and ideologies, as is demonstrated in chapter 1's analysis of the significant contribution of the traditions of Chinese tragic (cross-sex) romance narrative to the modern schoolgirl romance.

47 This chronology echoes the one in Sang's *The Emerging Lesbian*, for which she accounts with a similar historical logic (20–30).

48 Evans, *Women and Sexuality in China*, 206–12; see also Sang, *The Emerging Lesbian*, 163–74.

49 Chao, "Embodying the Invisible," chapters 6–7; Damm, "Same Sex Desire," 68–69.

50 Damm, "Same Sex Desire."

51 However, Chao notes one or two sensationalist media accounts of lesbianism as politically suspect gender inversion from the early 1980s ("Embodying the Invisible," 39–42).

52 See H. Leung, "Unsung Heroes"; Grossman, "Hong Kong Film"; McLelland, "Interview with Samshasha"; Hinsch, *Passions*, 162–71.

53 I have been told of the existence of a similar pulp novel, set in Hong Kong from around the same time, entitled *Nü xiang* (Women facing), but I have been unable to locate a copy of it; its apparent nonsurvival probably testifies to a cultural status similarly lowly to that of Xuan's novel.

54 For example, Peng's *Tongxinglian, zisha, jingshenbing*. Damm observes that Peng's psychoanalytic approach to homosexuality already featured in the Taiwanese press from the mid-1970s. See also Li, *Xing wenhua yanjiu baogao*.

55 On Taiwan, see Martin, *Situating Sexualities*. On Hong Kong, see D. Wong, "(Post-)identity Politics." On mainland China, see He, "Chinese Queer (Tongzhi) Women"; Xu, "Suppressed Voice or Silence by Choice?"; and Engebretsen, "Lesbian Identity." Lesbian communities emerged slightly later in mainland China than in Taiwan and Hong Kong, becoming much more visible and active since the spread of Internet communication post-1995.

56 The Republican period refers to the years between 1911 (the overthrow of the Qing

dynasty and the founding of the Republic of China) and 1949 (the Communist Revolution and the founding of the People's Republic of China).

57 There are of course many instances of treatments of this topic that do not conform to the models analyzed here; in fiction, consider, for instance, Li Ang's novel *Huajian mi qing* (Bewitching Love), Yi Shu's novel *Xu—* (Shhh—), and Yan Geling's novella "Bai she" (White Snake); in film, consider experimental lesbian features like Yau Ching's *Ho yuk* (Let's Love Hong Kong) and Zero Chou's *Si jiaoluo* (Corner's); soft porn films such as Chu Yuan's *Ai nu* (Intimate Confessions of a Chinese Courtesan) and Chu Yen-ping's *Nü huan* (Lady in Heat); and Cui Yan's drama about Chinese women in Canada, *Luo niao* (Chinese Chocolate).

58 This is particularly notable in differences between the mainland Chinese examples, on the one hand, and those from Taiwan and Hong Kong on the other since between 1949 and the mid-1980s cultural cross-flows were significantly greater between the latter two areas than they were between either of these and the People's Republic. See Gold, "Go with Your Feelings."

59 Silvio, "Reflexivity"; H. Leung, "Unsung Heroes"; and Sang, *The Emerging Lesbian*, 164–65.

60 For example, Chu T'ien-hsin's *Fangzhoushangde rizi*, which includes "Waves Scour the Sands," discussed in this volume, was republished by Shanghai Wenyi Chubanshe in 2001. Indeed, the fiction of Chu T'ien-hsin and Chu T'ien-wen has garnered significant attention in mainland Chinese literary circles since the 1980s. See, for example, discussions in Yang, "Shen qing zai jie"; An Xingben, "Queshide beige"; and Zhu, "Cong ernü siyu dao juancun chuanqi."

61 Examples of these literary cross-flows include the publication of the lesbian-themed collection *Jing yu shui* (Mirror and Water), edited by the mainland author Hong Ying and published by the Taiwanese press Jiuge in 1999; also the Hong Kong gay and lesbian publisher Worldson's (Huasheng) publication of the Three Places, One Heart series (*San di tong xin*), which collected lesbian- and gay-themed short stories by writers in all three areas in single volumes.

62 A tendency toward regional Chinese identification across geopolitical boundaries in gay and lesbian activism and subcultures is evident in the Chinese Tongzhi Conference (*Huaren tongzhi jiaoliu dahui*) series, organized by a group in Hong Kong but incorporating participants from all three areas as well as the worldwide Chinese diaspora. The first conference took place in Hong Kong in 1996; the second and third, in 1998 and 1999, again in Hong Kong; the fourth, in Taiwan in 2001; and the fifth, in Hong Kong in 2004. See the Tongzhi Conference Web site at http://www.tongzhiconference.com.

63 Tu, "Cultural China."

64 Li Mingying, "Miandui xuesheng tongxinglian yigan."

65 Shen Yuexing, *Zheli, meiyou nansheng*, 279–80. The two chapters devoted to same-sex romance in Shen's book are a fascinating generic mixture of memorial schoolgirl romance—written by the students themselves and comparable in their

confessional, sentimental tone to a classic example of the genre like Lu Yin's "Lishi de riji" (discussed in chapter 1)—and a kind of rhetorical damage-control effected by Shen's own psychological interpretations, inserted contrapuntally at crucial moments, which seek anxiously to assure the reader of the clear distinction between her students' passionate sentiments and "true" homosexuality. See 260–307. For a similar account, see also the anonymous article on a popular psychology Web site in China under the emphatic title "Closeness between Intimate Friends of the Same Sex Is Not Homosexuality" (*Tongxing miyou changsheng haogan bing fei tongxinglian*).

66. Shen Yuexing makes this distinction even more explicitly on p. 268.

67 The 1970s emergence of the subgenre is seen in the publication of works including Yashiro Masako's *Secret Love* (1970); Yamagishi Ryoko's *The Two in the White Room* (1971); and *The Rose of Versailles* (1972–73), *Brother, Dear Brother* (1974), and other series by Ikeda Riyoko. See Dollase, "Mad Girls in the Attic," 233; Fujimoto, *Watashi no ibasho wa doko ni aru no*, 180; Welker, "Drawing Out Lesbians"; and Ogi, "Gender Insubordination," 180–83. Many thanks to Taeko Yamada for her translation of Fujimoto.

68 Wei, "Shaping a Cultural Identity," 68–69; see also Lent, "Local Comic Books" and "Comics in East Asian Countries," and Ng, "A Comparative Study of Japanese Comics" and "The Impact of Japanese Comics."

69 For example, Ikeda Riyoko's *Brother, Dear Brother* was originally circulated in Taiwan as a pirate manga entitled *The Blue Orchid Cotillion* (*Qinglan yuanwuqu*) before screening in anime form on the Japanese NHK cable channel in 1991–92 and later on the local network CTS. (See the detailed *Rose of Versailles* fan site maintained by one Taiwanese fan, BYS [Xiao Yin]. The site includes information about the translation of Ikeda's works into Chinese and their circulation in Taiwan.) More recently, the anime by Satoru Nagasawa, *Maria-sama ga miteru* (The Gaze of the Virgin Mary), based on Oyuki Konno's novel, has been broadcast in Taiwan prior to its release as a manga series. The first volume was published in 2005 by Tong Li Comics. Other Japanese school-based GL (Girl's Love) manga series currently circulating in Chinese translation include Kimino Sakurako's *Strawberry Panic!* (Taiwan edition 2007–) and Hakamada Mera's *Our Last Season* (Taiwan edition 2006–).

70 Notable examples include the *Eko eko azarak* films from Japan (*Wizard of Darkness*, 1995, and *Birth of the Wizard*, 1996, both dir. Sato Shimako) and the *Yeogo goedam* trilogy from Korea (*Whispering Corridors*, 1998, dir. Park Ki-hyung; *Memento Mori*, 1999, dir. Kim Tae-Yong and Min Kyu-Dong; *The Wishing Stairs*, 2003, dir. Yun Jae-yeon).

71 Taiwanese director Arthur Chu's (Qu Youning) film *Sharen jihua* (My Whispering Plan) (2002) adapts this genre to a Taiwan setting. The introverted schoolgirl Jane (Peggy Young) plots to murder her popular best friend, Sunny (Sherlly Hsieh) when she becomes jealous of her friendships with other girls and her interest in boys. But the film stops well short of the full-scale horror of the Japanese and

Korean films: Jane doesn't actually murder Sunny, and her disturbed psychological state is explained in the film by an extrinsic cause (the forced evacuation and razing of her family home), rather than as a product of her same-sex attraction.

72 See, for example, Cornbug's melancholic, psychological-realist *Xuejie* (2002); Ranblue's light-hearted, comedic *Wo ai lanqiu meishaonü* 1 and 2 (2003); and Mayberight's *Wode xinli zhi you ni meiyou ta* 1 and 2 (2003). The lesbian undertones in Japanese campus-based girls' love manga have also been drawn out more fully in Taiwanese artist Fanny Shen's two-volume series *Yi beizi shouzhe ni* (1997–98), which similarly articulates the schoolgirl romance narrative with a more specifically and self-consciously lesbian identity and cultural politics.

73 See Zhang Qiaoting, *Xunfu yu dikang*; Kam, "TB zhe xingbie"; Tong, "Being a Tomboy"; and P. Leung, "Unruly Same-Sex Intimacies."

74 Zhang Qiaoting concludes that although Bei Yi Nü authorities demonstrate strong anxiety over the potential for homosexuality (*tongxinglian*) to be publicly seen as occurring at the school, nonetheless in certain limited ways the school functions as a temporary haven for same-sex attracted students, distanced as it is from the even more stringent surveillance of the family while also relatively insulated from the enforced heterosexual system of adult society (*Xunfu yu dikang*, chapters 4 and 5).

75 P. Leung, "Unruly Same-Sex Intimacies."

76 Kam cites Ng Kit-fan's 1996 popular-fictional schoolgirl romance "The Pure Country" ("Chuncuide guodu") as reflective of aspects of actual school cultures in Hong Kong ("TB zhe xingbie," 9). Popular lesbian author Ng Kit-fan's pen name is a homophone for the Cantonese phrase "refusing marriage," marking a thematic consistency with the early-twentieth-century schoolgirl romances in the framing of schoolgirl romance as marriage resistance (see chapter 1). The Women Coalition of Hong Kong, which conducted the Hong Kong Women Who Have Same-Sex Desires Oral History Project (1950–2004), published the findings in a booklet, *Tamende nüqing yinji* (2005); see especially the section on schoolgirl romance (14–15). See also D. Wong, "Beyond Identity Politics."

77 This is with the exception of the 1970s tomboy melodramas discussed in chapter 4, which do cast the tomboy as a socially marginal figure—as indeed she has tended to be, to judge by the scarcity of representations focusing on her experience.

Chapter One: Tragic Romance

Some material from two sections of this chapter appears in different and condensed form in Martin, "Trans-Asian Traces" and "Stigmatic Bodies."

1 Hinsch, *Passions*, 169.

2 For a discussion of critiques of Hinsch's position, see Martin, *Situating Sexualities*, 31–33. Hong Kong commentator Chou Wah-shan, who espoused a view closely related to Hinsch's in his Chinese book *Houzhimin tongzhi*, has partially revised his

argument in his more recent English book, *Tongzhi*. However, Chou's argument in the latter book is inconsistent, drawing heavily as it does on the work of a range of other scholars whose views are at times opposed. The problem is especially apparent in chapter 1, where Chou tries to argue simultaneously that "the modern Chinese history of sexuality cannot be captured by any simple 'Western colonizer versus Chinese colonized' . . . dichotomy" (55) and that Republican Chinese intellectuals adopted the Western "sexologist's pathologization of homosexuality" (49) and that "there was little discussion among Chinese intellectuals of homo, hetero, bi or the entire notion of sexual orientation" (50). In proposing the last point, Chou draws heavily on Frank Dikötter's brief section on homosexuality in *Sex, Culture and Modernity*. The shortcomings of Dikötter's research have been pointed out in detail by Sang (*The Emerging Lesbian*, 99–126).

3 Sedgwick, *Epistemology of the Closet*, 44.

4 Sang, *The Emerging Lesbian*, 16–17.

5 Sedgwick, *Epistemology of the Closet*, 45. See also, for example, Julian Carter's analysis of how the complexity of conceptualizations and practices of white women's same-sex erotic and affective relations in the early-twentieth-century United States belies the idea that "sexuality as we know it" in the modern period could be reducible to any simple, singular formulation ("On Mother-Love"). Others have questioned the assumption that normativity coincides exactly with something called "heterosexuality" in the modern West. For example, Paul Kelleher draws attention to Foucault's neglect of the cultural valence of sentiment in his concentration on sexuality: "By returning to the literary-historical context of sentimentalism [since the seventeenth century], we discover that what looks and feels like normative affection or 'sexuality' is not reducible only to the opposition between 'homo' and 'hetero.' In other words, normative figurations of mind, body, and social relation may not be strictly synonymous with heterosexuality as such, and the equation of heterosexuality with normativity . . . necessarily entails a historical remainder. Sentimentalism, I suggest, enables us to account for this remainder" ("If Love Were All," 151). Cf. discussion below and in chapter 2 on the central role of sentiment in both Chinese popular romance genres and the Chinese "going-in story."

6 For a concise example of this approach, see Fuss, "Introduction."

7 See Martin, *Situating Sexualities*, conclusion. I draw the idea of the proximate from Jonathan Dollimore's discussion of the perverse dynamic (*Sexual Dissidence*, 33); however, where Dollimore uses the term in a deconstructive sense, to denote the presence of the "other" within the "same," I am appropriating the term as a descriptor for historical processes—a related but not identical usage.

8 I am not proposing that universalizing understandings are uniquely Chinese; what distinguishes these examples from Western ones are the specific ways in which universalizing and minoritizing accounts mix and trouble one another.

9 See Plummer, *Telling Sexual Stories*.

10 Sang, *The Emerging Lesbian*, 102–3; Hinsch, *Passions*; Chou, *Tongzhi*, 13–55.

11 Gregory Pflugfelder emphasizes that the Japanese translation of European sex-ology in the early twentieth century involved a very selective process of reading and interpretation; as a result, he argues, modern Japanese sexological concepts, including dōseiai, cannot be presumed to be identical to the European concepts that they translated. *Cartographies of Desire*, 235–85.

12 See Pflugfelder, "'S' Is for Sister"; Robertson, "Yoshiya Nobuko," 159; and Chalmers, "Tolerance, Form and Female Dis-ease," paragraphs 16–17.

13 Furukawa, "The Changing Nature of Sexuality," 115. Note that Pflugfelder constructs the cause-and-effect relationship the other way around: "The emergence in the late nineteenth century of the new sexological model, with its theoretical equation of male and female 'same-sex love,' played a key role in elevating the visibility of intimate female-female relations within the social imaginary, and accorded them for the first time in the history of Japanese erotic discourses an integral place within authoritative cultural mappings of sexuality" ("'S' Is for Sister," 10). For Furukawa, the actual social prominence of intimate relations between schoolgirls served as impetus for the coinage of the term dōseiai; for Pflugfelder, it was the translation of sexology, including the term dōseiai, that led to the new social prominence of intimate relations between schoolgirls. This distinction notwithstanding, the authors concur in their proposal that the novel concept of dōseiai is entangled from the outset with public imaginings of schoolgirls' relations with each other.

14 Pflugfelder, *Cartographies of Desire*, 248.

15 Ueno, "Self-Determination on Sexuality?" 319; see also McLelland, *Reconstructing Sex and Gender in Japan 1945–55*.

16 Aoyama, "Transgendering shōjo shosetsu," 52; Robertson, "Yoshiya Nobuko" and *Takarazuka*, 61–73; and Dollase, "Early Twentieth Century Japanese Girls' Magazine Stories." Aoyama notes that the term shōjo appears to have entered common usage around 1900.

17 Dollase, "Early Twentieth Century Japanese Girls' Magazine Stories."

18 This emphasis is demonstrated by a sustained spate of sexological and quasi-sexological articles on this topic in the Japanese popular press, as well as feminist journals, between about 1910 and the mid-1930s. Furukawa cites multiple examples of popular Japanese journalism on love between girls published between 1910 and 1912; see also P. Wu, "Performing Gender," 67–72; Pflugfelder's extended discussion of early-twentieth-century Japanese journalistic accounts of same-sex love among schoolgirls in "'S' Is for Sister"; Robertson, "Dying to Tell"; and Frühstück, *Colonizing Sex*, 68–70.

19 Furukawa, "The Changing Nature of Sexuality," 115. For example, Furukawa cites the sexologist Yasuda Tokutaro, writing in 1935, when the cultural obsession with love between girls had already been current for almost twenty years: "Nan-shoku is already practiced only infrequently, as a barbaric feudal hangover, or as a substitute eroticism in puberty. But if one looks at the social pages of the newspapers these days, there are numerous double suicides of female lovers. [Dōseiai]

gives the appearance of being monopolized by girls." Note that the use of the English term "lesbianism" in the quote in the translated text above is misleading in its connotations of the modern, Western-style sexual identity; it would probably be more accurate to say "female same-sex love." See also Pflugfelder, "'S' Is for Sister," 18–19, and P. Wu, "Performing Gender," 67–68.

20 Pflugfelder, "'S' Is for Sister," 46.

21 Ibid., 11–17, 39ff. See also Robertson, "Dying to Tell," 54–59.

22 Pflugfelder, "'S' Is for Sister," 17. Pflugfelder connects these constructions of feminine versus masculine *dōseiai* to the European sexological theory of the two genders as complementary opposites. This is indeed a very notable tendency—for example, in Ellis's biological gender determinism (on Ellis's views on feminine gender and female homosexuality, see Smith-Rosenberg, *Disorderly Conduct*, 275–80). Pflugfelder's argument is thus not that the construction of girls as sentimental and sexually passive is uniquely Japanese but that the European sexological construction of femininity along these lines was taken up with particular enthusiasm in the already receptive Japanese context. See also Furukawa, "The Changing Nature of Sexuality,"115–16; McLelland, "From Sailor-Suits to Sadists," 3–7; and Frühstück, *Colonizing Sex*, 69–70. P. Wu notes the existence of a markedly pathologizing journalistic discourse on "revolting lesbianism," in relation to love-suicides, around 1911 ("Performing Gender," 67–72) but also observes the commonness of romantic idealization of female same-sex attachment in Meiji-era literature by both male and female authors (74).

23 Note that the Japanese terms *dōseiai* and *shōjo* are translated into modern Chinese terms (*tongxing'ai* and *shaonü*) using the same Chinese character forms—that is, they are orthographically identical. For a basic account of the cultural construction of adolescence in Republican China through the translation of Western medical discourse, see Dikötter, *Sex, Culture and Modernity*, 146–79. However, Dikötter strangely overlooks the profusion of Republican-era discussions of same-sex love between adolescent girls, declaring that "female homosexuality was rarely discussed in Republican China" (141).

24 Sang, *The Emerging Lesbian*, 122. On the Japanese translation of European sexology in the early twentieth century and the development of a Japanese sexological discourse, see Pflugfelder, *Cartographies of Desire*, 235–85; Furukawa, "The Changing Nature of Sexuality," 117–22; and Angles, "Writing the Love of Boys," 3–8.

25 Sang, *The Emerging Lesbian*, 107–13.

26 Ibid., 106–26.

27 Ibid., 112–13; on Furuya, see Pflugfelder, "'S' Is for Sister," 40–42.

28 Pflugfelder, "'S' Is for Sister," 41.

29 Sang, *The Emerging Lesbian*, 127–60. See also Larson, *Women and Writing*, 84–91.

30 Leo Ou-fan Lee observes that the tendency to idealize women as embodiments of spiritual love in 1920s Chinese modernist fiction, a tendency he connects with the contemporaneous strong interest in and translations of Western romantic

fiction, amounts to an almost total reversal of the association of women with the purely carnal in premodern Chinese literature (*Romantic Generation*, 266–68).

31 See, for example, the structuring opposition between masculine carnal love (*routi lianai*) and feminine spiritual love (*jingshen lianai*) in Chu T'ien-hsin's "A Story of Spring Butterflies."

32 Song, *Fragile Scholar*, 19–41.

33 McMahon, *Misers, Shrews*, 99–149.

34 Song, *Fragile Scholar*, 19–36. It is interesting to note Song's observation that the scholar in the scholar-beauty romance, whose good looks hinge on his delicate effeminacy, bears an intertextual relation to the Chinese homoerotic tradition and that this image of male beauty reflects a specifically male notion of the sexually desirable male body (125–56). Note also McMahon's observation that given the beauty's tendency to mimic masculine traits in both dress and literary talent in the "chaste" beauty-scholar romance, "the relationship between the beauty and the scholar takes on the characteristics of the friendship between two literati men" (*Misers, Shrews*, 99). If the apparently heterosexual romance of the scholar-beauty story indeed masks an underlying male homoeroticism, then this is interesting to bear in mind in relation to my argument below that the May Fourth women writers' schoolgirl romances effectively re-homosexualize the cross-sex romance narrative, albeit in a different way.

35 McMahon, *Misers, Shrews*, 100–103, 122–23.

36 Link, *Mandarin Ducks*, 62–63. Note the distinction between the homophones *ai4qing*, "romantic love," and *ai1qing*, "tragic love."

37 Ibid., 64–78.

38 Ibid., 70–71; Hsia, "Hsu Chen-ya's Yu-li hun," 213–14; see also L. Lee, *Romantic Generation*, 257–74.

39 A comparable structure of feeling arguably continues in some twentieth-century popular romances; see the discussion of Qiong Yao in chapter 2.

40 Hsia, "Hsu Chen-ya's Yu-li hun," 214.

41 Link connects them, on one hand, with the scholar-beauty tradition, and, on the other, with the increased interest in and translation of Western romantic fiction from around the turn of the century (*Mandarin Ducks*, 8–9, 54, 60–62).

42 Hsia, "Hsu Chen-ya's Yu-li hun," 201, 214, 235–40; L. Lee, *Romantic Generation*, 44–46. However, as Timothy C. Wong observes, Hsia offers little justification for the inclusion of "erotic" as a descriptor for a tradition that emphasizes spiritual and emotional love over bodily desire (*Stories for Saturday*, 46); henceforth, I will refer to the tradition Hsia describes as that of the "tragic-love story" or "tragic-love fiction."

43 See J. Chen, "Zhou Shoujuan's Love Stories"; Gimpel, *Lost Voices of Modernity*, 92–108; and Link, *Mandarin Ducks*, 61.

44 Link, *Mandarin Ducks*, 58, 62.

45 Jianhua Chen argues that butterfly author Zhou Shoujuan's fiction indigenized

Western-style cultural modernity through "native values" and literary aesthetics and modernized the *caizi-jiaren* form by using contemporary urban settings and championing the ideology of romantic love ("Zhou Shoujuan's Love Stories," 357–59).

46 Chow, *Woman*, 34–83. Comparably, Hsia proposes that *Yu li hun* in fact exposes the morbidity and destructiveness of the feudal code of feminine virtue that it seems to uphold in its representation of the heroine's, widow Li-niang's, spotless moral conduct ("Hsu Chen-ya's *Yu-li hun*," 224–25). See also Gimpel's discussion of the progressive explorations of various tenets of modern femininity—free marriage, the equality of the sexes, the injustice of polygamous marriage—in a range of stories and articles published in the butterfly journal *Xiaoshuo yuebao* (Short Story Magazine) between 1910 and 1914 (*Lost Voices of Modernity*, 92–108).

47 Larson, *Women and Writing*, 84–91; L. Lee, *Romantic Generation*, 262–66.

48 Larson, *Women and Writing*, 88ff. On writers' complex negotiations with ideologies of gender in the context of cultural and literary modernization in the Republican era, see also Yue, "Gendering the Origins of Modern Chinese Fiction," and L. Liu, "Invention and Intervention." For a detailed discussion of the influence of European romanticism on the Chinese literary modernists, see L. Lee, *Romantic Generation*, 275–96. Lee's description of the 1920s as a "romantic decade" in China's literary history rests on his observation of the male May Fourth authors' privileging of individual, subjective experience over objectivity and rational analysis, of emotional over ritual response, and of a utopian and only ever hazily defined yearning radically to overhaul existing social systems (295).

49 On the cultural, political, and literary construction of the New Woman, see Stevens, "Figuring Modernity"; C-k. S. Chan, "The Language of Despair"; Peng Hsiao-yen, "The New Woman" and *Haishang shuo qingyu*.

50 Larson, *Women and Writing*, 92.

51 See also Lieberman, *The Mother and Narrative Politics*, 104–33.

52 Larson, *Women and Writing*, 107–10; Sang, *The Emerging Lesbian*, 133–50. See also Chien, *He chu shi nü'er jia*, 13–39. Chien analyzes the representation of "female same-sex friendship" in works by Feng Yuanjun, Lu Yin, and Ding Ling, going so far as to propose that "'Lishi's Diary' could be called the first story in modern Chinese literature to present a positive view of female homosexual love . . ., and to critique traditional, heterosexual marriage from the perspective of a female homosexual" (22–23). In contrast to Chien's minoritizing reading of Lishi as a female homosexual, however, what I propose is most interesting about "Lishi's Diary" is precisely its implicitly *universalizing* view of same-sex love: far from singling Lishi out as an unusual variation on normal feminine sexuality, the story presents her rather as an ordinary schoolgirl not notably different from her classmates. Chien's assumption that Lu's story courageously rebels against "the upholders of traditional Confucian (homophobic) morality" (23) is also questionable since it was not until the period that the story was written—the

1920s—that the minoritizing concept of homosexuality as a condition affecting a particular, delimited group of individuals—and hence the possibility for homophobia—made an entry into Republican Chinese culture. These literary works' representations of marriage as traumatically unfulfilling in comparison with premarital same-sex relations echo some comparable portrayals in the case histories collected in Zhang Jingsheng's *Sex Histories*, published in 1926. See Leary, "Sexual Modernism," 332–38.

53 Larson, *Women and Writing*, 88–89.

54 Ibid., 90.

55 Ling's story, "Shuo you zheme yihui shi," whose title Sang translates as "Rumor Has It That Something Like This Happened," has been translated by Amy D. Dooling and Kristina M. Torgeson as "Once upon A Time" in their *Women Writing in Modern China*, 185–95. The story provides a particularly clear illustration of the association of the new ideology of romantic love—whether cross-sex or, as in this case, same-sex—with cultural Westernization. Not only does the story's central couple play the parts of Romeo and Juliet in a school production of Shakespeare's play, but also, tellingly, the young women tend to lapse into English when speaking to each other of love and the emotions. For example, the entire length of Yunluo's impassioned confession of love for Yingman appears in English: "*My God, how can I live without you! I love you. Say you love me, my love*" (Dooling and Torgeson, trans., "Once upon a Time," 190–91; Ling, "Shuo you zheme yihui shi," 124). Foreshadowing some of the late-twentieth-century examples of schoolgirl romance, Ling's story also mixes the two dominant tropes of female same-sex love: romantic friendship and secondary gender. The central couple is distinguished in lightly—yet noticeably—gendered terms: Yingman, who plays Romeo in the school play, is described as a "tall, outgoing northerner," while Yunluo (Juliet) is "delicate and vulnerable" (Dooling and Torgeson, trans., "Once upon a Time," 185, 186).

56 Chow, "Virtuous Transactions." However, Chow's analysis arguably tends to underplay the historical specificity of Ling's stories, presenting them as the work of a "Chinese woman" about "Chinese women" very generally, rather than seeing them in context as the works of a modernist author engaged, along with other modernist women writers of her time, in a social critique of quite specific feudal marriage practices.

57 Dooling and Torgeson, trans., "Once upon a Time," 195.

58 Among May Fourth examples, Lu Yin's "Lishi's Diary," with its flashback structure, prefigures the late-twentieth-century memorial mode most strongly; Ling's title, "Once upon a Time," suggests a certain aura of pastness, although the narrative of the story itself is not as overtly memorial as "Lishi's Diary" and the contemporary examples by Chu T'ien-hsin and Wong Bikwan discussed in chapter 2.

59 Lu Yin, *Lu Yin zizhuan*, 53.

60 Dooling and Torgeson, *Women Writing*, 136.

61 Lu describes how, during her middle-school years, "[This relative of my aunt] knew that I enjoyed novel reading and lent me the new copy of *Jade Pear Spirit* that he had recently bought. What this novel describes are the tribulations of a senti-mental [*duoqing*] yet ill-fated heroine; the story is extremely tragic, and as I read it I shed not a few tears. Later, when I returned the book to him, I suppose there must still have been some tear stains on it, for he asked my younger sister what had happened—had I cried when I read the book?—and my sister said, 'Cry! Did she ever—she couldn't even eat anything for a whole day!'" (Lu Yin, *Lu Yin zizhuan*, 42).

62 Zhang Manjuan describes "Lishi's Diary" as "a classic tragedy" in its depiction of the ill-fated love between Lishi and Yuanqing ("Yu Dafu," 5).

63 On butterfly heroines' forced marriages to the wrong men, see Chow's discussion of Li Dingyi's *Shuang yi ji* and *Qian jin gu*, (*Woman*, 58–63); on heroines' tendency to die for love, see Link on *Yu li hun* (*Mandarin Ducks*, 43); for an example of a butterfly tragic-love story illustrating both points, see Yan Fusun, "The Bridal Palanquin."

64 Lu Yin, *Lishi de riji*, 47.

65 See Chow (*Woman*, 70–71) and Hsia ("Hsu Chen-ya's Yu-li Hun," 233–34) on Mengxia and Liniang's chaste relations in *Yu li hun*. Frank Dikötter offers a gen-eral discussion of the sexological construction of gender as biologically imma-nent, and especially the construction of women as sexually passive, through a selective survey of Republican-era sex education materials; *Sex, Culture and Moder-nity*, 14–61. As discussed above, this idea also relates to a similar discourse on women's sexual passivity in Japanese-derived materials around the same time.

66 Cf. Chow on *Yu Li Hun* in *Woman*, 71, and Yan Fusun, "The Bridal Palanquin."

67 Lu Yin, "Lishi de riji," 48.

68 The modern fashion for sending plum blossom draws on fifth-century author Sheng Hongzhi's *Jingzhou ji* (Records of Jingzhou), which describes the scholar Lu Kai sending branches of the early spring flowers from his native Jiangnan region to his beloved and greatly missed friend Fan Ye in Chang'an; it implies a sentimental friendship between intellectuals. Thanks to Cuncun Wu.

69 Lu Yin, "Lishi de riji," 57.

70 Sedgwick, "Introduction: Axiomatic," in *Epistemology of the Closet*.

71 Sang, *The Emerging Lesbian*, 312n56.

72 Ellis, *Studies*, 216.

73 Sang, *The Emerging Lesbian*, 113–18.

74 Ellis, "School-Friendships," in *Studies*, 374. See also the universalizing account of schoolgirl lesbian behavior included in Chang Ching-sheng, *Sex Histories*, 54–56. For further accounts of the temporary-phase model of homosexuality by Zhang Jingsheng and other Republican Chinese writers, see Peng Hsiao-yen, "Sex Histo-ries: Zhang Jingsheng's Sexual Revolution"; Leary, "Sexual Modernism," 332–44 and 370; and Dikötter, *Sex, Culture and Modernity*, 139–40.

75 For a summary of the somewhat divergent views of Krafft-Ebing and Ellis on the nature and expression of sexual inversion in women, see Smith-Rosenberg, *Disorderly Conduct*, 267–88.

76 Sang mentions this story briefly in *The Emerging Lesbian*, 153–54.

77 The class designations of the three central characters (the girls Li Wenqing, Zheng Xiuyue, and Feng Shifen) are a key element of the story's leftist and proto-nationalist ideological framework. Yu wrote that he intended them to represent rural gentry capitalists, indecisive elements in the petite bourgeoisie, and revolutionary elements in the petite bourgeoisie respectively (Yu quoted in Zhang Manjuan, "Yu Dafu," 2).

78 Yu, "Ta shi yige ruo nüzi," 281–82, 308.

79 Ibid., 310.

80 McMahon, *Misers, Shrews*, 44.

81 See also Ding, *Obscene Things*, 241, and Martin, *Situating Sexualities*, 119–40, on Taiwanese author Chen Xue's queer redeployment of the *enü*.

82 I am suggesting a comparable ideological function for Li Wenqing to that which Lisa Moore reads in the similarly masculinized and abjected character Harriot Freke in Maria Edgworth's 1801 novel *Belinda*, whom she proposes serves to "mark the boundary between 'virtuous' and 'indecent' female friendship" ("Something More Tender Still," 29).

83 Yu, "Ta shi yige ruo nüzi," 313–14.

84 On this passage see also Zeng, "Xunzhao mizangzhongde baoli jingji chang."

85 My argument here is therefore at variance with Sang's (*The Emerging Lesbian*, 153–54) and represents an elaboration of my own earlier argument in "Stigmatic Bodies." I thank Liu Jen-peng for pointing out to me the importance of taking seriously Li Wenqing's peculiar polysemy.

86 Yu, "Ta shi yige ruo nüzi," 324.

87 But on the complexity of Krafft-Ebing's theory of inversion, which does not in fact equate straightforwardly with sexual desire exclusively for the same sex, see Storr, "Transformations."

88 Ding, *Obscene Things*, xii. The term Chen Huiwen uses is *yinnü*; Ding uses the more standard classical term *yinfu* (Chen Huiwen, "Cainü, yinnü, ruonü xingxiangde jiangou").

89 The examples Chen Huiwen cites are of Widow Li in chapter 28 of the Qing dynasty novel *Lin Lan Xiang* (Three women named Lin, Lan, and Xiang, author unknown), who played sex games with a maidservant involving a dildo, and of the old woman in the first chapter of the seventeenth-century novel *Yu shi ming yan* (Stories to Enlighten, by Feng Menglong), who, when young, seized the chance of the men being absent from the house to sleep with a female relative ("Cainu, yinnu, ruonu xingxiangde jiangou").

1 Chu T'ien-hsin, interview with Martin. Zhang Qiaoting's late-1990s ethnographic study of elite-educated, lesbian-identifying young women in Taipei also shows that the works by Chu, along with Cao Lijuan's "The Maidens' Dance," hold great significance for some of her interviewees and according to them helped catalyze their lesbian identification (Zhang, *Xunfu yu dikang*, 5/13–5/16 and 5/29n6).

2 See, for example, Ranblue's *Wo ai lanqiu mei shaonü* (I Love The Beautiful Basketball Girl); Mayberight's *Wode xinli zhi you ni meiyou ta* 1 and 2 (Only You); and Cornbug's *Xuejie* (My Elder Schoolmate).

3 Recent works by a younger generation of lesbian authors in Taiwan have tended to appropriate aspects of the schoolgirl romance narrative to distinct effect rather than reproducing it faithfully in all of its key elements. Both Tze-lan Sang and Liou Liang-ya link Qiu Miaojin's novel, *Eyu shouji* (The Crocodile's Journal), with this narrative. Specifically, Liou compares the novel with Chu T'ien-hsin's "Lang tao sha" (Waves Scour the Sands) in that both can be read as examples of the "T-po campus romance" (*Yuwang gengyishi*, 84–85; see also Sang, *The Emerging Lesbian*, 270). For detailed discussions of Qiu's novel, see Sang, *The Emerging Lesbian*, 255–74 and Martin, *Situating Sexualities*, 215–35. Elements of Chen Xue's "Searching for the Lost Wings of the Angel" also echo the schoolgirl romance narrative insofar as the story's protagonist is of school age and attends school and college during the period of the story's events (see Martin, *Situating Sexualities*, 119–40). Ironic traces of the narrative are also found in Hong Ling's "Poem from the Glass Womb" in the section where the young woman Aquaria attends school and college and seduces a series of classmates who are described as "little girls like white butterflies," in a tongue-in-cheek reference to Chu T'ien-hsin's "A Story of Spring Butterflies" (Hong, 199).

4 See Hong Ling's critique of this desexualizing tendency, "Leise yu bianzi de jiaohuan," 95–97. Zhang Qiaoting makes a related critique but concedes that lesbian readers nevertheless find important emotional resources in schoolgirl romances (*Xunfu yu dikang*, 5/14).

5 In Chu's "A Story of Spring Butterflies," the narrator infamously compares women with the inert chemical elements, as distinct from men, who represent the reactive ones: "Among chemical elements [lesbians] are inert with inert, creating no reaction, producing no spark, emitting no fantastic colors" (87); "inert element with inert element, they don't ardently pursue sexual activity" (88). Comparably, the narrator in Wong Bikwan's "She's a Young Woman and So Am I" relates, in regard to her relationship with her classmate Jihang, "We had neither done anything like kissing or caressing nor had we ever felt the need for it. Those so-called lesbian intimacies accompanied by moans and mutterings are merely a fantastic scenario men have imagined for the sake of feasting their eyes. Jihang and I had never done anything like that" (40; trans. Ding).

6 Cao's "The Maidens' Dance" is a classic schoolgirl romance. Its story stretches

over about twelve years, beginning when Tong Suxin and Zhong Yuan are six-teen and in school and ending with Zhong Yuan gone to the United States and Tong Suxin pregnant with her husband's child. The story includes the following scene:

> Zhong Yuan opened her backpack, felt about inside, and produced a bottle of olive oil. She unscrewed the cap, poured a few drops into her palm, then moved behind me to rub it in.
>
> I think Zhong Yuan's fingertips must have felt my sweaty back instantly tense up; she may even have felt my trembling. I squirmed about incessantly—I was eighteen, but aside from my mother and little sister, this was the first time anyone had touched my naked flesh, and what's more this person was Zhong Yuan. "You're so ticklish!" Zhong Yuan's laughing voice floated over my shoulder.
>
> Zhong Yuan held my shoulder, gently caressing my back—I was tempo-rarily removed from the clamor of voices and the hot sun and sea breeze of the beach, and a hot current from who knows where engulfed my whole body, as if it meant to boil me over and melt me through. Zhong Yuan's hands slid across my back, right—left—up—down. . . . My gasping pores inhaled her warm breath. It was as if she had ten million fingers, pinching, rubbing, crawl-ing; my body began to slide downward, boom, boom, my heartbeat urged me, urged me . . . ah, I was melting into a puddle of water, there on the sand. (25–26; my trans.)

Clearly enough, the narrator's sexual desire is the primary subject of this lengthy description. Zhao Mei's "Sui feng piao qu" (Gone With the Wind) includes the following comparable, proto-sexual scene between the two main characters:

> Qing had wanted to find out if [the protagonist's] legs were suited to ballet dancing, but in looking at her legs Qing discovered the bloody purple and blue bruises and wounds that were all over them. Qing raised her eyes to look at her. That deep, shining, limpid blue. Qing's eyes looked at her. And she shook her head. She couldn't tell Qing about her mother's savage beating. Qing lowered her head and caressed the purple and blue bruises on her legs. Qing even kissed her many wounds. Qing's movements were very gentle, but she continued to touch her incessantly. Qing's touch made her heart feel like waving grass. All itchy and tingling. She was very tense, but at the same time she yearned for this care and protection. (179)

7 This is the case, for example, in Zhao Mei's "Sui feng piao qu" (Gone with the Wind), Wong Bikwan's "She's a Young Woman and So Am I," and Chu's "A Story of Spring Butterflies."

8 For example, in Chu's "Waves Scour the Sands," see discussion below. For fur-ther discussion of T/po secondary gender in relation to Qiu Miaojin's writing, see Martin, "Stigmatic Bodies."

9 An example of a story mixing both models is Ng's "Chuncuide guodu" (The Pure Country), while Cao's "The Maidens' Dance" could be read as a T/po narrative (and its adaptation for Taiwan television certainly presents it this way; see chapter 4), although its characterization of the gender distinction between its two main characters is less marked than in Chu's "Waves Scour the Sands."

10 On romantic nostalgia, memory, and utopianism, see Starobinski, "The Idea of Nostalgia," esp. 89–95.

11 A posthumously published quasi-autobiographical story by Eileen Chang, "Tongxue shaonian dou bu jian" (My Prosperous Classmates) (the story within the book of the same title), provides an exemplary illustration of this tendency. Chang's story paints an intriguing picture of girls' schooling in the Republican period. The story's protagonist attends a girls' boarding school in Shanghai in the 1930s in which she matter of factly states that "homosexuality was all the rage [*tongxingliande fengqi . . . sheng*]." While the protagonist outgrows her crush on an elder schoolmate, her best friend, though she marries, spends her whole life without finding a love to compare with her adolescent love for her dorm-mate. Reflecting on her infatuation with her classmate, Chang's young protagonist muses, "Love with a purpose is not true love. All those women of an age to pursue love and marriage are thinking only of themselves — or else they are thinking of their family's and society's injunction to continue the family line [*chuan zong jie dai*]. That isn't true love" (E. Chang, "Tongxue shaonian dou bu jian" 10, 19). Many thanks to Wang Yin and Chen Yushin for bringing to my attention this fascinating recent example of schoolgirl romance along with Zhou's review of it cited below. For a reading of Chang's representation of same-sex love between women in this story and critical responses to it, see also Chen Yushin, "Passionate Friendship." For a reading of Chang's representation of same-sex love between women in some other stories, see Chang Hsiao-hung, A Queer Family Romance, 1–26.

12 Very much like Woolf's Mrs. Dalloway as discussed by Annamarie Jagose, these narratives "[confine] homosexuality to the register that enables its most voluble articulation — that of memory" (Inconsequence, 82).

13 Cf. Sang, The Emerging Lesbian, 270.

14 In this, the Chinese schoolgirl romance narratives have something in common with twentieth-century Euro-American narratives of homosexual experience in adolescence as analyzed by Angus Gordon in "Plastic Identities." Gordon observes that adolescent homosexuality is "a category . . . subject to a characteristic temporal displacement: that is, as something that typically becomes apprehensible only at a distance, looking back" (10). Yet interestingly, Gordon notes that there is a bias toward male protagonists in the twentieth-century Western canon of fictional accounts of adolescence (24). While some Chinese-language homosexual memorial narratives do have male protagonists (e.g., Lin Yuyi's "The Boy in the Pink Orchid Tree" and Lin Chun Ying's "Who Is Singing?"), the preponderance of female protagonists marks an interesting distinction between the Chinese literary narratives and their Euro-American counterparts.

15 Ellis, *Studies*, 216; emphasis added.

16 Taiwanese literary critic Zhou Fen-ling's review of Eileen Chang's "Tongxue shaonian dou bu jian" repeats Ellis's rhetorical move here, quite against the promptings of Chang's text itself:

> For women, [schoolgirl homosexuality] is an unspeakable secret of adolescence. If love is a secret religion [*mijiao*] between two people, then homosexual love is a secret within the secret. In Eileen Chang's story, the protagonist's possession of this kind of adolescent secret is no barrier to her becoming a wife and mother, but deep in her heart she's always making a comparison: heterosexuality is filthy and changeable; in contrast, homosexuality is aesthetic, spiritual, and steadfast. In the face of all life's disappointments and cruelties, this spiritual secret is her only comfort. . . . "Tongxue shaonian dou bu jian" follows the darkened pathways of the unconscious, with a middle-aged woman reminiscing about adolescent secrets; all of this remembering takes place in the unconscious. ("Fangxiangde mijiao," 1–2)

This willful emphasis on the supposed secrecy and unconscious character of re-membered schoolgirl romance is sharply at variance with the refreshing candor of Chang's text (see note 11 discussing the text).

17 Jagose, *Inconsequence*, 81–82.

18 Fuss, "Fallen Women."

19 Ibid., 60.

20 Gordon, "Plastic Identities."

21 Ibid., 46.

22 Ibid., 13. See also Gallop, *Around 1981*, 177–205, for another critique of Freud's developmentalist narrative on "temporary" adolescent lesbianism. Relatedly, in *Come As You Are*, Judith Roof proposes that Freud's narrative of sexuality naturalizes heterosexual primacy by means of the perversions. In this argument, the perversions are necessary to the story of sexuality, enabling a heroic heterosexuality to triumph over these obstacles, all the more convincingly to arrive at its predestined terminus of biological reproduction. However, in the *Three Essays*—the text on which Roof largely bases her broader critique of Freud's supposed naturalization of heterosexual outcomes—Freud is considerably more ambivalent on the question of heterosexuality's inevitability than Roof allows. This is particularly apparent in his footnoted elucidation of his theory of primordial bisexuality, in which he observes that "psycho-analysis considers that a choice of an object independently of its sex . . . is the original basis from which, and as a result of restriction in one direction or the other, both the normal and the inverted types develop. Thus from the point of view of psycho-analysis the exclusive sexual interest felt by men for women is also a problem that needs elucidating and is not a self-evident fact based upon an attraction that is ultimately of a chemical nature" (Freud, *Three Essays*, 23–24n1). See also Gordon's critique of Roof, "Plastic Identities," 19–20.

23 If a tendency to naturalize heterosexual outcomes to adolescent homosexual experience is found even in Freud's own complex and ambivalent writings on the subject, then as both Henry Abelove and Jonathan Dollimore have shown, this tendency becomes quite unequivocal in many post-Freudian appropriations of psychoanalytic theory for cruder teleologies of psychosexual development. See Abelove, "Freud." Against the common pathologization of homosexuality in post-Freudian psychoanalysis, these critics underscore a counter-narrative running through Freud's writings on the perversions. But see Gordon ("Plastic Identities," 46–47) on the limitations of Dollimore's rehabilitation of Freud. For a reading of the ideological complexity of Freud's writing on adolescent female homosexuality specifically, see Roof, *A Lure of Knowledge*, 174–215. In this work, Roof proposes that "Lesbian sexuality is in Freud . . . though usually transitory, . . . an ambivalent stage where oppositions, inevitable developments, and confining gender roles are broken open, allowing for multiple coexisting possibilities. This suggests that representations of lesbian sexuality in Freud's work do disturb the gendered dualities of sexual difference by breaking open the closure of oppositions, enacting a model — a time — for the perpetual interplay of knowledge and desire. Adolescent and premature, the figure of the lesbian represents a subversive operation created by increasing possibilities rather than by delaying an inevitable trajectory" (212). See also Marcuse, *Eros and Civilization*.

24 On the dissemination of Freudian thought in China between 1919 and 1949, see Jingyuan Zhang, *Psychoanalysis in China*, esp. 5–35 and 103–29.

25 Chu, interview with Martin, 8–9. Chu's story was republished in her *Fangzhou-shangde rizi*, 103–27.

26 Chu, interview with Martin, 10.

27 On the lavish use of exclamation points in May Fourth fiction due to the "ferociousness of the [new] outburst of personal emotions," see L. Lee, *Romantic Generation*, 263.

28 These complementary gendered roles correspond to the local subcultural secondary genders of T (tomboy) and *po* (woman).

29 Chu, "Waves Scour the Sands," 31.

30 Cf. Lu Yin, "Lishi's Diary":

> *15th of the first lunar month*: The day after learning that Yuanqing will leave I fell ill. Yuanqing accompanies me constantly, but this only makes my heart ache worse than ever! We have passed these last few days like condemned criminals. Ai! I remember summer that year, when after the rain tearful willow fronds weakly swayed, beyond the steps crickets chirped their secrets to one another, and Yuanqing and I sat leaning, one against the other, on the pale blue railing fence. Yuanqing said very clearly to me then: "I just want to find comfort for my soul; as for that terrifying thing, marriage, I'll avoid it at all costs." Today those words are nothing but the depleted traces of a vanished past! ("Lishi de riji," 56)

31 Chu, "Waves Scour the Sands," 25.

32 Ibid., 18, 26.

33 The lines are from Li Shangyin's (813–858 CE) "Jin Qin"; in C. T. Hsia's analysis, Li's poetry is exemplary of the melancholic "sentimental-erotic tradition" in Chinese literature ("Hsu Chen-ya's Yu-li Hun"). The poem is translated by Xu Yuanzhong as "The Sad Zither" (Xu, Lu, and Wu 300 Tang Poems, 352).

34 Roof, Come As You Are, introduction and chs. 1 and 3.

35 Chu, "Waves Scour the Sands," 32.

36 For a critical discussion of the sacrificial requirements of classical feminine virtue, see Chow, Woman, 50–83.

37 Chu, "Waves Scour the Sands," 25.

38 See the introduction for a discussion of The Love Eterne and its meteoric impact in Taiwan.

39 Zhang Yan writes Qi a letter from southern Taiwan, which she ritually preserves and memorizes; Qi gives a red rose to Zhang Yan on their final day of school.

40 On xunqing in the late-Qing tragic romance Huayue hen, see Hsia, "Hsu Chen-ya's Yu-li Hun, 216–18.

41 On Qiong Yao, see Lang, "San Mao and Qiong Yao" and "Taiwanese Romance"; Lee, "'Modernism' and 'Romanticism' in Taiwan Literature"; and Nielsen, "Caught in the Web of Love."

42 Lin Fang-mei, "Social Change," 197–200. See also the Chinese edition of this work, Jiedu Qiong Yao aiqing wangguo.

43 Lin Fang-mei, "Social Change," 218–41.

44 It is worth noting that Chu herself is the daughter of a family thoroughly steeped in elite literary culture, the child of celebrated mainland émigré author Chu Hsi-ning and well-known translator of Japanese literature Liu Musha.

45 Lin Fang-mei, "Social Change," 191–92.

46 Ibid., 103.

47 Chu, "Waves Scour the Sands," 26.

48 Chu, interview with Martin, 9; Qiu, (Bu)tong guo nüren guazao, 128–29; Lin Fang-mei, "Social Change," 66.

49 Although in reality Chinese romance genres already contain traces of transfigured homoeroticism; see discussion in note 34 of chapter 1 on Song Geng's treatment of the homoerotic subtext of the premodern beauty-scholar romance. The long-standing poetic tradition in which the male poet ventriloquizes the voice of a pining female lover already implies the appropriation of another's voice to express one's sentiments; in premodern times, the form was used to express the concerns of male literati to the emperor, in relation to whom the poet would place himself in a hierarchically lower—thus feminine—position, so that the discourse of romantic cross-sex love was used allegorically to refer to a homosocial relation between men. See Song, Fragile Scholar, 51–60 and 132–33.

50 The centrality of sentiment in "Waves" and its debt to older literary tropes of

duoqing (sentimentality), qing (love), and chou (sorrow) suggest a possible comparison with Paul Kelleher's conception of sentiment as that "remainder" within modern Western subjective normativity that is not encompassed by heterosexuality: a kind of lingering cultural and subjective "leftover" after the imposition of the modern hetero/homo sexual epistemology ("If Love Were All"). One might speculate that contemporary Chinese schoolgirl romances illustrate something similar, both in their evocation of premodern sentiment over modern sexuality and in their tendency to frustrate a clear-cut homo-hetero divide. On this reading, "Waves" would indicate the gap between sentiment and sexuality and suggest, along the lines that Kelleher argues in a Euro-American context, that attending to the (central) cultural place of feminine same-sex *sentimentality* reveals the inadequacy of a dogged focus on hetero- versus homo-*sexuality*. The affective formation in question—which might be dubbed homo-sentimentality—further shores up a universalizing epistemology since although it is undoubtedly a form of erotic love, it is conceived neither as "a sexuality" nor as something whose experience is confined to a clear-cut minority of women.

51 Chu, interview with Martin, 11.

52 In Roof's terms, these narratives might be described, similarly to Colette's "The Secret Woman," as "narrative[s] in which the middle . . . finally seems to escape the end," or again, like Monique Wittig's and Nicole Brossard's experimental lesbian fictions, as "inscrib[ing] the lesbian as a moment of perpetual play defying closure and the ideological investments such closure signifies" (*Come As You Are*, 44, 129). Yet the very popularity and relative ubiquity of the Chinese-language schoolgirl romance narratives marks a significant difference from the more experimental or "minor" examples of Euro-American fiction discussed by Roof. In other words, I think these stories bespeak an alternative form or emphasis *within* hegemonic sexual epistemology, rather than only a marginal critique directed at a monolithically dominant "hetero-narrative."

53 In this, the female homoerotic ellipsis in these stories differs in an important way from Harriette Andreadis's proposal of "erotic ellipsis" as a term designating the "unnaming" of the lesbian possibility in early modern English literature. See Andreadis, *Sappho in Early Modern England*, 1–24.

54 Chu, interview with Martin, 8.

55 Ibid., 10.

56 For a more detailed biography of Wong, see Sieber, *Red Is Not the Only Color*, 193–95. For critical interpretations of Wong's fiction, see, for example, Lau, "The 'Little Woman' as Exorcist," and Asker's response, "Eating Babies ." In Chinese, see Cai, *Gangren xushi*, 131–42 and 155–61, and "Jiazu siyu," 61–63; Huang Wanhua, "Nüxing wenxue"; Liou, "Aiyu zai Xianggang" in *Qingse shijimo*; and Hou, "Xianggang, zhengzhi, mei xingzhe."

57 Hou, "Xianggang, zhengzhi, mei xingzhe," 64.

58 For discussion of lesbian representation in *The Picture of Female Virtue*, see ibid., 66–68, and Liou, *Qingse shijimo*, 184–85. The novel tells the stories of three gen-

erations of Hong Kong women whose lives span the hundred years from the final decade of the Qing dynasty to the end of the twentieth century. The section "My Mother" includes the story of two women in postwar Hong Kong, Daixi and Yinzhi, who were passionately in love with each other but forcibly parted by marriage.

59 Wong's story was originally published in Wong Bikwan (Huang Biyun), *Ta shi nüzi, wo ye shi nüzi*. The Chinese version is cited below in cases where specific Chinese terms are being discussed.

60 Yi Shu is a popular Hong Kong romance novelist for whom Wong Bikwan has publicly expressed her contempt (Lau, "The 'Little Woman' as Exorcist," 157). On Yi Shu, see Lin Fang-mei, "Social Change," 282ff. and 304ff.

61 Wong Bikwan, trans. Ding, "She's a Young Woman and So Am I," 18.

62 For example, when Saisai first discovers that Jihang has been exchanging sex with men for money, the drunken Jihang tells her, "Yip Saisai, I am merely an ordinary [*shisu*] person," before tossing a handful of coins at her in reproach for her implicit condemnation (Wong, "Ta shi nüzi," 6).

63 In an internal monologue directed at Jihang, Saisai states, "I am merely an unassuming [*anfen*] girl who wants a simple [*danchun*] emotional bond with another human being"; later, she reflects on a similar theme: "What I wanted from life was very simple [*jianpu*]." (ibid., 7 and 11).

64 Wong Bikwan, trans. Ding, "She's a Young Woman and So Am I," 45.

65 Ibid., 47.

66 Sieber, *Red Is Not the Only Color*, 20.

67 For example, see Wong Bikwan, trans. Ding, "She's a Young Woman and So Am I," 45. Cf., for example, E. Chang, "Love in a Fallen City": Bai Liusu's lover, from whom she is vainly awaiting a marriage proposal before she will sleep with him, accuses her of seeing marriage as merely "long-term prostitution" (82).

68 Wong Bikwan, trans. Ding, "She's a Young Woman and So Am I," 47–48.

69 Ibid., 39, 42–43, 44; see also Sieber, *Red Is Not the Only Color*, 20.

70 Wong Bikwan, trans. Ding, "She's a Young Woman and So Am I," 43.

71 Ibid., 46–47.

72 Ibid., 42, 44, 46 (Wong orig. p. 15), 47.

73 In recent years, Yi Shu herself has touched on the lesbian topic—for example, in her family melodrama novel *Shhh—* (2007), (*Xu—*), which hints strongly at the possibility of a female same-sex relationship developing after the narrative's conclusion.

74 S. Chang, "Yuan Qiongqiong," 218.

75 Chang left Shanghai for Hong Kong in 1952; in Hong Kong she began writing in English; in 1955, she moved on again to the United States, where she lived quietly until her death forty years later. L. Lee, *Shanghai Modern*, 268; J. Chen, "Zhou Shoujuan's Love Stories," 361; N. Huang, "Eileen Chang," 458. On Chang, see also David Der-wei Wang's forewords to Chang, *The Rice-Sprout Song* and *The Rouge of the North*; Hsia, "Eileen Chang"; and Chow, *Woman*, 84–120; several translations

of Chang's Chinese essays and stories were published along with critical and biographical articles in a special memorial issue of *Renditions* (number 45, Spring 1996).

76 Lim, "Reading 'The Golden Cangue.'"

77 See Hsia, "Eileen Chang," 397–98.

78 E. Chang, quoted in Chang Hsiao-hung, *Zilian nüren*, 83.

79 See Chow, *Woman*, 84–120, and Chang Hsiao-hung, *Zilian nüren*, 80–87.

80 Chow, *Woman*, 84–120. Wang Xiaoming makes a related point about the way Chang's writing effectively bypasses the structuring meta-narratives of Chinese modernity—social and historical progress, ideology, politics, race, the nation, intellectual enlightenment, social criticism, and political revolution ("The 'Good Fortune' of Eileen Chang," 138).

81 Commentators on Chang's fiction are divided on the question of its critical effect. Wang Xiaoming argues that since Chang's writing shows such a pervasive lack of faith in the idea of historical progress, it is difficult to interpret it as social criticism ("The 'Good Fortune' of Eileen Chang," 139); Hsia takes a similar line ("Eileen Chang," 414–15). Commentators who focus specifically on Chang's representation of gendered experience, in contrast, tend to read in it an implicit critique of—even a protest against—the dehumanizing effects of the social and familial gender system; see, for example, Lim, "Reading 'The Golden Cangue,'" and Chow, *Woman*.

82 See Hou's discussion of the stylistic shadow of Chang in the works of Wong Bikwan and other Hong Kong women writers ("Xianggang, zhengzhi, mei xing-zhe," 33–36) and S. Chang, "Yuan Qiongqiong."

83 Since the story is narrated in the first person from Saisai's perspective, this intense sensory fixation on Jihang's physical presence also eroticizes a relationship that Saisai insists elsewhere has nothing to do with sex.

84 Wong Bikwan, trans. Ding, "She's a Young Woman and So Am I," 37.

85 Ibid., 38–39.

86 Ibid., 39.

87 The feminine transactions we see in Chang and Wong might be called "worldly transactions," in distinction from Rey Chow's "virtuous transactions"; while the latter concern women's self-insertion into the traditional system of feminine moral virtue, the former concern the decidedly less virtuous but equally unavoidable self-insertion by women into the system of modern patriarchal relations.

88 E. Chang, "Tongxue shaonian dou bu jian,"58–59.

89 Sang, *The Emerging Lesbian*, 100, 125.

Chapter Three: Postsocialist Melancholia

1 See J. Zhang, "Breaking Open"; Zhong, "Sisterhood?"; Sang: "At the Juncture" and *The Emerging Lesbian*, 163–222; Hong Ying, "Dalu nüxing zuojia nüxing zhi ai"; and Dai, "Rewriting Chinese Women," 204 and 205n14.

2 Liu Suola, "Lan tian lü hai," *Shanghai Literature* 6 (1985): 12–29. Subsequent page references to the story are to the 1988 Taiwan edition of Liu's collection *Ni bie wu xuanze*.

3 For further discussion of this transition and a summary of the extant research, see Sang, *The Emerging Lesbian*, 163–74. Thanks to Chris Berry for his revelation of the discussions about same-sex love in commercial popular health magazines in Beijing in this period.

4 One possible exception is Nie, who writes of "Blue Sky" that "the 'I' [narrator] is utterly neurotic, with a kind of hysterical sentiment toward her homosexual-style partner [*tongxinglian shide duixiang*], Manzi" ("Wuaizhongde tuwei," 6).

5 Hong Ying, *Jing yu shui*, 3–4.

6 Ibid., 6. Hong's introduction abruptly brushes aside the significance of female homoeroticism in the seventeenth-century classic *Liaozhai zhiyi* (5) and pays scant attention to other possible premodern and Republican representations of sex or sexual desire between women. For a detailed discussion of "lesbian" themes in premodern and May Fourth Chinese writing, see Sang, *The Emerging Lesbian*, chapters 1 and 2.

7 I allude here to Jing Wang's analysis of the successive waves of intellectual "fevers" (*re*) that swept through China's intellectual circles in this decade: "culture fever," "methodology fever," and so on (*High Culture Fever*).

8 For further discussion, see ibid.; Wang Ning, "Confronting Western Influence"; and X. Zhang, *Chinese Modernism*, esp. 150–57.

9 Shu-mei Shih underscores the parallels between the 1920s–1930s and the 1980s–1990s by pointing out mainland Chinese intellectuals' two consecutive engagements with Western modernity and modernism, first in the context of China's semi-colonization by European and Japanese powers, then in the context of China's cultural internationalization in the "New Era" (*The Lure of the Modern*, vii–xiii and 377). See also quotations from Liu Xiaobo in notes and text below.

10 This is Jing Wang's translation of the term (*High Culture Fever*, 145).

11 The point is made clearly in a 1986 article by Liu Xiaobo, specifically with reference to the cultural syncretism of the mid-1980s writing of Liu Suola, among others:

> The vertical axis of self-criticism must draw support from the horizontal axis of absorbing the foreign. For every people, reevaluation of the home culture can only proceed meaningfully with the aid of foreign culture. As in the May Fourth period, in the New Era, modern and contemporary Western culture provides the best point of reference for contemporary Chinese people to effect self-conscious self-reflection. In light of this reference point, the shortcomings of traditional Chinese culture stand out ever more clearly. As a result, there has arisen a tendency to borrow and learn [*jiejian*] from certain aspects of modern Western culture in order to criticize the traditions of the home culture. . . . However, this foreign influence is by no means monolithic or imposed without choice. Instead, it is a composite influence taken up by choice in

the context of the actual conditions of the anti-feudalist China of the reforms era. ("Yizhong xinde shenmei sichao," 40)

12 See K. Liu, "Subjectivity"; Liu Zaifu, "The Subjectivity of Literature Revisited"; and J. Wang, *High Culture Fever*, 195–232.

13 Liu Zaifu, "The Subjectivity of Literature Revisited," 59; K. Liu and Tang, "Introduction," 12. Jing Wang observes that Liu Zaifu's discussion of subjectivity is constantly on the verge of becoming a discussion of a more universalist kind of "humanity" (*High Culture Fever*, 206).

14 Rofel, *Other Modernities*, 217–56.

15 See J. Zhang: *Psychoanalysis in China*, chs, 1 and 4, and "Psychoanalysis in the Chinese Context," 8–9.

16 See, for example, Zhao Xianzhang, "Lun Fuluoyide de wenyi xinlixue fangfa," 110–18, which introduces theories of the unconscious and its formation through repression, the interpretation of dreams, and the relationship between psychoanalysis and Marxism. See also Wang Ning's discussion of the Freudian influence on New Era writers in "Confronting Western Influence," esp. n. 12.

17 For example, Liu Zaifu appeals to Freudianism explicitly as a theory that might usefully have complicated Marx's writing on the human subject had it been available at the time of his writing ("The Subjectivity of Literature Revisited," 65). Introducing Freudian theory to an academic, literary-critical readership in 1987, Zhao Xianzhang frames Freud's writing using terms such as "human character/personality" (*renge*), with which he habitually glosses the less familiar term "psychology" (*xinli*), and proclaims the usefulness of Freud's theories in allowing one to understand "the (original) self [*ziwo*] of all of humankind [*renlei*]" ("Lun Fuluoyide de wenyi xinlixue fangfa," 110, 118). *Renge*, *ziwo* and *renlei* are terms strongly associated with concurrent popular and academic discussions on the liberation of human subjectivity from state repression.

18 See Rofel, *Other Modernities*, 298n2–3. On the general utopianism of the intellectual project of cultural enlightenment in the early to mid-1980s, see J. Wang, *High Culture Fever*, 37–117.

19 J. Wang, *High Culture Fever*, 206ff.

20 Li Jie, "Liu Suola xiaoshuo lun," 121.

21 Liu Xiaobo, "Yizhong xinde shenmei sichao," 38.

22 Ibid., 42. Cf. Jing Wang's critique of Liu Xiaobo's overemphasis of the enlightenment moment in Liu Suola at the expense of the anti-enlightenment moment (*High Culture Fever*, 175–76).

23 Liu Beixian's fleeting mention of the novella is typical in this regard ("Liu Suola pingzhuan," 158), but cf. Xiao, who atypically frames "Blue Sky" as equally noteworthy as "You Have No Other Choice" though does not analyze it at length ("Jin nian feilixing zhuyi xiaoshuode pipan," 14).

24 See L. Lee, *Romantic Generation*, pp. 257–74.

25 Chinese critics writing in the 1980s generally take "You Have No Other Choice"

to be Liu's representative work for the period; unfortunately, however, it is not included in Martha Cheung's collection of translations.

26 On the *xungen pai* and its complex relation to modernism, see J. Wang, *High Culture Fever*, 213–24. As representative of the hotly contested modernist school, Liu's fiction catalyzes some of the key cultural and intellectual tensions of the New Era. In the late 1980s, Liu became a key target in the debate over "pseudomodernism" (*wei xiandai pai*), which, insofar as it crystallized anxieties about cultural modernization as Westernization, responds to the philosophical and stylistic syncretism of Liu's writing. (See Zhao Mei's insightful retrospective critique of the pseudomodernism debate, "Xianfeng xiaoshuode zizu yu fufan," and Jing Wang's extended discussion in *High Culture Fever*, 162–77.) The charge of pseudomodernism was generally made in relation to Liu's nonrealist literary style, which incorporates stream-of-consciousness and nonlinear narrative structure. In adopting this style, Liu was accused of having produced an inferior and forced imitation of contemporary Western fiction. (For an example of a proto-pseudomodernism critique of Liu's stylistic derivativeness, see Li Jie, "Liu Suola xiaoshuo lun.") For Jing Wang, on the other hand, Liu's writing exemplifies her generation's "spiritual crisis" as it suffered from the attenuated collapse of viable philosophical and artistic frameworks at the national level within which to situate its life and work (*High Culture Fever*, 144). See also Wu Liang, who describes Liu's protagonists as suffering "a sadness resulting from the lack of any belief" ("Re-membering the Cultural Revolution," 132).

27 Liu Suola, *Ni bie wu xuanze*. See Cheung "Introduction"; McDougall and Louie, *The Literature of China*, 414–15 and 445; Zhao Mei, "Xianfeng xiaoshuode zizu yu fufan," 34.

28 Liu Suola, "Lan tian lü hai," 143. Jing Wang (*High Culture Fever*) reads the tension between idealism and anti-idealism in this story as exemplary of Liu's generation's "spiritual crisis" in the wake of the defeat of Maoist utopianism. See also Wang Xiaoming, who argues that Manzi's idealized image can be read as the expression of a "self-defense instinct" on the part of a narrator/author unwilling to face her own existential despair ("Pibeide xinling," 71).

29 When Manzi sang in a tearful, husky voice after her boyfriend deserted her when she became pregnant, the narrator confesses: "That was the most moving singing style I'd heard in my whole life, and I almost wanted to imitate it to sing all my songs. . . . Of course, while she was singing, Manzi could never have imagined I'd sink so low as to consider imitating her" (Liu, "Lan tian lü hai," 161). The novella's diegetic thematization of the authenticity/imitation dialectic in the personae of Manzi and the narrator respectively echoes the meta-textual critical debates over pseudomodernism sparked by Liu's own stylistic syncretism.

30 Cf. the discussion of Hong Kong author Wong Bikwan's "She's a Young Woman and So Am I" in chapter 2.

31 Liu Suola, "Lan tian lü hai," 145.

32 Stewart, *On Longing*, 23.

33 Ibid., 135–38.

34 Ibid., 23.

35 Cheung, "Introduction," xiii; McDougall and Louie, *The Literature of China*, 415.

36 Liu Suola, "Lan tian lü hai," 192.

37 The perplexing excessiveness of the narrator's grief over Manzi's death and the strange forms that this grief takes lead Martha Cheung, in the absence of a more convincing motivating cause, to ask in relation to this story, "Where does genuine grief end and self-indulgence begin? How does one draw the line?" ("Introduction," xv). In this reading, the most that the narrator's inexplicable psychic disturbance could signal is "self-indulgence"; I argue that the story's lingering on this disturbance suggests, instead, a Freudian economy in which her repressed desire exacts from the narrator a psychic toll.

38 These critics are Li Jie and Liu Xiaobo respectively. See also Wang Ning's discussion of the influence of Freudianism in New Era fiction, including that of Liu Suola ("Confronting Western Influence").

39 Freud, "Mourning and Melancholia," 245.

40 Liu Suola, "Lan tian lü hai," 144.

41 Ibid., 167–68.

42 Ibid., 159.

43 Ibid., 175.

44 Ibid., 173.

45 Ibid., 147.

46 Ibid., 160.

47 Ibid., 189.

48 Ibid., 146.

49 Ibid.

50 Butler, "Imitation and Gender Insubordination." The singer is later described as "the woman-man who imitated a woman singing" (*mofang nüren changge de nü nanren*; Liu Suola, "Lan tian lü hai," 160). In contrast to the alignment of the (implicitly homosexual) "womanish man" singer of Cantopop with the cheaply imitative, Manzi, the object of the narrator's own proto-homosexual love, is consistently aligned with the other side of the novella's central authenticity/imitation dialectic.

51 This enigmatic admonition also brings to mind Manzi's and the narrator's own gender crossings elsewhere—for example, when the narrator dresses as a boy to walk Manzi through the park at night (see above); when the narrator recalls the time she and Manzi "imitated the big boys on the street" in smoking cigarettes; and at the story's conclusion, where the narrator reveals she is wearing a man's shirt (Liu Suola, "Lan tian lü hai," 156–57, 191). However, the passage discussed in the text above is colored by the modern Chinese rhetorical tradition of pressing the effeminate or cross-dressed man into service as a signifier of spiritual bankruptcy; see Siu Leung Li's discussion of this device at work in Lu Xun (*Cross-Dressing in Chinese Opera*, 15–26) and Liu Zaifu's citation of Chen Yan'ge's similar

move in a 1950s article ("The Subjectivity of Literature Revisited," 60). The young women's cross-dressing does not seem weighted with comparable negative significance.

52 Liu Suola, "Lan tian lü hai," 186–88.

53 Cf. Julia Kristeva's analysis of the relation between melancholia and language in *Black Sun*, 33–68.

54 Li Ziyun, "Nüzuojia zai dangdai wenxueshi suo qide xianfeng zuoyong," 9.

55 Foucault, *The History of Sexuality*, vol. 1, 35.

56 Ibid.

57 J. Wang, *High Culture Fever*, ch. 5; Rofel, *Other Modernities*, ch. 7.

58 However, as homosexual, the repressed lesbian desire posited by this novella troubles the presumptive naturalness of gender on which, as Rofel has shown, both popular and official discourses of "human nature" increasingly came to rest in the post-Mao period. Insofar as normative gender rests on the presumed complementarity of masculine and feminine persons and bodies, to suggest that sexual desire may occur between members of the same gender, as this novella does, perplexes such a conceptual system. (As if symbolically acting out the disturbance to normative gender caused by the emergence of *tongxinglian*, the narrator of "Blue Sky" is represented as occupying a constantly shifting position in relation to the poles of masculinity and femininity, evidenced most clearly in the novella's attention to her clothing.) If what Rofel calls the "postsocialist allegory of [Chinese] modernity" rests on the positing of an essential and natural gender that was repressed by Maoism, then Liu's novella offers a counter-allegory, or embryonic reverse discourse, on PRC modernity structured around a different kind of repressive hypothesis (Rofel, *Other Modernities*, 217). Here it is homosexual desire rather than "natural," dimorphous, complementary gender that is constructed as repressed. Such a construction contests the emergent allegory of gender repression that Rofel describes—an allegory whose fervent excavation of the naturalness of heterosexual sex and gender serves to render all the more unnatural the possibility of same-sex love. Yet the novella makes this contestation by borrowing the postsocialist allegory's own tools: the hydraulic metaphor of repression, along with its built-in presumption of repression's necessary failure.

59 J. Wang, *High Culture Fever*, 138.

60 I draw here on Leo Ou-fan Lee's efficient characterization of the key elements of 1920s Chinese literary romanticism, including subjectivism, emotionalism, appeals to authenticity, utopian yearnings, and reference to foreign and Western art and thought (*Romantic Generation*, 294–95).

Chapter Four: No Future

1 For a more detailed discussion of the tensions between T/po and bu fen cultures and an overview of research on this topic in Taiwan, see Martin, "Stigmatic Bodies."

2 Chao, "Embodying the Invisible"; Zheng, *Nü'er quan*, 130–51; Gian, "Huanchu nütongzhi," 79–99. See also Lü, "Taiwan nütongzhi jiuba zhi yanjiu."

3 Zheng, *Nü'er quan*, pp. 130–31; Chao, "Embodying the Invisible," 17; Lü, "Taiwan nütongzhi jiuba zhi yanjiu."

4 Chao, "Embodying the Invisible," 17; Zheng, *Nü'er quan*, 132.

5 Chao, "Embodying the Invisible," 30, 37–38, 155.

6 Gian includes a table with twenty-four such micro-classifications. "Huanchu nütongzhi," 94–95.

7 Tong, "Being a Tomboy," 78–112.

8 Kam, "Recognition through Mis-recognition."

9 See Martin, "That Global Feeling," on the 2004–2005 Chinese-language lesbian Internet survey project, and Engebretsen, "Lesbian Identity ."

10 The Taiwanese lesbian Internet scene developed several years prior to the mainland Chinese one, and despite the comparatively tiny size of Taiwan's population (23 million), at the time of writing it remains a central—if not *the* central—site for Chinese-language lesbian Internet communication. See Berry and Martin, "Syncretism and Synchronicity."

11 Anonymous respondent to Martin's survey, October 20, 2003; original response in Chinese. For a discussion of the intertextual, transcultural citations performed by the term *lazi*, see Berry and Martin, "Syncretism and Synchronicity."

12 Anonymous respondent to Martin's survey, October 9, 2003; original response in English.

13 However, the conceptual linkage between the inherently minoritizing category of "female homosexuals" (*nütongxinglianzhe*) and female masculinity is notable in mass-media reporting. On Taiwanese print media representations of lesbianism as female masculinity in the 1980s, see Chao, "Embodying the Invisible," 39ff.; on a similar situation in Hong Kong media today, see Kam, "Recognition through Mis-recognition," 8. But see my discussion in the introduction on why this popular conceptual linkage of *nütongxinglianzhe* with female masculinity does not exhaust the field of female homoerotic representation since the dominant, universalizing model of erotic love between women is fundamentally at odds with the inherently minoritizing identity category of *nütongxinglianzhe*. That is, while the idea of "lesbians"—*when conceived as a distinct sexual minority*—may well be overdetermined by an image of female masculinity, the broader cultural construction of sexual love between women is not overdetermined in that way.

14 Liu Jenpeng, Ding, and Parry, "Xieshide qihuan jiegou."

15 L. Williams, *Playing the Race Card*.

16 Yu, "Ta shi yige ruo nüzi," 310.

17 Eribon, *Insult*, 16; emphasis added.

18 See also Martin, "Stigmatic Bodies."

19 However, this is not to say that tomboy melodrama is the only form that melodrama takes in representations of female homoeroticism; sometimes it is conventionally feminine women, as representatives of femininity in general, whose

injury provides melodrama's structuring tension. This is the case, for example, with the focus on physical injury to female bodies by an unjust patriarchal society in Alice Wang's *Love Me If You Can*, discussed in the introduction. In this film, Ying is cruelly beaten by her father, whose gambling debts she is working to pay off, and the camera focuses on her bruised and bloody back in a shower scene; San is constantly suffering accidental physical injury; San's friend She Shih is violently attacked by her male creditors; and both Ying and San are savagely beaten by a mob of gangsters (She Shih's creditors) and then drowned in the film's truly harrowing climax. A similar specular logic of feminine injury is notable in Jacob Cheung Chi Leung's *Zi shu* (Intimates), with Foon tending to Wan's wounded back, on which the camera similarly lingers in one of the flashback sections. Another comparable text in this regard is Pai Hsien-yung's story "Gu lian hua" (Love's lone flower, 1970) and its 2005 adaptation as both a sixteen-part television drama and a feature film by Tsao Jui-yuan (discussed in this book's epilogue). Pai's story focuses on love between sing-song girls. The protagonist Yun Fang's first love is Wu Bao, a girl with whom she works in 1940s Shanghai; Wu Bao dies young, and later, after fleeing to Taiwan in the 1949 post–civil war exodus, Yun Fang has a second same-sex relationship, this time with Juan-juan, a co-worker in a Taipei wine house during the 1950s. Both Wu Bao and Juan-juan are physically abused by their male clients, and both the film and the television series linger in particular over the scenes of Juan-juan's violent physical abuse. With their emphasis on women's collective injury at the hands of men and the efforts of women to protect one another by means of their love, texts like these constitute a distinct form of female homoerotic melodrama, one that focuses on the vulnerability to injury inherent in the experience of being a woman within patriarchal society, as distinct from the tomboy melodramas that are the focus of this chapter, which focus more specifically on the distinctive perils of embodying female masculinity.

20 I am grateful to Chris Berry for suggesting this connection.

21 L. Williams, *Playing the Race Card*, xiv.

22 Brooks, *The Melodramatic Imagination*, 27; emphasis added.

23 L. Williams, *Playing the Race Card*, 29–30.

24 Ibid., 15–16.

25 On the eclipse of opera films and spoken drama films by family melodramas, mandarin duck and butterfly films, social problem films, and slapstick comedies in the early 1920s, see Hu, *Projecting a Nation*, 56–61. A history of the melodramatic mode in early-century Chinese cinema would also point to many of the films of the leftist film movement of the 1930s and 1940s, with their championing of the proletariat and peasants as suffering underdogs (for example, Cheng Bugao's *Chun can* [Spring Silkworms, 1933] and Zheng Junli's *Wuya yu maque* [Crow and Sparrows, 1949]). See Hu, *Projecting a Nation*, chs. 4–6. But even more interesting in terms of the project at hand are those 1930s films that I would like to call "melodramas of the sexually outcast woman." Examples of this category include

Wu Yonggang's *Shennü* (The Goddess, 1934) and Yuan Muzhi's *Malu tianshi* (Street Angel, 1937), both of which feature self-sacrificing female prostitutes as embodiments of quasi-divine moral virtue (in *Street Angel*, this is in the persona of a secondary character—the female protagonist's elder sister—who sacrifices herself for her sister). I highlight these examples because their spectacularization of the suffering of virtuous women whose sexual behavior falls "outside the circle" of normative feminine sexual conduct suggests an interesting resonance with the examples of tomboy melodrama that I discuss below. For a discussion of *The Goddess* as exemplary of the Chinese filmic indigenization of the melodramatic mode, see Rothman, "The Goddess."

26 In addition to the mass-cultural texts I discuss below, one also thinks, again, of Qiu Miaojin's more high-brow fiction with its insistent return to the spectacle of the suffering tomboy, as at the conclusion to her novel *Eyu shouji* (The Crocodile's Journal), where the crocodile/lesbian protagonist self-immolates, Frankenstein-style, in a makeshift boat pushed out to sea, or even in the life story of Qiu herself as it was publicly fictionalized in the posthumously published novel *Mengmate yishu* (Montmartre Testament), which culminates in the author/protagonist's anguished suicide.

27 Martin, *Situating Sexualities*, 215–51.

28 Gledhill, "Rethinking Genre," 240.

29 L. Williams, *Playing the Race Card*, 25.

30 Lin Fang-mei, "Social Change," 166–67; Liu Jenpeng, Ding, and Parry, "Xieshide qihuan jiegou."

31 Lin Fang-mei, "Social Change," 166–67.

32 Nanqi was a major popular press during the 1970s; as well as romances, it published popular martial arts fiction, including Jin Yong's works.

33 Xuan, *Yuan zhi wai*, 34–35. The four consecutive references to Meijia's "maternal" nature are on p. 33.

34 Ibid., 334.

35 Ibid., 1. This is a slight modification of the translation given by Liu Jenpeng, Ding, and Parry, "Xieshide qihuan jiegou."

36 Liu Jenpeng, Ding, and Parry, "Xieshide qihuan jiegou." The novel's cover—which shows a beautiful but remote European-style castle framed by a square window of flowers—perhaps supports this interpretation.

37 Xuan, *Yuan zhi wai*, 42–43.

38 Later on, it turns out Yu Ying was wrong about Meijia: she really can't bring herself to have sexual relations with men and returns to women after only a brief sortie into heterosexuality.

39 The figure of the melodramatic tomboy that emerges so powerfully from the pages of *Outside the Circle* has something in common with the image of the "doomed lesbian" described by Vicinus as emerging in Europe and the United States in the 1930s ("They Wonder," 251–52). In Vicinus's account, the lesbian as "*femme damnée*" was a widely recognizable public image by the 1950s—due in no

small part to the influence of pulp fiction—and her imagined life, like those of Yu Ying in *Outside the Circle* and Angel Ding in *The Unfilial Daughter* (discussed below), was characterized above all by defiance and loneliness. Vicinus is careful to point out, however, that the doomed lesbian was not simply a literary invention but reflected, to a large degree, the actual restriction of life choices for lesbians in this time period. Similarly, I propose, the prevalence of a comparable image in the case of tomboy representation in late-century Chinese public cultures cannot be explained away as simply a "negative stereotype" because it also enables and even encourages the reader's or spectator's critique of the real social conditions that make the experience of the sex/gender transgressive woman so believably difficult.

40 The feminine pronoun is used here advisedly, given the generic association of *Yuan zhi wai*, by virtue of its author and publisher, with popular romance fiction.

41 Xuan, *Yuan zhi wai*, 24–25.

42 Ibid., 333–34.

43 Liu Jenpeng, Ding, and Parry, "Xieshide qihuan jiegou." The novel's conclusion also exemplifies a melodramatic affective and narrative structure. Linda Williams writes as follows: "Melodramatic climaxes that end in the death of a good person . . . offer paroxysms of pathos and recognitions of virtue compensating for individual loss of life. But if we persist in calling these paroxysms of pathos sentimental, we relegate them to a realm of passivity that misses the degree to which sentiment enables action. . . . Melodrama . . . most typically offers combinations of pathos *and* action. Virtuous sufferer and active hero may be divided into conventional male and female roles or combined in the same person" (*Playing the Race Card*, 24). In *Yuan zhi wai*, Yu Ying takes the role of both the suffering victim, toward whom the novel's reader is encouraged to extend sympathy, and the active hero, who "rescues" the victim (herself) by removing herself once and for all from the intolerably humiliating situation of being the butt of society's jokes. In this, Yu Ying exemplifies particularly literally the combination of conventional masculine and feminine melodramatic roles in the "third gender" of tomboy.

44 Crown is Taiwan's best-known publisher of romance fiction, associated as it is with Chinese-language "romance queen" Qiong Yao (see Lang, "San Mao and Qiong Yao"). In the 1990s, Crown also began to make forays into queer fiction, publishing works by Chen Xue, Hong Ling, and Chi Ta-wei. *The Unfilial Daughter* includes a preface by Zhang Manjuan, currently one of Taiwan's best-selling romance writers.

45 Telephone interview with Zhuang Mingzhu, director of programming, TTV, December 12, 2003.

46 See, for example, the introduction to the series at the following mainland Chinese lesbian Web site: http://movie.lalaclub.com/movie.asp?id=25.

47 Other texts mentioned included the American film *Boys Don't Cry* (three mentions) and the Canadian film *When Night Is Falling* (two mentions). A more complete analysis of the results of this survey, which obtained both long- and short-answer

responses to a series of questions on women's experience of using the Chinese-language lesbian Internet from a total of 117 women across mainland China, Taiwan, Hong Kong, and the worldwide Chinese diaspora, is in Martin, "That Global Feeling."

48 Wang Chun-chi, "Zhuliuzhongde panni."

49 Angel's mother's use of Minnan (or "Taiwanese") language, as well as adding color and spice to her insults, also marks her abject class status according to the logic of this series, in which poverty, vulgarity, the dysfunctional family, and Taiwaneseness are contrasted with middle-class life, gentility, and Mandarin-speaking culture (but see Liu Jenpeng and Ding, "Reticent Poetics," on the more reticent but nonetheless real violence of Zhan Qing-qing's Mandarin-speaking middle-class family, who effectively compel their daughter to suicide). I use the term "village" here advisedly; the story is set in the Taipei of about thirty-five years ago, where outside the small commercial and administrative center, rustic, village-like neighborhoods directly abutted agricultural land.

50 On this aspect of melodrama see, for example, Brooks, The Melodramatic Imagination, 16ff., and Gledhill, "The Melodramatic Field," 21.

51 For a more detailed critique of Du's novel's treatment of Angel's mother, see Liu Jenpeng and Ding, "Reticent Poetics," esp. 39–51.

52 Cf. Liu Jenpeng and Ding: "[The Unfilial Daughter] could . . . be read as rehearsing a dominant narrative logic whereby the wronged daughter's accusation against an abusive mother/family is authorized by her eventual, tragically fated death" ("Reticent Poetics," 39).

53 An evil mother like Angel Ding's represents the antithesis of the saintly paragon of maternal virtue portrayed in Wu Yonggang's 1934 film The Goddess (see notes 25 and 64). Indeed, it is tempting to see the modern idealized mother and the demonized one as two sides of the same coin, and the naming of these characters lends weight to this hypothesis: while in Wu's film it is the self-sacrificing mother who is deified as "the goddess," (shennü), in The Unfilial Daughter it is the mother's very evilness that guarantees her long-suffering daughter's deification, as "Angel" (Tianshi). On idealized mothers in Republican Chinese cultural production, see also Lieberman, The Mother and Narrative Politics.

54 Lieberman observes the preponderance of absent or unavailable mothers to New Women daughters in the female-authored modernist fiction of that period, attributing it to the precariousness of new women's place in Chinese modernism (The Mother and Narrative Politics, 16 and 104–33). Yet Lieberman's choice of Lu Yin's "Lishi's Diary" as an exemplification of this argument also points to the discursive linkage of deficient mothering with same-sex loving daughters specifically (113–16).

55 For a detailed analysis of this story, see Martin, Situating Sexualities, 119–40.

56 L. Williams, Playing the Race Card, 31.

57 Zhang, "Wuke nizhuande mingyun," 5.

58 Cesario, untitled; emphasis added.

59 This populist encapsulation of the novel's narrative logic is also useful in the way it captures *The Unfilial Daughter*'s melodramatic logic: the reader articulates the symbolic sense in which Angel's death from cancer asks to be read as a response to her familial and social situation, which is of course not literally true. The "no future" temporality of tomboy melodrama resonates, to a degree, with Lee Edelman's discussion of the constitutive imaginative association of homosexuality with a threat to futurity that is linked to homosexuality's supposed threat to reproductive heterosexuality in Euro-American representations (*No Future*).

60 I say that the tomboy's future is a blank rather than simply saying that her future is death because I think it is the tomboy's disappearance, more than her death per se, that most defines her narrative end (recall Chu T'ien-hsin's "Waves Scour the Sands," discussed in chapter 2). After all, the tomboy does not always die; sometimes she just goes to America (see the discussion of *The Maidens' Dance* [telemovie] in chapter 5).

61 Xuan, *Yuan zhi wai*, 332.

62 This observation would apply as well to Qiu Miaojin's high-brow tomboy-themed fiction.

63 In positing mass-cultural melodrama as a symbolic processing of actual social violence and inequality, this reading broadly echoes Linda Williams's interpretation of "racial melodrama" in the American film. It also illustrates once more the persistent "familialization" of the homosexual topic in Chinese representations (cf. Berry, "Asian Values, Family Values," and Martin, *Situating Sexualities*, 117–84).

64 Cf. Wang Chun-chi, "Zhuliuzhongde panni." The distinction I draw here is comparable to that drawn by Rothman between the literal and the filmic levels of Wu Yonggang's melodrama of suffering femininity, *The Goddess*. Rothman writes: "Taken literally, *The Goddess* affirms a woman's self-denial, but *as a film*, it affirms the woman's self" ("*The Goddess*," 69). By "literally," I understand Rothman to refer to the most obvious, crudest "message" of the film's narrative and especially its conclusion; by "as a film" I understand his reference to be to the less explicit yet more powerful overall affective impact of the film's treatment of character throughout.

65 I define *Blue Gate Crossing* as a teenpic in line with Cook and Bernink's discussion ("Teenpics")—that is, because it is a film centering on teenage characters directed in large part toward an adolescent audience. Of the various subgenres of teenpic that Cook and Bernink discuss, Yee's film is closest to the "rite of passage" narrative (219). See also Doherty, *Teenagers and Teenpics*. For a more detailed and multidimensional analysis of this film, see Martin, "Taiwan (Trans)National Cinema."

66 Appropriately, given her forthright, tomboyish personality, Meng Kerou's name is a homophone for "ferocity triumphs over gentleness."

67 This is an (ill-founded) hope that Kerou shares with Yu Ying, who tries the same strategy early on in *Outside the Circle*.

68 Martin, *Situating Sexualities.*

69 Martin, "Taiwan (Trans)National Cinema."

70 This undecidability is reflected in the responses of Taiwanese viewers, who are split on the question of whether or not Kerou will remain same-sex attracted. See ibid.

Chapter Five: Television as Public Mourning

1 Recently several popular lesbian Internet teen novels based on schoolgirl romance narratives have also been published in book form; these include Ranblue's *Wo ai lanqiu meishaonü*; Mayberight's *Wode xinli zhi you ni meiyou ta* 1 and 2; and Cornbug's *Xuejie*. Further filmic examples are discussed in chapter 6.

2 Martin, *Situating Sexualities.*

3 Martin, "Taiwan's Literature of Transgressive Sexuality."

4 For a detailed discussion of T/po genders, see chapter 4.

5 These are China Television System (CTS), TTV, China Television Company (CTV), and Formosa Television (FTV). Established on the basis of the Public Television Law passed in 1997, PTS was set up with the aid of a government grant. See Government Information Office, *Taiwan Yearbook 2003.*

6 Public Television Service Taiwan, *Public Television Service Foundation Annual Report 2002,* 22.

7 Both *Crystal Boys* and *The Maidens' Dance* also fit with PTS's policy of producing an annual quota of dramas based on adaptations of Taiwanese literature. Jessie Shih, discussion with Martin, December 9, 2003, Taipei.

8 Both programs achieved their ratings in 10 p.m. Sunday time slots. *The Maidens' Dance* had been aired six times on PTS at the time of my discussion with Shih and other PTS staff in December 2003. Note that numbers of people viewing the program via Internet video streaming do not show up in the ratings figures. One thousand DVDs of the film were also produced and marketed via the Internet; almost all had been sold by December 2003. Ratings figures, sales information, and information on the lack of conservative backlash courtesy of PTS.

9 Detailed analyses of audience demographics for these telemovies *Waves* are not available; this statement is based on PTS's analysis of the audience for its drama programs collectively, which shows that 56 percent of viewers of the station's dramas are women. A largely female audience is also suggested by the online discussion of *Waves* at PTS's "PTS Drama" BBS forum; the majority of posts appear to be from women viewers. *Waves*' director Lisa Chen Xiuyu also conducted a small-scale Internet survey that revealed that most viewers of this program were women between the ages of 20 and 35, with a sprinkling of teenage girls (Lisa Chen Xiuyu interview with Martin, December 19, 2003).

10 The films are both strongly marked by cultural nostalgia for a pre-urban, central Taiwanese village idyll. For a discussion of nostalgia for imperial "Japaneseness" in *The Maidens' Dance*, see Martin, "Trans-Asian Traces." That article also discusses

stylistic "Japanization" in *The Maidens' Dance* through its hybridized manga aesthetic, which draws indirectly on Japanese *shōjo ai* manga style.

11 Such a view is proposed by *Waves'* director, Lisa Chen Xiuyu, who sees the telemovie not as a lesbian film per se but as an example of the female friendship film (*nüxing qingyi pianzi*) (Lisa Chen Xiuyu interview with Martin, December 19, 2003). On the history and generic characteristics of the "woman's film" understood as a subgenre of melodrama, see, for example, Haskell's classic essay, "The Woman's Film," in Haskell, *From Reverence to Rape*; Hollinger, *In the Company of Women*, esp. introduction and ch. 1; Leibowitz, "Apt Feelings"; and the essays collected in Gledhill, *Home Is Where the Heart Is*. Melodrama as a "women's genre" has usually been considered in television in relation to the soap opera form rather than the telemovie (see, for example, Landy, *Imitations of Life*; see also the discussion in chapter 4 of the Taiwanese serial drama *The Unfilial Daughter* as an example of television melodrama). Note that this usage of the term "melodrama" as a *generic* marker of the "woman's film"/"women's television" differs from melodrama understood as a *mode*, defined by the representation of virtue accruing from unjust injury and suffering, on which, in chapter 4, I have followed Linda Williams's definition (see *Playing the Race Card*, 16–23 and 303n7). In some respects, the feminine-centered narratives of memorial schoolgirl romance discussed in this chapter and in chapters 1–3 conform to Williams's delineation of the central features of melodrama: they commence and seek to return to a "space of innocence" (the utopia of feminine youth); their pathos-filled endings work according to the temporal logic of the "too late" (youth's utopia is lost forever); and their form borrows from but is not reducible to realism (ibid., 28–42). However, it is my contention that the tomboy narratives discussed in chapter 4 conform more fully than these feminine-centered narratives to the melodramatic mode since in addition to the features mentioned, they also exemplify Williams's other two key features of the mode: the focus on recognizing the occulted virtue of victim-heroes (the tomboys themselves) and the Manichean conflict between good (the virtuous, suffering tomboys) and evil (social opprobrium, presented either directly or indirectly).

12 Zhang Qiaoting, *Xunfu yu dikang*. See further discussion of Zhang's ethnographic research on homoerotic schoolgirl cultures in Taipei in the introduction.

13 The memorialism so notable in *The Maidens' Dance* is equally in evidence in Tsao's more recent endeavor, the 2005 adaptation of Pai Hsien-yung's story, *Gu lian hua*, "Love's Lone Flower," as both a sixteen-part TV series and a feature film (see note 19 in chapter 4 and see the epilogue). Pai's original story already conforms to the memorial mode, first in that Yun Fang's love for Juan-juan in the present constantly recalls her earlier love for Wu Bao and second in the cultural nostalgia of a story written in 1970 recalling the Shanghai of the 1940s and the Taipei of the 1950s. Tsao's lush filmic and televisual adaptations of Pai's story strongly foreground this cultural nostalgia; other examples of this emergent genre that one is tempted to call the "*qipao* period pic" would be Hou Hsiao-hsien's *Haishang hua*

(Flowers of Shanghai), Wong Kar-wai's *Huayang nianhua* (In the Mood for Love), and Ang Lee's *Se, jie* (Lust, Caution).

14 The characters of Tong's full name mean literally "Pureheart Child"; in its association of adolescent femininity with childlike purity the name encapsulates a central ideological structure of the schoolgirl romance. Coincidentally—or perhaps not—the *yuan* character in Zhong Yuan's given name is the same as a character in the given name of one of the schoolgirl lovers in Lu Yin's "Lishi's Diary": Yuanqing.

15 On narrative's default heterosexual presumption, see Roof, *Come As You Are*. In her interpretation of the relentless memorialization of the lesbian in Euro-American representation, Jagose proposes that such memorialization at once has the disciplinary function of quarantining the lesbian in the past, and also ensures that the unquiet ghost of her supposedly banished memory can never be finally laid to rest in the present (*Inconsequence*, 77–100). If the opening shot of *The Maidens' Dance* illustrates the former aspect of this double function, then its closing shot is clearly more concerned with the latter.

16 Holmlund, *Impossible Bodies*, 31–50, quote on 33; see also Hollinger, *In the Company of Women*, 139–78.

17 Holmlund, *Impossible Bodies*, 31–50.

18 Hollinger (*In the Company of Women*, 146) uses this phrase in her critique of *Personal Best*.

19 White, "Girls Still Cry", 217.

20 White, ibid., 218.

21 The centrality in these telemovies of the desiring gaze at the tomboy on the part not only of her feminine sweetheart but also, by strong implication, of the spectator, makes clear that the "backward glance" of female homoerotic representation that is this book's subject indicates not just the mournful look of memory but also the desiring look of erotic appreciation. This latter sense perhaps has something in common with Mark Turner's use of the same phrase to indicate the sexualized, spatial gay male gaze (Turner, *Backward Glances*), albeit that in another sense, the male pleasures of gay cruising of which Turner writes appear, in their defining spontaneity and presentness, quite different to the insistently memorial feminine pleasures represented in these texts.

22 Cao, "Tongnü zhi wu," 17.

23 Doane, "The 'Woman's Film'," 286; emphasis added.

24 White, "Girls Still Cry," 218; emphasis added.

25 Another exemplary recent instance of this narrative is found in the Shaw Brothers' film *Shuang zhuo* (Twin Bracelets, 1991), based on the 1986 short story by mainland Chinese author Lu Zhaohuan. Set during the 1980s in a small fishing community in Hui'an in which strict ethnic custom dictates that husbands and wives must live separately, the film stages a critique of the harshness of the local marriage customs, setting these against the strong loving bonds between two young women, Huihua and Xiugu, whose vow to remain unmarried and live as "sister-

spouses" (*jiemei fuqi*) is defeated by the pressures toward cross-sex marriage. Here too memory plays a central role: on the day that the girls make their vow, Huihua emphasizes to Xiugu the importance that they remember this vow, come what may; later, when Xiugu weds, Huihua is agonized by what she perceives as her sweetheart's forgetfulness of their former love. The film's clearest critique is of the inhumanity of the specific marriage structure in Hui'an, but this enables it to contrast enforced cross-sex marriage with painfully renounced female same-sex love in a particularly stark manner. In a twist that echoes Shen Yijun's watery fate in *Voice of Waves*, Huihua ultimately chooses to drown herself in the ocean rather than continue to be subjected to the violently patriarchal marriage custom. For an excellent analysis of audience receptions of the film in Taiwan and China, see Friedman, "Another Kind of Love?"

26 This viewer goes on to complain that *The Maidens' Dance* was unconvincing compared to her own memories. Nonetheless, the fact that the film evokes these memories is illustrative of my broader point about the tendency of the films to evoke lesbian reminiscence as a viewer response. Lesbian, "*Tongnü zhi wu* kehua nühaimende qinggan bu ju shuifuli." The following responses are all taken from the same forum. Lisa Chen Xiuyu revealed in an interview that when researching for the film, she discussed it with many of her colleagues and friends, all of whom recognized people similar to the three major characters from personal experience. She expressed the hope of reaching as broad an audience as possible among Taiwanese women by presenting characters to whom most women could relate (Lisa Chen Xiuyu interview with Martin, December 9, 2003).

27 Dog, "Yibu pian yiding dou hui you zhengfan liangmian pingjia."

28 Maomao, "Bu jiande bu xuyao."

29 Waiting, "*Tongnü zhi wu* you weidao."

30 Mianbao, "Nanian xiatian langsheng qiaotong wode xin."

31 Nanian, "*Nanian xiatiande langsheng*."

32 Keleguo, "Re: *Nanian xiatiande langsheng*."

33 I place "heterosexuality" within quotation marks in cases where I am referring to nonlesbian adult recollectors of adolescent same-sex love. This is because although such recollectors—fictional and actual—do sometimes identify themselves as heterosexual (*yixinglian*), the "heterosexuality" that they embody seems to me differentiated in important respects from the kind of heterosexuality that is normative in Euro-American contexts, which tends to define itself through anxious preclusion of the possibility of same-sex attraction. In some cases, these adult recollectors never use the word "heterosexual" at all; for example, one viewer of the Taiwanese TV series identifies herself simply as "not a lesbian," and the protagonist of *The Maidens' Dance*, although she loves first her female friend and then her male fiancé, does not refer to herself using the language of sexual identity at all. Given these complications, it seems wise to refer to the sexuality of these nonlesbian recollectors of adolescent same-sex love as "heterosexual" only with caution. Indeed, the universalizing model of lesbian attraction drawn on

both by the schoolgirl romance television productions themselves and by many of their viewers (see below) renders problematic both the implicitly minoritizing and identitarian language of "homosexuality" and its reciprocally defined counterpart, "heterosexuality."

34 Observing the double valency of these narratives and the forms of personal identification that they elicit in viewers tends to contradict the conclusion reached by Jolly in "Coming Out of the Coming Out Story." Jolly reads Chinese American novelist Anchee Min's *Red Azalea* as a "going-in" story (477) that sees its protagonist sexually involved with first a woman and later a man yet "remain[s] very far from the scenario of coming out, in which, by contrast, essentialist definitions of sexuality support a plot in which one sexual object (even if never a desired one) is renounced for another and the private sphere is publicized" (490). Thus far, Jolly's argument is defensible. What is less convincing is her leap from here to the support of Chou Wah-shan's culturally essentialist proposal that "coming out is a western formula not simply transferable to other contexts" (490). In fact, as these TV productions and their enthusiastic consumption by self-identifying lesbians in both Taiwan and mainland China demonstrate, the actual conditions of intercultural flow in the contemporary world are such that it is extremely difficult to maintain belief in any indigenous cultural context—certainly not the mythical "China" that Chou invents—untainted by "western formulae."

35 "Metaphysics of identity" in relation to sexuality and the coming-out narrative is Fuss's term, *Inside/Out*, 1.

36 In "Television/Feminism," Torres proposes that the 1980s American drama *Heart-Beat* similarly encodes both a universalizing and a minoritizing model of lesbianism; however, the way it encodes those models differs significantly from the Taiwanese telemovies. *HeartBeat* features one out lesbian character (Marilyn) working in a feminist medical practice with a group of straight women doctors. Torres argues that the series alternates between a universalizing construction of Marilyn's lesbianism, which frames it as an expression of feminism, and a minoritizing construction that uses Marilyn's sexual specificity as a means to contain the homophobic anxieties inevitably raised by the situation of an all-woman medical practice. If we were to pursue Torres's question, which concerns the degree of progressiveness versus conservatism of televisual lesbian representations, in relation to the Taiwanese programs, we would come up, like Torres, with a conflicted picture. On the one hand, the minoritization of the tomboy and the attribution of a marital future to her young feminine lover in these programs could be seen as a reiteration of one "conservative" model of lesbian relations proposed in early European sexology: lesbianism as either pathological—a congenital state of sexual inversion—or insubstantial—a situational and temporary youthful behavior (cf. discussion of Ellis in chapter 1). And yet by universalizing the sexual desire of the feminine woman for the tomboy, the Taiwanese telemovies demonstrate a key distinction from the American series as analyzed by Torres; apparently these productions—and the responses to them from

nonlesbian-identifying viewers — are unaffected by any homophobic imperative to demarcate and contain the space of lesbian possibility by minoritizing lesbian desire per se; what is minoritized is not sexual desire between women but tomboy gender. The situation where the tomboy is represented as a sex-gender minority while her feminine lover is represented effectively as "any woman" recalls something like the triumphant paradox of that T-shirt that reads "I'm not a lesbian (but my girlfriend is)." Like *HeartBeat* in Torres's analysis, the Taiwanese telemovies thus unsurprisingly appear as complexly ambivalent rather than straightforwardly "conservative" or "progressive" — but they are ambivalent in interestingly distinctive ways.

37 I also take this approach because, as I have demonstrated above, the films themselves consistently invite spectatorial identification with their feminine, "heterosexual"-to-be protagonists.

38 Plummer, *Telling Sexual Stories*, 34; emphasis in original.

39 "Coherence system" is Linde's term, meaning "a means for understanding, evaluating, and constructing accounts of experience"; quoted in Liang, "Conversationally Implicating Lesbian and Gay Identity," 303. On "interpretive communities," see Plummer, *Telling Sexual Stories*, 22.

40 On the narrative organization and sexual epistemology of the coming-out story, see also Gordon, "Turning Back"; Creet, "Anxieties of Identity"; and Roof, *Come As You Are*, 104–7.

41 Plummer, *Telling Sexual Stories*, 33.

42 Butler: *Gender Trouble*, 57–65; *Bodies That Matter*, 233–36; *Psychic Life*, 132–66.

43 Butler, *Psychic Life*, 136.

44 Ibid., 138.

45 Ibid.

46 Ibid., 147; first emphasis in original; second emphasis added.

47 These narratives obviously deal with same-gender erotic attachments experienced in adolescence, rather than with what Butler's psychoanalytic framework advances as the "original" same-gender erotic attachment: that between the infant and the same-gender parent. The protagonists love their sweethearts quite precisely *as tomboy classmates*; faced with the narratives' abundant indications of the social specificity of this relation, it would make little sense to try forcing a reading of these women as the protagonists' "mother substitutes." However, interestingly, mother-daughter eroticism has indeed been a central subject of some recent Taiwanese lesbian fiction; see, for example, Chen Xue's "Searching for the Lost Wings of the Angel" and Hong Ling's "Poem from the Glass Womb."

48 Butler, *Psychic Life*, 140.

49 For Freud, "melancholia is in some way related to an object-loss which is withdrawn from consciousness, in contradistinction to mourning, in which there is nothing about the loss that is unconscious" ("Mourning and Melancholia," 245).

50 The prevalence of similar images of mournful femininity inspired the title of this chapter. With a nod to Dyer's work in "The Image of the Sad Young Man," I mean to propose that the "image of the sad young (same-sex attracted) woman" is a staple of contemporary Chinese forms of representation and that, as in Dyer's analysis of the sad young man, this image exerts a strong identificatory pull on many of its consumers (Dyer, *The Matter of Images*). For a discussion of the image of the sad young man in East Asian film, see Berry, "Happy Alone?"

51 On social memory as a series of practices, see Chris Healy: "Social memory is made up of relatively discrete instances in a network of performances: enunciations in historical writing, speaking, (re)enactment, (re)presentation and so on; the surfaces of historical discourses; the renderings of memory practices" (*From the Ruins of Colonialism*, 4–5).

52 See, for example, Chou, *Tongzhi*.

53 See Sedgwick, "Queer Performativity," 14–15.

54 In "Queer Performativity," Sedgwick frames a related difficulty in the post-Butlerian uses to which the theory of performativity has been put, which she argues often result in a kind of "good dog/bad dog" criticism that, in its obsession with the question of the subversiveness/conservatism of a given cultural product, effectively reinstates the repressive hypothesis. In the ongoing debates over the relative homosexual "tolerance" of various societies — East versus West, past versus present — we find an analogue of this impasse in a kind of "good culture/bad culture" paradigm. For key examples of the "tolerance" argument vis-à-vis "traditional China" as distinct from the repressive "modern West," see Chou, *Tongzhi*, 13–55, and Hinsch, *Passions*, 162–71. For a review of critical treatments of Chou's privileging of a reified (and largely illusory) tradition of Chinese "silent tolerance" (*moyan kuanrong*) of homosexuality, see Martin, *Situating Sexualities*, 31–33.

55 Cf. Sang, *The Emerging Lesbian*, 100 and 122–25.

56 In this structural sense of being fundamentally incoherent, modern Chinese discourses on sexuality are like their Western counterparts (Sedgwick, *Epistemology of the Closet*, 67–90); what is distinctive, as I have tried to show, lies in their particular emphases and micro-level organization.

Chapter Six: Critical Presentism

1 In August 2005, the inaugural Asian Lesbian Film Festival was held in Taipei, sponsored by the Gender and Sexuality Rights Association, Taiwan, and showcasing a range of recent short films from the region, many of them made by self-identifying lesbian filmmakers (see the festival Web site at http://www.gsrat.net). The festival represents part of the same emergent regional lesbian film movement that also produced the three films discussed in detail in the latter part of this chapter.

2 See, for example, White, *UnInvited*; Wilton, *Immortal, Invisible*; Weiss, *Vampires and Violets*; Kabir, *Daughters of Desire*; Hoogland, *Lesbian Configurations*, 24–42.

3 De Lauretis, "Sexual Indifference and Lesbian Representation," 152.

4 White, *UnInvited*, xvii.

5 Ibid., 2. On lesbian spectres in Euro-American cinema, see also Mayne, *Framed*, 41–64, on Henri-Georges Clouzot's *Les diaboliques*.

6 Weiss, *Vampires and Violets*, 137–61.

7 On the troubled relations between lesbian representation and the exploitative masculinist gaze in cinema, see also Mayne, *Framed*, 149–60; Roof, *A Lure of Knowledge*, 15–89; Merck, *Perversions*, 162–76.

8 The recent emergence of a lesbian-themed feature film from the PRC owes much to both the strange situation vis-à-vis "underground" filmmaking in the PRC — such that films can be made unofficially if the filmmaker is determined enough but cannot secure domestic theatrical release without Film Bureau approval (see discussion below) — and to the popular emergence of the homosexual topic into public discourse after four decades of censorship (see Sang, *The Emerging Lesbian*, 163–74). In Taiwan, before the lifting of martial law in 1987, the Government Information Office regulated the production of both literature and film and forbade the production of films and stories that were contrary to "cultural morality" or portrayed "vulgar gestures or acts" and erotic scenes (Lan Tsu Wei, "The Role of Government"; Chao, "Embodying the Invisible," 189). This system was revised shortly after 1987 and replaced with a category system demarcating three levels of restriction based on film content (Chao, 197). For detailed discussions of the representation of "lesbian," proto-lesbian, and transgender characters in popular Hong Kong cinema, see H. Leung, "Unsung Heroes," and Chao, "Embodying the Invisible," chapter 7.

9 Recent work by See Kam Tan and others on the potential for queer identifications to be made by spectators of cross-dressed Cantonese opera films takes an approach similar to White's in its insistence on the polysemic productiveness, rather than simple "repressiveness," of older films, in which direct representation of lesbianism was absent. (Tan and Aw, "Love Eterne" and "The Cross-Gender Performances of Yam Kim-Fei"). Aside from Stanley Kwan's documentary exploration in *Yang ± Yin* (1996), no comprehensive study of lesbian subtext in pre-1980s Chinese cinemas has yet been undertaken, though such a study is certainly imaginable, especially given the popularity of cross-dressing themes. This pertains not only to opera films; consider also, for example, Shanghai director Fang Peilin's 1936 box office hit *Huashen guniang* (Tomboy), in which one young woman falls in love with another under the illusion that her beloved is a boy; see Hu, *Projecting a Nation*, 112–13.

10 This is not to argue that the memorial mode is the *only* mode of lesbian representation in Chinese cinema, only that it is a very influential and far-reaching one. Representations of lesbianism in much popular Hong Kong cinema, for example,

are quite distinct and demand different interpretative strategies (for example, Chu Yuan's soft-porn period melodrama *Ai nu* (Intimate Confessions of a Chinese Courtesan, 1972); Ching Siu-tung's *Xiao ao jianghu 2* (Swordsman 2, 1992); Lee Wai-man and Ching Siu-tung's *Dongfang bu bai 2* (Swordsman 3, 1993); Fok Yiu-leung's *Chiluo gao yang* (Naked Killer, 1992); and Yip Wai-man's *Gu huo zai qing yi pian zhi hong xing shi san mei* (Portland Street Blues, 1998); for critical approaches to these films, see note 8 above. However, detailed consideration of these films falls outside the scope of the present study, which is conceived not as a comprehensive survey of *all* forms of lesbian representation in Chinese cinema, but of the cinematic manifestations of and responses to the memorial mode of lesbian representation specifically. See also introduction, note 57.

11 Helen Leung critiques the film's nostalgic fixation for precisely this failure to envisage the possibility of lesbian relations in Hong Kong's present ("Queer-scapes," 434–35.) Jacob Cheung Chi Leung returns to the theme of intimate emotional bonds between women in his more recent film *Huangxin jiaqi* (Midnight Fly, 2001), though here the friendship between the two central characters—a man's wife and his mistress—lacks explicit sexual, erotic, or romantic elements.

12 The strong tendency for lesbian-themed Chinese-language films to include historical content suggests, perhaps, a kind of "seeping out" of the memorial mode from the individual to the more broadly social level. As well as *Intimates* and *Murmur of Youth*, other examples of this kind of film include Mak Yan Yan's *Butterfly* (discussed below), with its revisiting of the Hong Kong popular movement supporting the student protests in Tian'anmen Square in 1989; Cheng Sheng-fu's 1992 film *Shisheng huamei* (The Silent Thrush), with its evocation of local Taiwanese history through the representation of Taiwanese opera tradition (see Silvio, "Lesbianism and Taiwanese Localism in *The Silent Thrush*"); Huang Yushan's *Shuang zhuo* (Twin Bracelets), with its focus on traditional marriage practices in the Hui'an area of mainland China (see chapter 5, note 25); and Hong Kong director Shu Kei's lesbian-themed opera film *Hu du men* (Stage Door, 1996) (see Grossman, "The Rise of Homosexuality"). The Taiwanese telemovies discussed in chapter 5 also show traces of Taiwanese localist nostalgia; see Martin, "Trans-Asian Traces." See also note 13 below.

13 Examples could be multiplied further. For example, Sylvia Chang's film *Ershi, sanshi, sishi* (Twenty Thirty Forty, 2004) is an exploration of women's emotional experience at three different stages of life. Predictably the theme of same-sex attraction is confined to the story of the two twenty-year-olds; the thirty- and forty-year-old women are concerned, by contrast, exclusively with the cross-sex relations of marriage, divorce, heterosexual dating, and so forth. Costume dramas in which women's same-sex love is linked with cultural nostalgia for the Republican era constitute what may be an emerging mini-genre. Aside from *Intimates*, other examples here include Hong Kong director Yon Fan's *You yuan jing meng* (Peony Pavilion, 2001) and Taiwanese director Tsao Jui-yuan's film version of Pai Hsien-yung's story "Gu lian hua" (Love's Lone Flower, 2005; concurrently

released as a television serial; see discussion in epilogue). All three films are marked by memorialism not just in their nostalgic depiction of the lush decadence of Republican-era entertainment culture but also in their narrative form and stories, structured as each narrative is by the flashback reminiscences of a central woman character about a now-departed female lover.

14 Background on the film's production and other information is from my interview with Chen Jofei, conducted on December 12, 2003, in Taipei.

15 Chen's comments resonate with the argument proposed in chapter 5 on how recent schoolgirl romance telemovies, with their loving portrayal of tomboy characters, "speak back" to the mass-cultural image of the tomboy as socially abjected and unloved, as discussed in chapter 4.

16 An interesting "pan-Chinese" linguistic effect is created in the film by the fact that while Josie Ho (Flavia) delivers her lines in Cantonese, Tian Yuan slips habitually into a northern-accented Mandarin.

17 Jin's breast bears a birthmark in the shape of a butterfly; hence the name of Chen Xue's original novella, "The Mark of the Butterfly."

18 The film suggests a clear parallel throughout between the PRC government's violation of the Tian'anmen Square protestors' human rights and the difficulties faced by the central lesbian characters. In this, the film exemplifies Andrew Grossman's observation of the tendency in 1990s Hong Kong cinema for "(homo)sexual freedom" to be pressed into service as a synecdoche of political freedom in the context of Hong Kong's uncertain political future as a territory of the PRC. See Grossman, "The Rise of Homosexuality."

19 Mak Yan Yan interview with Martin, April 18, 2005. A diegetic motivation for the look of these images is given later in the film when we see Flavia tearfully watching an old Super-8 film of herself and Jin on their first day of college.

20 Chow, "Nostalgia of the New Wave," 232.

21 This is, of course, a common theme in memorial schoolgirl romances more broadly; see, for example, the recurring image of the seaside holiday in Liu Suola's "Blue Sky Green Sea" and the image of Qi and Zhang Yan singing under the banyan tree in Chu T'ien-hsin's "Waves Scour the Sands."

22 Mak interview with Martin, April 18, 2005.

23 The conceptualization of memory as a "re-presentation" in the present rather than a direct link to the actual past is by now a dominant one within cultural memory studies; see, for example, Huyssen: Present Pasts, 3–4, and Twilight Memories, 2–3; Bal, "Introduction" vii–xvii.

24 Personal communication with Chen Xue, March 15, 2005.

25 A more recent film that takes up a very similar strategy is Zero Chou's Ci qing (Spider Lilies, Taiwan, 2007). Here, as in Alice Wang's film Love Me If You Can (discussed in the introduction), the narrative revolves around a young woman (Jade, played by Rainie Yang) trying to induce her same-sex childhood sweetheart (Takeko, played by Isabella Leong) to remember their former love and to reignite it in the present. Again the theme of memory versus forgetting is foregrounded

throughout the film—for example, in the theme song, in whose lyrics jasmine flowers, associated with Jade, symbolize memory, and in the leitmotif of the spider lily, associated with Takeko, which in Japanese folklore is said to induce forgetfulness in those journeying to the underworld. Unlike in *Love Me If You Can*, here the reminiscent heroine is able to reawaken her lover's memory, and as in *Butterfly*, the two women are reunited at the end of the film. As they lie in bed in the golden light of sexual afterglow in the penultimate scene, Takeko asks Jade, "Why do you remember everything?" to which Jade replies, rhetorically, "Would you rather choose to forget?"

26 Martin interview with Li Yu, Beijing, December 26, 2003. The following account of Li Yu's background and views on *Fish and Elephant* is based on the same interview.

27 Ibid.

28 Li has since directed two further feature films, *Hong yan* (Dam Street, 2005) and *Pingguo* (Apple, 2006).

29 Li Yu interview with Martin, 2003.

30 Shi Tou interview with Fran Martin, Beijing, December 24, 2003,; see appendix for the edited transcript.

31 Deren et al., "Poetry and the Film" 171–86. On the connection between Deren's and Deleuze's theories, see, for example, Brannigan, "Maya Deren."

32 Deleuze, *Cinema 2*, 1–24.

33 Deren et al., "Poetry and the Film," 174 and 177.

34 Ibid., 174.

35 Deleuze, *Cinema 2*. Deleuze's explanation for the shift from the movement-image to the time-image is broadly historical:

> Precisely what brings this cinema of action into question after the war is the ... rise of situations to which one can no longer react, of environments with which there are now only chance relations, of empty or disconnected any-space-whatevers replacing qualified extended space. It is here that situations no longer extend into action or reaction in accordance with the requirements of the movement-image. These are pure optical and sound situations, in which the character does not know how to respond, abandoned spaces in which he [*sic*] ceases to experience and to act so that he enters into flight, goes on a trip, comes and goes, vaguely indifferent to what happens to him, undecided as to what must be done. (*Cinema 2*, 272)

36 For Deleuze, what was significantly new in late-twentieth-century cinema was precisely its subordination of "movement"—narrative development—to the pure time of the "optical and sound image"; see note 35.

37 Deleuze, *Cinema 2*, 271.

38 Ibid.

39 Cui, "Li Yu he *Jinnian xiatian*."

40 Of course, in Deren's definition, subjective flashbacks (flashbacks to a certain

mood rather than a certain event) such as those in Butterfly could also be described as scenes in which the vertical dimension dominates the horizontal. But the kind of "vertical time" in which I am most interested here is produced by "vertical" treatments of the *present* moment; the scenes to which I am referring are clearly distinguished from subjective flashbacks by their attention to the present. Such presentism is particularly noteworthy in Fish and Elephant given the film's complete lack of flashbacks or indeed any reference at all to lesbianism as a memorial condition.

41 An exception is the final sex scene; here a more rapid pace is established by the use of mobile framing, shorter takes, and cutting. This is explainable since a sense of urgency needs to be developed to parallel the climax of Junjun's story in the siege scene, with which the sex scene is crosscut. Static framing and longish takes are used throughout the film, in various different scenes, but my argument is that the use of these techniques reaches a kind of apotheosis in the scenes of Xiao Qun's and Xiao Ling's intimacy, where they are combined with the visual/spatial elements discussed above. Both the spatial particularity and the vertical time of these scenes are indexed in the use of cigarette smoke in many of them. The smoke from the two women's cigarettes renders visible and prominent both the extension of the women's particular kind of space (by making empty space opaque) and the duration of the ecstatic moments of their intimacy (by moving when all else is all but motionless).

42 When questioned on her influences, Li immediately cited the male directors of the Taiwan New Wave, Hou Hsiao-hsien and Edward Yang, rather than the European New Wave directors from whose work Hou and Yang's style is routinely claimed to derive in Western criticism (for a critique of this tendency, see Martin, "The European Undead"). The Taiwan New Wave was also the first movement mentioned by Chen Jofei when questioned on the style of Incidental Journey. This suggests an interesting regional embedding of the meaning of "art film style," such that it may be associated immediately with Taiwan rather than Europe.

43 Weiss, Vampires and Violets, 109–12.

44 Li Yu interview with Martin, 2003.

45 This hybrid style marks a contrast with films like Hong Kong lesbian director Yau Ching's Ho yuk (Let's Love Hong Kong, 2001) and Taiwanese lesbian director Zero Chou's Si jiaoluo (Corner's, 2001), with their far fuller and self-conscious use of experimental style.

46 This systematic and seemingly inevitable subordination of women by a masculinist state system in Fish and Elephant echoes a similar situation in mainland Chinese author Liu Suola's novella "Blue Sky Green Sea," discussed in chapter 3. In that novella, the narrator's best friend, Manzi, dies as the result of a home abortion that she performed on herself, too frightened to visit a hospital after once being berated "like a dog" by a moralistic doctor who discovered that she was unmarried yet sexually active. (Liu Suola, Blue Sky Green Sea and Other Stories, 37.) It is interesting that in that novella, as in Li's film, some of the harshest expressions

of the extant sex-gender system are manifested in representatives of the state: doctors and police. This linkage of gender subordination with the state apparatus is far stronger in these texts than in the Taiwanese and Hong Kong examples considered in other chapters and no doubt indexes the structural particularity of the state-mediated sex-gender system in the post-Mao PRC.

Epilogue

1 Pai Hsien-yung, *Qingchun hudie gu lian hua.*
2 Pai's story is loosely based on historical fact: Lin San-lang is based on the real Taiwanese musician Yang San-lang. See Taiwan Public Television Service Online. *Love's Lone Flower* screened on PTS after its initial broadcast on CTS.
3 Sedgwick, "Introduction: Axiomatic" in *Epistemology of the Closet.*
4 The figure to which I refer is a close relative of the *po*, the tomboy's feminine lover. However, she is not quite identical with her since the *po* is sometimes also constructed on a minoritizing model — that is, as a member of a minority group of feminine women who are attracted to masculine women rather than to men.
5 See chapter 5, note 25.
6 *Spider Lilies* is discussed in chapter 6, note 25.
7 See, for example, the lively discussions between Taiwanese and mainland audiences of *Spider Lilies* at the film's discussion forum (http://www.wretch.cc/blog/spiderlily). A hot topic of discussion in 2007 was the ethics of mainland viewers' downloading pirated copies of the film, in light of the extreme unlikelihood of an official release in the People's Republic, on the one hand, and everyone's desire to support the filmmakers, on the other.
8 For examples, see the introduction.

Appendix

1 Susan Jolly; see Ge Youli and Susan Jolly, "East Meets West Feminist Translation Group."
2 Yau Ching, dir., *Let's Love Hong Kong*, 2001, and Li Yu, dir., *Fish and Elephant*, 2001.

Filmography

Note: Includes both films and television programs.

Avnet, Jon, dir. *Fried Green Tomatoes*. United States, 1992.

Chang, Sylvia 張艾嘉, dir. *Ershi, sanshi, sishi* 二十三十四十 (Twenty Thirty Forty). Hong Kong/Taiwan/Japan, 2004.

Chen Jofei 陳若菲, dir. *Hai jiao tian ya* 海角天涯 (Incidental Journey). Taiwan, 2001.

Chen Xiuyu Lisa 陳秀玉, dir. *Nanian xiatiande langsheng* 那年夏天的浪聲 (Voice of Waves). Telemovie. Taiwan: PTS, 2002.

Cheng Bugao 程步高, dir. *Chun can* 春蠶 (Spring Silkworms). China, 1933.

Cheng Sheng-fu 鄭勝夫, dir. *Shisheng huamei* 失聲畫眉 (The Silent Thrush). Taiwan, 1992.

Cheung Chi Leung Jacob 張之亮, dir. *Huangxin jiaqi* 慌心假期 (Midnight Fly). Hong Kong, 2001.

———. *Zi shu* 自梳 (Intimates). Hong Kong, 1997.

Ching Siu-tung Tony 程小東, dir. *Xiao ao jianghu 2: Dongfang bu bai* 笑傲江湖 2—東方不敗 (Swordsman II). Hong Kong, 1992.

Chou, Zero 周美玲, dir., *Ci qing* 刺青 (Spider Lilies). Taiwan, 2007.

———. *Si jiaoluo* 私角落 (Corner's). Taiwan, 2001.

Chu, Arthur 瞿友寧, dir. *Sharen jihua* 殺人計畫 (My Whispering Plan). Taiwan, 2002.

Chu Yen-ping 朱延平, dir. *Nü huan* 女歡 (Lady in Heat). Taiwan, 1998.

Chu Yuan 楚原, dir. *Ai nu* 愛奴 (Intimate Confessions of a Chinese Courtesan). Hong Kong, 1972.

Cui Yan 催燕, dir., *Luo niao* 落鳥 (Chinese Chocolate). Canada, 1996.

Deitch, Donna, dir. *Desert Hearts*. United States, 1986.

Fang Peilin 方沛霖, dir. *Huashen guniang* 化身姑娘 (Tomboy, or Miss Changebody). China, 1936.

Fok Yiu-leung Clarence 霍耀良, dir. *Chiluo gao yang* 赤裸羔羊 (Naked Killer). Hong Kong, 1992.

Hou Hsiao-hsien 候孝賢, dir. *Haishang hua* 海上花 (Flowers of Shanghai). Taiwan, 1998.

Huang Yushan 黃玉珊, dir. *Shuang zhuo* 雙鐲 (Twin Bracelets). Hong Kong, 1991.

Khoo, Eric, dir. *Be with Me*. Singapore, 2005.

Kim Tae-Yong and Min Kyu-Dong, dirs. *Yeogo goedam 2* (Memento Mori). South Korea, 1999.

Ko Yi-zheng 柯一正, dir. *Ninü* 逆女 (The Unfilial Daughter). Television drama series. Taiwan: TTV, 2001.

Kurys, Diane, dir. *Entre nous*. France, 1983.

Kwan, Stanley, dir. *Yang ± Yin: Gender in Chinese Cinema*. Hong Kong, 1996.

Lee Ang 李安, dir. *Se, jie* 色，戒 (Lust, Caution) United States/China/Taiwan/Hong Kong, 2007.

Lee Wai-man Raymond, and Tony Ching Siu-tung 李惠民，程小東, dirs. *Dongfang bu bai 2: Feng yun zai qi* 東方不敗2—風雲再起 (Swordsman III: The East Is Red). Hong Kong, 1993.

Li Han Hsiang 李翰祥, dir. *Liang Shanbo yu Zhu Yingtai* 梁山伯與祝英台 (The Love Eterne). Hong Kong, 1962.

Li Yu 李玉, dir. *Hong yan* 紅顏 (Dam Street). China, 2005.

———. *Jinnian xiatian* 今年夏天 (Fish and Elephant). China, 2001.

———. *Pingguo* 蘋果 (Apple). China, 2006.

Lin Cheng-sheng 林正盛, dir. *Meili zai change* 美麗在唱歌 (Murmur of Youth). Taiwan, 1997.

McLaughlin, Sheila, dir. *She Must Be Seeing Things*. United States, 1987.

Mak Yan Yan 麥婉欣, dir. *Hudie* 蝴蝶 (Butterfly). Hong Kong, 2004.

Park Ki-hyung, dir. *Yeogo goedam* (Whispering Corridors). South Korea, 1998.

Peirce, Kimberly, dir. *Boys Don't Cry*. United States, 1999.

Rozema, Patricia, dir. *When Night Is Falling*. Canada, 1995.

Sato Shimako, dir. *Eko eko azarak 1* (Wizard of Darkness). Japan, 1995.

———. *Eko eko azarak 2* (Birth of the Wizard). Japan, 1996.

Sayles, John, dir. *Lianna*. United States, 1983.

Shu Kei 舒琪, dir. *Hu du men* 虎度門 (Stage Door). Hong Kong, 1996.

Towne, Robert, dir. *Personal Best*. United States, 1982.

Tsao Jui-yuan 曹瑞原, dir. *Gu lian hua* 孤戀花 (Love's Lone Flower). Television drama series. Taiwan: CTS, 2005.

———. *Gu lian hua* 孤戀花 (Love's Lone Flower). Taiwan, 2005.

———. *Niezi* 孽子 (CrystalsBoys). Television drama series. Taiwan: PTS, 2003.

———. *Tongnü zhi wu* 童女之舞 (The Maidens' Dance). Telemovie. Taiwan: PTS, 2002.

Wang, Alice, 王毓雅, dir. *Fei yue qing hai* 飛躍情海 (Love Me If You Can). Taiwan, 2003.

Wong Kar-wai 王家衛, dir. *Huayang nianhua* 花樣年華 (In the Mood for Love). Hong Kong, 2000.

Wu, Alice, dir. *Saving Face*. United States, 2004.

Wu Yonggang 吳永剛, dir. *Shennü* 神女 (The Goddess). China, 1934.

Yau Ching 游靜, dir. *Ho yuk* 好郁 (Let's Love Hong Kong). Hong Kong, 2001.

Yee Chih-yen 易智言, dir. *Lanse da men* 藍色大門 (Blue Gate Crossing). Taiwan/France, 2002.

Yip Wai-man Raymond 葉偉民, dir. *Gu huo zai qing yi pian zhi hong xing shi san mei* 古惑仔情義篇之洪興十三妹 (Portland Street Blues). Hong Kong, 1998.

Yon Fan 楊凡, dir. *You yuan jing meng* 遊園驚夢 (Peony Pavilion). Hong Kong, 2001.

Yuan Muzhi 袁牧之, dir. *Malu tianshi* 馬路天使 (Street Angel). China, 1937.

Yun Jae-yeon, dir. *Yeogo goedam 3* (The Wishing Stairs). South Korea, 2003.

Zheng Junli 鄭君里, dir. *Wuya yu maque* 烏鴉與麻雀 (Crow and Sparrows). China, 1949.

...

Selected Bibliography

Abelove, Henry. "Freud, Male Homosexuality, and the Americans." In Abelove et al., *Lesbian and Gay Studies Reader*, 381–93.

Abelove, Henry, Michele Aina Barale, and David M. Halperin, eds. *The Lesbian and Gay Studies Reader*. New York: Routledge, 1993.

An Keqiang 安克強. *Hong taiyangxiade hei linghun: Zhongguo dalu tongzhi xianxiang baodao* 紅太陽下的黑靈魂：中國大陸同志現場報導 (Black Shadows under the Red Sun: A Report of the Situation of Mainland Chinese Gays). Taipei: Re'ai, 1997.

An Xingben 安興本. "Queshide beige yu nanmingde mengmo: Taiwan dang dai tongxinglian wenxue lun" 缺失的悲歌与難鳴的夢魘－台灣當代同性戀文學論 (The Lost Tragic Song and the Wordless Nightmare: Contemporary Taiwan Homosexual Literary Theory). *Dangdai zuojia pinglun* 當代作家評論 6 (1992): 99–105.

Andreadis, Harriette. *Sappho in Early Modern England: Female Same-Sex Literary Erotics 1550–1714*. Chicago: University of Chicago Press, 2001.

Angles, Jeffrey M. "Writing the Love of Boys: Representations of Male-Male Desire in the Literature of Muruyama Kaita and Edogawa Ranpo." PHD dissertation, Ohio State University, 2003.

Aoyama, Tomoko. "Transgendering *shōjo shosetsu*: Girls' inter-text/sex-uality." In *Genders, Transgenders and Sexualities in Japan*. Ed. Mark McLelland and Romit Dasgupta, 49–64. London: Routledge, 2005.

Asker, D. B. D. "Eating Babies Is Right and Wrong or Neither of the Above: Jonathan Swift and Huang Biyun." *Journal of Modern Literature in Chinese* 3, no. 2 (January 1999): 131–43.

Bal, Mieke. "Introduction." In *Acts of Memory: Cultural Recall in the Present*. Ed. Mieke Bal, Jonathan Crewe, and Leo Spitzer. Hanover, N.H.: University Press of New England, 1999.

Barlow, Tani, ed. *Gender Politics in Modern China: Writing and Feminism.* Durham: Duke University Press, 1993.

Berry, Chris. "Happy Alone? Sad Young Men in East Asian Gay Cinema." *Journal of Homosexuality* 39, no. 3/4 (2000): 187–200.

———. "Asian Values, Family Values: Film, Video and Lesbian and Gay Identities." *The Journal of Homosexuality* 40, no. 3/4 (2000): 211–32.

Berry, Chris, and Fran Martin. "Syncretism and Synchronicity: Queer'n' Asian Cyberspace in 1990s Taiwan and Korea." In *Mobile Cultures: New Media in Queer Asia.* Ed. C. Berry, F. Martin, and A. Yue, 87–114. Durham: Duke University Press, 2003.

Bland, L., and Doan, Laura, eds. *Sexology in Culture: Labelling Bodies and Desires.* Cambridge: Polity Press, 1998.

Brannigan, Erin. "Maya Deren, Dance, and Gestural Encounters in Ritual in Transfigured Time." *Senses of Cinema* 22 (2002). Available at http://www.sensesofcinema.com/contents/02/22/deren.html. Accessed August 16, 2006.

Brooks, Peter. *The Melodramatic Imagination: Balzac, Henry James, Melodrama, and the Mode of Excess.* New Haven: Yale University Press, 1976.

Burston, Paul, and Colin Richardson, eds. *A Queer Romance: Lesbians, Gay Men and Popular Culture.* London: Routledge, 1995.

Butler, Judith. *Bodies That Matter: On the Discursive Limits of "Sex."* New York: Routledge, 1993.

———. *Gender Trouble: Feminism and the Subversion of Identity.* New York: Routledge, 1990.

———. "Imitation and Gender Insubordination." In Fuss, *Inside/Out,* 13–31.

———. *The Psychic Life of Power: Theories in Subjection.* Stanford: Stanford University Press, 1997.

Cai Yihuai 蔡益懷. *Gangren xushi: Ba, jiuling niandai Xianggang xiaoshuo zhong de "Xianggang xingxiang" yu xushi fanshi* 港人敘事：八九十年代香港小說中的"香港形象"與敘事範式 (Hong Kong Narratives: The "Image of Hong Kong" and Narrative Form in Novels from the Eighties and Nineties). Hong Kong: Hong Kong Writers' Association, 2001.

———. "Jiazu siyu: Lienü tu yu Shi Xiang Ji" 家族私語：《烈女圖》與《拾香紀》(Family Secrets: Portraits of Virtuous Women and Shi Xiang Ji). *Xianggang Wenxue* 香港文學 189 (September 2000): 61–63.

Cao Lijuan. "Dance of a Maiden." Trans. Shou-fang Hu-Moore. *The Chinese Pen: Contemporary Chinese Literature from Taiwan* 30, no. 1 (2002): 71–102.

———. "Tongnü zhi wu" 童女之舞 (The Maidens' Dance). In *Tongnü zhi wu* 童女之舞 (The Maidens' Dance), 14–49. Taipei: Datian, 1998.

Carter, Julian. "On Mother-Love: History, Queer Theory and Nonlesbian Identity." *Journal of the History of Sexuality* 14, nos. 1/2 (January/April 2005): 107–38.

Castle, Terry. *The Apparitional Lesbian: Female Homosexuality and Modern Culture.* New York: Columbia University Press, 1993.

Cesario. Untitled commentary on Ninü 逆女 (The Unfilial Daughter). Available at http://www.books.com.tw/exep/prod/booksfile.php?item=0010023515. Accessed April 7, 2005.

Chalmers, Sharon. "Tolerance, Form and Female Dis-ease: The Pathologisation of Lesbian Sexuality in Japanese Society." *Intersections* 6 (2004). Available at http://www.sshe.murdoch.edu.au/intersections/issue6/chalmers.html.

Chan, Chak Lui. "'Interesting' Gender-Crossing: A Case of Cantonese Opera in Hong Kong." Paper presented at Sexualities, Genders and Rights in Asia: First International Conference of Asian Queer Studies, Bangkok, 2005.

Chan, Ching-kiu Stephen. "The Language of Despair: Ideological Representations of the 'New Woman' by May Fourth Writers." In Barlow, *Gender Politics*, 13–32.

Chang Ching-sheng (Zhang Jingsheng). *Sex Histories: China's First Modern Treatise on Sex Education*. Trans. Howard Levy. Yokohama: self-published, 1967. Orig. 1926.

Chang, Eileen 張愛玲. "The Golden Cangue." Trans. Eileen Chang. In *Twentieth Century Chinese Stories*. Ed. C. T. Hsia. New York: Columbia University Press, 1971. Orig. 1943.

———. "Love in a Fallen City." Trans. Karen Kingsbury. *Renditions* 45 (spring 1996): 61–149. Orig. 1943.

———. *The Rice-Sprout Song*. Berkeley: University of California Press, 1998. Orig. 1955.

———. *The Rouge of the North*. Berkeley: University of California Press, 1998. Orig. 1967.

———. *Tongxue shaonian dou bu jian* 同學少年都不賤 (My Prosperous Classmates). Taipei: Crown, 2004.

———. "Traces of Love." Trans. Eva Hung. *Renditions* 45 (spring 1996): 112–27. Orig. 1945.

Chang Hsiao-hung 張小虹. Guaitai jiating luomanshi 怪胎家庭羅曼史 (A Queer Family Romance). Taipei: Shibao, 2000.

———. *Zilian nüren* 自戀女人 (The Narcissistic Woman). Taipei: Lianhe Wenxue, 1996.

Chang, Sung-sheng Yvonne. "Yuan Qiongqiong and the Rage for Eileen Zhang among Taiwan's *Feminine* Writers." In Barlow, *Gender Politics*, 215–37. Durham: Duke University Press, 1993.

Chao, Antonia Yengning. "Embodying the Invisible: Body Politics in Constructing Contemporary Taiwanese Lesbian Identities." PHD dissertation, Cornell University, 1996.

Chen Huiwen 陳慧文. "'Cainü,' 'yinnü,' 'ruonü' xingxiangde jiangou—Yu Dafu 'Ta shi yige ruo nüzi' zhong de nüxing xushu" 才女，淫女，弱女形象的建構—郁達夫 《 她是一個弱女子 》 中的女性敘述 (The Construction of Images of Talented Women, Lascivious Women and Weak Women: The Narration of the Female in Yu Dafu's "She Was A Weak Woman"). Unpublished paper. Available at http://sex.ncu.edu.tw/course/liou/4_Papers/Paper_04.html. Accessed August 11, 2004.

Chen, Jianhua. "Zhou Shoujuan's Love Stories and Mandarin Ducks and Butterflies Fiction." In Mostow, *Columbia Companion*, 355–63.

Chen Xue 陳雪. "Hudie de jihao" 蝴蝶的記號 (The Mark of the Butterfly). In *Mengyou 1994* 夢遊1994 (Sleepwalking 1994), 113–91. Taipei: Yuanliu, 1994.

———. "Searching for the Lost Wings of the Angel." Trans. F. Martin. In Martin, *Angelwings*, 167–87.

Chen Yushin. "Passionate Friendship: Schoolgirl Romance and Female Homosexuality in May Fourth Era China." Paper presented at Sexualities, Genders and Rights in Asia: First International Conference of Asian Queer Studies, Bangkok, 2005.

Cheung, Martha. "Introduction." In Liu Suola, *Blue Sky Green Sea and Other Stories*, ix–xxv. Trans. Martha Cheung. Hong Kong: Renditions Paperbacks, 1993.

Chi, Pang-yuan, and David Der-wei Wang, eds. *Chinese Literature in the Second Half of a Modern Century: A Critical Survey*. Bloomington: Indiana University Press, 2000.

Chien Ying-ying 簡瑛瑛. *He chu shi nü'er jia: Nüxing zhuyi yu Zhong Xi bijiao wenxue* 何處是女兒家: 女性主義與中西比較文學 (Feminism and East/West Comparative Literature Studies). Taipei: Lianhe Wenxue, 1998.

Chou Wah-shan 周華山. *Beijing tongzhide gushi* 北京同志的故事 (Beijing Gays' Stories). Hong Kong: Xianggang Tongzhi Yanjiushe, 1996.

———. *Houzhimin tongzhi* 後殖民同志 (Postcolonial *Tongzhi*). Hong Kong: Xianggang Tongzhi Yanjiushe, 1997.

———. *Tongzhi: The Politics of Same-Sex Eroticism in Chinese Societies*. New York: Haworth Press, 2000.

Chow, Rey. "Nostalgia of the New Wave: Structure in Wong Kar-wai's *Happy Together*." *Camera Obscura* 42 (1999): 30–49.

———. "Virtuous Transactions: A Reading of Three Stories by Ling Shuhua." In Barlow, *Gender Politics*, 90–105.

———. *Woman and Chinese Modernity: The Politics of Reading between West and East*. Minneapolis: University of Minnesota Press, 1991.

Chu T'ien-hsin 朱天心. "Chunfeng hudie zhi shi" 春風蝴蝶之事 (A Story of Spring Butterflies). In *Xiang wo juancunde xiongdimen* 想我眷村的兄弟們 (Thinking of My Brothers in the Veterans' Neighborhood), 199–221. Taipei: Maitian, 1992.

———. *Fangzhoushangde rizi* 方舟上的日子 (Days on the Ark). Shanghai: Shanghai Wenyi Chubanshe, 2001.

———. Interview with Fran Martin accompanying Martin's translation of "Waves Scour the Sands." *Renditions* 63 (spring 2005): 7–12.

———. "Lang tao sha" 浪淘沙 (Waves Scour the Sands). In *Fangzhoushangde rizi* 方舟上的日子 (Days on the Ark), 103–27. Taipei: Yuanliu, 1993. Orig. 1974.

———. "A Story of Spring Butterflies." Trans. Fran Martin. In Martin, *Angelwings*, 75–93.

———. "Waves Scour the Sands." Trans. Fran Martin. *Renditions* 63 (spring 2005): 13–32.

Connery, Christopher. "The Oceanic Feeling and the Regional Imaginary." In *Global/*

Local: *Cultural Production and the Transnational Imaginary*. Ed. Rob Wilson and Wimal Dissanayake, 284–311. Durham: Duke University Press, 1996.

Cook, Pam, and Mieke Bernink. "Teenpics." In *The Cinema Book*. Ed. P. Cook and M. Mernink, 218–22. London: BFI Publishing, 1999.

Cornbug 玉米虫. *Xuejie* 學姐 (My Elder Schoolmate). Taipei: Hongse Wenhua Chuban, 2002.

Creekmur, Corey K., and Alexander Doty, eds. *Out in Culture: Gay, Lesbian, and Queer Essays on Popular Culture*. Durham: Duke University Press, 1995.

Creet, Julia. "Anxieties of Identity: Coming Out and Coming Undone." In *Negotiating Lesbian and Gay Subjects*. Ed. M. Dorenkamp and R. Henke, 179–99. New York: Routledge, 1995.

Cui Zi'en 崔子恩. "Li Yu he Jinnian xiatian" 李玉和《今年夏天》 (Li Yu and *Fish and Elephant*). Manuscript passed on privately to the author. Also available at http://www.menggang.com/movie/china/liyu/fishelephnt/fishelephnt-c.html. Accessed August 22, 2006.

Dai Jinhua. "Rewriting Chinese Women: Gender Production and Cultural Space in the Eighties and Nineties." Trans. Yu Ning with Mayfair Yang. In *Spaces of Their Own: Women's Public Sphere in Transnational China*. Ed. Mayfair Mei-hui Yang, 198–99. Minneapolis: University of Minnesota Press, 1999.

Damm, Jens. "Same Sex Desire and Society in Taiwan, 1970–1987." *China Quarterly* (March 2005): 67–81.

de Lauretis, Teresa. "Film and the Visible." In *How Do I Look? Queer Film and Video*. Ed. Bad Object Choices Collective, 223–64. Seattle: Bay Press, 1991.

———. *The Practice of Love: Lesbian Sexuality and Perverse Desire*. Bloomington: Indiana University Press, 1994.

———. "Sexual Indifference and Lesbian Representation." In Abelove et al., *Lesbian and Gay Studies Reader*, 141–58.

Deleuze, Gilles. *Cinema 2: The Time-Image*. Trans. Hugh Tomlinson and Robert Galeta. Minneapolis: University of Minnesota Press, 1989.

Deren, Maya, Arthur Miller, Dylan Thomas, Parker Tyler, and Willard Maas. "Poetry and the Film: A Symposium," organized by Amos Vogel. In *Film Culture*. Ed. P. Adams Sitney, 171–86. London: Secker and Warburg, 1971.

Dikötter, Frank. *Sex, Culture and Modernity in China: Medical Science and the Construction of Sexual Identities in the Early Republican Period*. London: Hurst, 1995.

Ding, Naifei. *Obscene Things: Sexual Politics in Jin Ping Mei*. Durham: Duke University Press, 2002.

Doan, Laura. "'Acts of Female Indecency': Sexology's Intervention in Legislating Lesbianism." In Bland and Doan, *Sexology in Culture*, 199–213.

Doane, Mary Anne. "The 'Woman's Film': Possession and Address." In Gledhill, *Home Is Where the Heart Is*, 283–98.

Dog. "Yibu pian yiding dou hui you zhengfan liangmian pingjia—wo kan *Tongnü zhi wu*" 一部片一定都會有正反兩面評價 - 我看 "童女之舞" (Any Film Has Both a Positive and a Negative Interpretation—My Views on *The Maidens' Dance*).

Rensheng Juzhan Taolunqu 人生劇展討論區 (Public Television Service). Posted October 11, 2002.

Doherty, Thomas. *Teenagers and Teenpics: The Juvenilization of American Movies in the 1950s.* Boston: Unwin Hyman, 1988.

Dollase, Hiromi Tsichuya. "Early Twentieth Century Japanese Girls' Magazine Stories: Examining Shōjo Voice in Hanamomogatari (Flower Tales)." *Journal of Popular Culture* 36, no. 4 (2003): 724–55.

———. "Mad Girls in the Attic: Louisa May Alcott, Yoshiya Nobuko and the Development of Shojo Culture." PHD dissertation, Purdue University, 2003.

Dollimore, Jonathan. *Sexual Dissidence: Augustine to Wilde, Freud to Foucault.* Oxford: Clarendon Press and Oxford University Press, 1991.

Dooling, Amy D. and Kristina M. Torgeson, eds. *Women Writing in Modern China.* New York: Columbia University Press, 1998.

Doty, Alexander. *Making Things Perfectly Queer: Interpreting Mass Culture.* Minneapolis: University of Minnesota Press, 1993.

Du Xiulan 杜修蘭. *Ninü* 逆女 (The Unfilial Daughter). Taipei: Crown, 1996.

Duberman, M., M. Vicinus, and G. Chauncey Jr., eds. *Hidden from History: Reclaiming the Gay and Lesbian Past.* New York: Penguin, 1989.

Dyer, Richard. *The Matter of Images: Essays on Representation.* London: Routledge, 1993.

Edelman, Lee. *No Future: Queer Theory and the Death Drive.* Durham: Duke University Press, 2004.

Edgeworth, Maria. *Belinda.* London: Pandora, 1986.

Ellis, Havelock. *Studies in the Psychology of Sex,* vol. 2. New York: Random House, 1910/1936.

Engebretsen, Elisabeth. "Lesbian Identity and Community Projects in Beijing: Notes from the Field on Studying and Theorizing Same-Sex Cultures in the Age of Globalization." Paper presented at Sexualities, Genders and Rights in Asia: First International Conference of Asian Queer Studies, Bangkok, 2005.

Eribon, Didier. *Insult and the Making of the Gay Self.* Durham: Duke University Press, 2004.

Evans, Harriet. *Women and Sexuality in China: Dominant Discourses on Female Sexuality and Gender Since 1949.* Cambridge: Polity Press, 1997.

Faderman, Lillian. *Surpassing the Love of Men: Romantic Friendship and Love between Women from the Renaissance to the Present.* New York: Morrow, 1981.

Farwell, Marilyn R. *Heterosexual Plots and Lesbian Narratives.* New York: New York University Press, 1996.

Foucault, Michel. *The History of Sexuality.* Vol. 1: *An Introduction.* Trans. Robert Hurley. London: Penguin, 1981.

Freud, Sigmund. "Mourning and Melancholia." Trans. James Strachey. In *The Standard Edition of the Complete Psychological Works of Sigmund Freud,* vol. 14. Ed. J. Strachey, A. Freud, A. Strachey, and A. Tyson, 243–58. London: Hogarth Press, 1957.

———. *Three Essays on the Theory of Sexuality.* Trans. James Strachey. New York: Basic Books, 1962.

Friedman, Sara. "Another Kind of Love?: Debating Homosexuality and Same-Sex Intimacy through Taiwanese and Chinese Film Reception." In *Media, Erotics, and Transnational Asia*. Ed. Louisa Schein and Purnima Mankekar. Durham: Duke University Press, forthcoming.

Frühstück, Sabine. *Colonizing Sex: Sexology and Social Control in Modern Japan*. Berkeley: University of California Press, 2003.

Fujimoto Yukari. *Watashi no ibasho wa doko ni aru no—Shojo manga utsuru kokaru no katachi*. Tokyo: Gakuyo Shobo, 1998. Partial trans. Taeko Yamada, 2003.

Furukawa Makoto. "The Changing Nature of Sexuality: The Three Codes Framing Homosexuality in Modern Japan." Trans. Angus Lockyer. *U.S.-Japan Women's Journal, English Supplement* 7 (1994): 98–127.

Fuss, Diana. "Fallen Women: 'The Psychogenesis of a Case of Homosexuality in a Woman.'" In Fuss, *Identification Papers*, 57–82. New York: Routledge, 1995.

———. "Introduction." In Fuss, *Inside/Out*, 1–10.

———, ed. *Inside/Out: Lesbian Theories, Gay Theories*. New York: Routledge, 1991.

Gallop, Jane. *Around 1981: Academic Feminist Literary Criticism*. New York: Routledge, 1992.

Ge Youli and Susan Jolly. "East Meets West Feminist Translation Group: A Conversation between Two Participants." In Hsiung et al., *Chinese Women Organizing*, 61–75.

Gian Jiashin 簡家欣. "Huanchu nütongzhi: Jiuling niandai Taiwan nütongzhide lunshu xinggou yu yundong jijie" 喚出女同志：九0年代台灣女同志的論述形構與運動集結 (Bringing out Taiwan Lesbians: The Lesbian Discourses and Movements in Taiwan [1990–1996]). Master's thesis, National Taiwan University, 1996.

Gimpel, Denise. *Lost Voices of Modernity: A Chinese Popular Fiction Magazine in Context*. Honolulu: University of Hawaii Press, 2001.

Gledhill, Christine. "Rethinking Genre." In *Reinventing Film Studies*. Ed. C. Gledhill and L. Williams, 221–43. London: Arnold, 2000.

Gledhill, Christine, ed. *Home Is Where the Heart Is: Studies in Melodrama and the Woman's Film*. London: BFI Publishers, 1987.

———. "The Melodramatic Field: An Investigation." In Gledhill, *Home Is Where the Heart Is*, 5–39.

Gold, Thomas B. "Go with Your Feelings: Hong Kong and Taiwan Popular Culture in Greater China." *China Quarterly* 136 (1993): 907–25.

Gordon, Angus. "Plastic Identities: Adolescence, Homosexuality, and Contemporary Culture." PHD dissertation, University of Melbourne, 1997.

———. "Turning Back: Adolescence, Narrative, and Queer Theory." *GLQ* 5 (1999): 1–24.

Government Information Office. *Taiwan Yearbook 2003*. http://www.gio.gov.tw/taiwan-website/5-gp/yearbook/chpt17.htm#3. Accessed February 18, 2005.

Grossman, Andrew. "Hong Kong Film." GLBTQ.com. Accessed August 15, 2005.

———. "The Rise of Homosexuality and the Dawn of Communism in Hong Kong Film: 1993–1998." *Journal of Homosexuality* 39 (2000): 3–4, 149–86.

Guo Lianghui 郭良蕙. *Disan xing* 第三性 (The Third Sex). Taipei: Shibao Wenhua, 1985.

Hakamada Mera 夸田米良. *Our Last Season* (manga series) 最後的制服 Trans. Huang Yiping 黃翊蘋 (Taiwan edition). Taipei: Jianrui, 2007.

Halperin, David M. "Is There a History of Sexuality?" In Abelove et al., *Lesbian and Gay Studies Reader*, 416–31.

Haskell, Molly. *From Reverence to Rape: The Treatment of Women in the Movies*. New York: Penguin, 1974.

He Xiaopei. "Chinese Queer (Tongzhi) Women Organizing in the 1990s." In Hsiung et al., *Chinese Women Organizing*, 41–59.

Healy, Chris. *From the Ruins of Colonialism: History as Social Memory*. Cambridge: Cambridge University Press, 1997.

Hinsch, Bret. *Passions of the Cut Sleeve: The Male Homosexual Tradition in China*. Berkeley: University of California Press, 1990.

Hollinger, Karen. *In the Company of Women: Contemporary Female Friendship Films*. Minneapolis: University of Minnesota Press, 1998.

Holmlund, Chris. *Impossible Bodies: Femininity and Masculinity at the Movies*. London: Routledge, 2002.

Hong Ling 洪凌. "Leise yu bianzi de jiaohuan" 蕾絲與鞭子的交歡 (An Intercourse between Lace and Whip). In *Leise yu bianzi de jiaohuan: Dangdai Taiwan qingse wenxue lun* 蕾絲與鞭子的交歡：當代台灣情色文學論 (An Intercourse between Lace and Whip: Contemporary Taiwan Literary Critical Discourse on Erotic Writing). Ed. S. Lin and Y. Lin 林水福，林燿德, 91–127. Taipei: Shibao, 1997.

———. "Poem from the Glass Womb." Trans. Fran Martin. In Martin, *Angelwings*, 189–212.

Hong Ying 虹影. "Dalu nüxing zuojia nüxing zhi ai" 大陸女作家女性之愛 (Women's Love in the Works of Mainland Women Writers). In Hong Ying, *Jing yu shui*, 3–17.

———, ed. *Jing yu shui: Dalu nü zuojia nüxing zhi ai xiaoshuo xuan* 鏡與水：大陸女作家女性之愛小說選 (Mirror and Water: Selected Stories about Women's Love by Mainland Women Writers). Taipei: Jiuge, 1999.

Hoogland, Renée C. *Lesbian Configurations*. New York: Columbia University Press, 1997.

Hou Li-zhen 候麗貞. "Xianggang, zhengzhi, mei xingzhe—Huang Biyun xiaoshuo yanjiu" 香港，政治，媚行者—黃碧雲小說研究 (Hong Kong, Politics, Fascinating Walker: Research on the Novels of Wong Bikwan). Master's thesis, Tamkang University, 2002.

Hsia, C. T. (1999). "Eileen Chang." In *A History of Modern Chinese Fiction*, 3d ed., 389–431. Bloomington: Indiana University Press, 1999.

———. "Hsu Chen-ya's *Yu-li Hun*: An Essay in Literary History and Criticism." In

Chinese Middlebrow Fiction from the Ch'ing and Early Republican Eras. Ed. T. U-Y. Liu, 199–240. Hong Kong: Chinese University Press, 1984.

Hsiung, Ping-chun, Maria Jaschok, and Cecilia Milwerts, eds. *Chinese Women Organizing: Cadres, Feminists, Muslims, Queers.* Oxford: Berg, 2001.

Hu, Jubin. *Projecting a Nation: Chinese National Cinema before 1949.* Hong Kong: Hong Kong University Press, 2003.

Huang, Nicole. "Eileen Chang and Alternative Wartime Narrative." In Mostow, *Columbia Companion*, 458–62.

Huang Wanhua 黃萬華. "Nüxing wenxue: Fuchu lishi dibiaode ling yi han yi" 女性文學：浮出歷史地表的另一含義 (Women's Literature: Another Implication of Its Emergence into History). *Xianggang wenxue* 香港文學 215 (November 2002): 27–33.

Huyssen, Andreas. *Present Pasts: Urban Palimpsests and the Politics of Memory.* Stanford: Stanford University Press, 2003.

———. *Twilight Memories: Marking Time in a Culture of Amnesia.* New York: Routledge, 1995.

Jagose, Annamarie. *Inconsequence: Lesbian Representation and the Logic of Sexual Sequence.* Ithaca, N.Y.: Cornell University Press, 2002.

———. *Lesbian Utopics.* New York: Routledge, 1994.

Jolly, Margaretta. "Coming Out of the Coming Out Story: Writing Queer Lives." *Sexualities* 4, no. 4 (2001): 474–96.

Kabir, Shameem. *Daughters of Desire: Lesbian Representations in Film.* London: Cassell, 1997.

Kam Yip-lo, Lucetta 金曄路. "Recognition through Mis-recognition: The Gender Identifications of Masculine Women in Hong Kong." In Martin et al., *Asia-PacifiQueer*, 99–116.

———. "TB zhe xingbie" TB 這性別 (This Gender Called TB). *E-Journal on Hong Kong Cultural and Social Studies* 2 (2002). http://www.hku.hk/hkcsp/ccex/ehkcss01/frame.htm?mid=1&smid=1&ssmid=7.

———, ed. 金曄路. *Yueliang de saodong: Ta-ta de chulian gushi—Women de zishu* (Torments of the Moon: Stories of First Lesbian Love). Hong Kong: Cultural Act Up, 2001.

Keleguo 可樂果. "Re: Nanian xiatiande langsheng. . . ." Re: 那年夏天的浪聲 . . . (Re: *Voice of Waves*. . . .). Rensheng Juzhan Taolunqu 人生劇展討論區 (Public Television Service). Posted October 14, 2002.

Kelleher, Paul. "If Love Were All: Reading Sedgwick Sentimentally." In *Regarding Sedgwick: Essays on Queer Culture and Critical Theory.* Ed. S. M. Barber and D. L. Clark, 143–62. New York: Routledge, 2002.

Kimino Sakurako 公野櫻子. *Strawberry Panic! Girls' School in Full Bloom* (manga series) 草莓狂熱. Trans. Liu Tingyu 劉廷宇 (Taiwan edition). Taipei: Jianrui, 2007.

Kristeva, Julia. *Black Sun: Depression and Melancholia.* Trans. Leon S. Roudiez. New York: Columbia University Press, 1989.

Lan Tsu-wei. "The Role of Government in the Development of the Taiwanese New Wave." In *The 20th Anniversary of Taiwan New Wave Cinema: Taiwanese Cinema, 1982–2002—From New Wave to Independent*. Catalogue of the Seventh Pusan International Film Festival, 2002. Available at http://www.asianfilms.org/taiwan/huigu/huigu5.html. Accessed September 21, 2004.

Landy, Marcia, ed. *Imitations of Life: A Reader on Film and Television Melodrama*. Detroit: Wayne State University Press, 1991.

Lang, Miriam. "San Mao and Qiong Yao: A 'Popular' Pair." *Modern Chinese Literature and Culture* 15, no. 2 (2003): 76–120.

———. "Taiwanese Romance: San Mao and Qiong Yao." In Mostow, *Columbia Companion*, 515–19.

Larson, Wendy. *Women and Writing in Modern China*. Stanford: Stanford University Press, 1998.

Lau, Joseph S. M. "The 'Little Woman' as Exorcist: Notes on the Fiction of Huang Biyun." *Journal of Modern Literature in Chinese* 2, no. 2 (January 1999): 149–63.

Leary, Charles Leland. "Sexual Modernism in China: Zhang Jingsheng and 1920s Urban Culture." PHD dissertation, Cornell University, 1994.

Lee, Leo Ou-fan. *The Romantic Generation of Modern Chinese Writers*. Cambridge, Mass.: Harvard University Press, 1973.

———. *Shanghai Modern: The Flowering of a New Urban Culture in China, 1930–1945*. Cambridge, Mass.: Harvard University Press, 1999.

———. "'Modernism' and 'Romanticism' in Taiwan Literature." In *Chinese Fiction from Taiwan: Critical Perspectives*. Ed. Jeanette L. Faurot, 6–30. Bloomington: Indiana University Press, 1980.

Leibowitz, Flo. "Apt Feelings, or Why Women's Films Aren't Trivial." In *Post-Theory: Reconstructing Film Studies*. Ed. D. Bordwell and N. Carroll, 219–29. Madison: University of Wisconsin Press, 1996.

Lent, John A. "Comics in East Asian Countries: A Contemporary Survey." *Journal of Popular Culture* 29, no. 1 (1995): 185–98.

———. "Local Comic Books and the Curse of Manga in Hong Kong, South Korea and Taiwan." *Asian Journal of Communication* 9, no. 1 (1999): 108–28.

———, ed. *Illustrating Asia: Comics, Humor Magazines, and Picture Books*. Honolulu: University of Hawaii Press, 2001.

Lesbian. "*Tongnü zhi wu kehua nühaimende qinggan bu ju shuifuli*" 童女之舞刻劃女孩們的情感不具說服力 (The Emotions of the Stereotyped Girls in *The Maidens' Dance* Are Unconvincing). Rensheng Juzhan Taolunqu 人生劇展討論區 (Public Television Service). Posted March 19, 2002.

Leung, Helen Hok-sze. "Queerscapes in Contemporary Hong Kong Cinema." *Positions: East Asia Cultures Critique* 9, no. 2 (2001): 423–47.

———. "Thoughts on Lesbian Genders in Contemporary Chinese Cultures." *Journal of Lesbian Studies* 6, no. 2 (2002): 123–33.

———. (2005). "Unsung Heroes: Reading Transgender Subjectivities in Hong Kong

Action Cinema." In *Masculinities and Hong Kong Cinema*. Ed. L. Pang and D. K.-m. Wong, 81–98. Hong Kong: Hong Kong University Press, 2005.

Leung, Pik-ki. "Unruly Same-Sex Intimacies: Schoolgirls' Tales and Practices of Transgressive Emotionality and Sexuality in Postsocialist China." Paper presented at Sexualities, Genders and Rights in Asia: First International Conference of Asian Queer Studies, Bangkok, 2005.

Li Ang 李昂. *Huajian mi qing* 花間迷情 (Bewitching Love). Taipei: Locus Publishing, 2005.

Li Jie 李絜. "Liu Suola xiaoshuo lun" 劉索拉小說論 (On Liu Suola's Fiction). Wenxue Pinglun 文學評論 1 (1986): 120–26.

Li Mingying 李明英. "Miandui xuesheng tongxinglian yigan" 面對學生同性戀疑惑 (Facing the Suspicion of Student Homosexuality). 2001. http://www.famplan.org.hk/sexedu/B5/article/Article_details.asp?arID=137. Accessed October 12, 2004.

Li, Siu Leung. *Cross-Dressing in Chinese Opera*. Hong Kong: Hong Kong University Press, 2003.

Li Yinhe 李銀河. *Xing wenhua yanjiu baogao* 性文化研究報告 (Research Report on Sexual Culture). Nanjing: Jiangsu Renmin Chubanshe, 2003.

Li Ziyun 李子云. "Nüzuojia zai dangdai wenxueshi suo qide xianfeng zuoyong" 女作家在當代文學史所起的先鋒作用 (The Avant-Garde Role Played by Women Writers in Contemporary Literary History). *Dangdai zuojia pinglun* 當代作家評論 6 (1987): 4–10.

Liang, A. C. "Conversationally Implicating Lesbian and Gay Identity." In *Reinventing Identities: The Gendered Self in Discourse*. Ed. M. Bucholtz, A. C. Liang, and L. A. Sutton. New York: Oxford University Press, 1999.

Lieberman, Sally Taylor. *The Mother and Narrative Politics in Modern China*. Charlottesville: University Press of Virginia, 1998.

Lim Chin-chown. "Reading 'The Golden Cangue': Iron Boudoirs and Symbols of Oppressed Confucian Women." Trans. Louise Edwards and Kam Louie. *Renditions* 45 (spring 1996): 141–49.

Lin Chun Ying. "Who Is Singing?" Trans. Fran Martin. In Martin, *Angelwings*, 155–65.

Lin Fang-mei 林芳玫. *Jiedu Qiong Yao aiqing wangguo* 解讀瓊瑤愛情王國 (Interpreting Qiong Yao's Romantic Kingdom). Taipei: Shibao, 1994.

———. "Social Change and Romantic Ideology: The Impact of the Publishing Industry, Family Organization and Gender Roles on the Reception and Interpretation of Romance Fiction in Taiwan." PHD dissertation, University of Pennsylvania, 1992.

Lin Yuyi. "The Boy in the Pink Orchid Tree." Trans. Fran Martin. In Martin, *Angelwings*, 127–53.

Ling Shuhua 凌叔華. "Once upon a Time." Trans. Amy A. Dooling and Kristina M. Torgeson. In Dooling and Torgeson, *Writing Women in Modern China*, 185–95.

———. "Shuo you zheme yihui shi" 說有這麼一回事 (Once upon a time). In Chen Xueyong 陳學勇 ed., *Ling Shuhua Wencun* 凌叔華文存. (A Collection of Ling Shu-hua's Writing), vol. 1, 117–28. Sichuan: Sichuan Wenyi Chubanshe, 1998.

Link, E. Perry. *Mandarin Ducks and Butterflies: Popular Fiction in Early Twentieth-Century Chinese Cities*. Berkeley: University of California Press, 1981.

Liou Liang-ya 劉亮雅. *Qingse shijimo: Xiaoshuo, xingbie, wenhua, meixue* 情色世紀末：小說、性別、文化、美學 (Gender, Sexuality, and the Fin de Siècle). Taipei: Jiuge, 2001.

———. *Yuwang gengyishi: Qingse xiaoshuode zhengzhi yu meixue* 慾望更衣室：情色小說的政治與美學 (Engendering Dissident Desires: The Politics and Aesthetics of Erotic Fictions). Taipei: Yuanzun, 1998.

Liu Beixian 劉北憲. "Liu Suola pingzhuan" 劉索拉評傳 (A Critique of Liu Suola). In *Zhongguo dangdai qingnian nüzuojia pingzhuan* 中國當代青年女作家評傳 (Critiques of Contemporary Young Chinese Women Writers), 152–65. Beijing: Zhongguo Funü Chubanshe, 1990.

Liu Dalin, Man Lun Ng, et al. *Sexual Behavior in Modern China: Report on the Nationwide Survey of 20,000 Men and Women (English Edition)*. New York: Continuum, 1997.

Liu Jenpeng and Ding Naifei. "Reticent Poetics, Queer Politics." *Inter-Asia Cultural Studies* 6, no. 1 (2005): 30–55.

Liu Jenpeng, Ding Naifei, and Amie Parry 劉人鵬，丁乃非，白瑞梅. "Xieshide qihuan jiegou yu qihuande xieshi xiaoying: Chong du T, po xushi" 寫實的奇幻結構與奇幻的寫實效應—重讀 T，婆敘事 (Realism's Fantasy Structures and Fantasy's Realist Effects: Reading T-po Narratives). In *Wangliang wen jing: Ku'er yuedu gonglue* 罔兩文景—酷兒閱讀攻略 (Penumbrae Query Shadow: Queer Reading Tactics), 107–44. Chungli: Zhongyang Daxue Xing/bie Yanjiushi, 2007.

Liu Kang. "Subjectivity, Marxism, and Cultural Theory in China." In K. Liu and Tang, *Politics*, 23–54.

Liu, Kang, and Xiaobing Tang. "Introduction." In K. Liu and Tang, *Politics*, 8–20.

———, eds. *Politics, Ideology, and Literary Discourse in Modern China: Theoretical Interventions and Cultural Critique*. Durham: Duke University Press, 1993.

Liu, Lydia H. "Invention and Intervention: The Female Tradition in Modern Chinese Literature." In Barlow, *Gender Politics*, 33–57.

Liu Suola 劉索拉. *Blue Sky Green Sea and Other Stories*. Trans. Martha Cheung. Hong Kong: Renditions Paperbacks, 1993.

———. "Lan tian lü hai" 藍天綠海 (Blue Sky Green Sea). In Liu Suola, *Ni bie wu xuanze*, 141–92. Orig. 1985.

———. *Ni bie wu xuanze* 你別無選擇 (You Have No Other Choice). Taipei: Xindi Wenhua Chuban, 1988.

Liu Xiaobo 劉曉波. "Yizhong xinde shenmei sichao: Cong Xu Xing, Chen Cun, Liu Suolade san bu zuopin tanqi" 一種新的審美思潮—從徐星，陳村，劉索拉的三部作品談起 (The Rise of a New Aesthetic: Starting from Three Works by Xu Xing, Chen Cun, and Liu Suola). *Wenxue pinglun* 文學評論 3 (1986): 35–43.

Liu Zaifu. "The Subjectivity of Literature Revisited." In K. Liu and Tang, *Politics*.

Lü Jinyuan 呂錦媛. "Taiwan nütongzhi jiuba zhi yanjiu" 台灣女同志酒吧之研究 (A Research Note on Taiwan's Lesbian Bars). *Cultural Studies Monthly* 文化研究月報 23 (2003). http://140.112.191.178/csa/journal/23/journal_park153.htm.

Lu, Tonglin, ed. *Gender and Sexuality in Twentieth-Century Literature and Society*. Albany: SUNY Press, 1993.

Lu Yin 盧隱. "Lishi de riji" 麗石的日記 (Lishi's Diary). In *Lu Yin Xuanji* 盧隱選集 (Selected Works by Lu Yin). Ed. Xiao Feng and Sun Ke 肖鳳，孫可, 47–113. Tianjin: Baihua Wenyi Chubanshe, 1983. Orig. 1923.

———. *Lu Yin zizhuan* 盧隱自傳 (Lu Yin's Autobiography). Shanghai: Di Yi Chubanshe, 1934.

Mak, Anson, Chou Wah-shan, and Jiang Jianbang, eds. 麥海珊, 周華山, 江建邦. *Xianggang tongzhi zhan chu-lai* 香港同志站出來 (Hong Kong Gays Stand Up). Hong Kong: Xianggang Tongzhi Yanjiu She, 1995.

Maomao 毛毛. "Bu jiande bu xuyao" 不見得不需要 (We Don't Necessarily Not Need it). *Rensheng Juzhan Taolunqu* 人生劇展討論區 (Public Television Service). Posted October 15, 2002.

Marcuse, Herbert. *Eros and Civilization: A Philosophical Inquiry into Freud*. London: Abacus, 1972.

Martin, Fran. "The European Undead: Tsai Ming-liang's Temporal Dysphoria." *Senses of Cinema* 27 (2003). Available at http://www.sensesofcinema.com/contents/03/27/tsai_european_undead.html. Accessed August 17, 2006.

———. *Situating Sexualities: Queer Representation in Taiwanese Fiction, Film and Public Culture*. Hong Kong: Hong Kong University Press, 2003.

———. "Stigmatic Bodies: The Corporeal Qiu Miaojin." In *Embodied Modernities: Corporeality, Representation and Chinese Cultures*. Ed. F. Martin and L. Heinrich, 177–94. Honolulu: University of Hawaii Press, 2006.

———. "Taiwan (Trans)National Cinema, or, The Far-Flung Adventures of a Taiwanese Tomboy." In *Cinema Taiwan: State of the Art, State of the Nation*. Ed. W. Lin, R. Rushou Chen, and D. W. Davis, 131–45. New York: Routledge, 2007.

———. "Taiwan's Literature of Transgressive Sexuality." In Martin, *Angelwings*, 1–28.

———. "That Global Feeling: Sexual Subjectivities and Imagined Geographies in Chinese-Language Lesbian Cyberspaces." In *Internationalizing Internet Studies*. Ed. Mark McLelland and Gerard Goggin, 285–301. New York: Routledge, 2008.

———. "Trans-Asian Traces: Watching Schoolgirl Romance on Taiwan Television." In *TransAsia Screens*. Ed. Chris Berry and Zhang Zhen. Hong Kong: Hong Kong University Press, forthcoming.

———, ed. *Angelwings: Contemporary Queer Fiction from Taiwan*. Honolulu: University of Hawaii Press, 2003.

Martin, Fran, Peter A. Jackson, Mark McLelland, and Audrey Yue, eds. *AsiaPacifiQueer: Rethinking Gender and Sexuality in the Asia-Pacific*. Urbana: University of Illinois Press, 2008.

Mayberight 小也. *Wode xinli zhi you ni meiyou ta 1* 我的心裡只有你沒有他 1 (Only You 1). Taipei: Jihe Chubanshe, 2003.

———. *Wode xinli zhi you ni meiyou ta 2* 我的心裡只有你沒有他 2 (Only You 2). Taipei: Jihe Chubanshe, 2003.

Mayne, Judith. *Framed: Lesbians, Feminists and Media Culture.* Minneapolis: University of Minnesota Press, 2000.

McDougall, Bonnie S., and Kam Louie. *The Literature of China in the Twentieth Century.* Gosford: Bushbooks, 1997.

McLelland, Mark. "From Sailor-Suits to Sadists: 'Lesbos Love' as Reflected in Japan's Postwar 'Perverse Press.'" *U.S.-Japan Women's Journal, English Supplement* 27 (2004): 3–26.

———. "Interview with Samshasha, Hong Kong's First Gay Rights Activist and Author." *Intersections* 4 (2000). http://wwwsshe.murdoch.edu.au/intersections/issue4/interview_mclelland.html.

———. *Reconstructing Sex and Gender in Japan 1945–55.* Unpublished manuscript.

McMahon, Keith. *Misers, Shrews, and Polygamists: Sexuality and Male-Female Relations in Eighteenth-Century Chinese Fiction.* Durham: Duke University Press, 1995.

Meese, Elizabeth A. *(Sem)Erotics: Theorizing Lesbian Writing.* New York: New York University Press, 1992.

Merck, Mandy. *Perversions: Deviant Readings.* New York: Routledge, 1993.

Mianbao 麵包. "Nanian xiatian langsheng qiaotong wode xin" 那年夏天浪聲敲痛我的心 (The *Voice of Waves* Wounded My Heart). Rensheng Juzhan Taolunqu 人生劇展討論區 (Public Television Service). Posted October 19, 2002.

Modleski, Tania. "Time and Desire in the Woman's Film." *Cinema Journal* 23, no. 3 (spring 1984): 19–30.

Moore, Lisa. "'Something More Tender Still Than Friendship': Romantic Friendship in Early-Nineteenth-Century England." In Vicinus, *Lesbian Subjects,* 21–40.

Mostow, Joshua. *The Columbia Companion to Modern East Asian Literature.* New York: Columbia University Press, 2003.

Nagasawa Satoru 長澤智. *The Gaze of the Virgin Mary* (manga series) 瑪莉亞的凝望. Trans. Cai Mengfang 蔡夢芳 (Taiwan edition). Taipei: Tong Li, 2005.

Nanian 那年. "Nanian xiatiande langsheng. . . ." 那年夏天的浪聲. . . . (*Voice of Waves. . . .*). Rensheng Juzhan Taolunqu 人生劇展討論區 (Public Television Service). Posted October 14, 2002.

Newton, Esther. *Margaret Mead Made Me Gay: Personal Essays, Public Ideas.* Durham: Duke University Press, 2000.

———. "The Mythic Mannish Lesbian: Radclyffe Hall and the New Woman." In Duberman et al., *Hidden from History,* 281–93.

Ng Kit-fan 吳潔芳. "Chuncuide guodu" 純粹的國度 (The Pure Country). In *Tata tatade gushi* 他他她她的故事 (His Stories, Her Stories). Ed. Lu Jianxiong 盧劍雄. Hong Kong: Worldson, 1996.

Ng, Wai-ming. "A Comparative Study of Japanese Comics in Southeast Asia and East Asia." *International Journal of Comic Art* (spring 2000): 45–56.

———. "The Impact of Japanese Comics and Animation in Asia." *Journal of Japanese Trade and Industry* (July/August 2002): 1–4.

Nie Mao 聶茂 (2002). "Wuaizhongde tuwei: Quanqiuhua jingzhaoxia dui Zhongguo xin shiqi xianfeng xiaoshuode huanyuanxing jiedu" 霧靄中的突圍—全球化鏡照下對中國新時期先鋒小說的還原性解讀 (Ambush in the Mist: A Reinterpretation of China's New Era Avant-Garde Fiction in the Light of Globalization). *Shiji zhongguo* 世紀中國, 2002. http://www.cc.org.cn/zhoukan/guancha yusikao/0207/0207121008.htm. Accessed June 1, 2003; site has since been closed down.

Nielsen, Inge. "Caught in the Web of Love: Intercepting the Young Adult Reception of Qiongyao's Romances On-line." *Acta Orientalia Academiae Scientarium Hungaricae* 51, nos. 3–4 (2000): 235–53.

Ogi, Fusami. "Gender Insubordination in Japanese Comics (Manga) for Girls." In Lent, *Illustrating Asia*, 171–86.

Ong, Aihwa, and Donald M. Nonini, eds. *Ungrounded Empires: The Cultural Politics of Modern Chinese Transnationalism*. New York: Routledge, 1997.

Pai Hsien-yung 白先勇. "Gu lian hua" 孤戀花 (Love's Lone Flower). In *Taipei People: Chinese-English Bilingual Edition*. Ed. G. Kao 臺北人, 229–57. Hong Kong: Chinese University Press, 1970.

———. *Qingchun hudie gu lian hua* 青春蝴蝶孤戀花 (Love's lone flower, butterfly youth edition). Taipei: Yuanliu, 2005.

Peng Hsiao-yen 澎小妍. *Haishang shuo qingyu: Cong Zhang Ziping dao Liu Na'ou* 海上說情慾：從張資平到劉吶鷗 (Shanghai Desire: From Zhang Ziping to Liu Na'ou). Taipei: Institute of Chinese Literature and Philosophy, Academia Sinica, 2001.

———. "The New Woman: May Fourth Women's Struggle for Self-Liberation." *Bulletin of the Institute of Chinese Literature and Philosophy* 6 (March 1995): 259–334.

———. "Sex Histories: Zhang Jingsheng's Sexual Revolution." *Tamkang Review* 30, no. 2 (1999): 71–98.

Peng Huai-chen 彭懷真. *Tongxinglian, zisha, jingshenbing* 同性戀, 自殺, 精神病 (Homosexuality, Suicide, and Mental Disorders). Taipei: Ganlan Jijinhui, 1983.

Pflugfelder, Gregory M. *Cartographies of Desire: Male-Male Sexuality in Japanese Discourse, 1600–1950*. Berkeley: University of California Press, 1999.

———. "'S' Is for Sister: Schoolgirl Intimacy and 'Same-Sex Love' in Early Twentieth-Century Japan." Unpublished paper, 2003.

Plummer, Kenneth. *Telling Sexual Stories: Power, Change, and Social Worlds*. London: Routledge, 1995.

Public Television Service Taiwan. *Public Television Service Foundation Annual Report 2002*. Taipei, 2002.

———. "Rensheng juzhan taolunqu" 人生劇展討論區 (Drama on PTS Internet BBS forum, 2000). http://www.pts.org.tw/php/board/index.php?LISTALL=1&FIRST =1&BMENB=104. Accessed September 15–24, 2003.

Qiong Yao 瓊瑤. *Tusi hua* 菟絲花 (The Dodder Flower). Taipei: Crown, 1993. Orig. 1964.

Qiu Guifen 邱貴芬. *(Bu)tong guo nüren guazao* （不）同國女人聒噪 (A Rabble of Women from Different Lands). Taipei: Yuanzun, 1998.

Qiu Miaojin 邱妙津. *Eyu shouji* 鱷魚手記 (The Crocodile's Journal). Taipei: Shibao, 1994.

———. *Mengmate yishu* 蒙馬特遺書 (Montmartre Testament). Taipei: Lianhe Wenxue, 1996.

Ranblue 海天一色. *Wo ai lanqiu mei shaonü 1 and 2* 我愛籃球美少女 (I Love the Beautiful Basketball Girl, vols. 1 and 2). Painchiao: Yashutang Wenhua, 2003.

Robertson, Jennifer. "Dying to Tell: Sexuality and Suicide in Imperial Japan." In *Queer Diasporas*. Ed. C. Patton and B. Sánchez-Eppler, 38–70. Durham: Duke University Press, 2000.

———. *Takarazuka: Sexual Politics and Popular Culture in Modern Japan*. Berkeley: University of California Press, 1998.

———. "Yoshiya Nobuko: Out and Outspoken in Practice and Prose." In *The Human Tradition in Modern Japan*. Ed. A. Welthall, 155–74. Wilmington, Del.: Scholarly Resources, 2002.

Rofel, Lisa. *Other Modernities: Gendered Yearnings in China after Socialism*. Berkeley: University of California Press, 1999.

Rohy, Valerie. *Impossible Women: Lesbian Figures and American Literature*. Ithaca, N.Y.: Cornell University Press, 2000.

Roof, Judith. *Come As You Are: Sexuality and Narrative*. New York: Columbia University Press, 1996.

———. *A Lure of Knowledge: Lesbian Sexuality and Theory*. New York: Columbia University Press, 1991.

Rothman, William. "The Goddess: Reflections on Melodrama East and West." In *Melodrama and Asian Cinema*. Ed. W. Dissanayake, 59–72. Cambridge: Cambridge University Press, 1993.

Sang, Tze-lan D. "At the Juncture of Censure and Mass Voyeurism: Narratives of Female Homoerotic Desire in Post-Mao China." *GLQ* 8, no. 4 (2002): 523–52.

———. *The Emerging Lesbian: Female Same-Sex Desire in Modern China*. Chicago: University of Chicago Press, 2003.

"Sanqian li renchao bo guang lian yan, shi zhang ruan chen qixiang wanqian" 三千里人潮 波 光 激 灩， 十 丈 軟 塵 氣 象 萬 千 (Spectacular Scenes as an Overflowing Tide of People Extends for a Thousand Miles). *Lianhe bao* 聯合報 (United Daily News), November 1, 1963. Available at http://tsk.ocean-pioneer.com/my2.htm. Accessed May 18, 2005.

Sedgwick, Eve Kosofsky. *Epistemology of the Closet*. Berkeley: University of California Press, 1990.

———. "Queer Performativity: Henry James's The Art of the Novel." *GLQ* 1, no. 1 (1993): 1–16.

Shen, Fanny 沈蓮芳. *Yi beizi shouzhe ni 1* 一輩子守著妳 1 (I'll Be Your Paradise 1). Taipei: Tongli Comics, 1997.

———. *Yi beizi shouzhe ni 2* 一輩子守著妳 2 (I'll Be Your Paradise 2). Taipei: Tongli Comics, 1998.

Shen Yuexing 沈月星, ed. *Zheli, meiyou nansheng: Laizi nüzhongde xinqing baogao* 這裡，沒有男生：來自女中的心情報告 (Here, There Are No Boys: A Report on the Emotional Life of a Girls' Middle School). Shanghai: Shanghai Kexue Jishu Wenxian Chubanshe, 2002.

Shih, Shu-mei. *The Lure of the Modern: Writing Modernism in Semicolonial China, 1917–1937.* Berkeley: University of California Press, 2001.

Sieber, Patricia, ed. *Red Is Not the Only Color: Contemporary Chinese Fiction on Love and Sex between Women, Collected Stories.* Lanham, Md.: Rowman and Littlefield, 2001.

Silvio, Teri. "Lesbianism and Taiwanese Localism in the Film *The Silent Thrush.*" In Martin et al., *AsiaPacifiQueer*, 217–34.

———. "Reflexivity, Bodily Praxis, and Identity in Taiwanese Opera." *GLQ* 5, no. 4 (1999): 585–604.

Smith-Rosenberg, Carroll. *Disorderly Conduct: Visions of Gender in Victorian America.* New York: A. A. Knopf, 1985.

Song Geng. *The Fragile Scholar: Power and Masculinity in Chinese Culture.* Hong Kong: Hong Kong University Press, 2004.

Starobinski, Jean. "The Idea of Nostalgia." *Diogenes* 54 (1966): 81–103.

Stevens, Sarah E. "Figuring Modernity: The New Woman and the Modern Girl in Republican China." *NWSA Journal* 15, no. 3 (2003): 82–103.

Stewart, Susan. *On Longing: Narratives of the Miniature, the Gigantic, the Souvenir, the Collection.* Durham: Duke University Press, 1993.

Storr, Merl. "Transformations: Subjects, Categories and Cures in Krafft-Ebing's Sexology." In Bland and Doan, *Sexology*, 11–26.

Tan, See Kam, and Annette Aw. "The Cross-Gender Performances of Yam Kim-Fei, or the Queer Factor in Postwar Hong Kong Cantonese Opera/Opera Films." *Journal of Homosexuality* 39, nos. 3–4 (2000): 201–11.

———. "Love Eterne: (Almost) a Heterosexual Love Story." In *Chinese Films in Focus: 25 New Takes.* Ed. C. Berry, 137–43. London: British Film Institute, 2003.

Tong Ka Man, Carmen. "Being a Tomboy: An Ethnographic Research of Young Schoolgirls in Hong Kong." Master's thesis, Hong Kong University, 2001.

"Tongxing miyou chansheng haogan bing fei tongxinglian" 同性密友產生好感并非同性戀 (Closeness between Intimate Friends of the Same Sex is Not Homosexuality). http://www.xinlihua.cn/xl/hlxl/view.php?id=1548. Accessed October 10, 2004.

Torres, Sasha. "Television/Feminism: Heartbeat and Prime Time Lesbianism." In Abelove et al., *Lesbian and Gay Studies Reader*, 176–85.

Tu, Wei-ming. "Cultural China: The Periphery as the Center." In *The Living Tree: The Changing Meaning of Being Chinese Today.* Ed. W.-m. Tu, 1–34. Stanford: Stanford University Press, 1994.

Turner, Mark. *Backward Glances: Cruising Queer Streets in London and New York.* London: Reaktion Books, 2004.

Ueno, Chizuko. "Self-Determination on Sexuality?: Commercialization of Sex among Teenage Girls in Japan," *Inter-Asia Cultural Studies* 4, no. 2 (2003): 317–24.

Vicinus, Martha. "Distance and Desire: English Boarding School Friendships, 1870–1920." In Duberman et al., *Hidden from History*, 212–29.

———. "Introduction." In Vicinus, ed., *Lesbian Subjects*, 1–12.

———. (1996). "'They Wonder to Which Sex I Belong': The Historical Roots of the Modern Lesbian Identity." In Vicinus, ed., *Lesbian Subjects*, 233–59.

Vicinus, Martha, ed. *Lesbian Subjects: A Feminist Studies Reader*. Bloomington: Indiana University Press, 1996.

Waiting. "Tongnü zhi wu you weidao" 童女之舞有味道 (*The Maidens' Dance* has character). Rensheng Juzhan Taolunqu 人生劇展討論區 (Public Television Service). Posted October 19, 2002.

Wang Chun-chi 王君琦. "Zhuliuzhongde panni: Jiedu Taiwan dianshiju Ninü de dikang yihan" 主流中的叛逆:解讀台灣電視劇《逆女》的抵抗意涵 (Lesbian Seeking Possible Resistance on Television: A Case Study of Ni-Nü). *Envisage: A Journal Book of Chinese Media Studies* 媒介擬想 3 (2005): 35–50.

Wang, David Der-wei. "Foreword." In E. Chang, *The Rice-Sprout Song*, vii–xxv.

———. "Foreword." In E. Chang, *The Rouge of the North*, vii–xxx.

Wang, Jing. *High Culture Fever: Politics, Aesthetics, and Ideology in Deng's China*. Berkeley: University of California Press, 1996.

Wang Ning. "Confronting Western Influence: Rethinking Chinese Literature of the New Period." *New Literary History* 24, no. 4 (autumn 1993): 905–27.

Wang Xiaoming 王曉明. "The 'Good Fortune' of Eileen Chang." Trans. Cecile Chuchin Sun. *Renditions* 45 (spring 1996): 136–40.

———. "Pibeide xinling: Cong Zhang Xinxin, Liu Suola he Can Xue de xiaoshuo tanqi" 疲憊的心靈—從張辛欣，劉索拉和殘雪的小說談起 (The Exhausted Spirit: Starting from the Novels of Zhang Xinxin, Liu Suola, and Can Xue). *Shanghai wenxue* 上海文學 128 (1988): 67–74.

Wee, Christopher Justin Wan-ling. "Buying Japan: Singapore, Japan and an 'East Asian' Modernity." *Journal of Pacific Asia* 4 (1997): 21–46.

Wei, Shu-chu. "Shaping a Cultural Identity: The Picture Book and Cartoons in Taiwan, 1945–1980." In Lent, *Illustrating Asia*, 64–80.

Weiss, Andrea. *Vampires and Violets: Lesbians in the Cinema*. London: Cape, 1992.

Welker, James. "Drawing Out Lesbians: The Blurred Representation of Lesbians in Shojo Manga." Paper presented at AsiaPacifiQueer 3: The Uses of Queer Asia: Research, Methods, and Diasporic Intellectuals, University of Melbourne, 2002.

White, Patricia. "Girls Still Cry." *Screen* 42, no. 2 (2001): 217–21.

———. *Uninvited: Classical Hollywood Cinema and Lesbian Representability*. Bloomington: Indiana University Press, 1999.

Williams, Linda. *Playing the Race Card: Melodramas of Black and White from Uncle Tom to O. J. Simpson*. Princeton: Princeton University Press, 2001.

Williams, Raymond. *The Long Revolution*. London: Chatto and Windus, 1961.

Wilton, Tamsin, ed. *Immortal, Invisible: Lesbians and the Moving Image*. London: Routledge, 1995.

Women Coalition of Hong Kong 香港會愛上女人的女人口述歷史計劃執行委員會. *Tamende nüqing yinji* 她們的女情印記 (A Record of Their Women-Love). Hong Kong: Women Coalition of Hong Kong. 2005.

Wong Bikwan 黃碧雲. *Lienü tu* 烈女圖 (The Picture of Female Virtue). Taipei: Titan, 1999.

———. (2001). "She's a Young Woman and So Am I." Trans. Naifei Ding. In Sieber, *Red Is Not the Only Color*, 37–48.

———. "Ta shi nüzi, wo ye shi nüzi" 她是女子，我也是女子 (She's a Young Woman and So Am I). In *Ta shi nüzi, wo ye shi nüzi* 她是女子，我也是女子 (She's a Young Woman and So Am I), 1–18. Taipei: Maitian, 1994.

Wong, Day. "Beyond Identity Politics: The Making of an Oral History of Hong Kong Women Who Have Same-Sex Desires." Paper presented at Sexualities, Genders and Rights in Asia: First International Conference of Asian Queer Studies, Bangkok, 2005.

———. "(Post-)Identity Politics and Anti-Normalization: (Homo)Sexual Rights Movement." In *Remaking Citizenship in Hong Kong: Community, Nation and the Global City*. Ed. A. S. Ku and N. Pun, 195–214. London: Routledge, 2006.

Wong, Timothy C., ed. *Stories for Saturday: Twentieth-Century Chinese Popular Fiction*. Honolulu: University of Hawaii Press, 2003.

Wu Chensheng and Chou Wah-shan 吳春生，周華山, eds. *Women huozhe!* 我們活著! (We Are Living!). Hong Kong: Xianggang Tongzhi Yanjiu She, 1996.

Wu Liang (2000). "Re-membering the Cultural Revolution." Trans. Shu Yunzhong. In Chi and Wang, *Chinese Literature in the Second Half of a Modern Century*, 124–36.

Wu, Peichen. "Performing Gender along the Lesbian Continuum: The Politics of Sexual Identity in the Seitô Society." *U.S.-Japan Women's Journal, English Supplement* 22 (2002): 64–86.

Xiao Ying 肖鷹. "Jin nian feilixing zhuyi xiaoshuode pipan" 近年非理性主義小說批判 (A Critique of Nonrationalist Fiction in Recent Years). *Wenxue pinglun* 文學評論 5 (1990): 5–23.

Xu Bin. "Suppressed Voice or Silence by Choice? Lesbians and the Emerging Lesbian Communities in Contemporary China." Paper presented at Sexualities, Genders and Rights in Asia: First International Conference of Asian Queer Studies, Bangkok, 2005.

Xu Yuanzhong, Lu Peixian, and Wu Juntao, eds. *300 Tang Poems: A New Translation*. Beijing and Hong Kong: Zhongguo Duiwai Fanyi Chuban Gongsi and Shangwu Yinshuguan, 1987.

Xuan Xiaofo 玄小佛. *Yuan zhi wai* 圓之外 (Outside the Circle). Taipei: Nanqi, 1976.

Yan Fusun. "The Bridal Palanquin." Trans. Timothy C. Wong. In T. Wong, *Stories for Saturday*, 49–60. Orig. 1921.

Yan Geling 嚴歌苓. *Bai she* 白蛇 (White Snake). Taipei: Jiuge, 1999.

———. "White Snake." In *White Snake and Other Stories*. Trans. Lawrence A. Walker, 1–64. San Francisco: Aunt Lute, 1999.

Yang Ming 楊明. "Shen qing zai jie, guyi zai mei–Cexie Zhu Tianxin" 深情在睫，孤意在眉—側寫朱天心 (Deep Love and Loneliness Close at Hand: On Chu T'ien-hsin). *Wenxun yuekan* 文訊月刊 25 (August 1986): 250–53.

Yi Shu 亦舒. Xu— 嘘— (Shhh—). Hong Kong: Cosmos Books, 2007.

Yu Dafu 郁達夫. "Ta shi yige ruo nüzi" 她是一個弱女子 (She Was a Weak Woman). In *Yu Dafu quanji* 郁達夫全集 (Complete Works of Yu Dafu), vol. 2, 279–375. Zhejiang: Zhejiang Wenyi Chubanshe, 1991. Orig. 1923.

Yue, Ming-bao. "Gendering the Origins of Modern Chinese Fiction." In T. Lu, *Gender and Sexuality*, 47–65.

Zeng Yanyu 曾燕瑀. "Xunzhao mizangzhongde baoli jingji chang—yuedu Yu Dafu 'Ta shi yige ruo nüzi'" 尋找迷藏中的暴力競技場—閱讀郁達夫〈她是一個弱女子〉 (Searching for the Arena of Violence at the Heart of the Riddle: Reading Yu Dafu's "She Was a Weak Woman"). Unpublished paper. Available at http://sex.ncu.edu.tw/course/liou/4_Papers/Paper_05.html. Accessed November 8, 2004.

Zhang Aizhu 張靄珠. "Xing fanchuan, yizhi kongjian, yu houzhimin bianzhuang huanghoude wenhua xianji" 性別反串、異質空間、與後殖民變裝皇后的文化羨嫉 (Cross-dressing, Heterotopias, and the Cultural Phenomenon of Post-colonial Drag Queens). *Chung-wai Literary Monthly* 29, no. 7 (2000): 137–57.

Zhang Jingsheng. *See* Chang Ching-sheng.

Zhang, Jingyuan. "The First Chinese Translation of Sigmund Freud." *Chinese Comparatist* 3, no. 1 (July 1989): 33–35.

Zhang, Jingyuan. "Breaking Open: Chinese Women's Writing in the Late 1980s and 1990s." In Chi and Wang, *Chinese Literature in the Second Half of a Modern Century*, 161–79.

———. *Psychoanalysis in China: Literary Transformations 1919–1949*. Ithaca, N.Y.: Cornell University Press, 1992.

———. "Psychoanalysis in the Chinese Context." *IIAS Newsletter* 30 (March 2003): 8–9.

Zhang Manjuan 張曼娟. "Wuke nizhuande mingyun" 無可逆轉之命運 (Irreversible Fate). In Du, *Ninü* 逆女, 3–5.

Zhang Manjuan 張曼娟. "Yu Dafu 'Ta shi yige ruo nüzi' de nüxing juese yu nütongxing'ai" 郁達夫〈她是一個弱女子〉的女性角色與女同性愛 (Female Roles and Lesbianism in Yu Dafu's "She Was A Weak Woman"). Paper presented at 110th Conference of the Chinese Department at Soochow University, Taiwan, 2003.

Zhang Qiaoting 張喬婷. *Xunfu yu dikang: Shi wei xiaoyuan nü jingying lazi de qingyu yayi* 馴服與抵抗：十位校園女菁英拉子的情慾壓抑 (Campus Memory: Identity and the Emerging of Lesbian Subjectivities in Taiwan). Taipei: Tangshan, 2000.

Zhang, Xudong. *Chinese Modernism in the Era of Reforms: Cultural Fever, Avant-Garde Fiction, and the New Chinese Cinema*. Durham: Duke University Press, 1997.

Zhao Mei 趙玫. "Sui feng piao qu" 隨風飄去 (Gone with the Wind). In Hong Ying, *Jing yu shui*, 167–88.

———. "Xianfeng xiaoshuode zizu yu fufan" 先鋒小說的自足與浮泛 (Self-sufficiency and Superficiality of Vanguard Novels). *Wenxue pinglun* 文學評論 1 (1989): 31–39.

Zhao Xianzhang 趙憲章. "Lun Fuluoyide de wenyi xinlixue fangfa" 論弗洛伊德的文藝心理學方法 (Freud's Psychological Methods for Literature and Art). *Wenxue pinglun* 文學評論 3 (1987): 110–18.

Zheng Meili 鄭美里. *Nü'er quan: Taiwan nütongzhide xingbie, jiating yu quannei shenghuo* 女兒圈：台灣女同志的性別、家庭與圈內生活 (Girls' Circle: Taiwan's Lesbians' Gender, Home Life, and Subcultural Practice). Taipei: Nüshu Wenhua, 1997.

Zhong Xueping. "Sisterhood? Representations of Women's Relationships in Two Contemporary Chinese Texts." In T. Lu, *Gender and Sexuality*, 157–73.

Zhou Fen-ling 周芬伶. "Fangxiangde mijiao" 芳香的祕教 (A Fragrant Esoteric Religion). Review of Eileen Chang's *Tongxue shaonian dou bu jian*. *Lianhe bao* 聯合報, April 4, 2004. Available at http://udn.com/NEWS/READING/X2/1937754.shtml. Accessed April 6, 2004.

Zhu Shuangyi 朱雙一. "Cong ernü siyu dao juancun chuanqi–Zhu Tianxin lun" 從兒女私語到眷村傳奇－朱天心論 (From the Secrets of Sons and Daughters to Legends of the Veterans' Neighborhood: On Chu T'ien-hsin). *Taiwan wenxue xuankan* 台灣文學選刊 7 (1994): 66–68.

Zimmerman, Bonnie. *The Safe Sea of Women: Lesbian Fiction 1969–1989*. Boston: Beacon Press, 1990.

Index

Evans, Harriet, 18

Eyu shouji (The Crocodile's Journal) (Qiu Miaojin novel), 222n.3, 238n.26

Faderman, Lillian, 9–10, 206n.17

Family Planning Association of Hong Kong, 21–22

Fei yue qing hai (Love Me If You Can) (film), 2–6, 14–15, 150, 236–37n.19, 251–52n.25

feminism: discussions of in contemporary China, 191, 194; first-wave, 13; in Japan, 33–34; lesbian, 9–10, 93; liberal, 73–74; poststructuralist, 94; second-wave, 16

femme film, Euro-American, 124–26

Foucault, Michel, 91–92, 235n.58

Freud, Sigmund, and Freudianism, 8, 27, 34, 52–53, 72, 79, 81, 82–92, 142, 225–26nn.22–24, 232nn.16–17, 234nn.37–38, 247n.49. See also melancholia; same-sex love, female: represented as repressed

Fried Green Tomatoes (film), 124

Friedman, Sara, 244–45n.25

friendship, romantic, 12–13, 33, 45, 46, 121

Furukawa Makoto, 33, 215n.13, 215–16n.19

Furuya Toyoko, 35

Fuss, Diana, 53

Gaze of the Virgin Mary, The (manga), 212n.69

gender, secondary, 12–14, 93–117, 119, 219n.55, 223–24nn.8–9. See also sexuality; tomboys

Gian Jia-shin, 93–94

Gide, André, 78

Gimpel, Denise, 218n.46

Gledhill, Christine, 100

going-in story, 26, 29–48, 49–74, 77, 124, 141–42, 246n.34

Gordon, Angus, 53, 224–25n.14, 226n.23

Grossman, Andrew, 251n.18

"Gu du" (Ancient Capital) (Chu T'ien-hsin story), 63

Gu huo zai qing yi pian zhi hong xing shi san mei (Portland Street Blues) (film), 249n.10

"Gu lian hua" (Love's Lone Flower) (Pai Hsien-yung story), 180, 236–37n.19, 243–44n.13

Gu lian hua (Love's Lone Flower) (TV and film adaptations), 180–83, 236–37n.19, 243–44n.13, 250–51n.13

Hai jiao tian ya (Incidental Journey) (film), 147, 153–57, 163, 166, 172, 179

"Haibin guren" (Old Acquaintances by the Seaside) (Lu Yin novella), 39

Haishang hua (Flowers of Shanghai) (film), 243–44n.13

Happy Together (film), 159, 163

Healy, Chris, 248n.51

HeartBeat (TV drama), 246–47n.36

Heller, Joseph, 78

Hinsch, Bret, 9, 29, 248n.54

Ho yuk (Let's Love Hong Kong) (film), 211n.57, 253–54n.45

Hollinger, Karen, 126

Holmlund, Chris, 124

homophobia, 19, 25, 45, 97–99, 185, 218–19n.52, 246–47n.36

homosexuality. See same-sex love, female: homosexuality and

Hong Kong cinema, 19, 20, 249nn.9–10. See also individual film titles

Hong Ling. See Hung, Lucifer

Hong lou meng (Dream of the Red Chamber) (Cao Xueqin novel), 38, 43

Hong yan (Dam Street) (film), 252n.28

Hong Ying, 76, 231n.6. See also Jing yu shui

Hou Hsiao-hsien, 253n.42

Fran Martin is a senior lecturer in cultural studies at the University of Melbourne. She has edited (with Larissa Heinrich) *Embodied Modernities: Corporeality, Representation, and Chinese Cultures* (2006) and (with Chris Berry and Audrey Yue) *Mobile Cultures: New Media in Queer Asia* (2003), and she has edited and translated the stories in *Angelwings: Contemporary Queer Fiction from Taiwan* (2003).

. . .

Library of Congress Cataloging-in-Publication Data

Martin, Fran, 1971–

Backward glances : contemporary Chinese cultures and the female homoerotic imaginary / Fran Martin.

p. cm. — (Asia-Pacific, culture, politics, and society)

Includes bibliographical references and index.

ISBN 978-0-8223-4668-5 (cloth : alk. paper)

ISBN 978-0-8223-4680-7 (pbk. : alk. paper)

1. Sex in popular culture—China. 2. Popular culture—China. 3. Lesbianism in motion pictures. I. Title. II. Series: Asia-Pacific.

HQ18.C6M35 2010

306.76′630951—dc22

2009042228